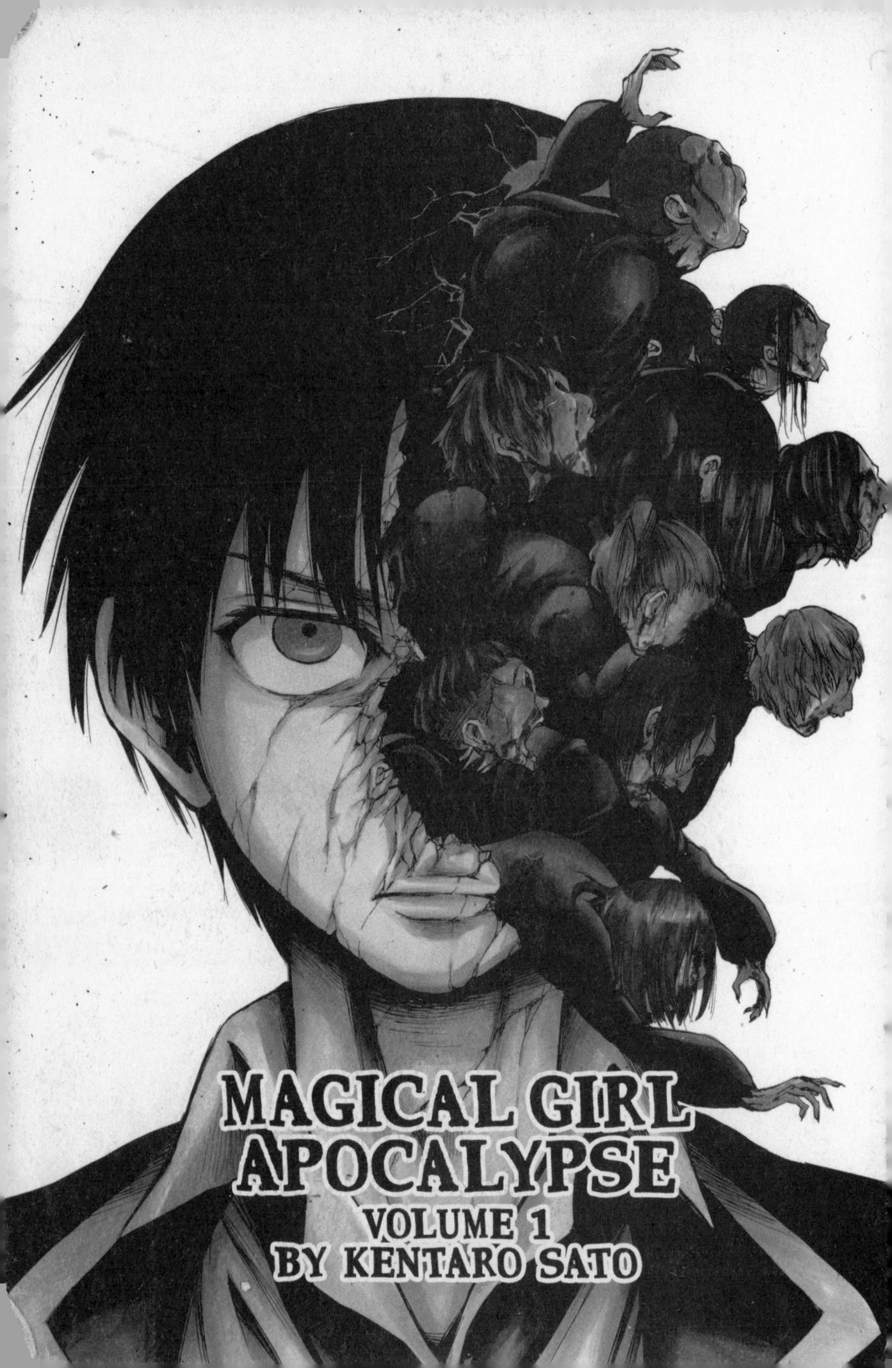
MAGICAL GIRL
APOCALYPSE
VOLUME 1
BY KENTARO SATO

SEVEN SEAS ENTERTAINMENT PRESENTS

MAGICAL GIRL APOCALYPSE

story and art by KENTARO SATO   VOLUME 1

TRANSLATION
Wesley Bridges

ADAPTATION
Janet Houck

LETTERING AND LAYOUT
Jaedison Yui

LOGO DESIGN
Phil Balsman

COVER DESIGN
Nicky Lim

PROOFREADER
Shanti Whitesides
Lee Otter

MANAGING EDITOR
Adam Arnold

PUBLISHER
Jason DeAngelis

MAHO SYOJYO OF THE END Volume 1
© Kentaro Sato 2013
Originally published in Japan in 2013 by Akita Publishing Co., Ltd..
English translation rights arranged with Akita Publishing Co., Ltd. through
TOHAN CORPORATION, Tokyo.

Seven Seas books may be purchased in bulk for educational, business, or
promotional use. For information on bulk purchases, please contact Macmillan
Corporate & Premium Sales Department at 1-800-221-7945 (ext 5442)
or write specialmarkets@macmillan.com.

Seven Seas and the Seven Seas logo are trademarks of
Seven Seas Entertainment, LLC. All rights reserved.

ISBN: 978-1-626920-78-1

Printed in Canada

First Printing: October 2014

10 9 8 7 6 5 4 3 2 1

FOLLOW US ONLINE: *www.gomanga.com*

READING DIRECTIONS

This book reads from *right to left*, Japanese style.
If this is your first time reading manga, you start
reading from the top right panel on each page and
take it from there. If you get lost, just follow the
numbered diagram here. It may seem backwards at
first, but you'll get the hang of it! Have fun!!

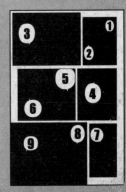

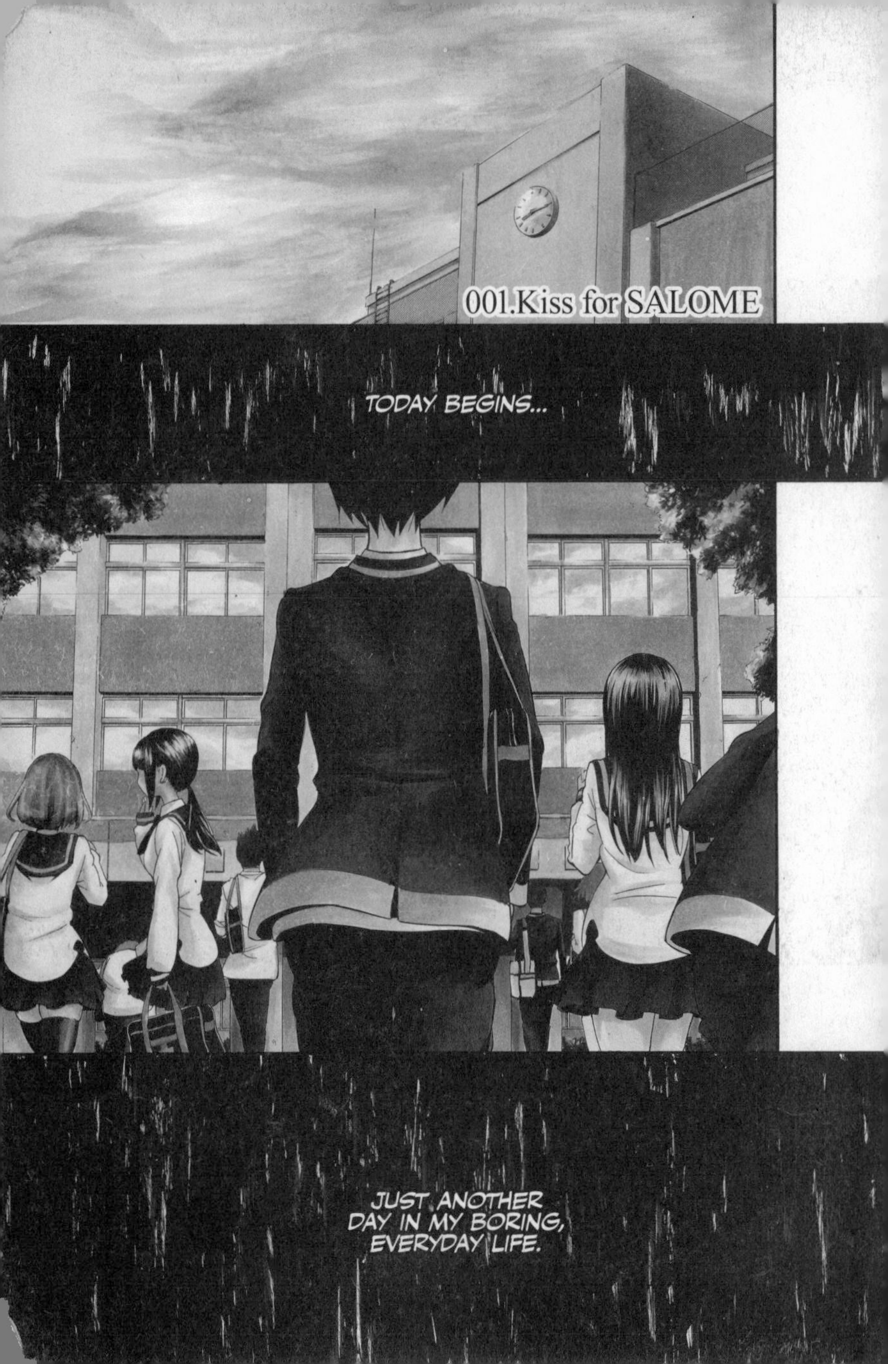
001.Kiss for SALOME
TODAY BEGINS...
JUST ANOTHER DAY IN MY BORING, EVERYDAY LIFE.

001.Kiss for SALOME

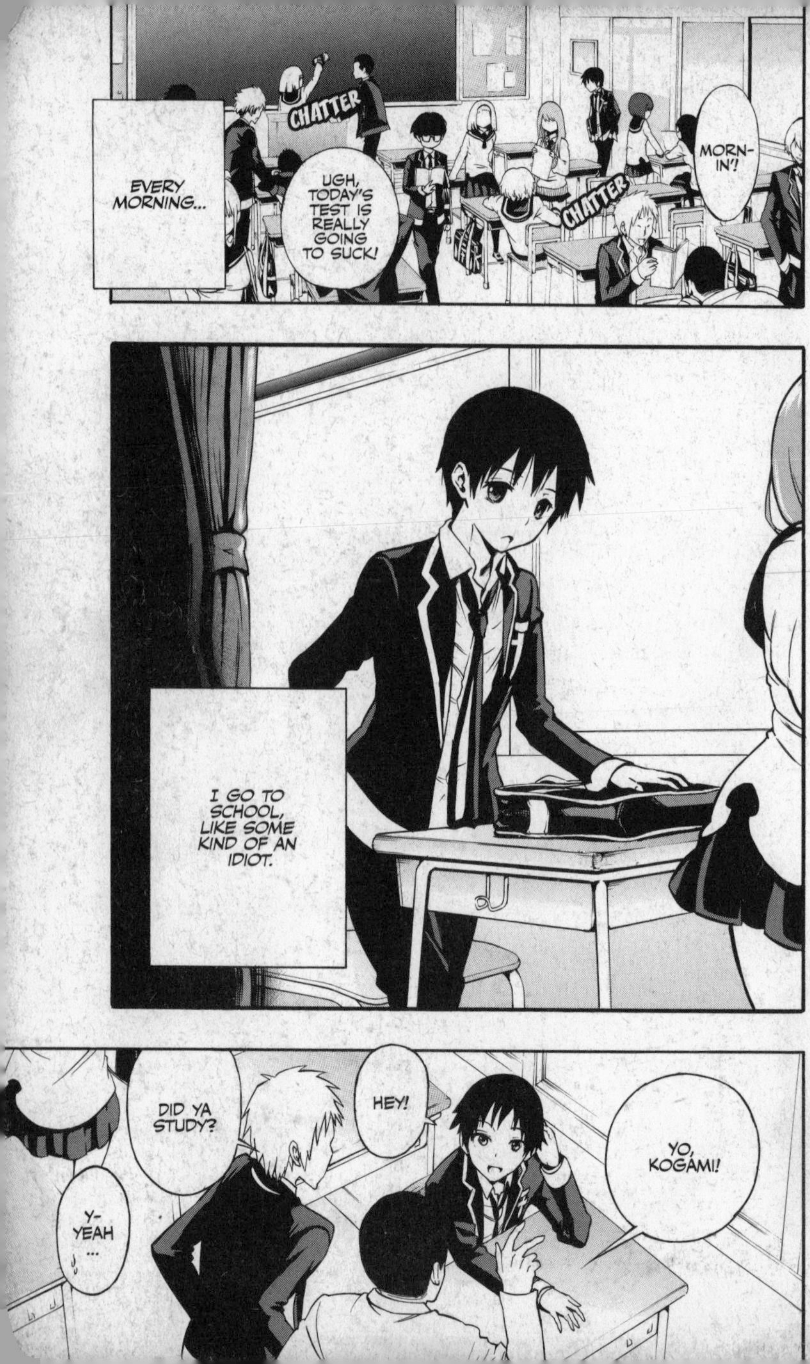
MORN-IN'!
CHATTER
UGH, TODAY'S TEST IS REALLY GOING TO SUCK!
CHATTER
EVERY MORNING...
I GO TO SCHOOL, LIKE SOME KIND OF AN IDIOT.
YO, KOGAMI!
HEY!
DID YA STUDY?
Y-YEAH ...

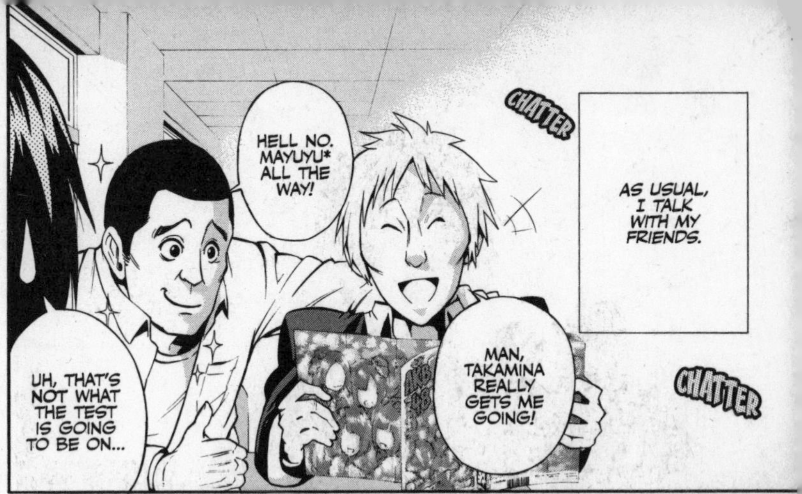
AS USUAL, I TALK WITH MY FRIENDS.
CHATTER
CHATTER
MAN, TAKAMINA REALLY GETS ME GOING!
HELL NO. MAYUYU* ALL THE WAY!
UH, THAT'S NOT WHAT THE TEST IS GOING TO BE ON...

*Minami Takamina and Mayu Wantanabe (a.k.a. Mayuyu) from the Japanese idol group AKB48.

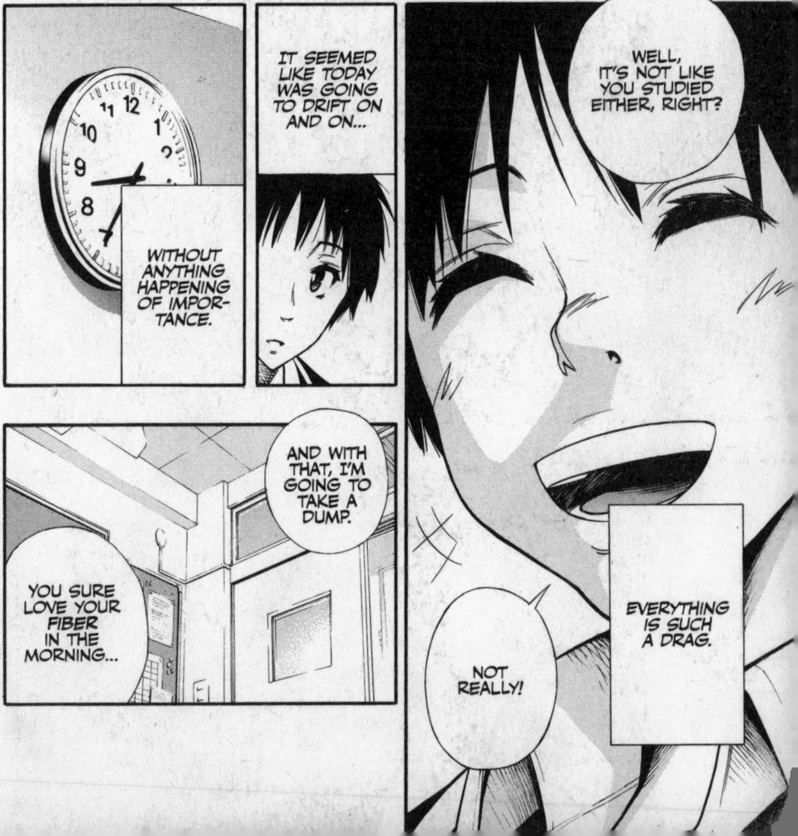
WELL, IT'S NOT LIKE YOU STUDIED EITHER, RIGHT?
EVERYTHING IS SUCH A DRAG.
NOT REALLY!
IT SEEMED LIKE TODAY WAS GOING TO DRIFT ON AND ON...
WITHOUT ANYTHING HAPPENING OF IMPORTANCE.
AND WITH THAT, I'M GOING TO TAKE A DUMP.
YOU SURE LOVE YOUR FIBER IN THE MORNING...

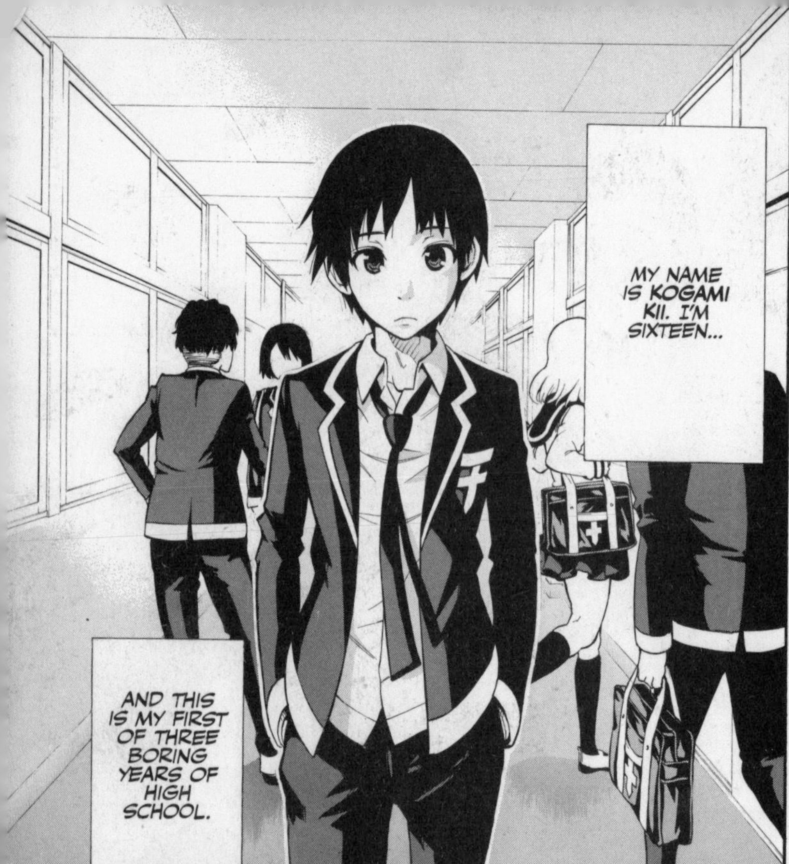
MY NAME IS KOGAMI KII. I'M SIXTEEN...
AND THIS IS MY FIRST OF THREE BORING YEARS OF HIGH SCHOOL.

*"Sen" is short for "sensei." It's like calling the teacher, "Mr. G."

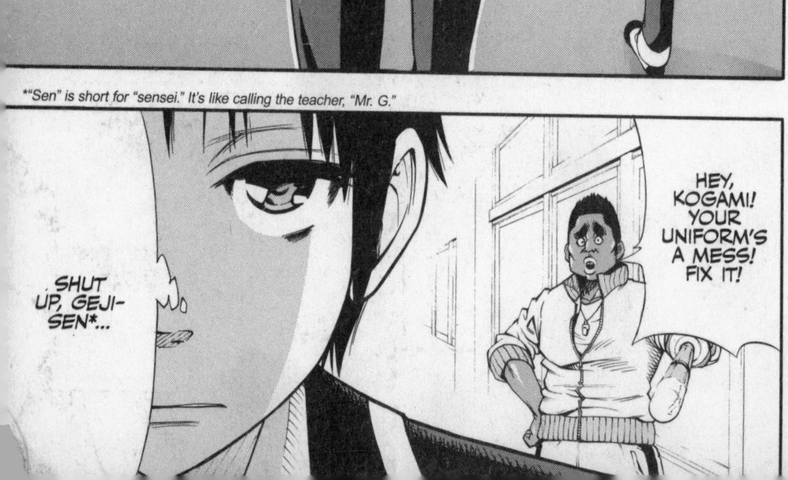
HEY, KOGAMI! YOUR UNIFORM'S A MESS! FIX IT!
SHUT UP, GEJI-SEN*...

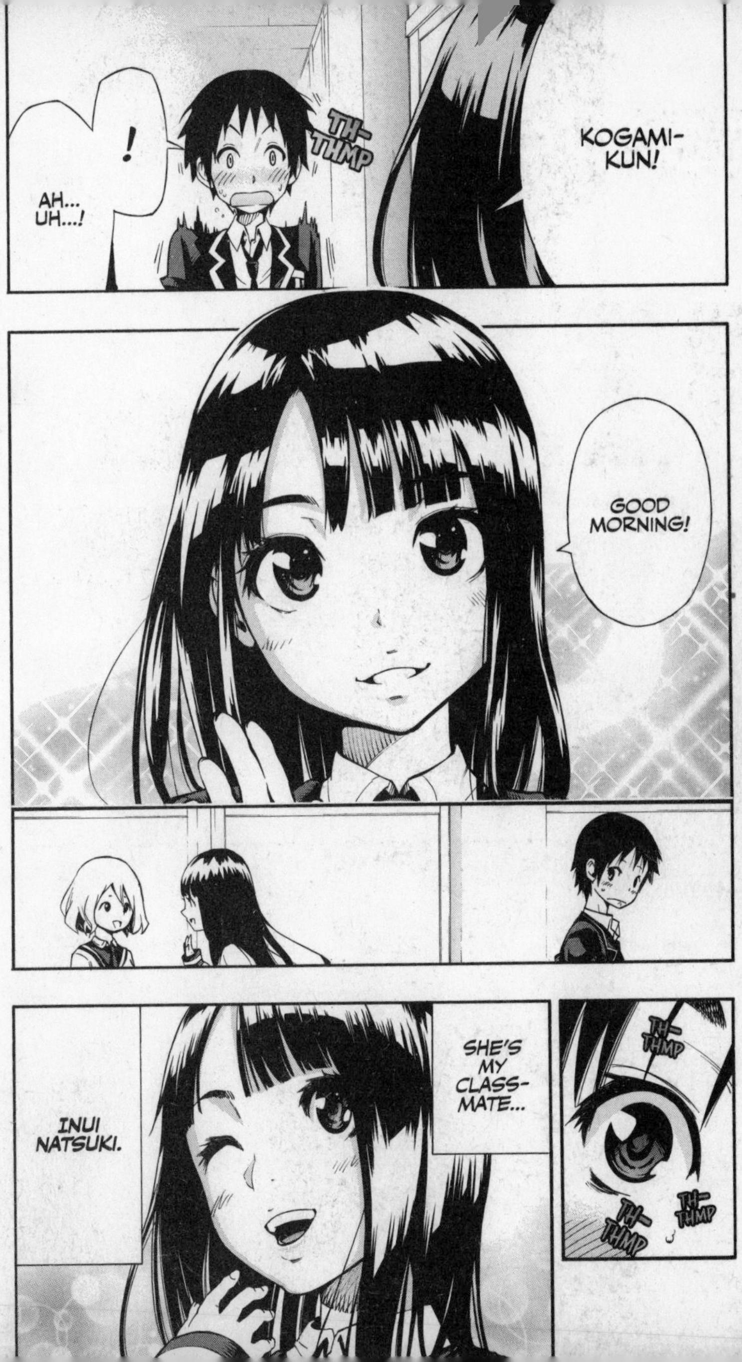
KOGAMI-KUN!
TH-THMP
!
AH... UH...!
GOOD MORNING!
TH-THMP
TH-THMP
TH-THMP
SHE'S MY CLASS-MATE...
INUI NATSUKI.

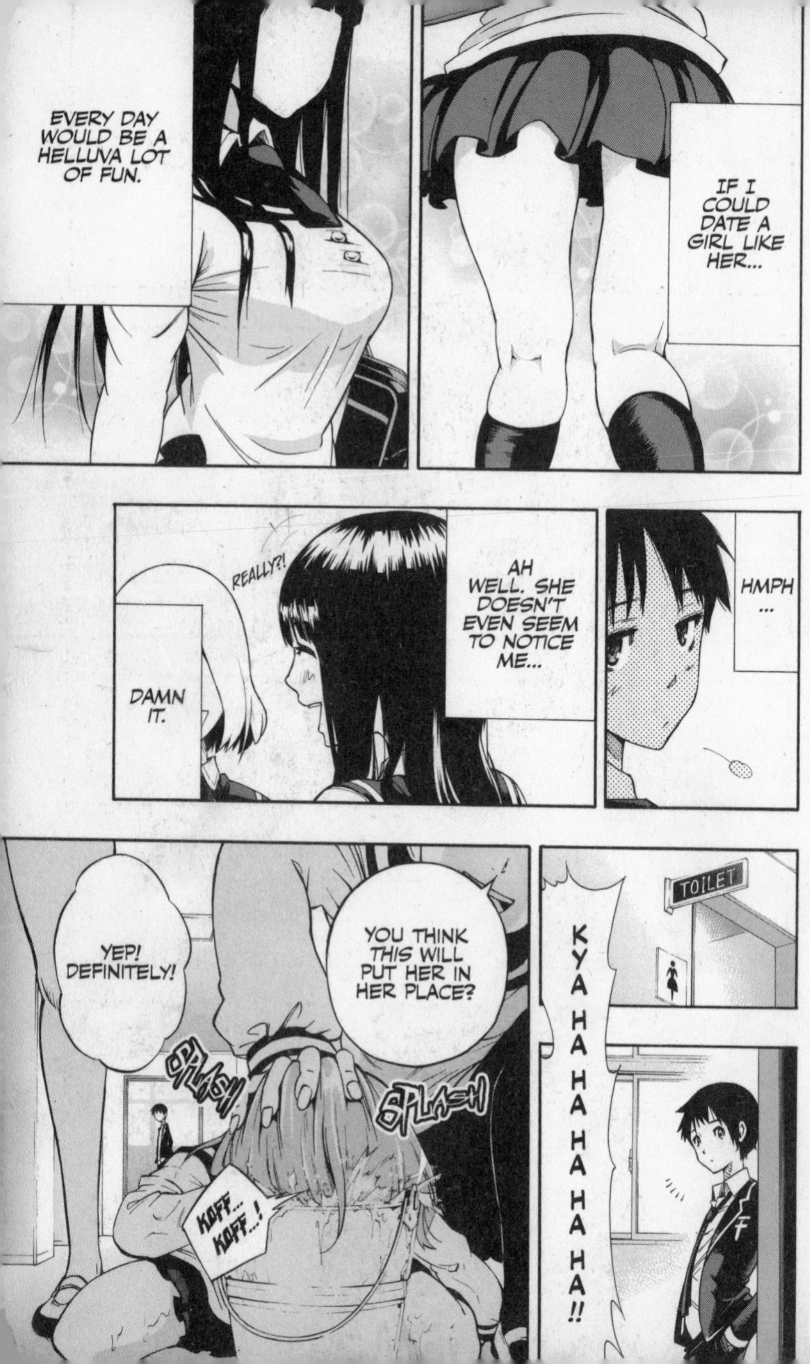
IF I COULD DATE A GIRL LIKE HER...
EVERY DAY WOULD BE A HELLUVA LOT OF FUN.
HMPH ...
AH WELL. SHE DOESN'T EVEN SEEM TO NOTICE ME...
REALLY?!
DAMN IT.
TOILET
KYA HA HA HA HA HA HA HA HA!!
YOU THINK THIS WILL PUT HER IN HER PLACE?
YEP! DEFINITELY!
SPLASH
SPLASH
KOFF... KOFF...!

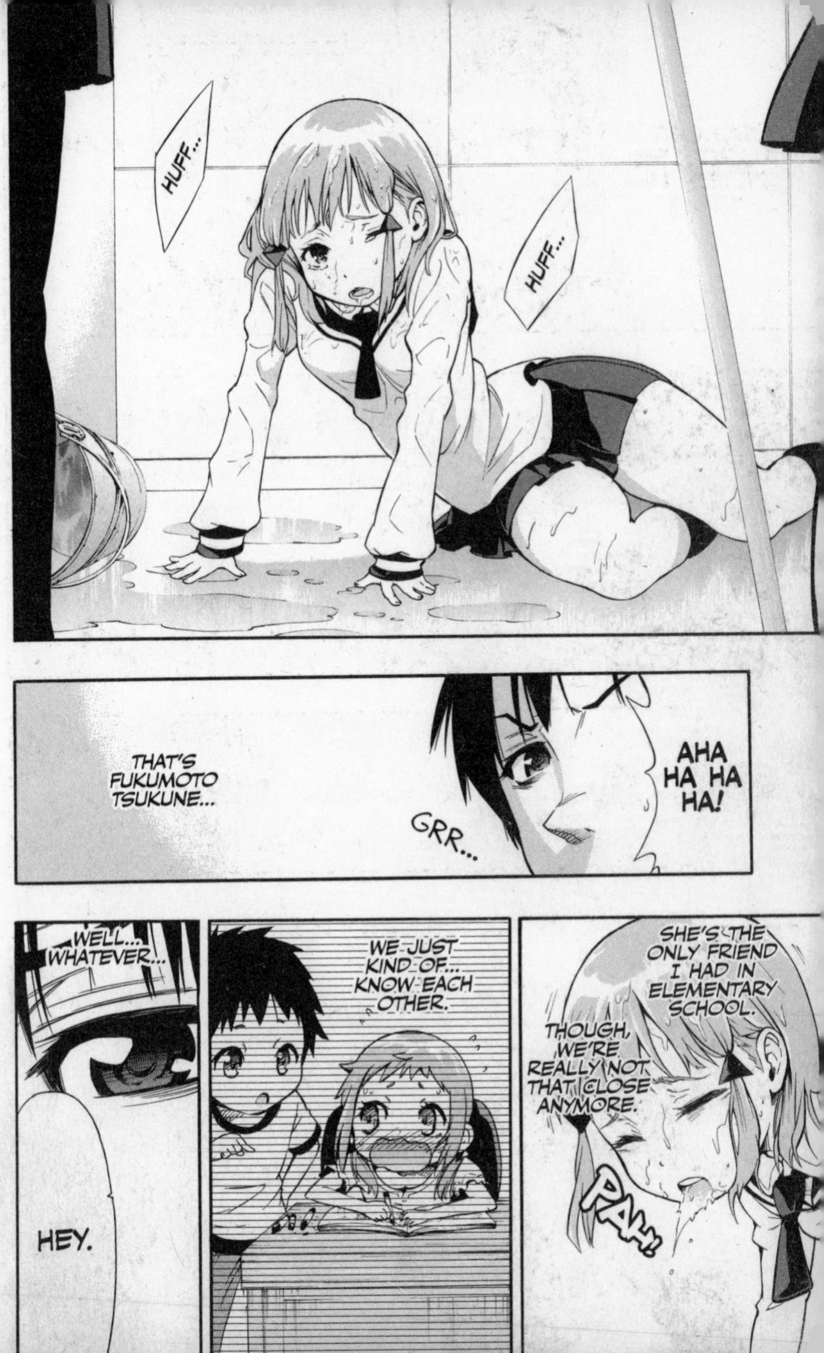
HUFF...
HUFF...
AHA HA HA HA!
THAT'S FUKUMOTO TSUKUNE...
GRR...
SHE'S THE ONLY FRIEND I HAD IN ELEMENTARY SCHOOL.
THOUGH, WE'RE REALLY NOT THAT CLOSE ANYMORE.
PAH!
WE JUST KIND OF... KNOW EACH OTHER.
WELL... WHATEVER...
HEY.

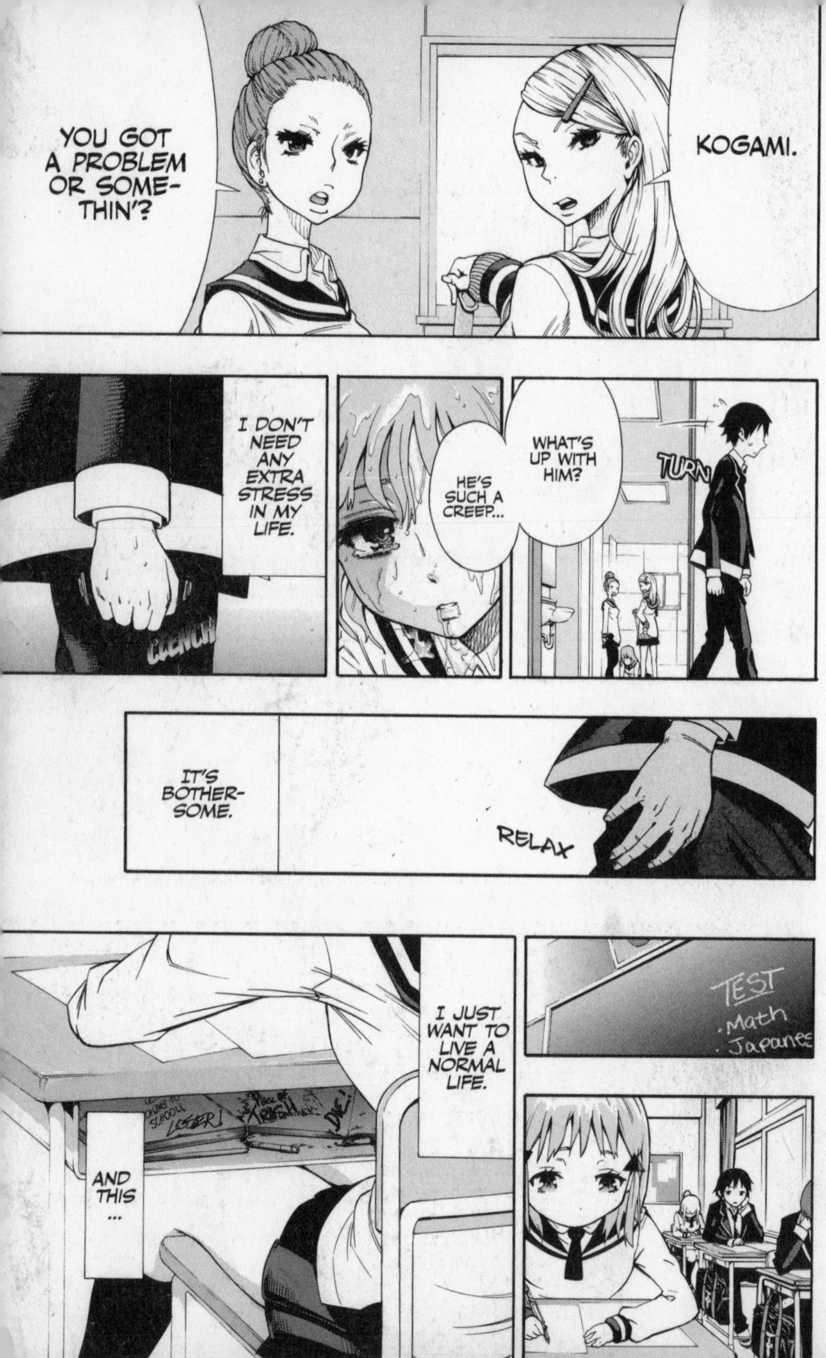
KOGAMI.
YOU GOT A PROBLEM OR SOME-THIN'?
TURN
WHAT'S UP WITH HIM?
HE'S SUCH A CREEP...
I DON'T NEED ANY EXTRA STRESS IN MY LIFE.
CLENCH
RELAX
IT'S BOTHER-SOME.
TEST
.Math
.Japanes
I JUST WANT TO LIVE A NORMAL LIFE.
LOSER!
DIE!
AND THIS...

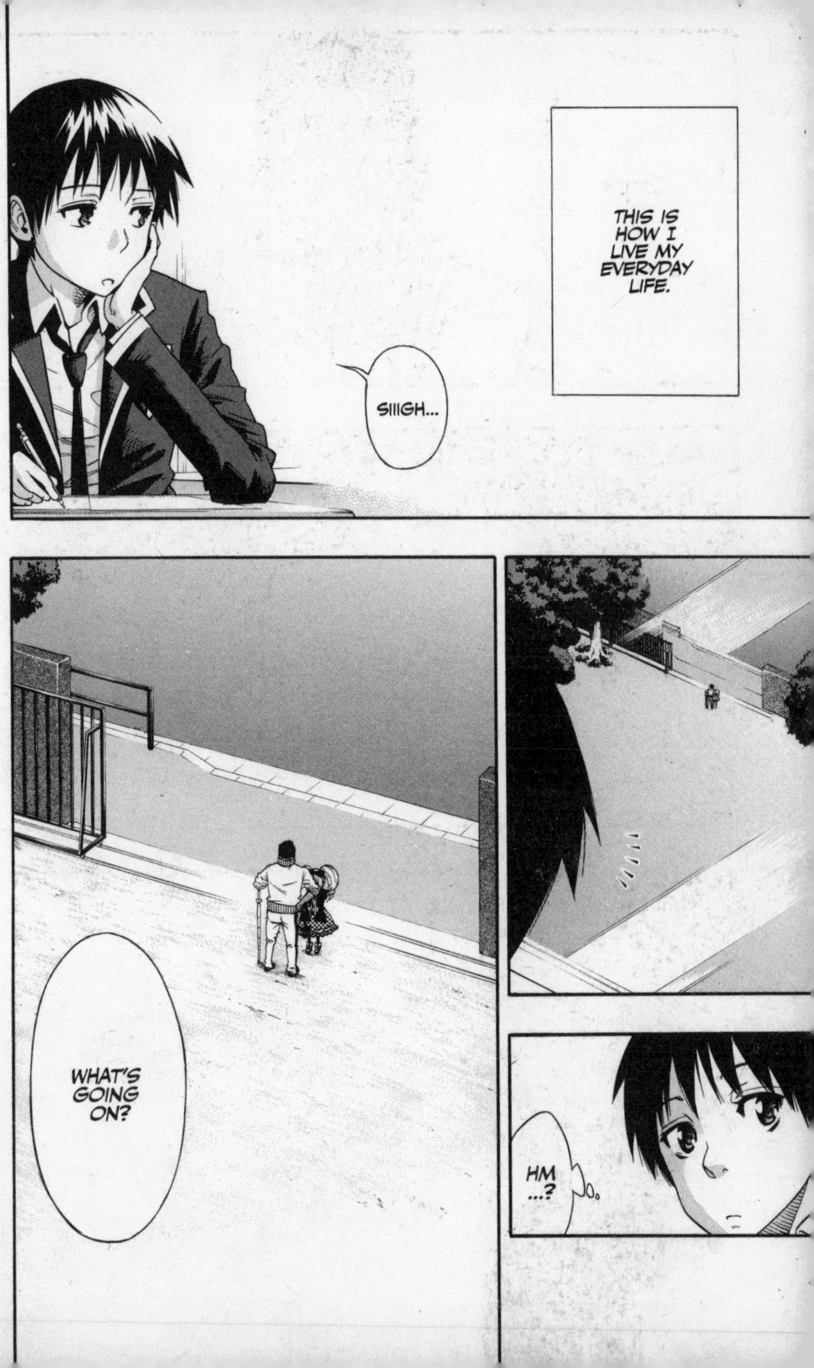
THIS IS HOW I LIVE MY EVERYDAY LIFE.
SIIIGH...
HM ...?
WHAT'S GOING ON?

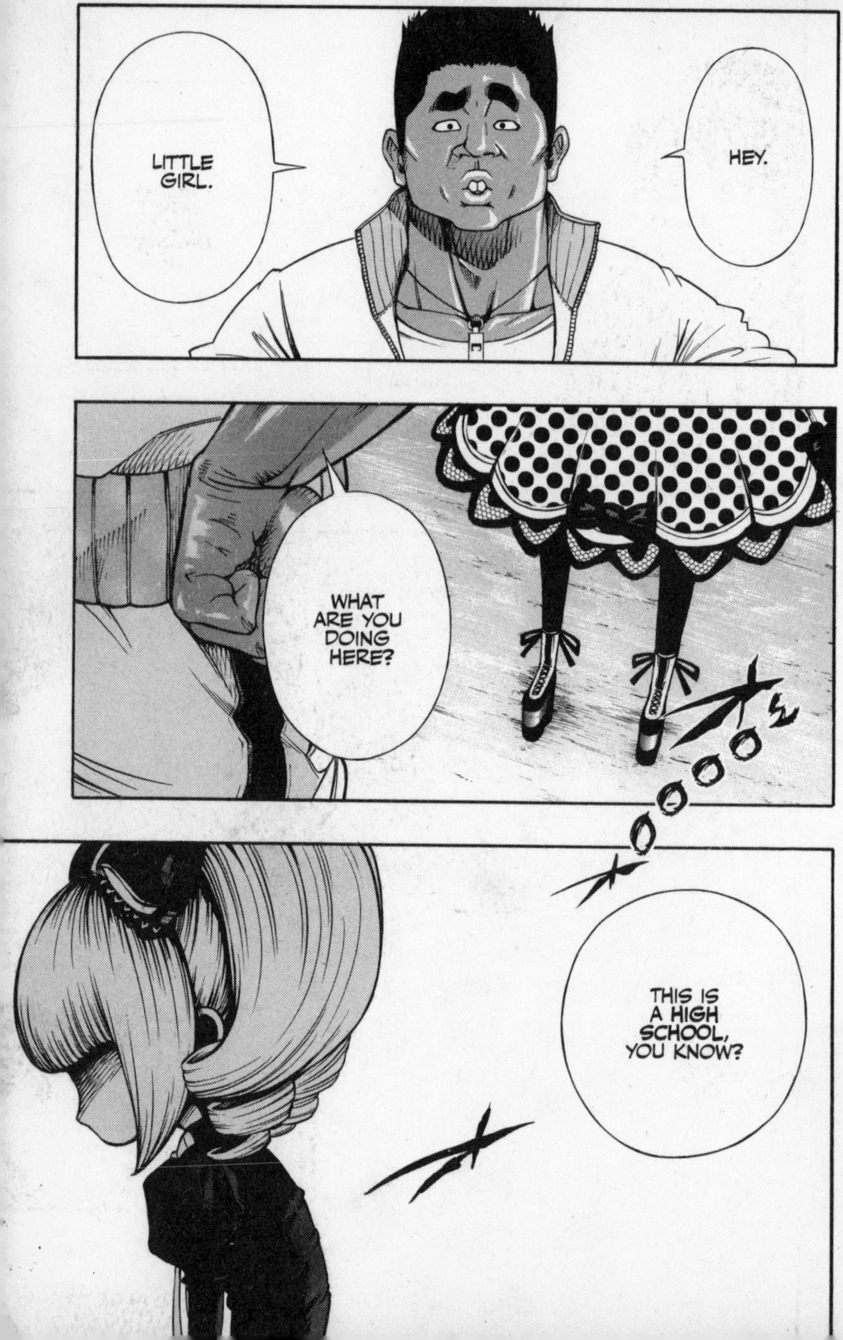
HEY.
LITTLE GIRL.
WHAT ARE YOU DOING HERE?
THIS IS A HIGH SCHOOL, YOU KNOW?

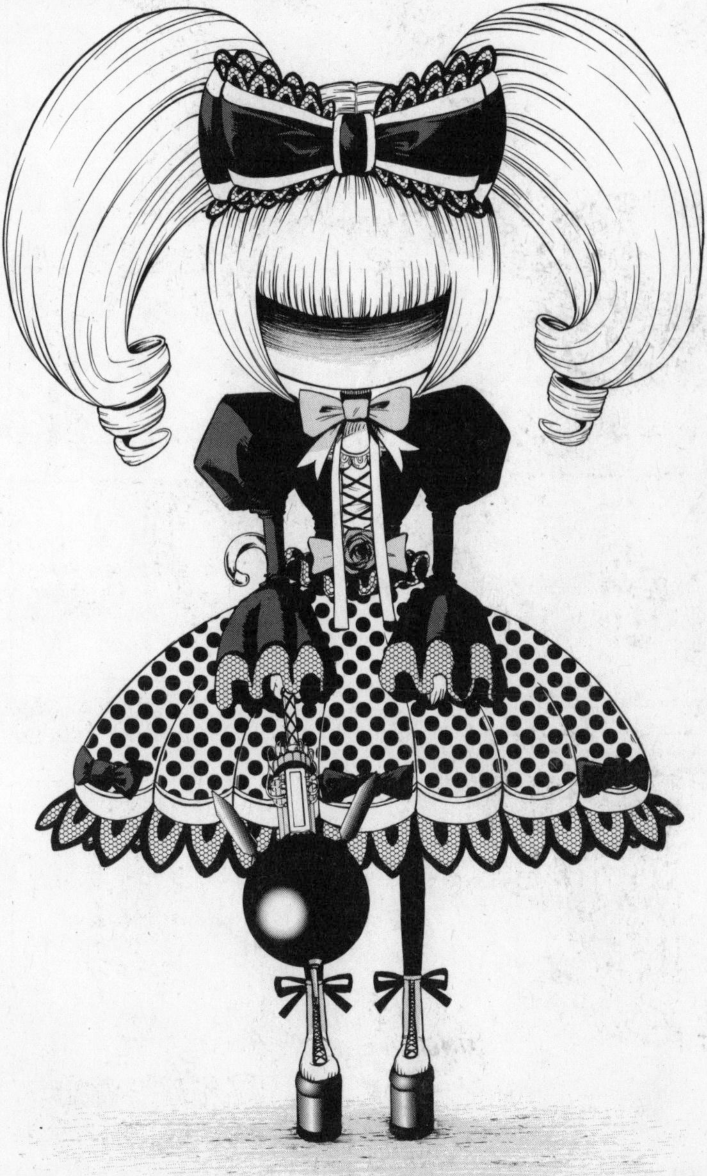

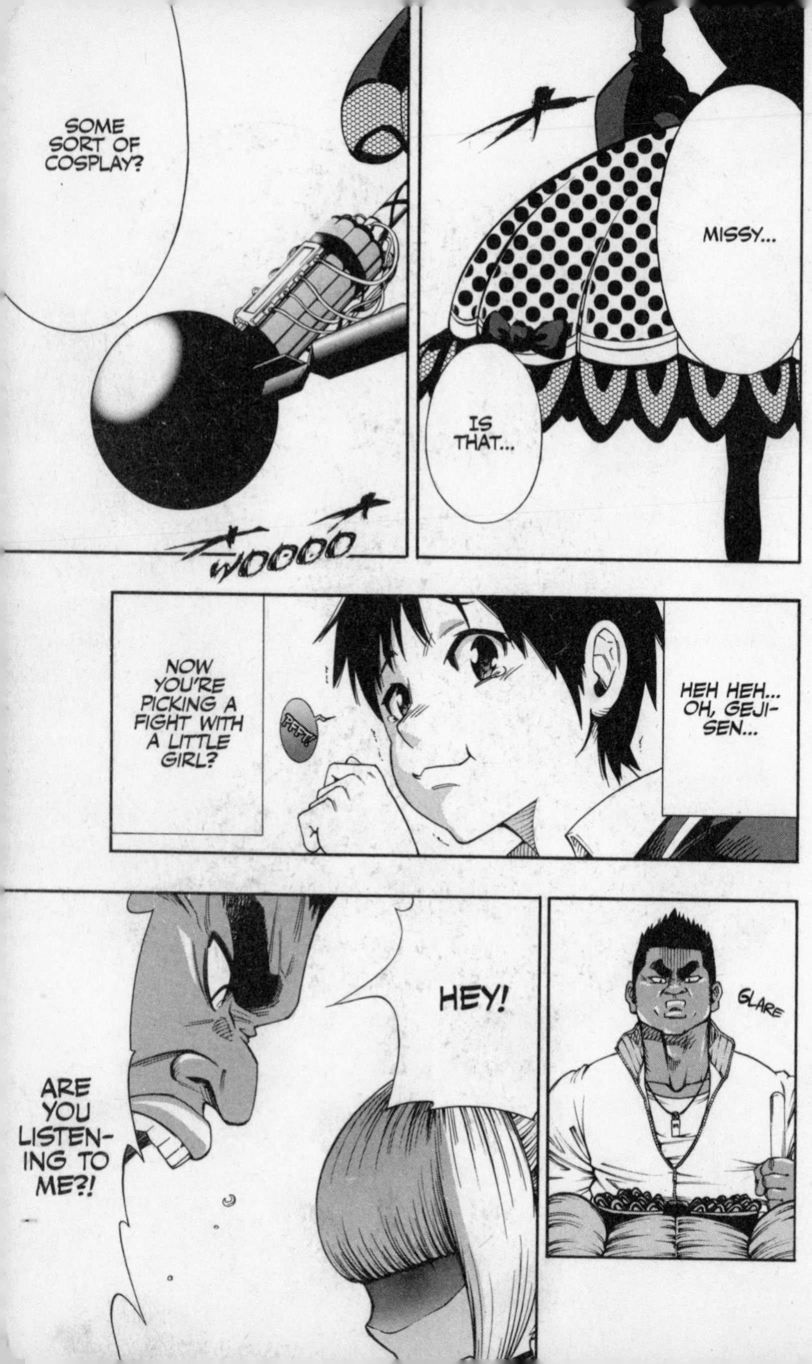
MISSY...
IS THAT...
SOME SORT OF COSPLAY?
WOOOO
HEH HEH... OH, GEJI-SEN...
PFFT!
NOW YOU'RE PICKING A FIGHT WITH A LITTLE GIRL?
GLARE
HEY!
ARE YOU LISTENING TO ME?!

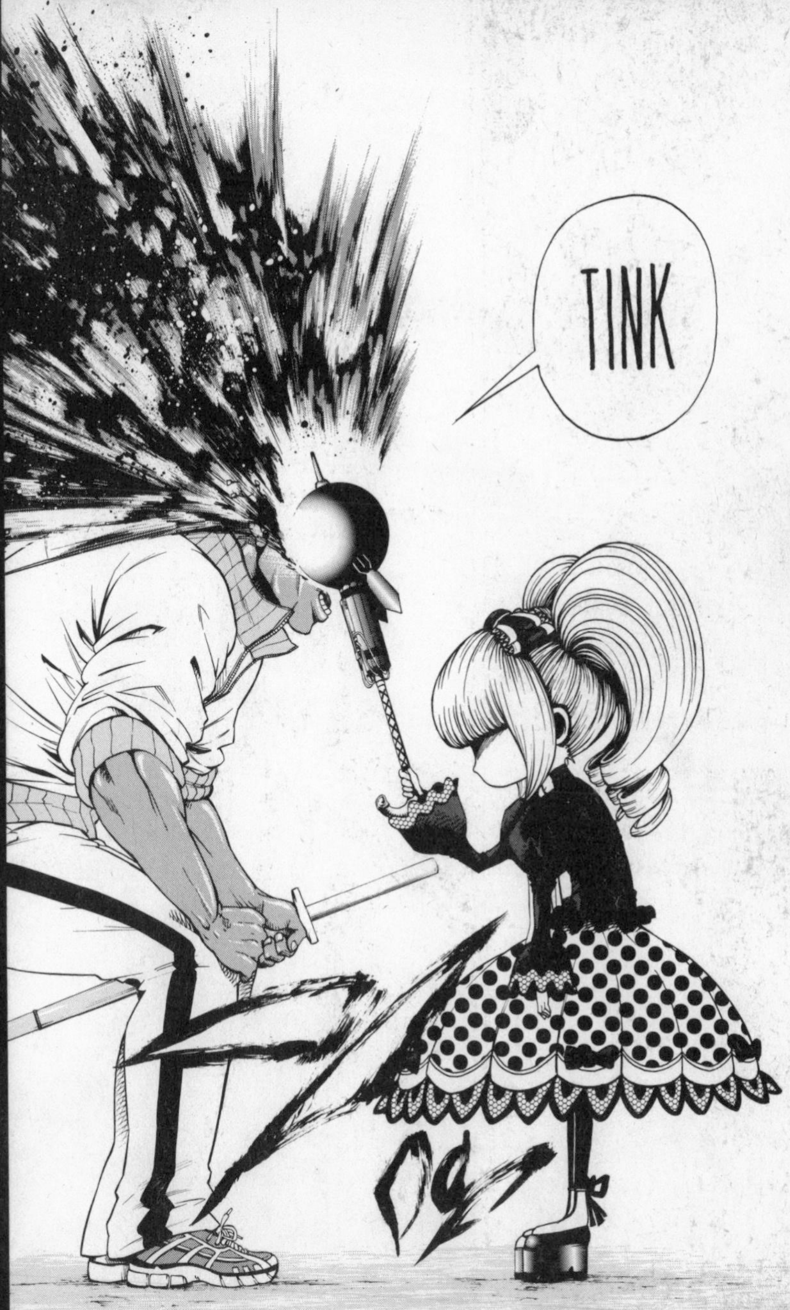
TINK

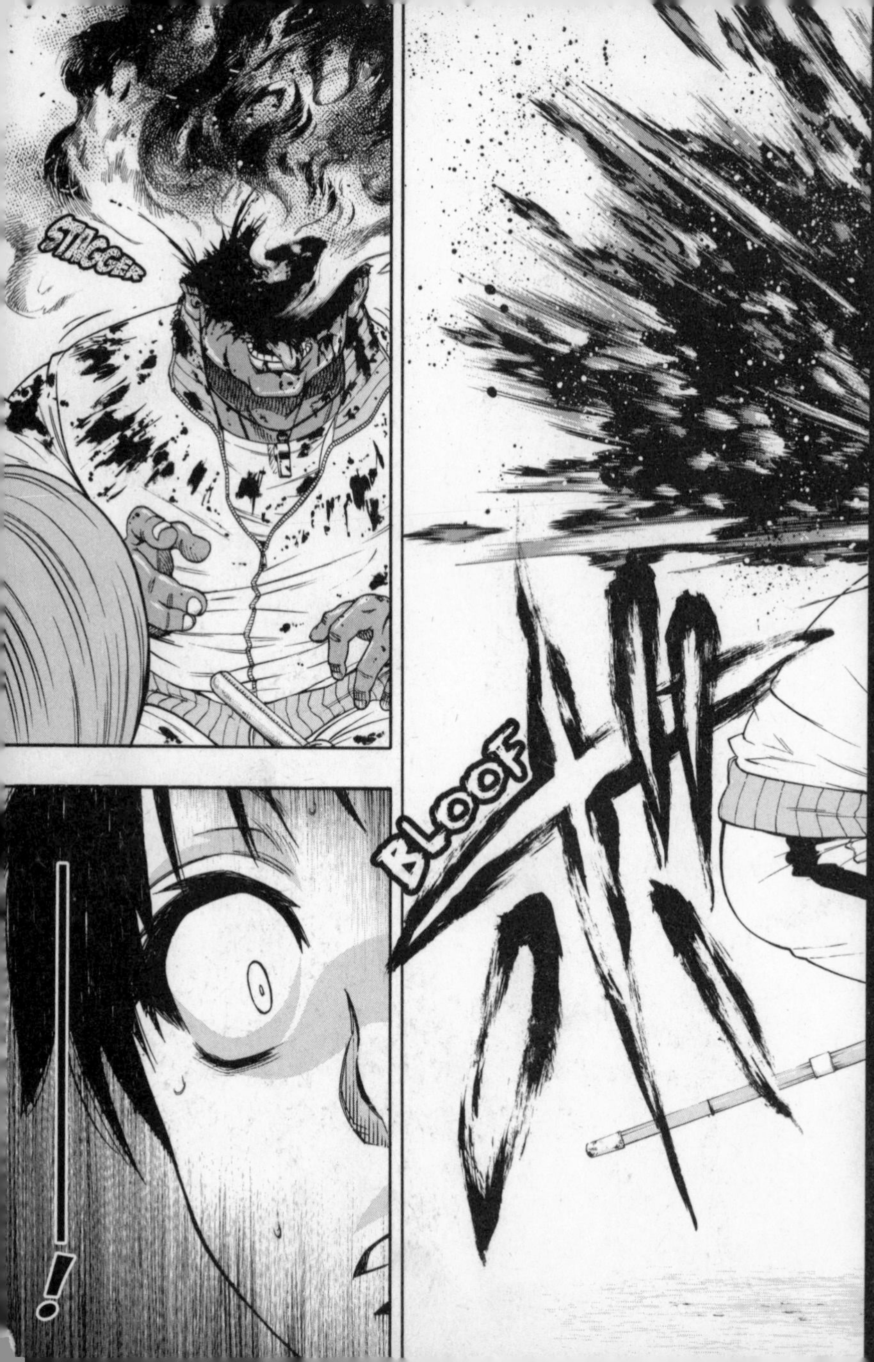
BLOOF
STAGGER
—!

SLUNK

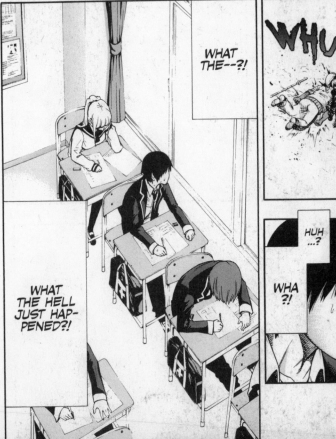

WHAT
THE--?!

WHUMP

WHAT
THE HELL
JUST HAP-
PENED?!

HUH
...?

WHA
?!

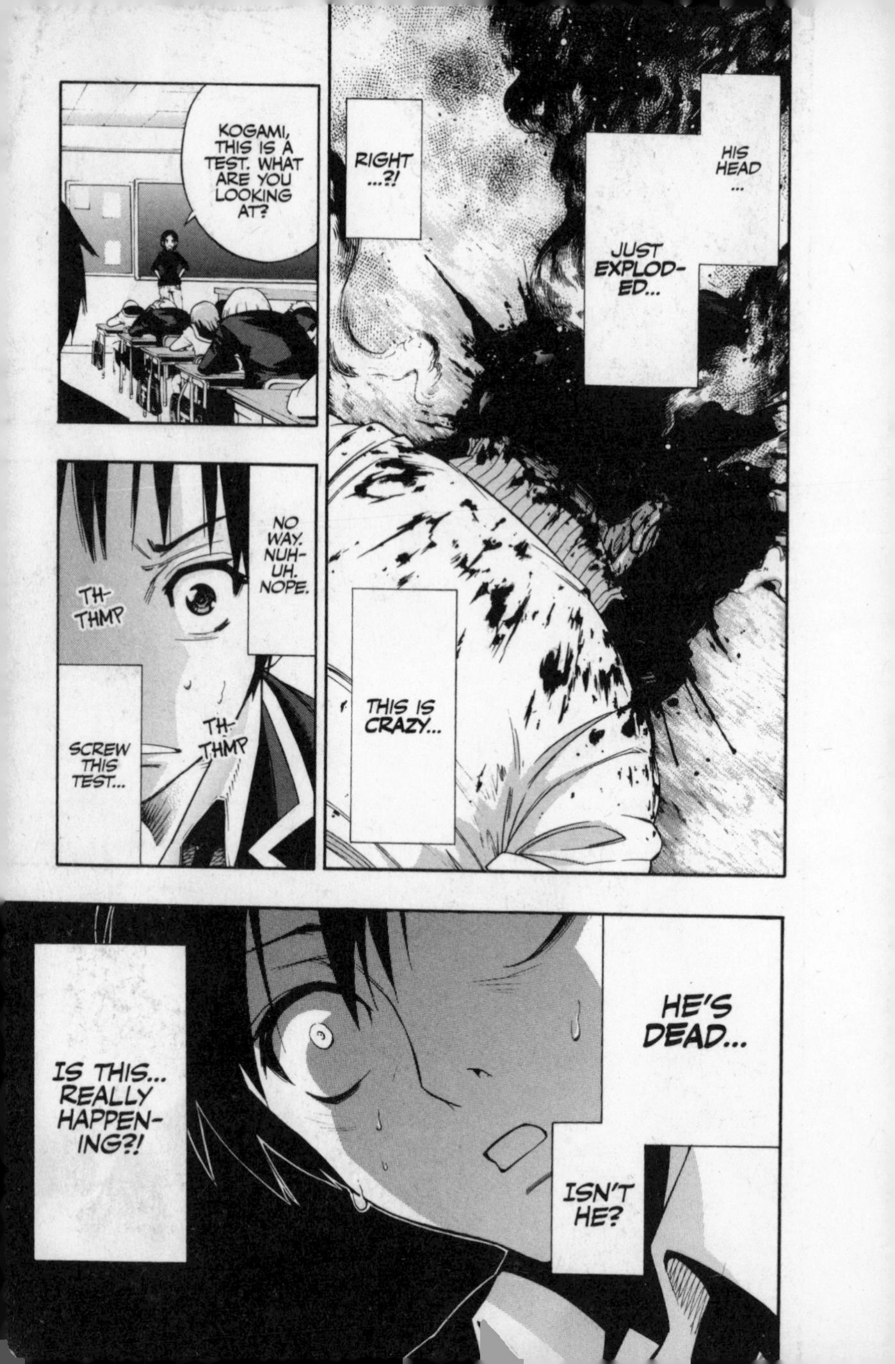
HIS HEAD ...
RIGHT ...?!
JUST EXPLODED...
THIS IS CRAZY...
KOGAMI, THIS IS A TEST. WHAT ARE YOU LOOKING AT?
NO WAY. NUH-UH. NOPE.
TH-THMP
TH-THMP
SCREW THIS TEST...
HE'S DEAD...
ISN'T HE?
IS THIS... REALLY HAPPENING?!

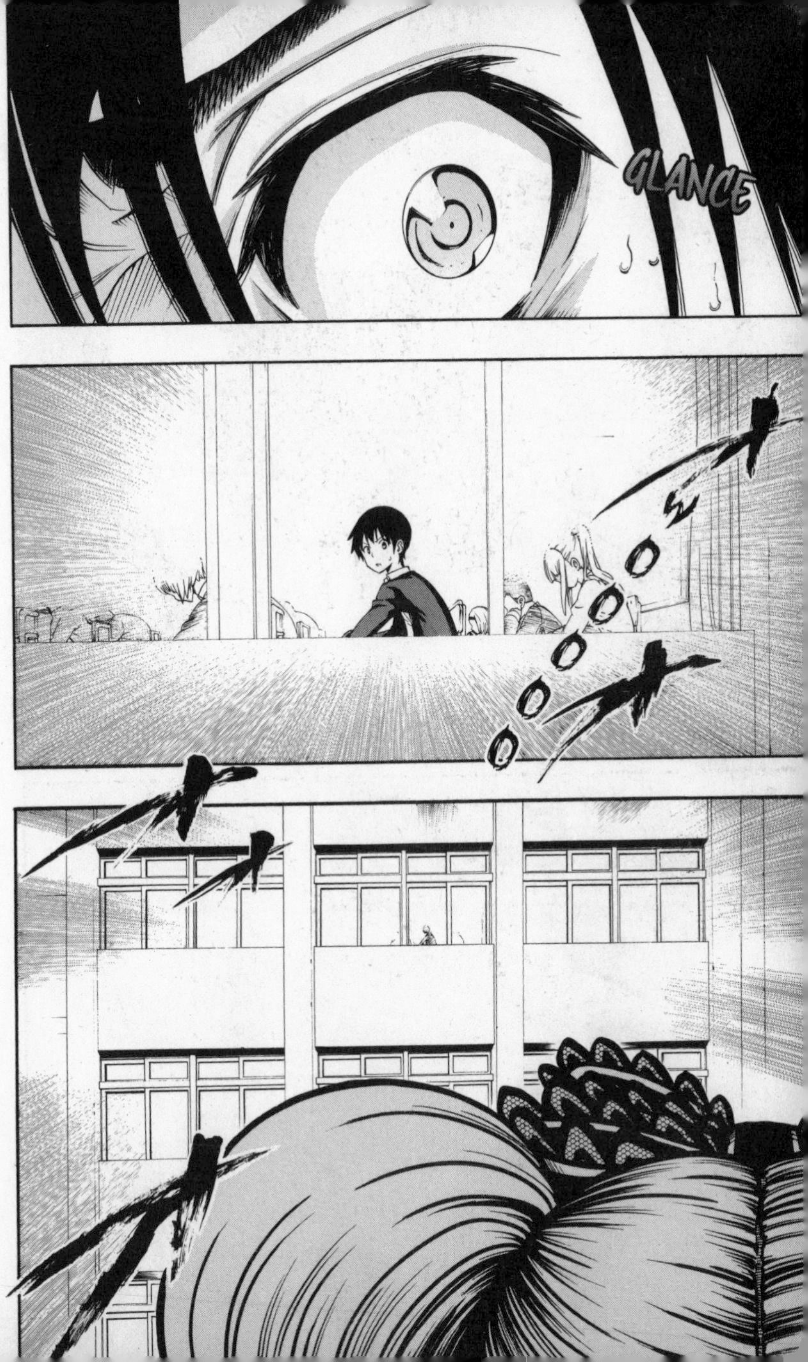
GLANCE

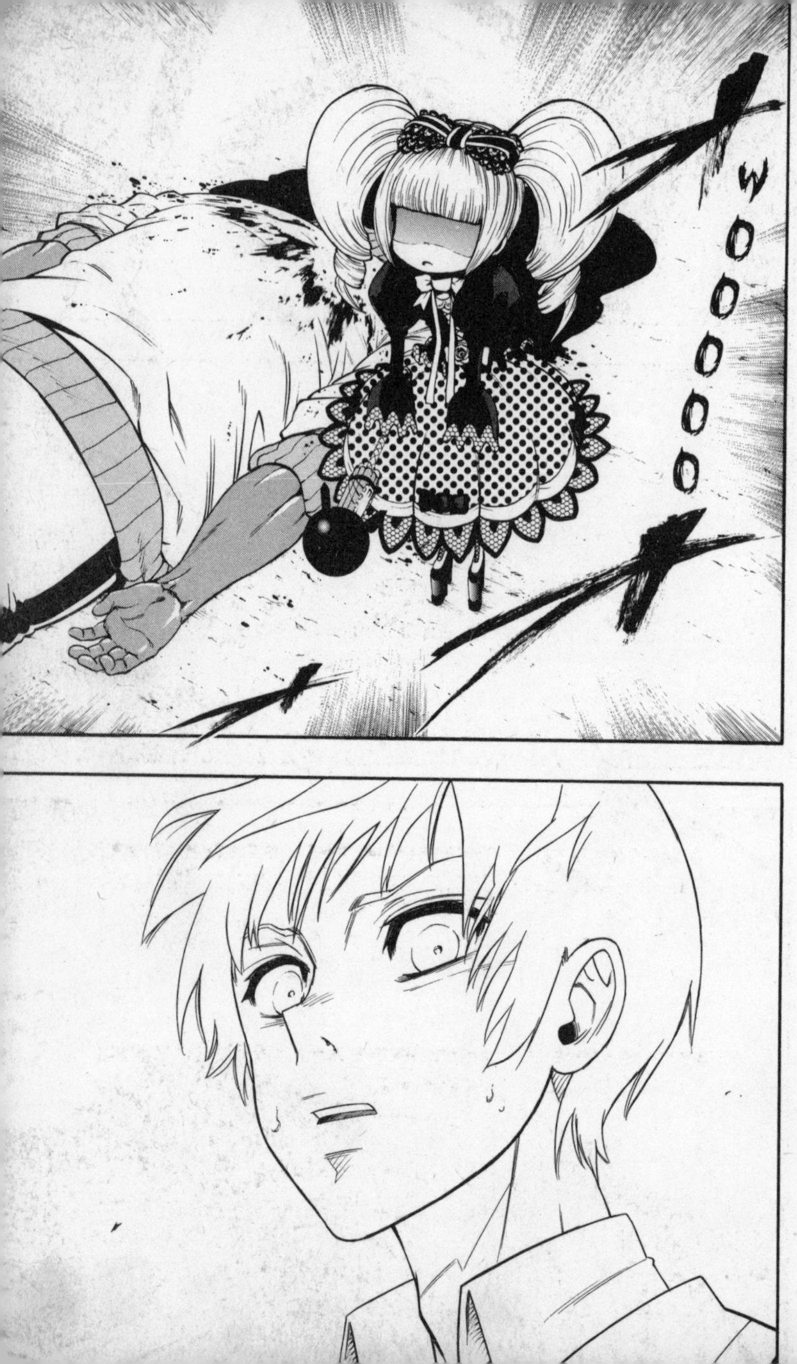
WOOOOO

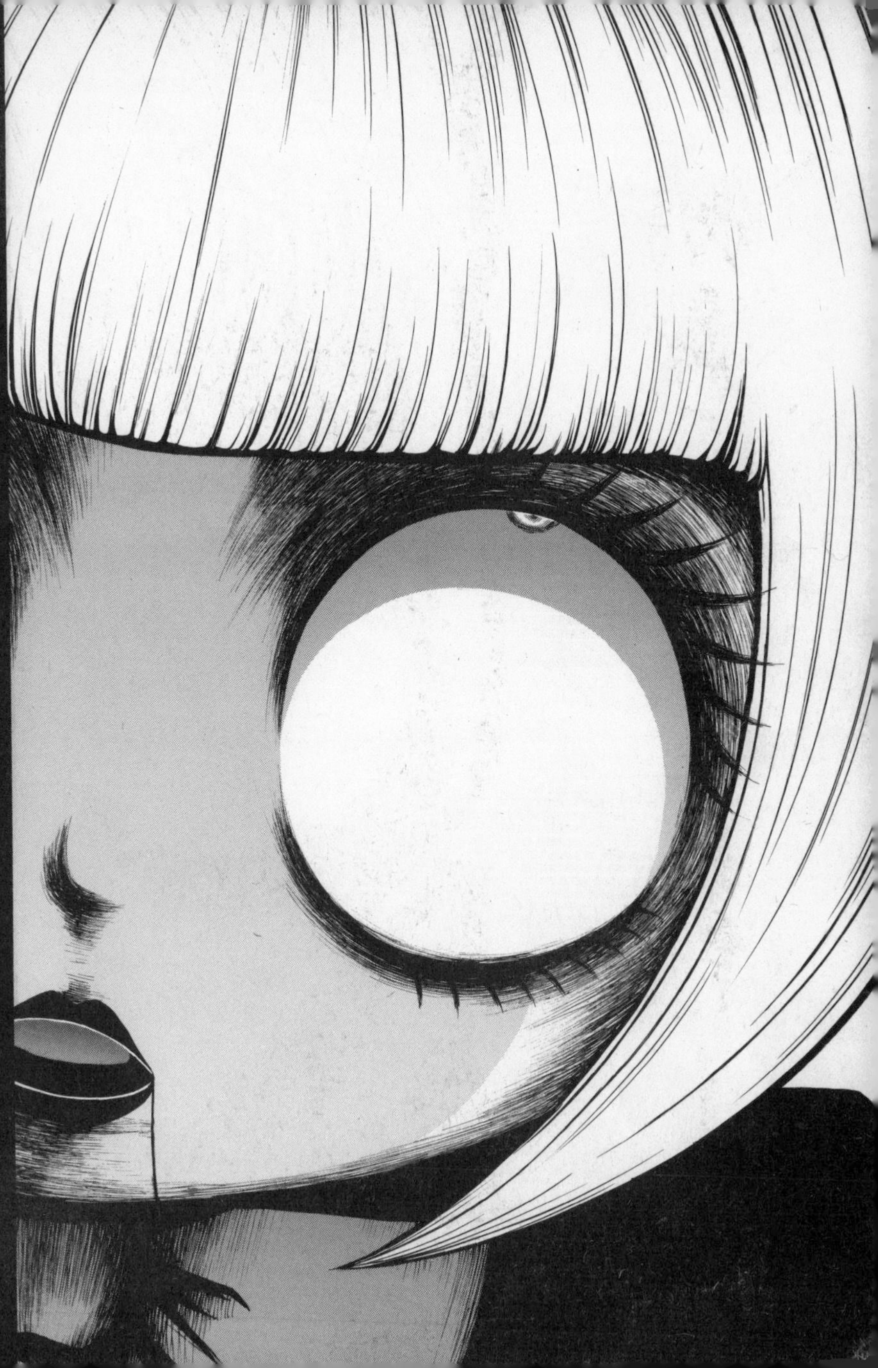

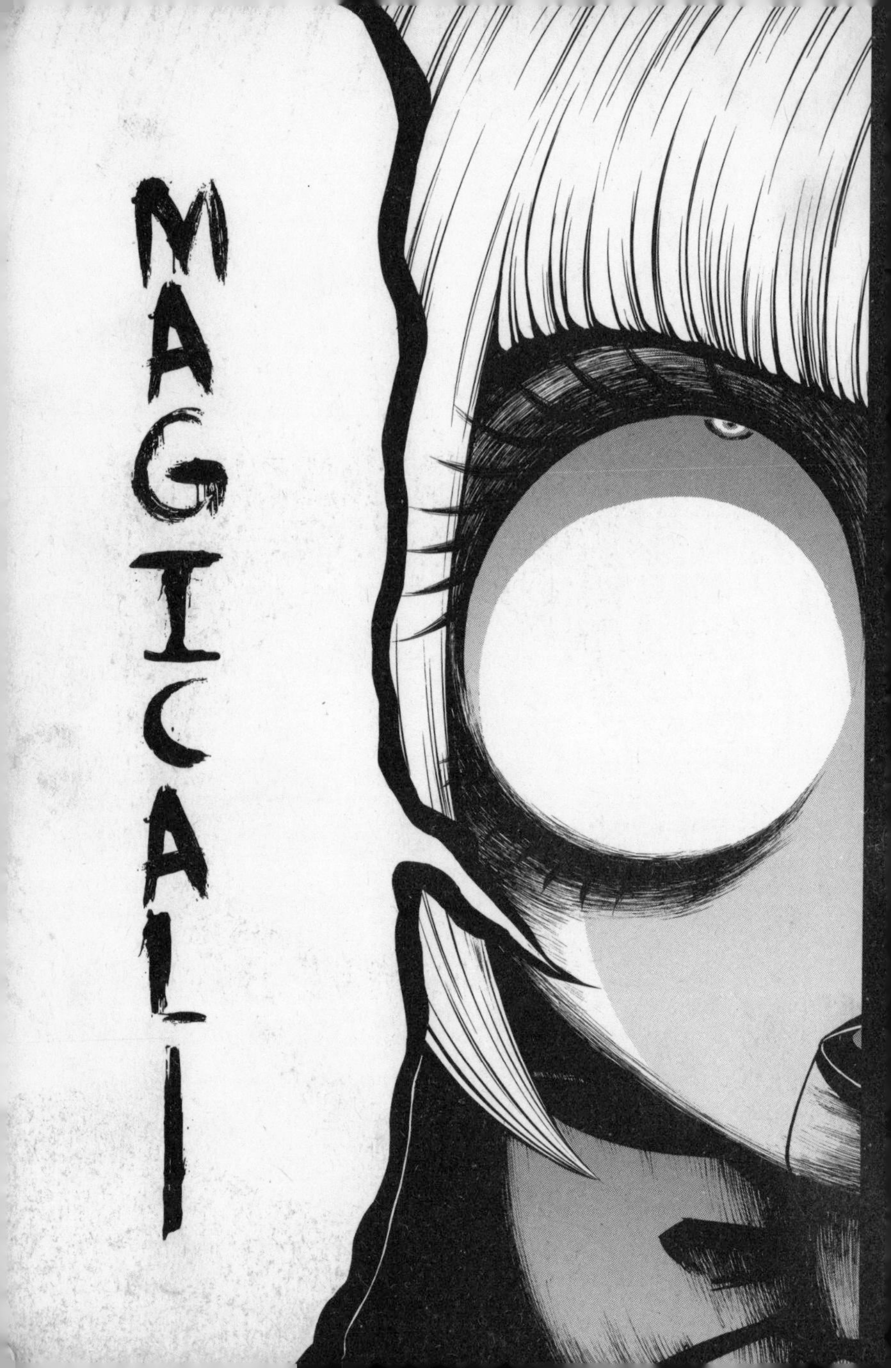
MAGICAL

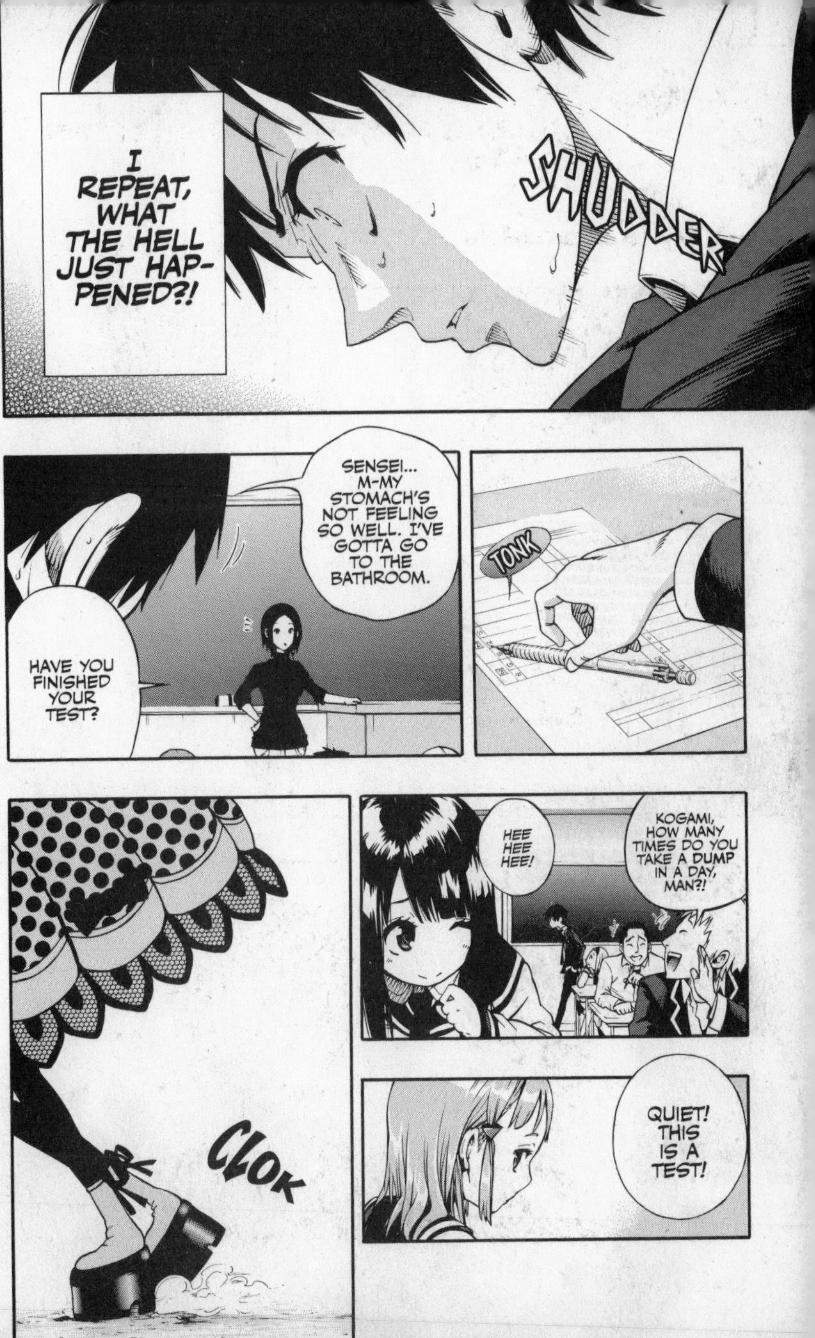
SHUDDER
I REPEAT, WHAT THE HELL JUST HAPPENED?!
TONK
SENSEI... M-MY STOMACH'S NOT FEELING SO WELL. I'VE GOTTA GO TO THE BATHROOM.
HAVE YOU FINISHED YOUR TEST?
KOGAMI, HOW MANY TIMES DO YOU TAKE A DUMP IN A DAY, MAN?!
HEE HEE HEE!
QUIET! THIS IS A TEST!
CLOK

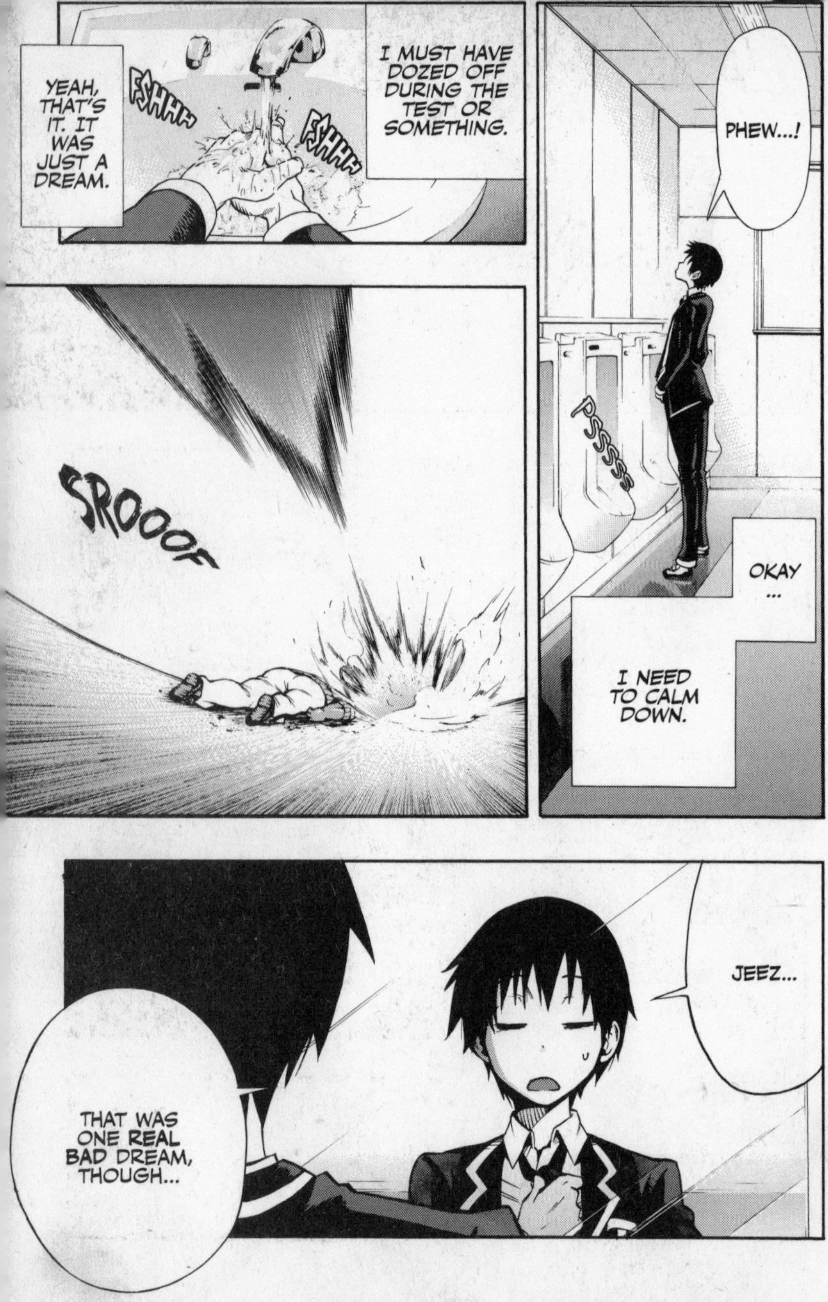
PHEW...!
PSSSSS
OKAY ...
I NEED TO CALM DOWN.
I MUST HAVE DOZED OFF DURING THE TEST OR SOMETHING.
FSHHH
FSHHH
YEAH, THAT'S IT. IT WAS JUST A DREAM.
SROOOF
JEEZ...
THAT WAS ONE REAL BAD DREAM, THOUGH...

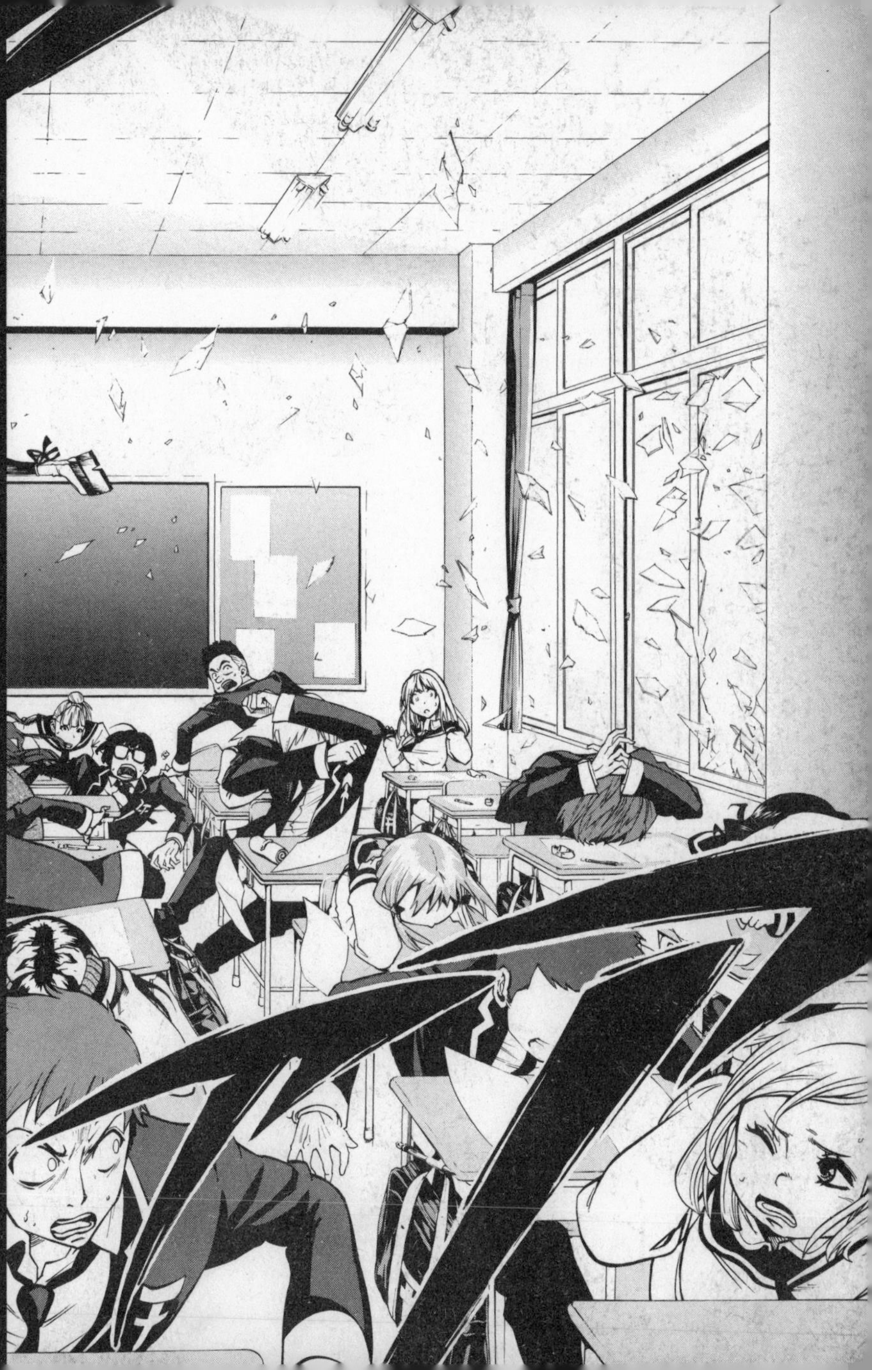

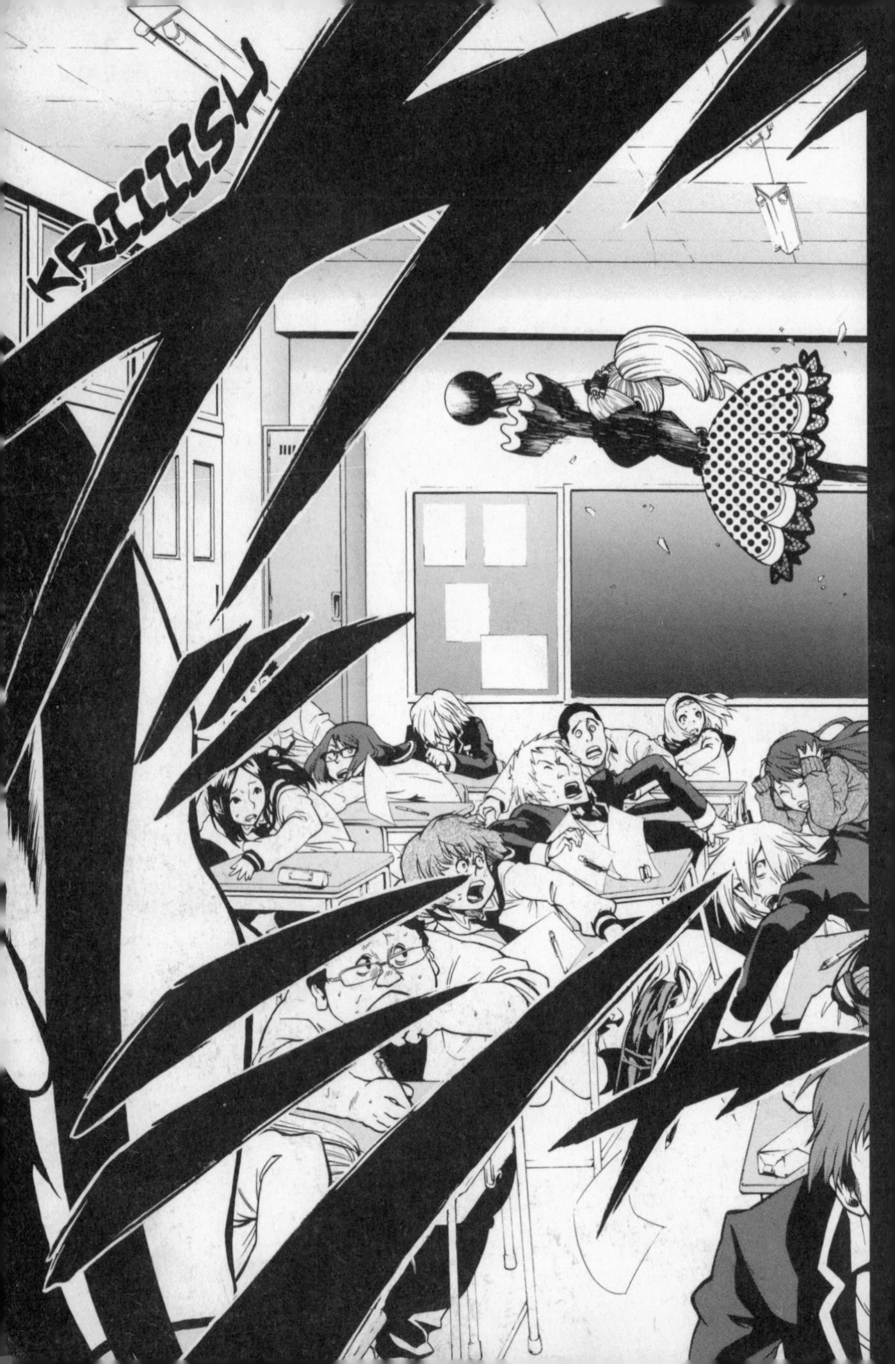
KRIIIISH

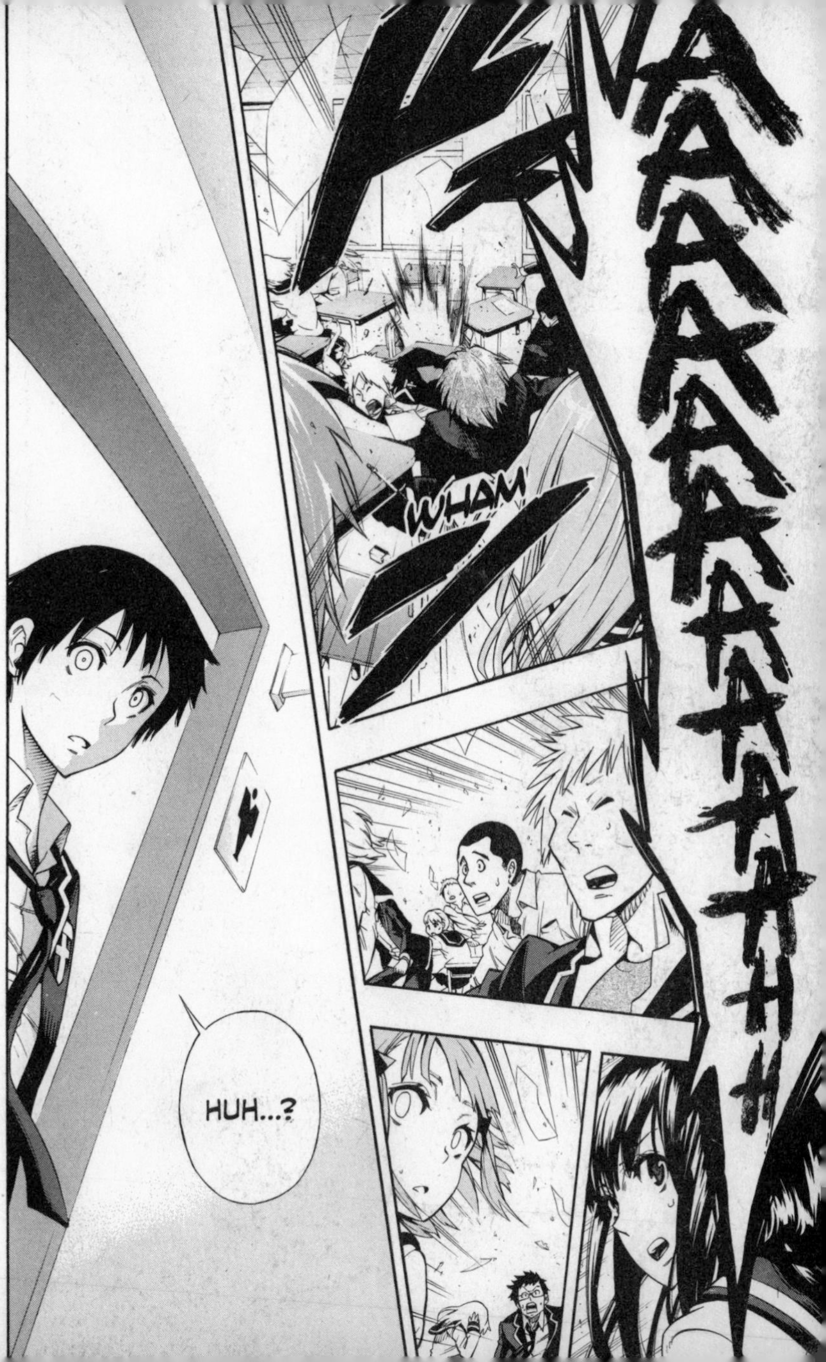
AAAAAAAAHHHHH
WHAM
HUH...?

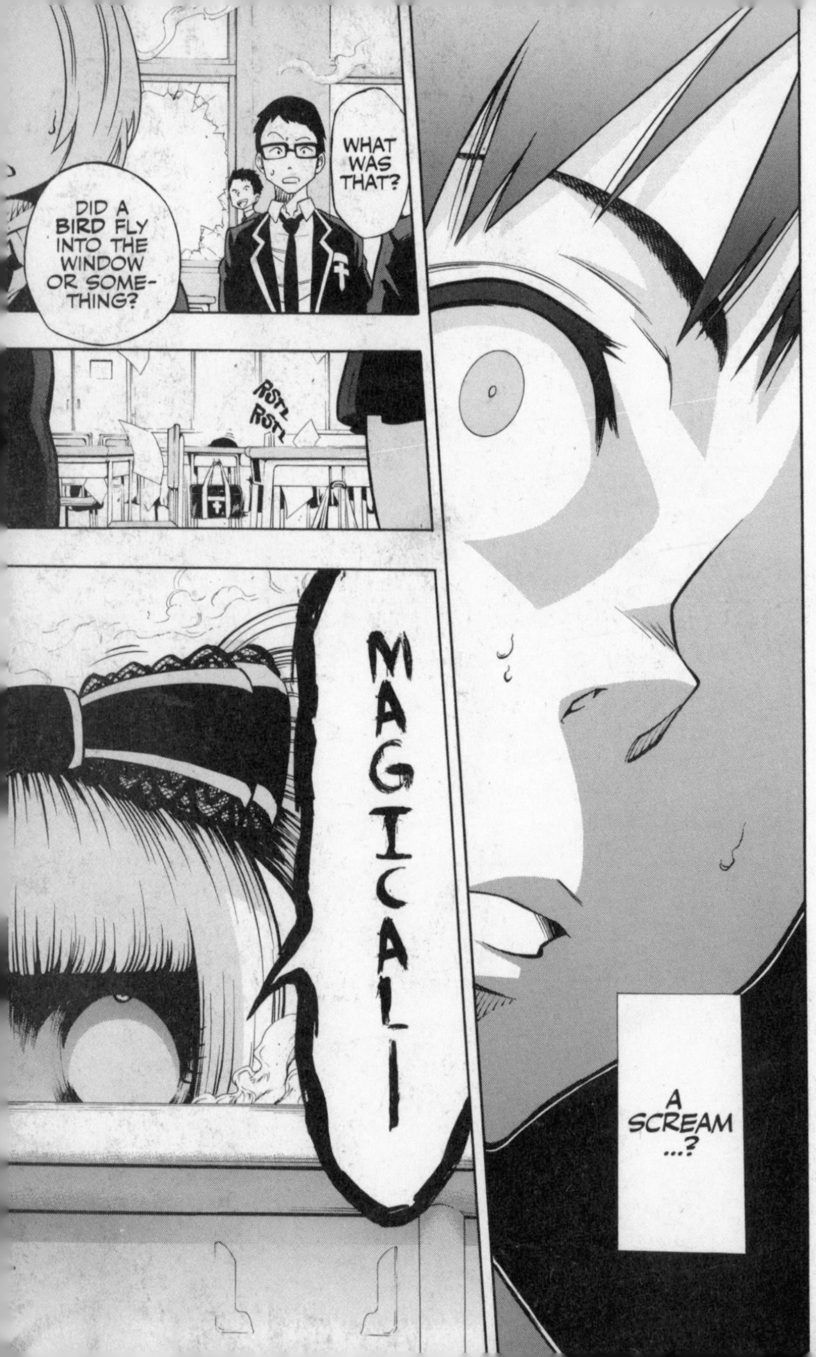
A SCREAM ...?
WHAT WAS THAT?
DID A BIRD FLY INTO THE WINDOW OR SOME-THING?
RSTL RSTL
MAGICAL!

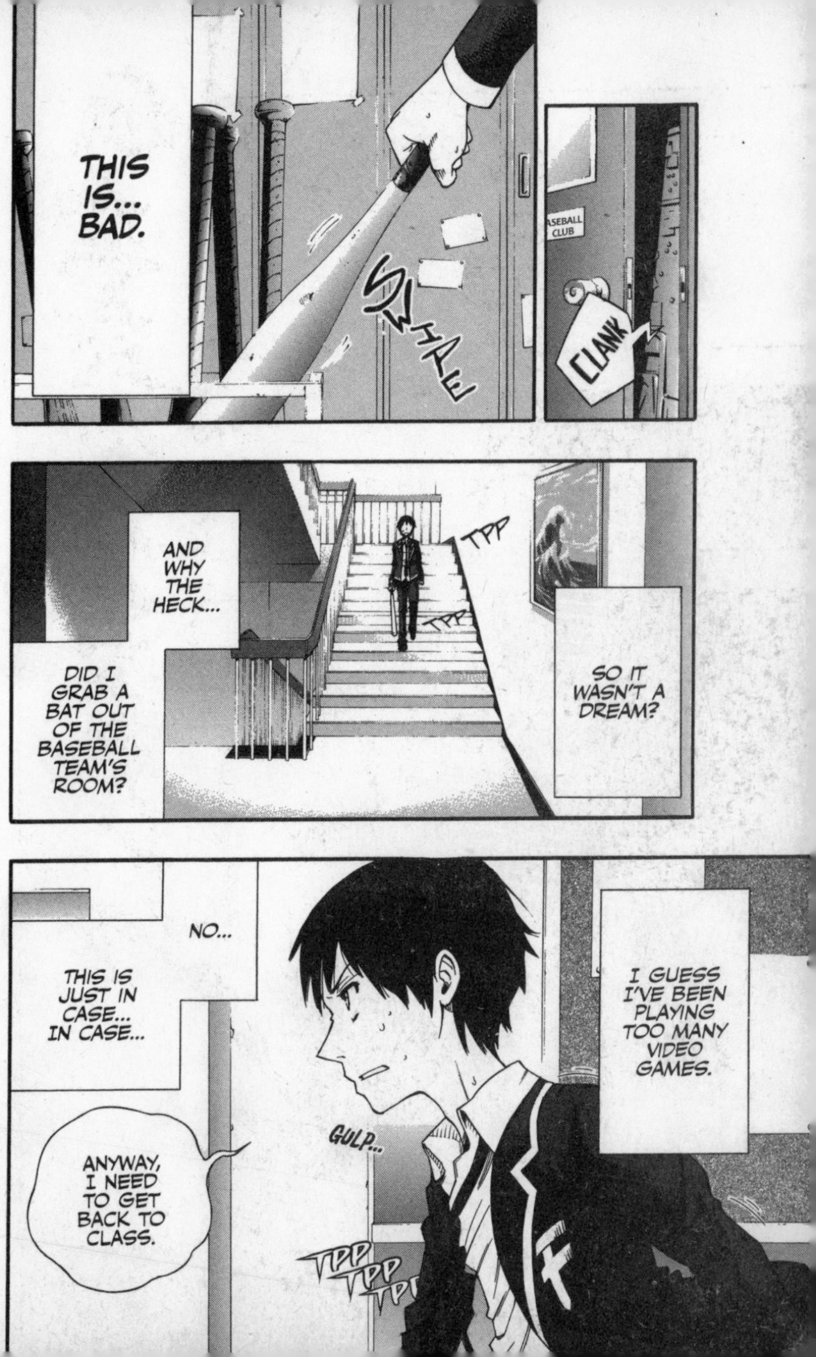
ASEBALL CLUB
CLANK
THIS IS... BAD.
SWIPE
TPP
SO IT WASN'T A DREAM?
AND WHY THE HECK...
DID I GRAB A BAT OUT OF THE BASEBALL TEAM'S ROOM?
TPP
I GUESS I'VE BEEN PLAYING TOO MANY VIDEO GAMES.
NO...
THIS IS JUST IN CASE... IN CASE...
GULP...
ANYWAY, I NEED TO GET BACK TO CLASS.
TPP TPP TPP

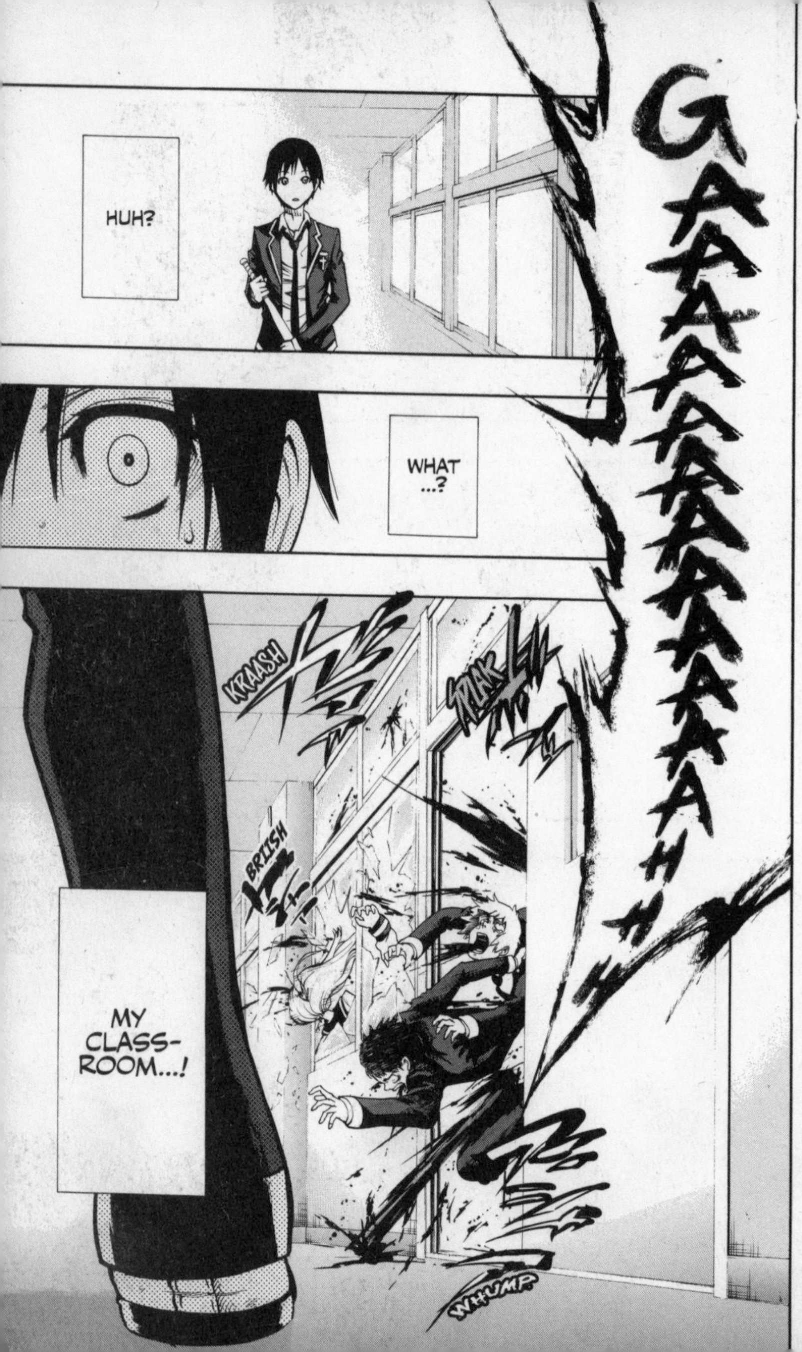
HUH?
GAAAAAAAAAAAAHHH
WHAT ...?
SPAK
KRAASH
BRIIISH
MY CLASS-ROOM...!
WHUMP

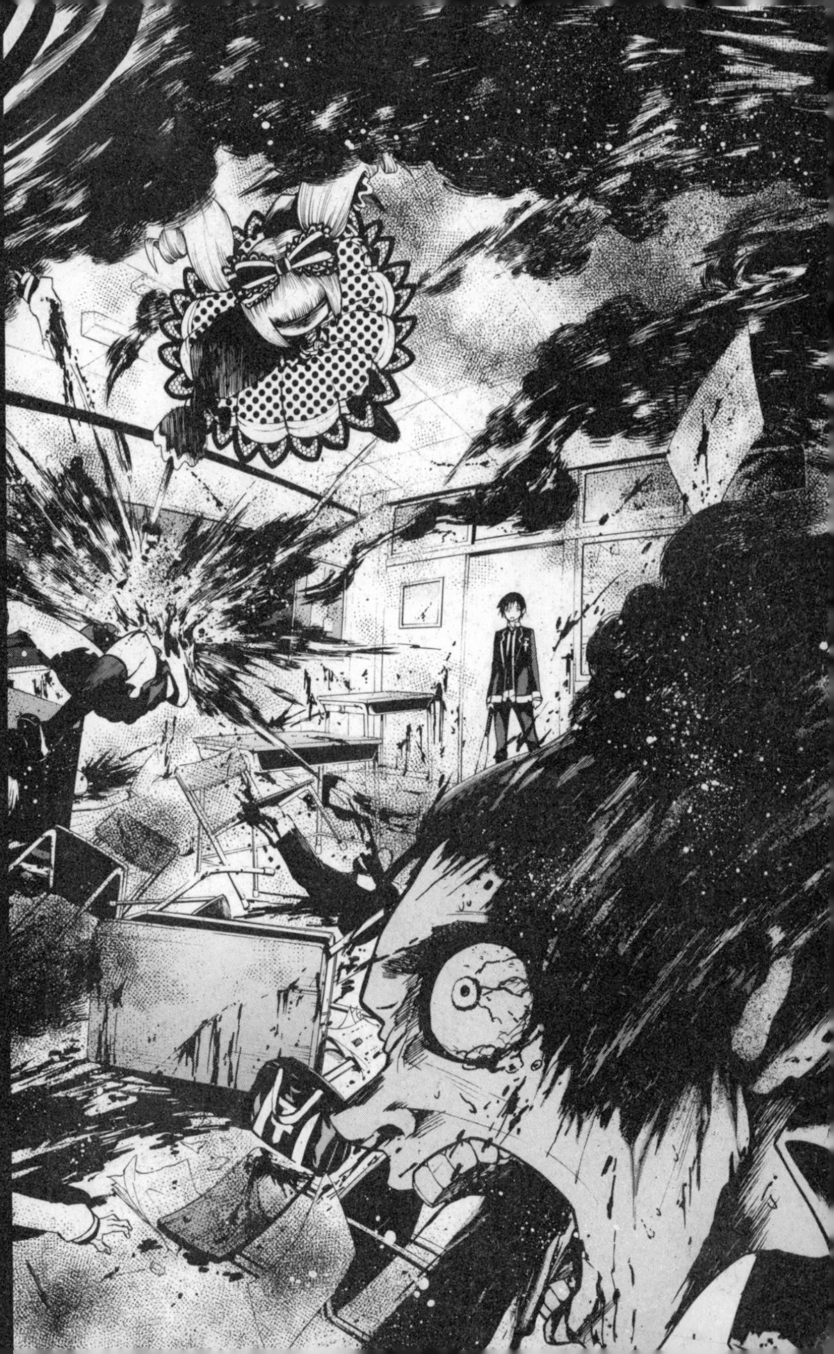

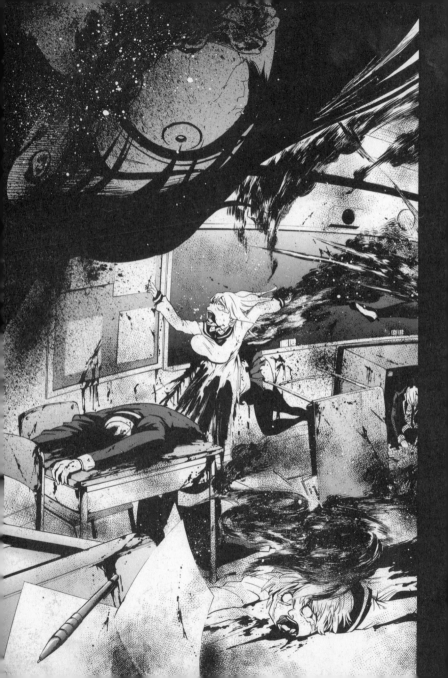

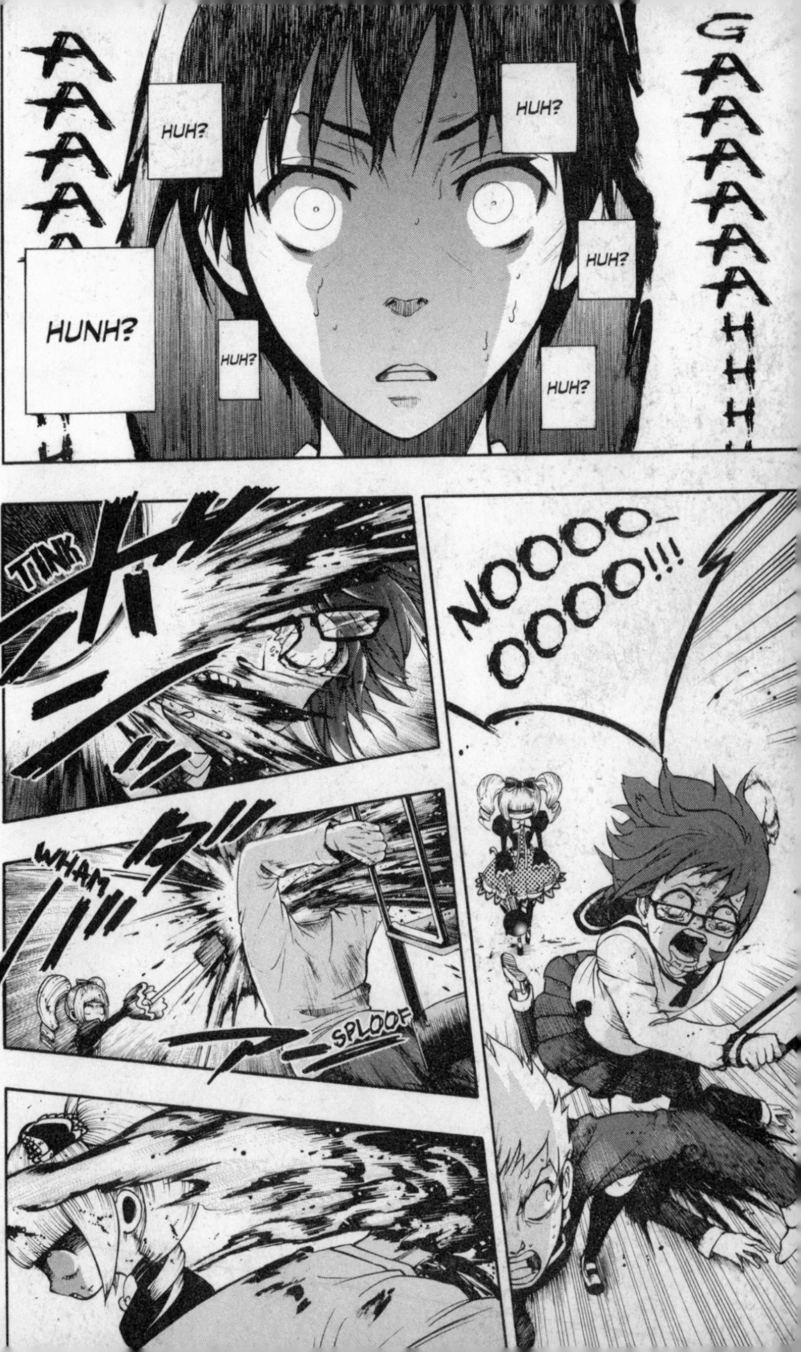
GAAAAAAHHH
HUH?
HUH?
HUH?
HUH?
HUH?
HUNH?
NOOOOO-
OOOOO!!!
TINK
WHAM
SPLOOF

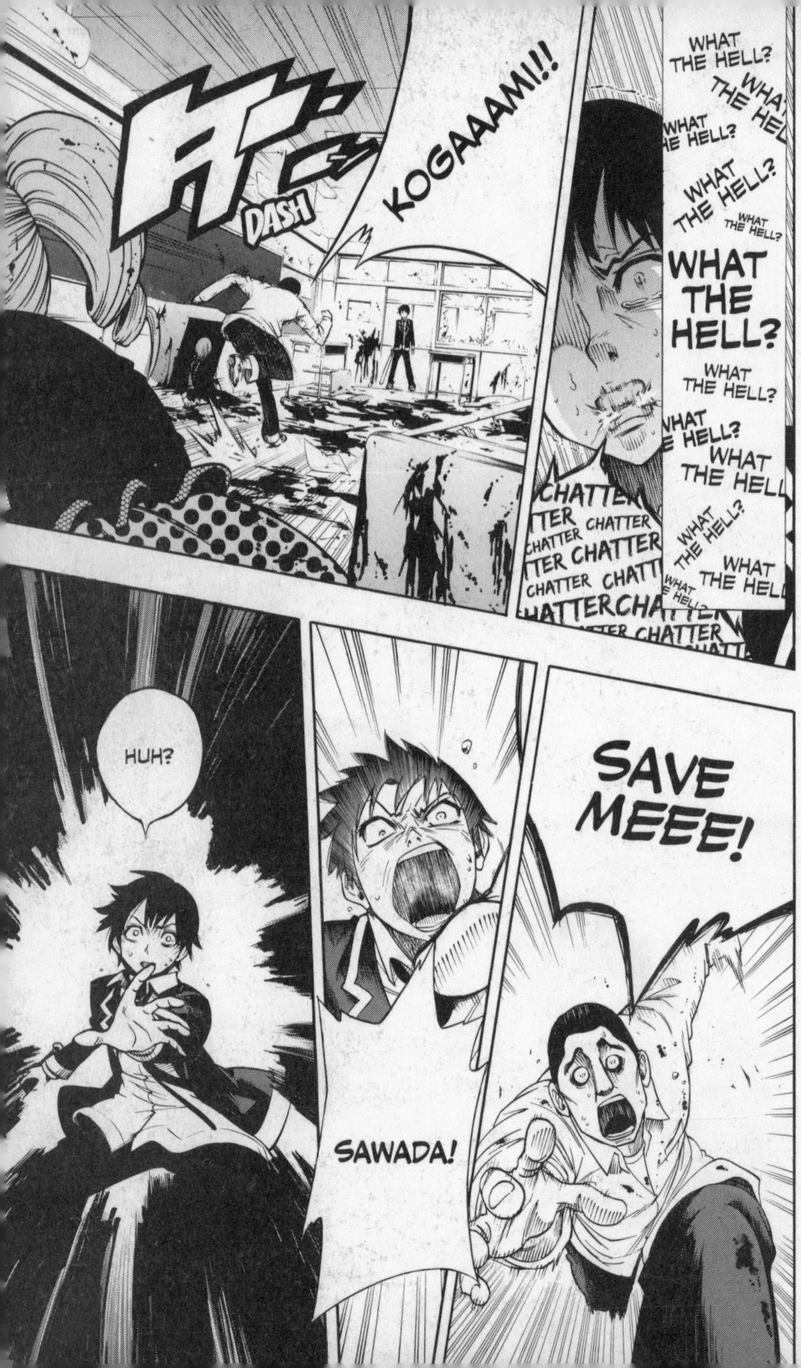
WHAT THE HELL?
WHAT THE HELL?
WHAT THE HELL?
WHAT THE HELL?
WHAT THE HELL?
WHAT THE HELL?
WHAT THE HELL?
WHAT THE HELL?
CHATTER
CHATTER
CHATTER
CHATTER
DASH
KOGAAAMI!!
SAVE MEEE!
SAWADA!
HUH?

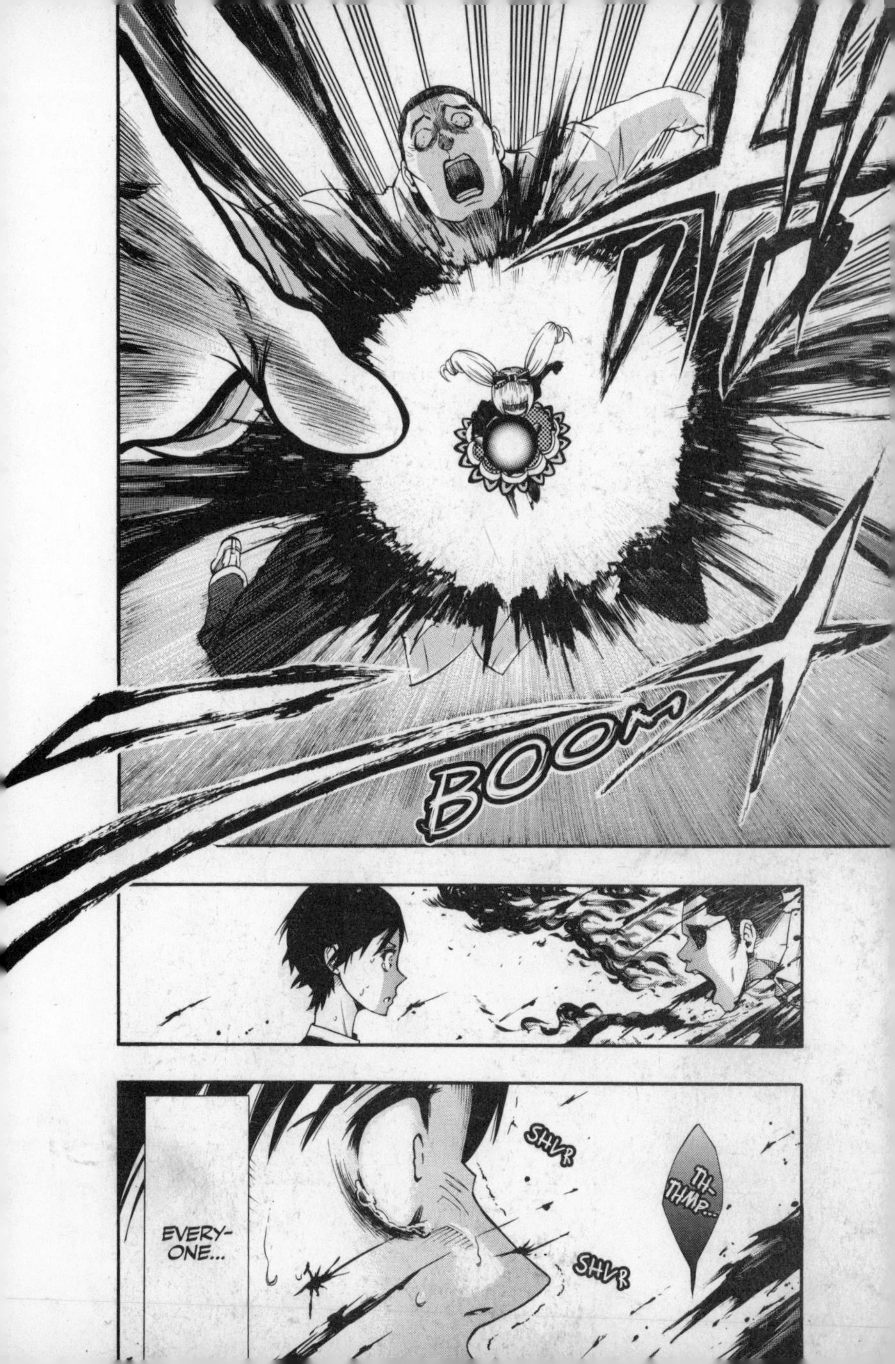
BOOM
SHVR
TH-THMP...
SHVR
EVERY-ONE...

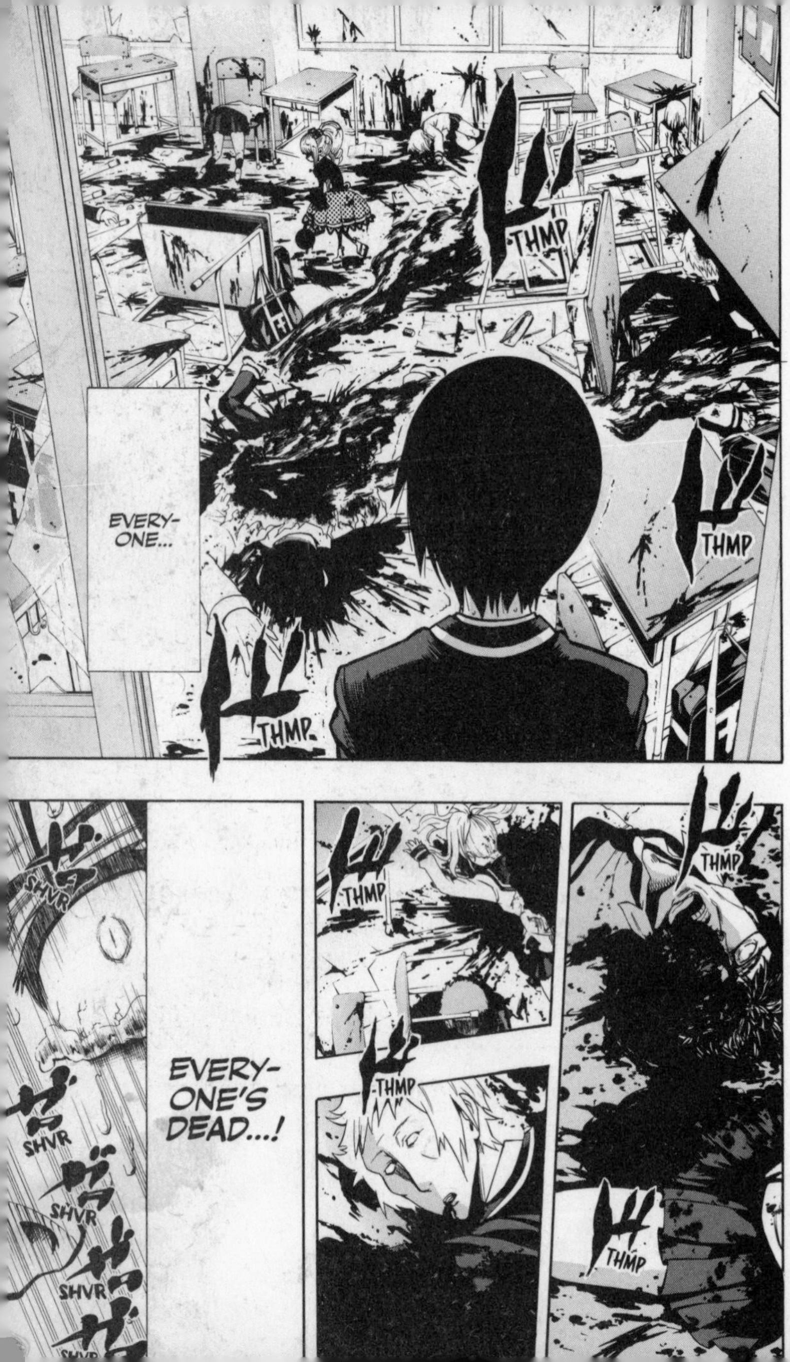
THMP
THMP
EVERY-ONE...
THMP
THMP
THMP
THMP
THMP
EVERY-ONE'S DEAD...!
SHVR
SHVR
SHVR
SHVR

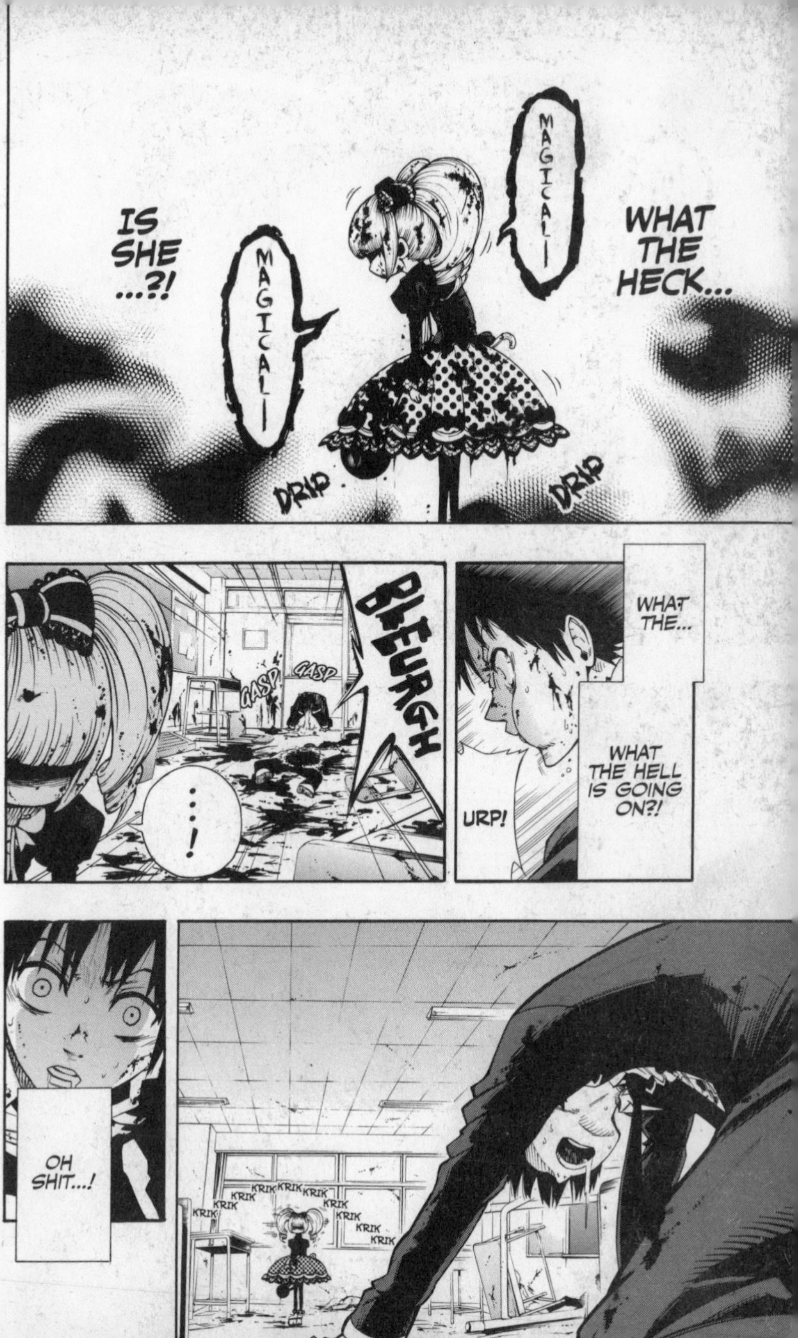
WHAT THE HECK...
MAGICAL!
MAGICAL!
IS SHE ...?!
DRIP
DRIP
WHAT THE...
WHAT THE HELL IS GOING ON?!
URP!
BLEURGH
GASP
GASP
...!
KRIK KRIK KRIK KRIK KRIK KRIK KRIK KRIK KRIK
OH SHIT...!

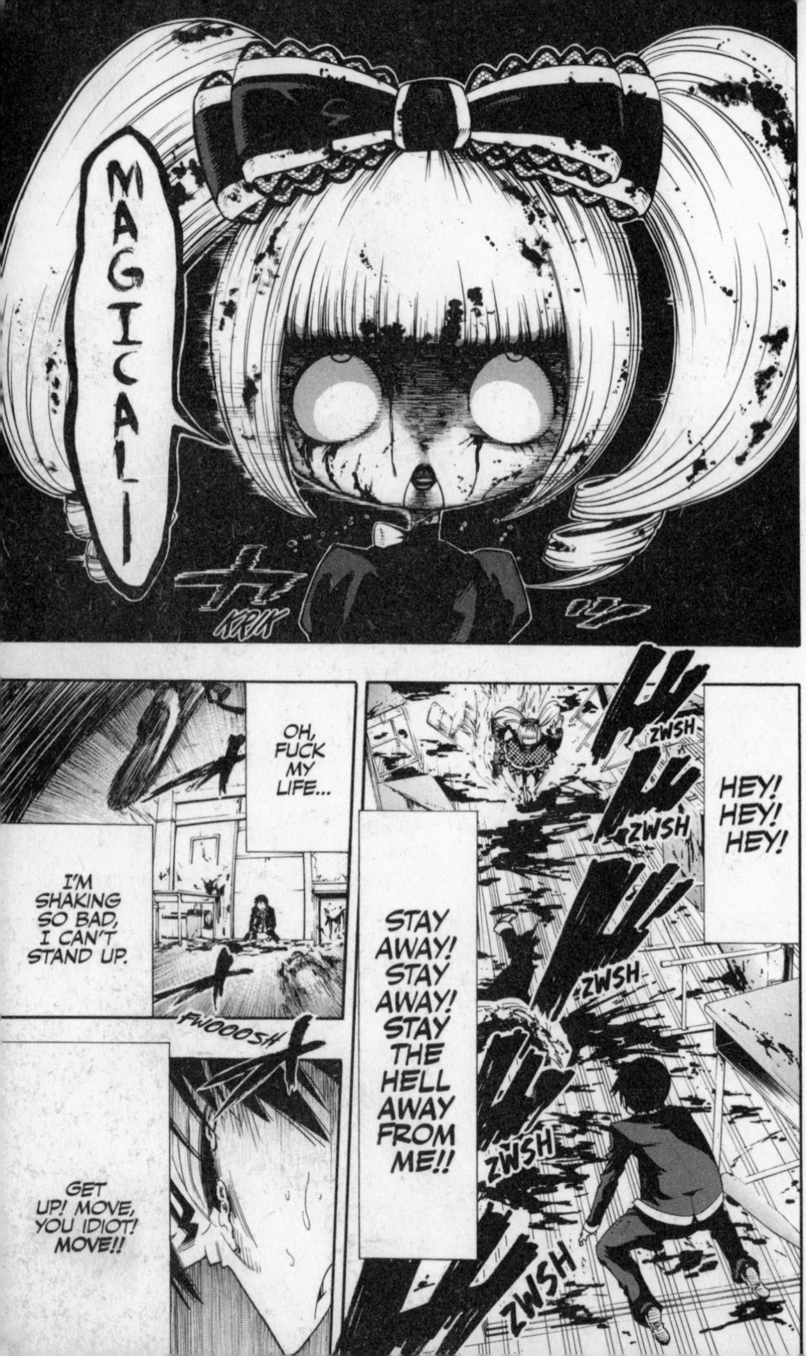
MAGICAL
KRIK
HEY! HEY! HEY!
ZWSH
ZWSH
ZWSH
STAY AWAY! STAY AWAY! STAY THE HELL AWAY FROM ME!!
ZWSH
ZWSH
ZWSH
OH, FUCK MY LIFE...
I'M SHAKING SO BAD, I CAN'T STAND UP.
FWOOOSH
GET UP! MOVE, YOU IDIOT! MOVE!!

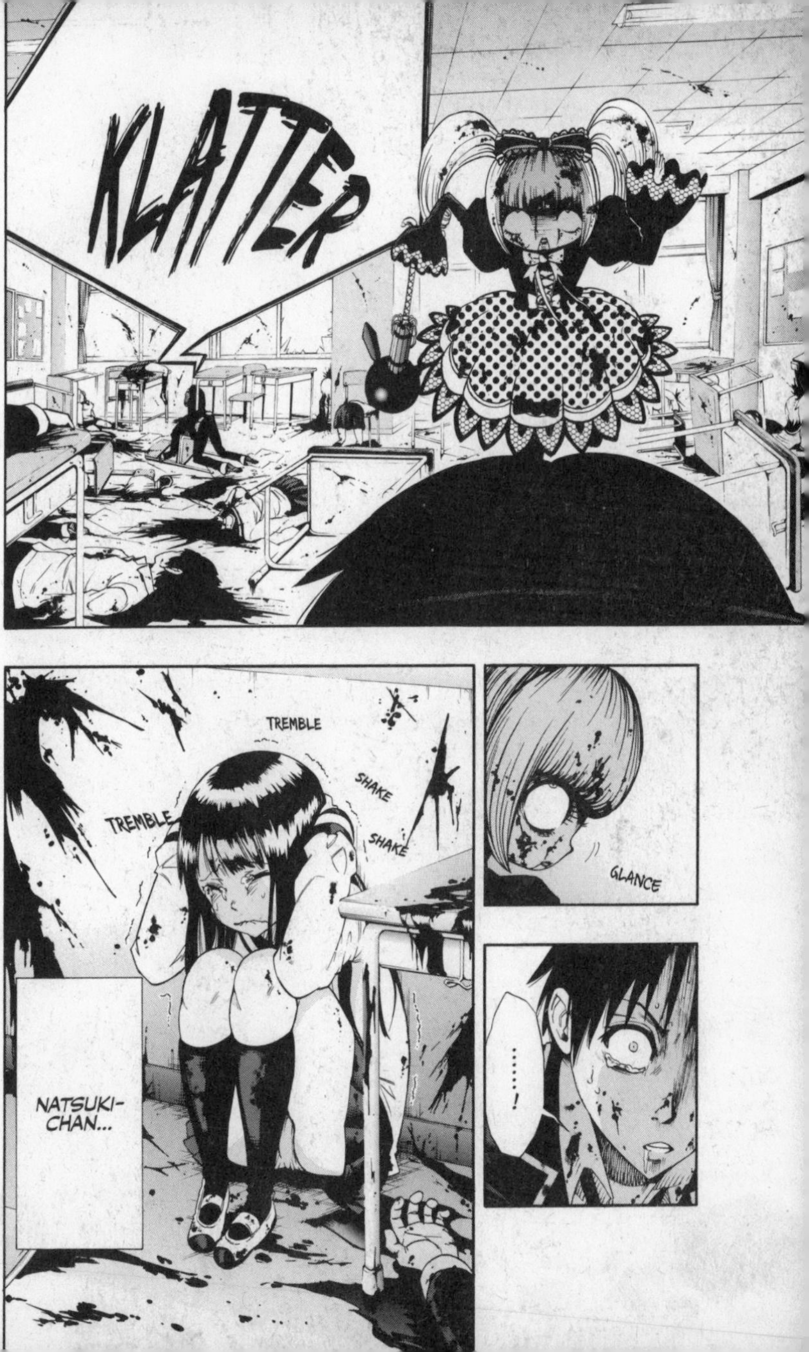
KLATTER
GLANCE
......!
TREMBLE
SHAKE
SHAKE
TREMBLE
NATSUKI-CHAN...

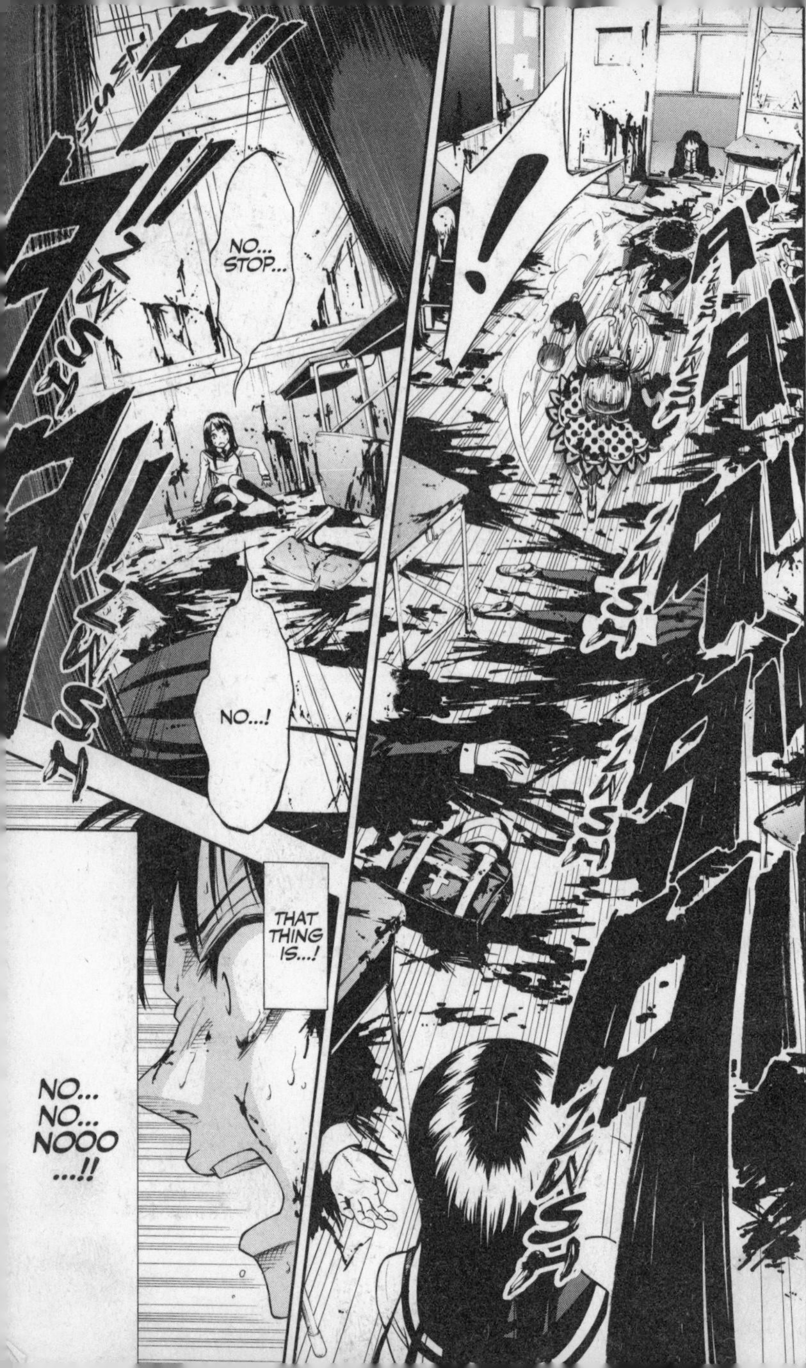
!
NO... STOP...
NO...!
THAT THING IS...!
NO... NO... NOOO ...!!

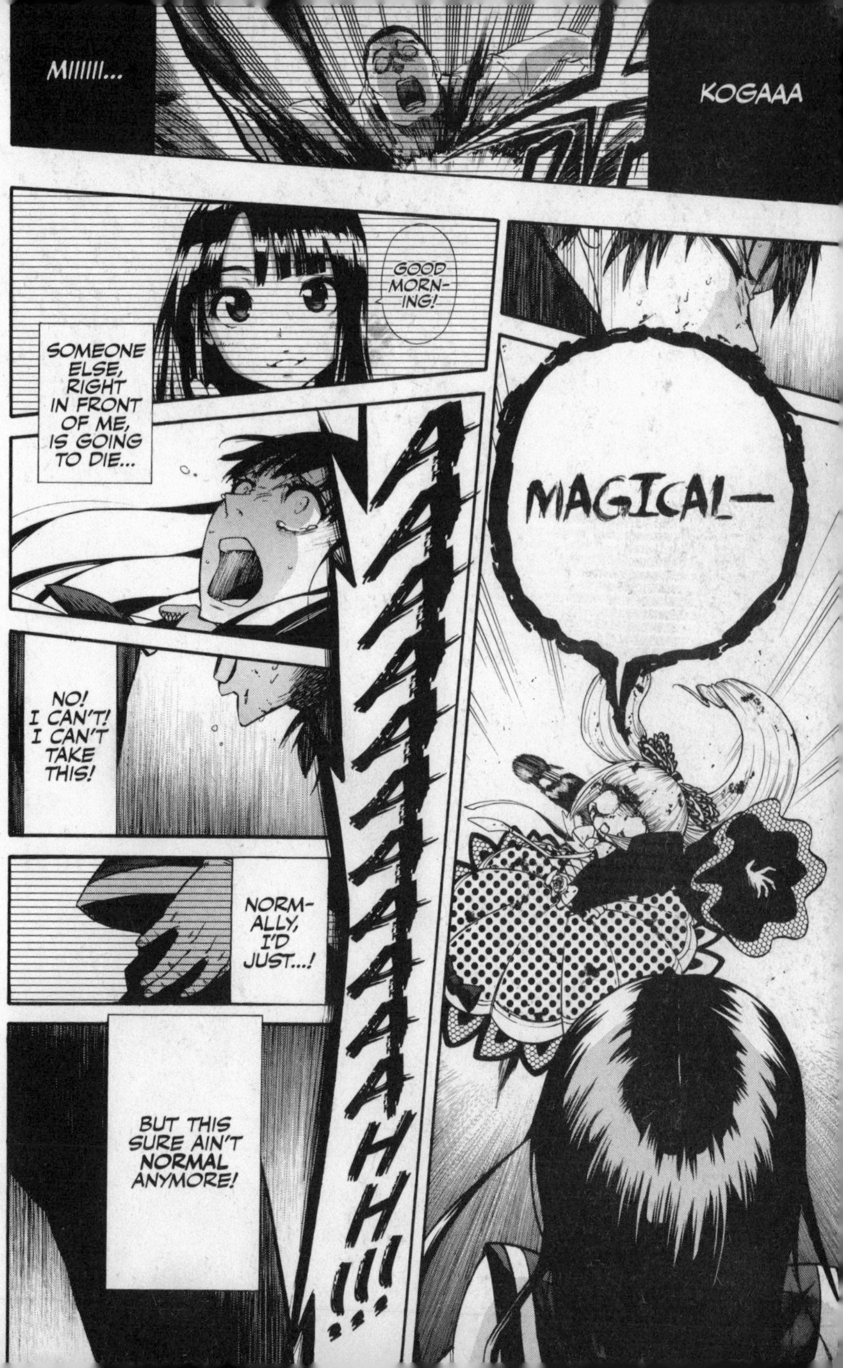
KOGAAA
MIIIII...
MAGICAL—
GOOD MORNING!
SOMEONE ELSE, RIGHT IN FRONT OF ME, IS GOING TO DIE...
AAAAAAAAAAAAAAAHH!!!
NO! I CAN'T! I CAN'T TAKE THIS!
NORMALLY, I'D JUST...!
BUT THIS SURE AIN'T NORMAL ANYMORE!

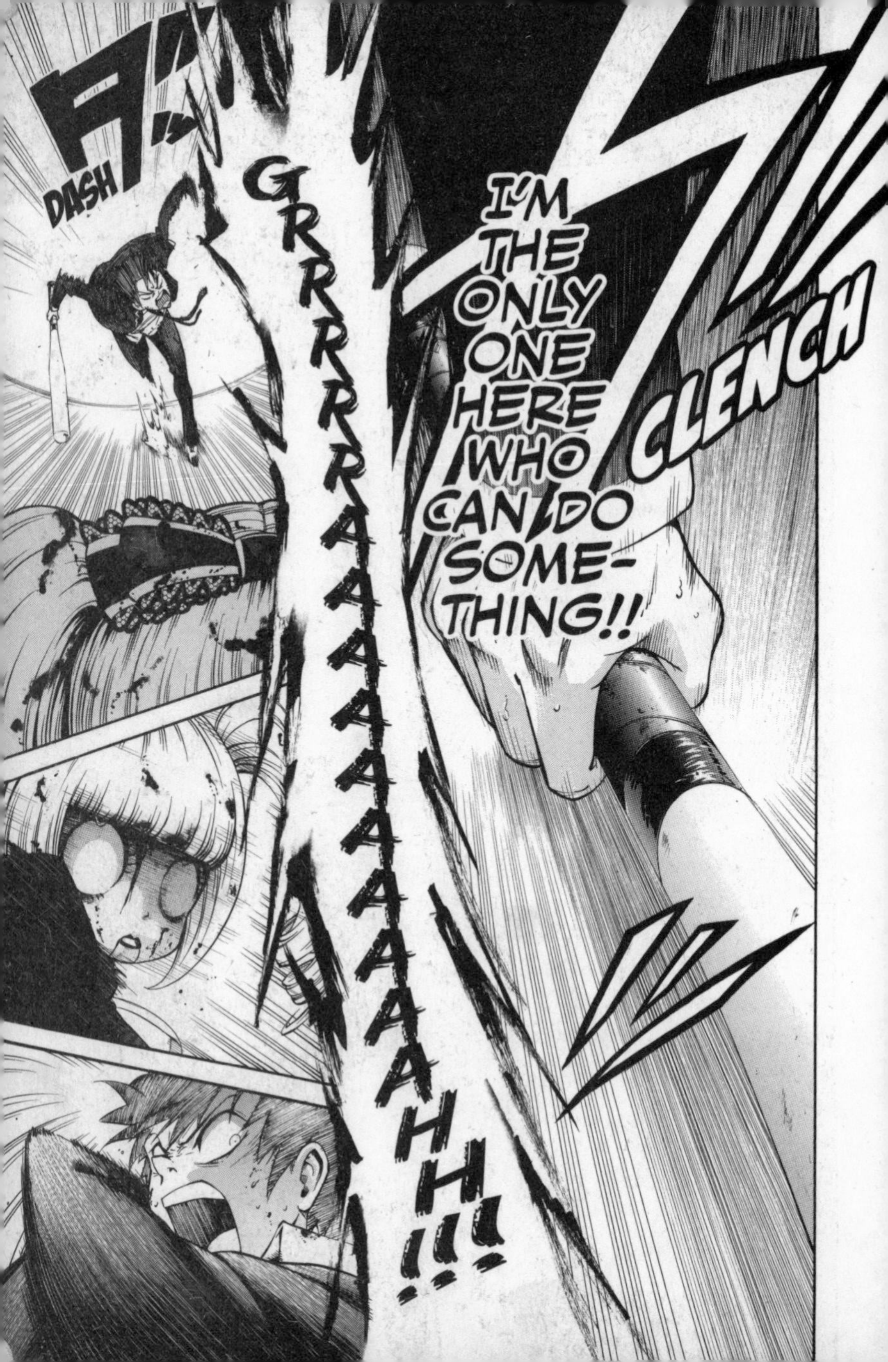
I'M THE ONLY ONE HERE WHO CAN DO SOME-THING!!
CLENCH
GRRRRRAAAAAAAAAAAAHH!!!
DASH

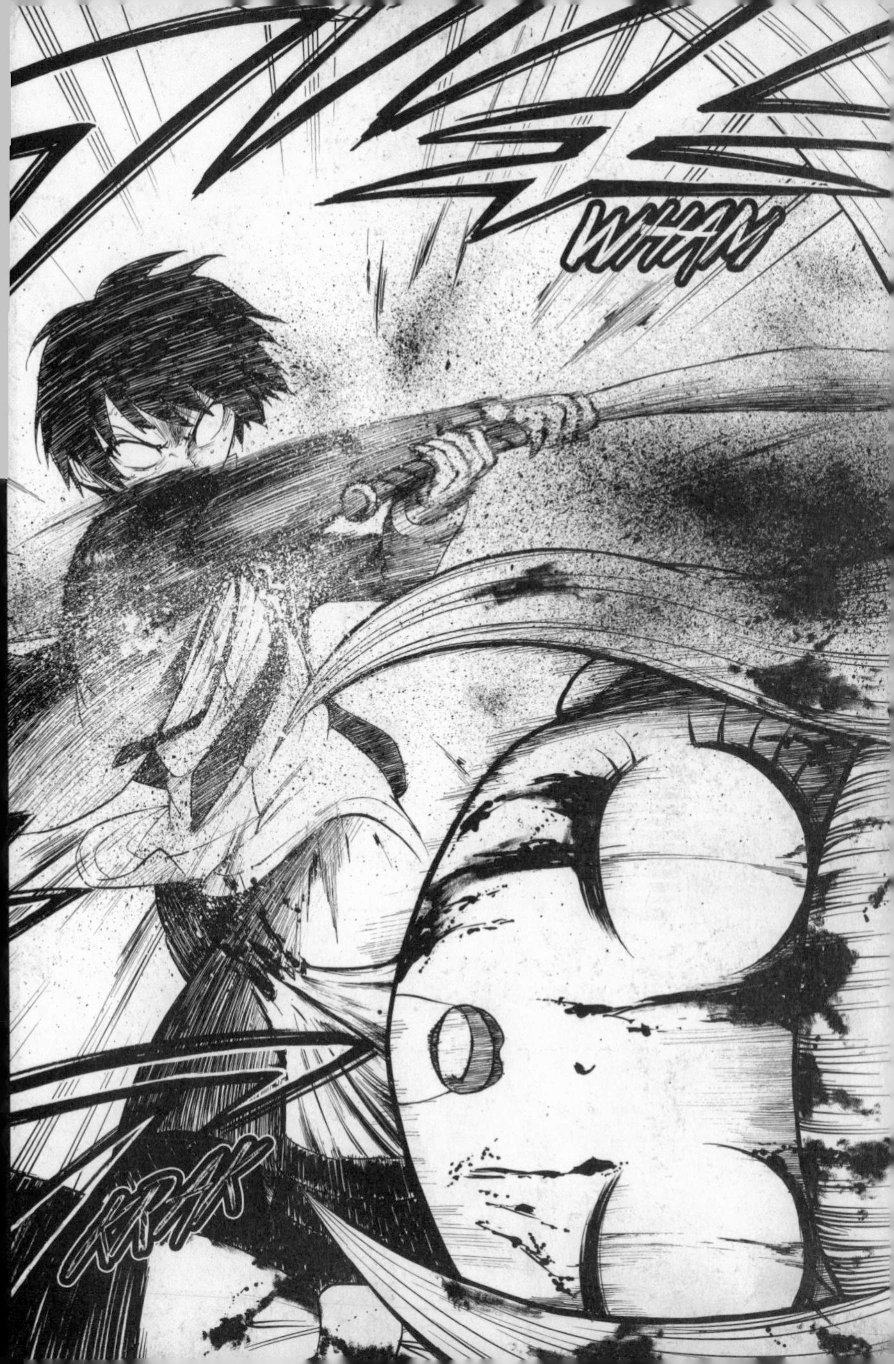
WHAM

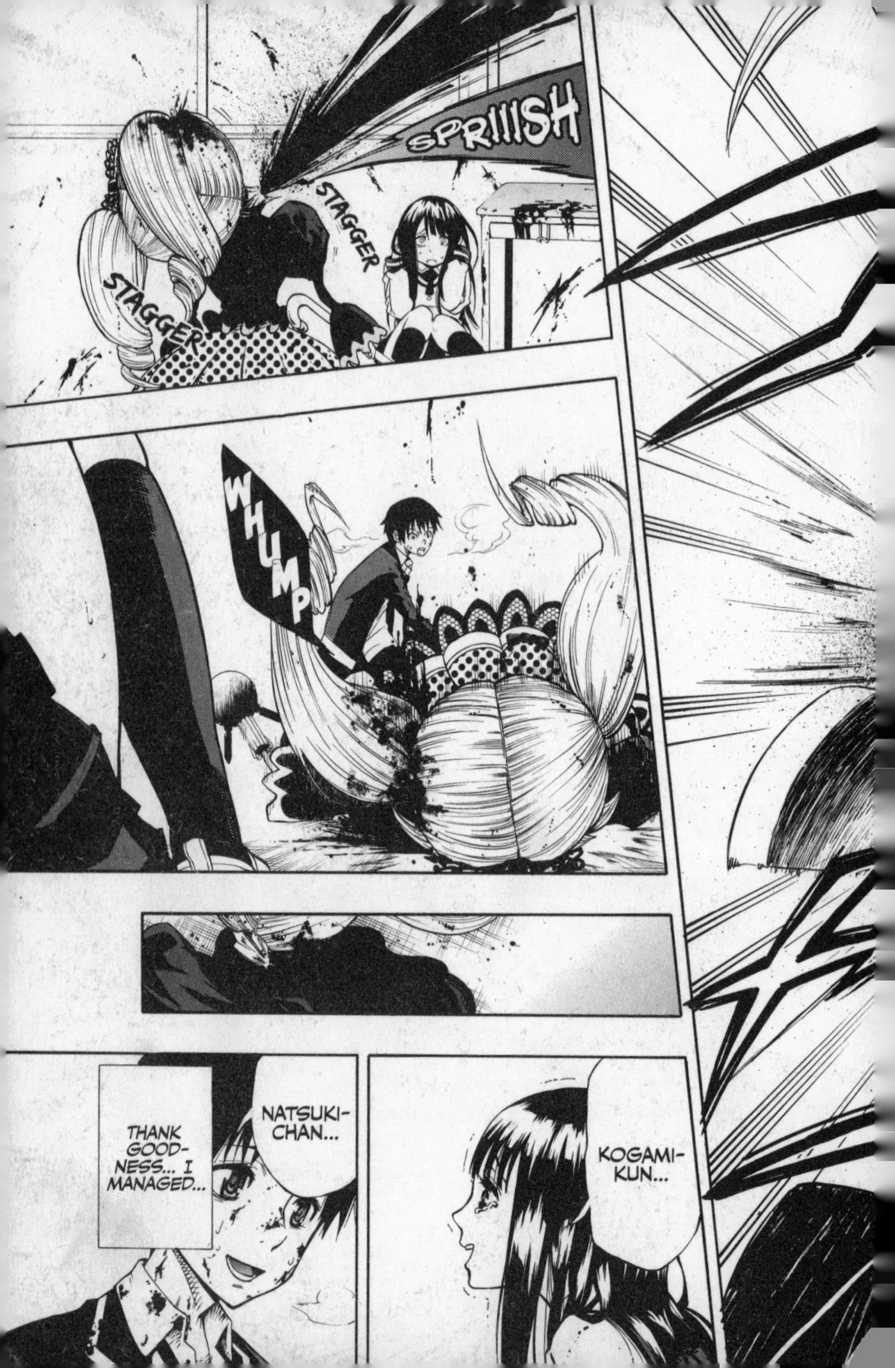
SPRIIISH
STAGGER
STAGGER
WHUMP
KOGAMI-KUN...
NATSUKI-CHAN...
THANK GOODNESS... I MANAGED...

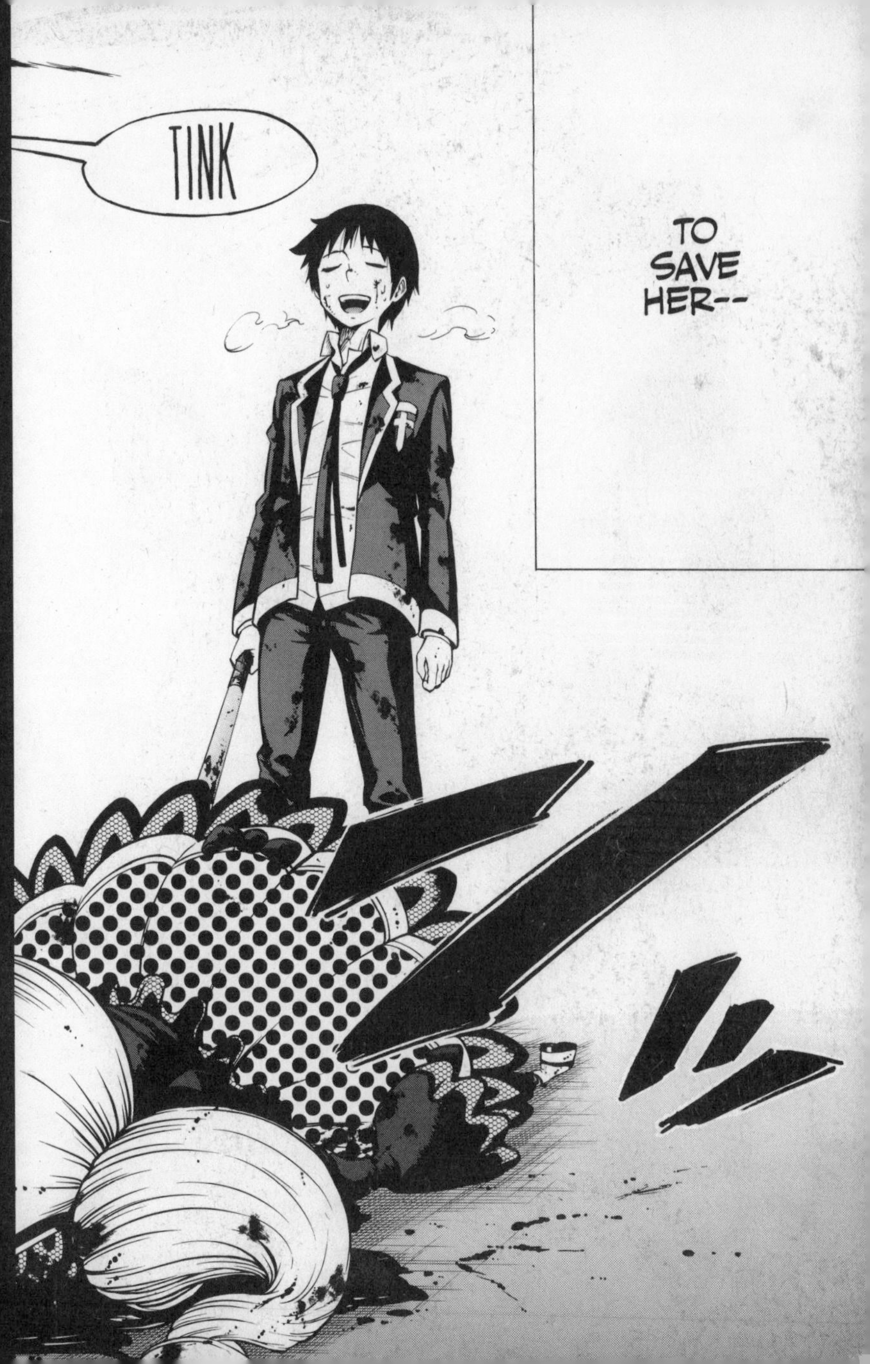
TO SAVE HER--
TINK

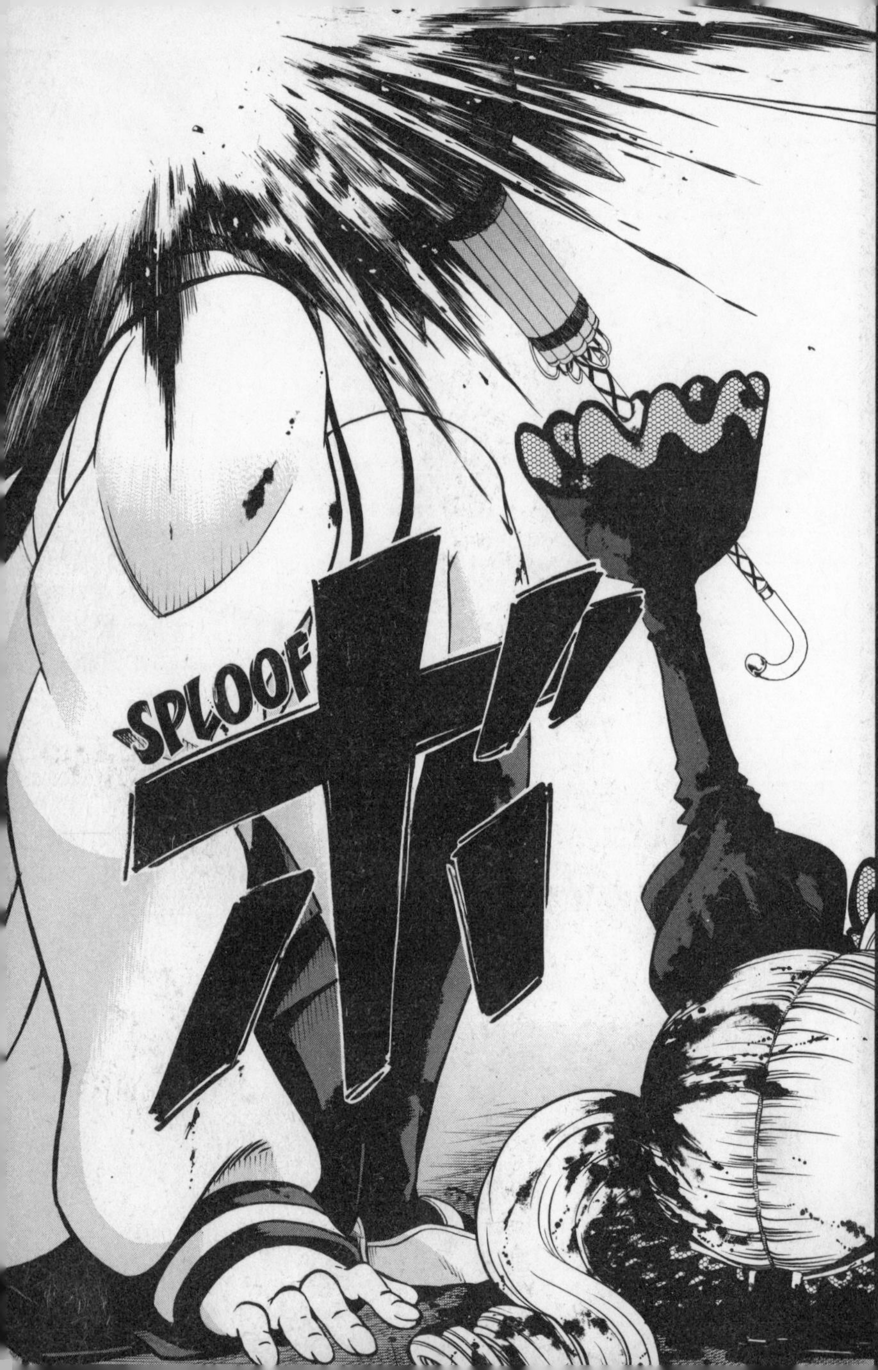
SPLOOF
ナバ

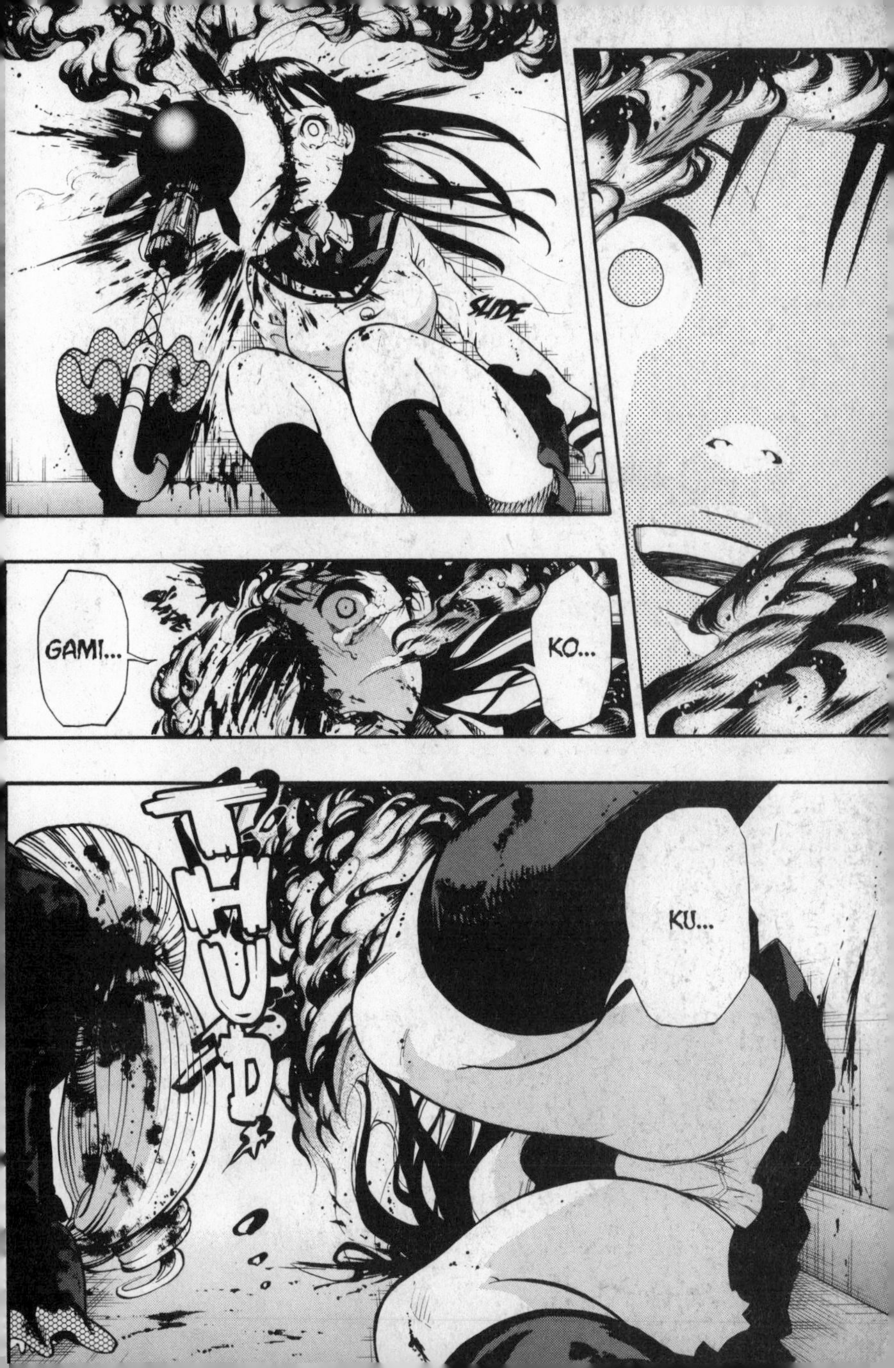
SLIDE
KO...
SLIDE
GAMI...
KU...
THUD

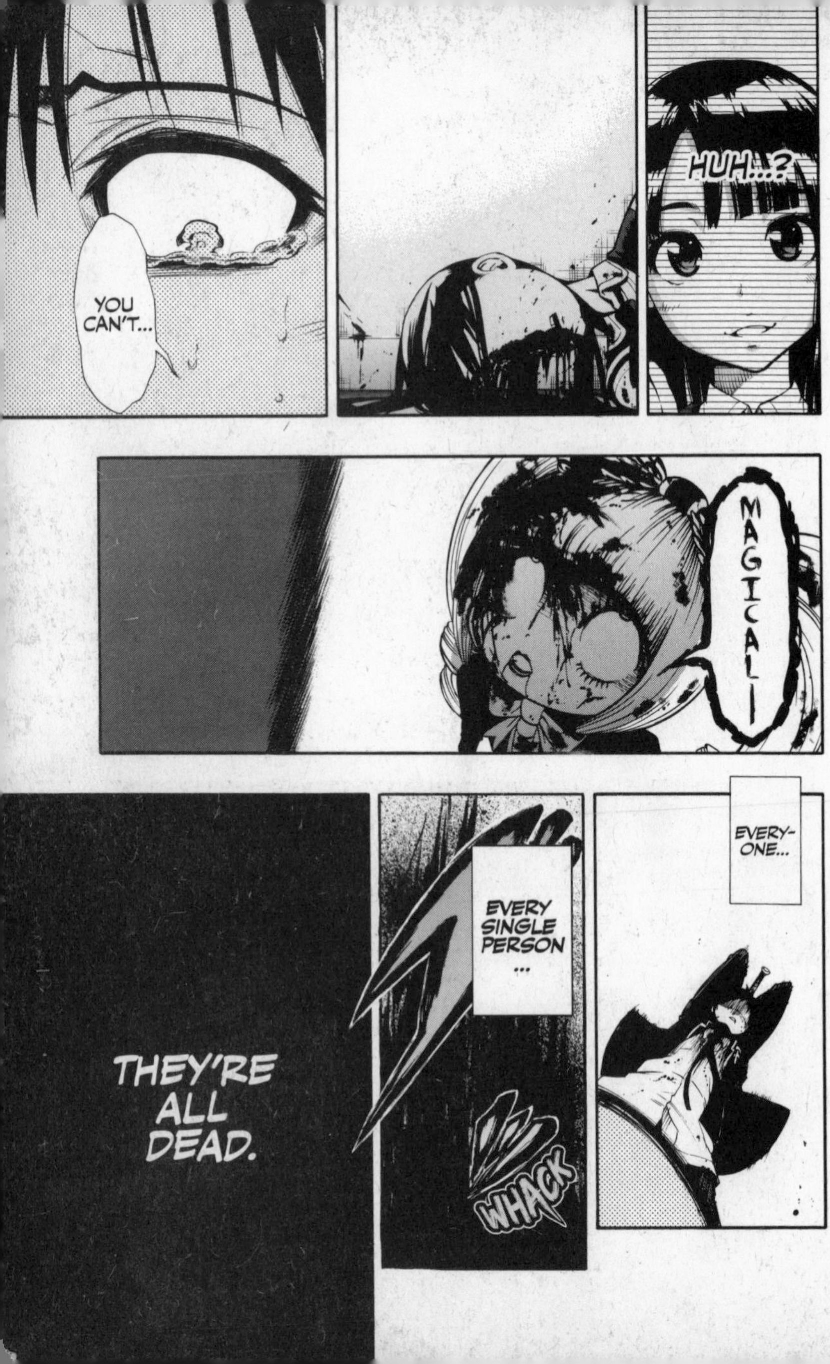
HUH...?
YOU CAN'T...
MAGICALI
EVERY-ONE...
EVERY SINGLE PERSON ...
WHACK
THEY'RE ALL DEAD.

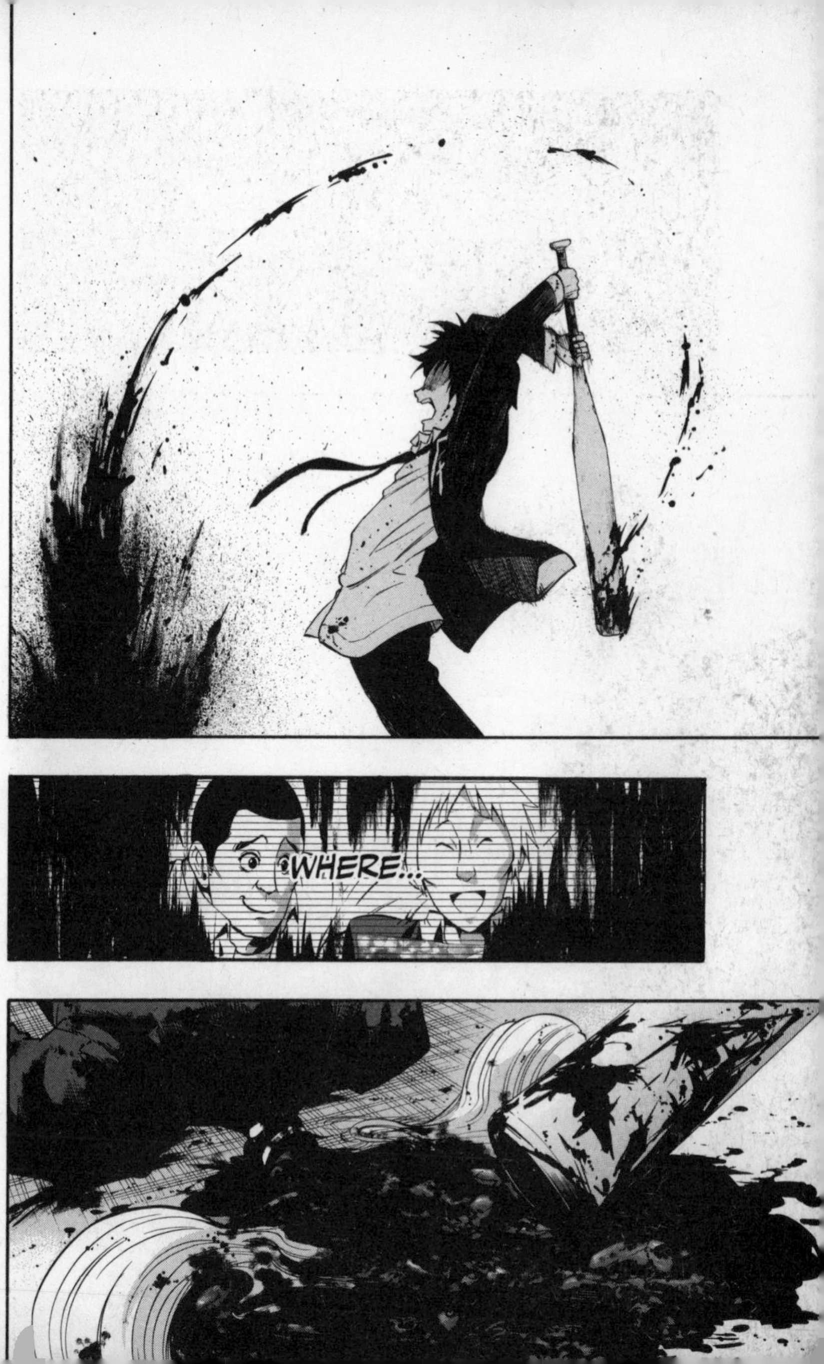
WHERE...

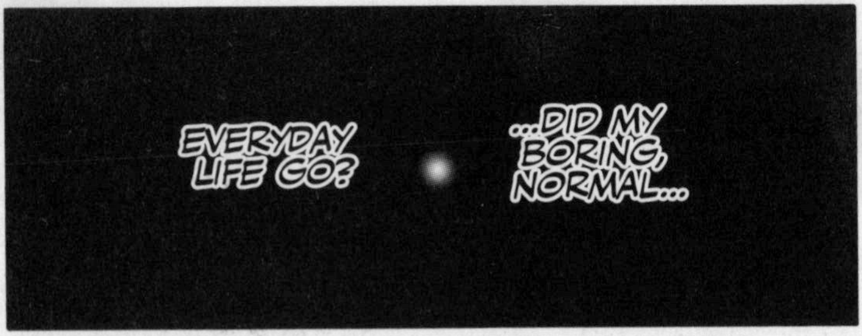
...DID MY BORING, NORMAL...
EVERYDAY LIFE GO?
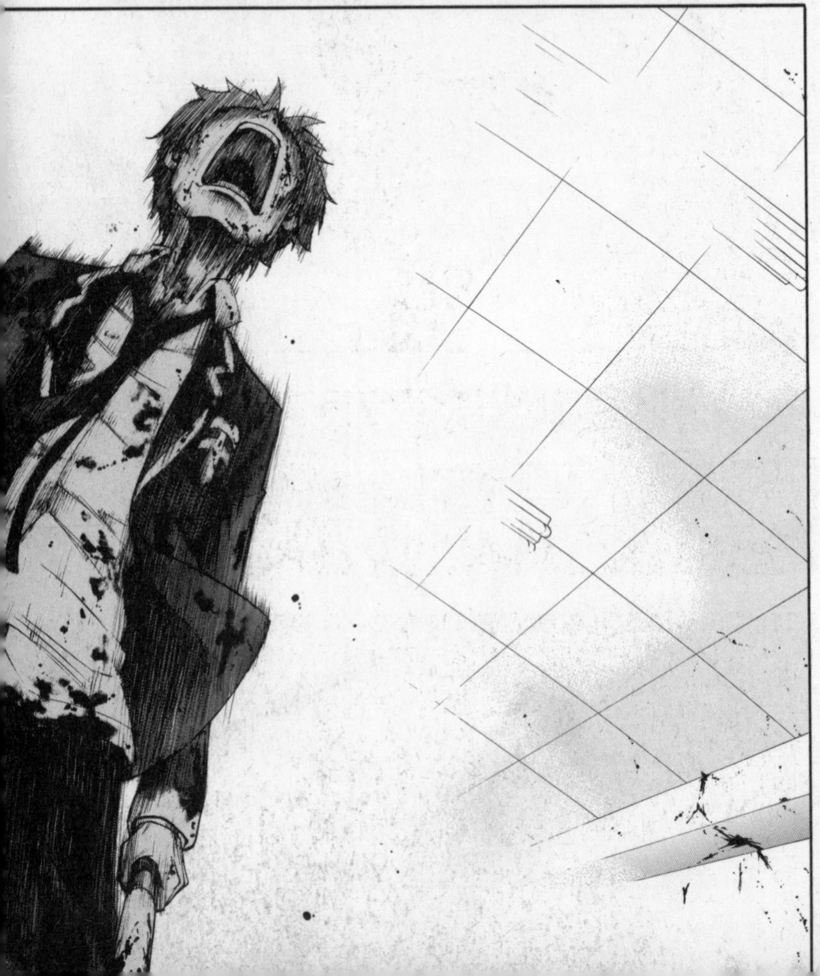

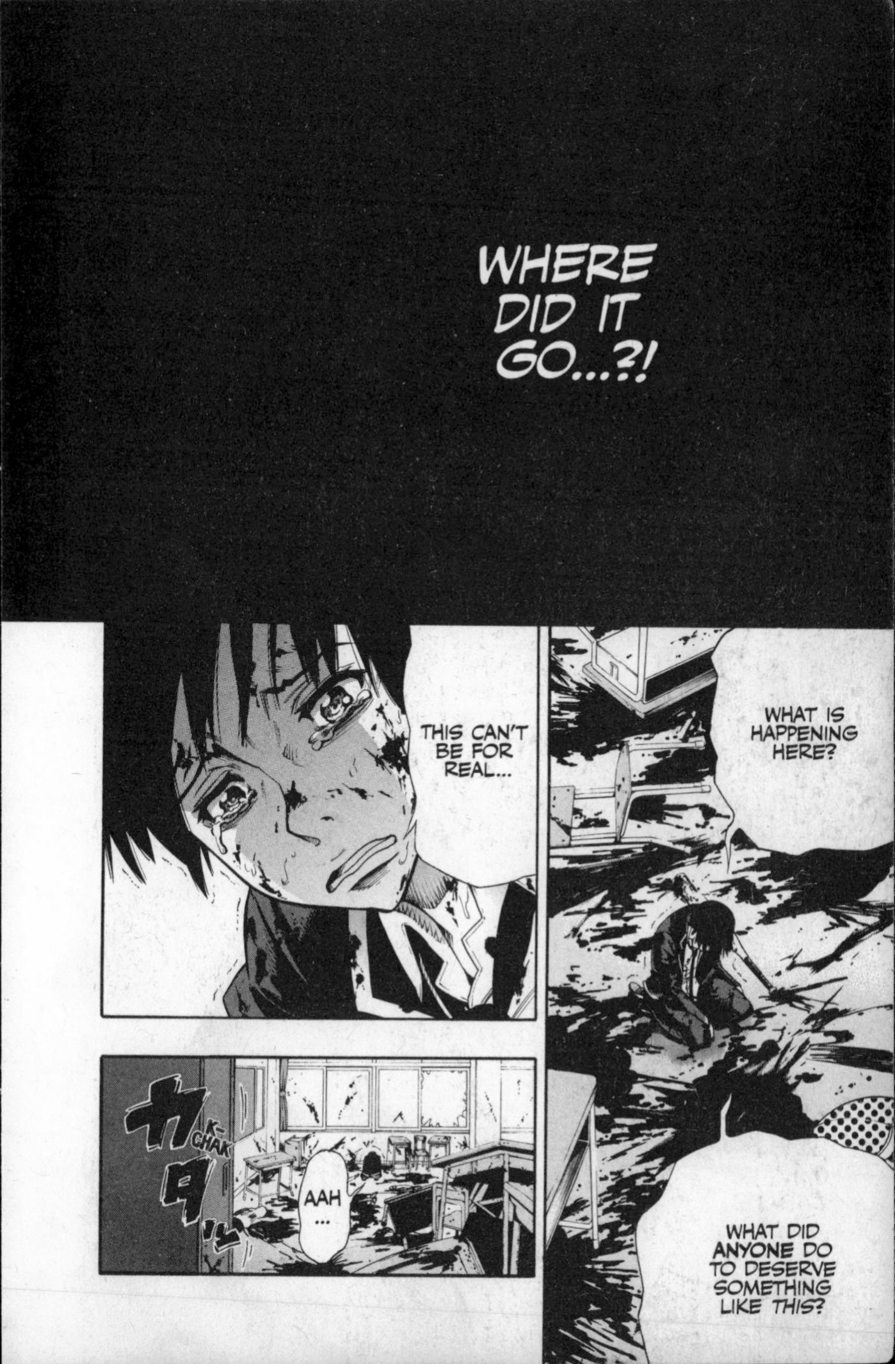
WHERE DID IT GO...?!
WHAT IS HAPPENING HERE?
WHAT DID ANYONE DO TO DESERVE SOMETHING LIKE THIS?
THIS CAN'T BE FOR REAL...
K-CHAK
AAH ...

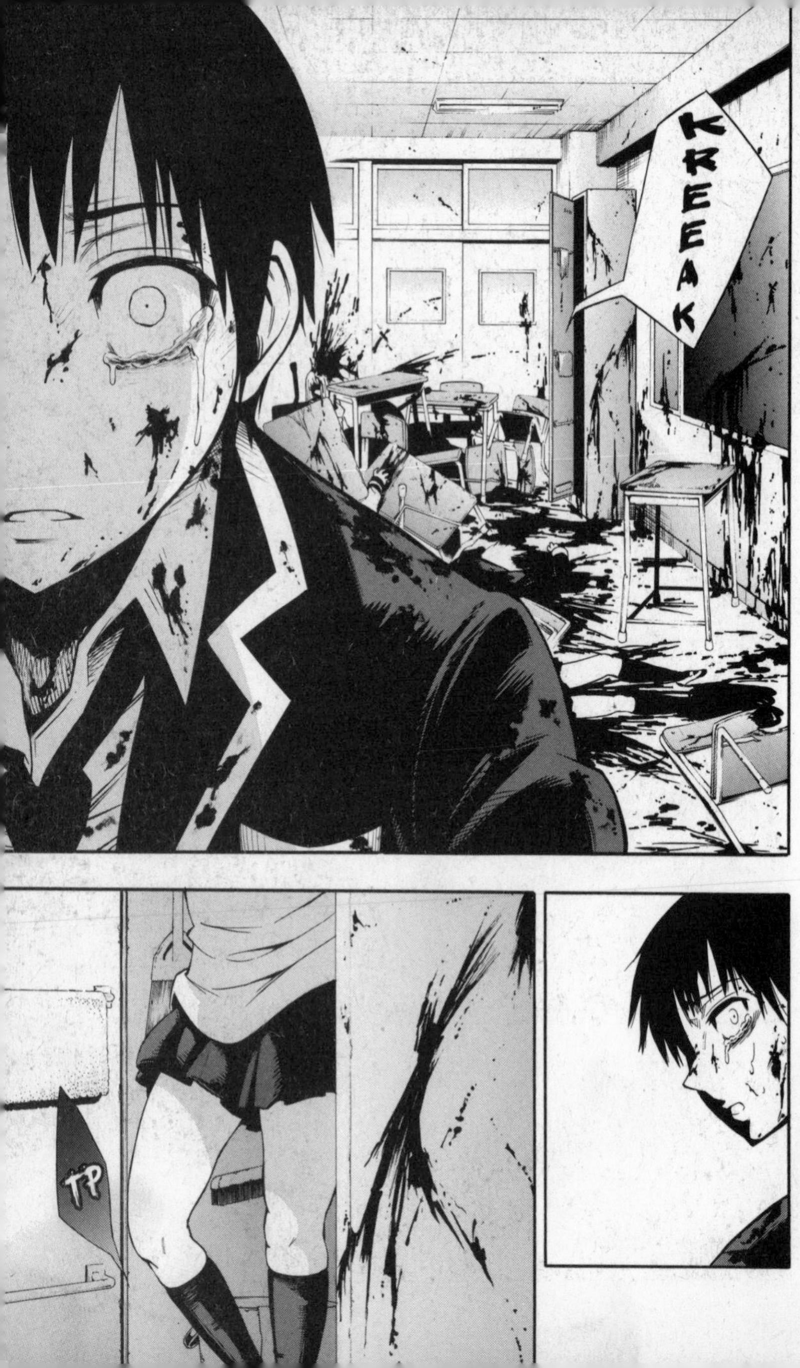
KREEAK
TP

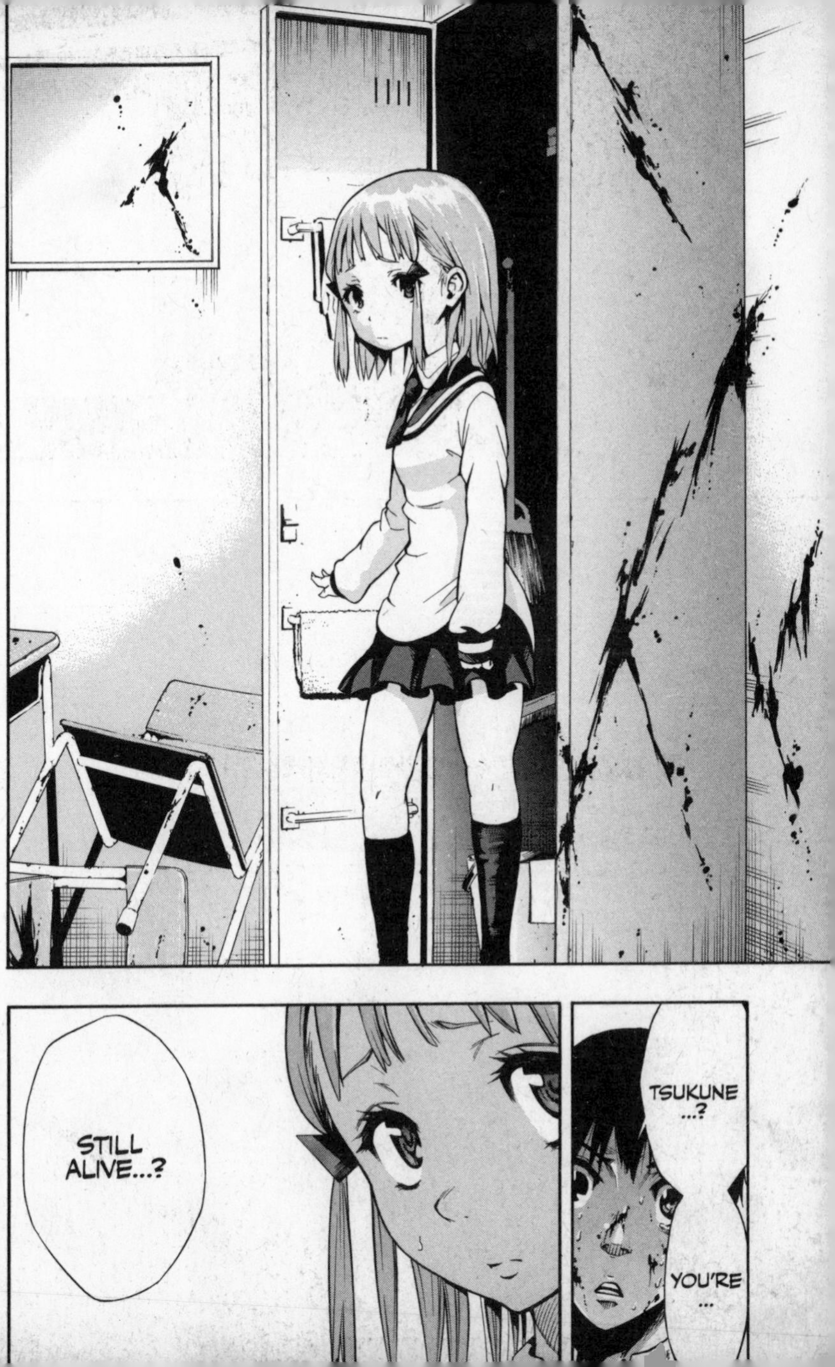
TSUKUNE ...?
YOU'RE ...
STILL ALIVE...?

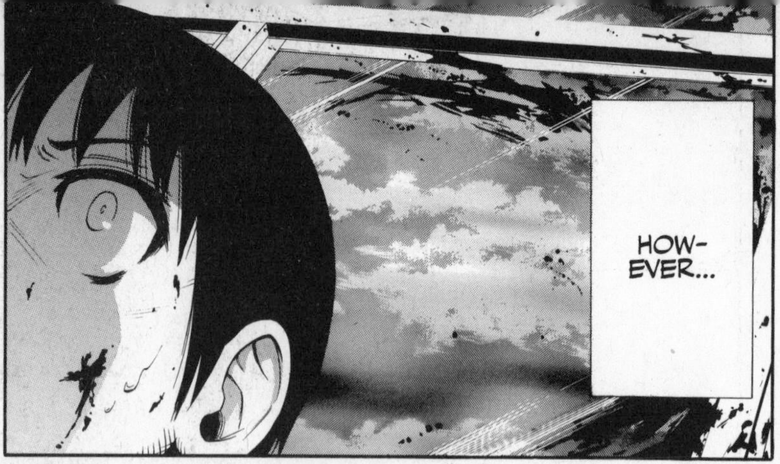
HOW-
EVER...

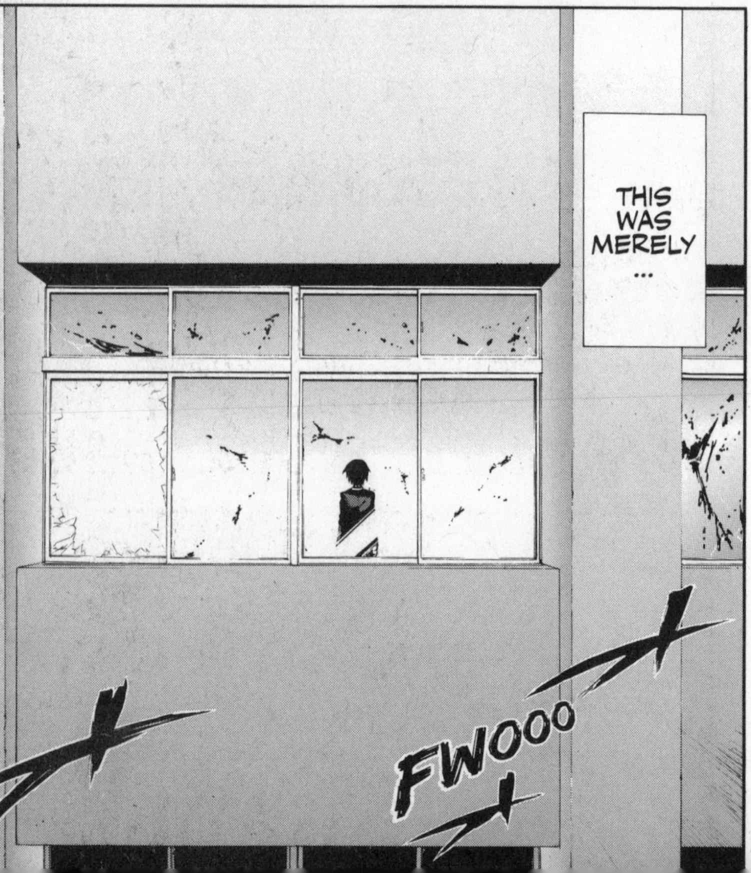
THIS
WAS
MERELY
...
FWOOO

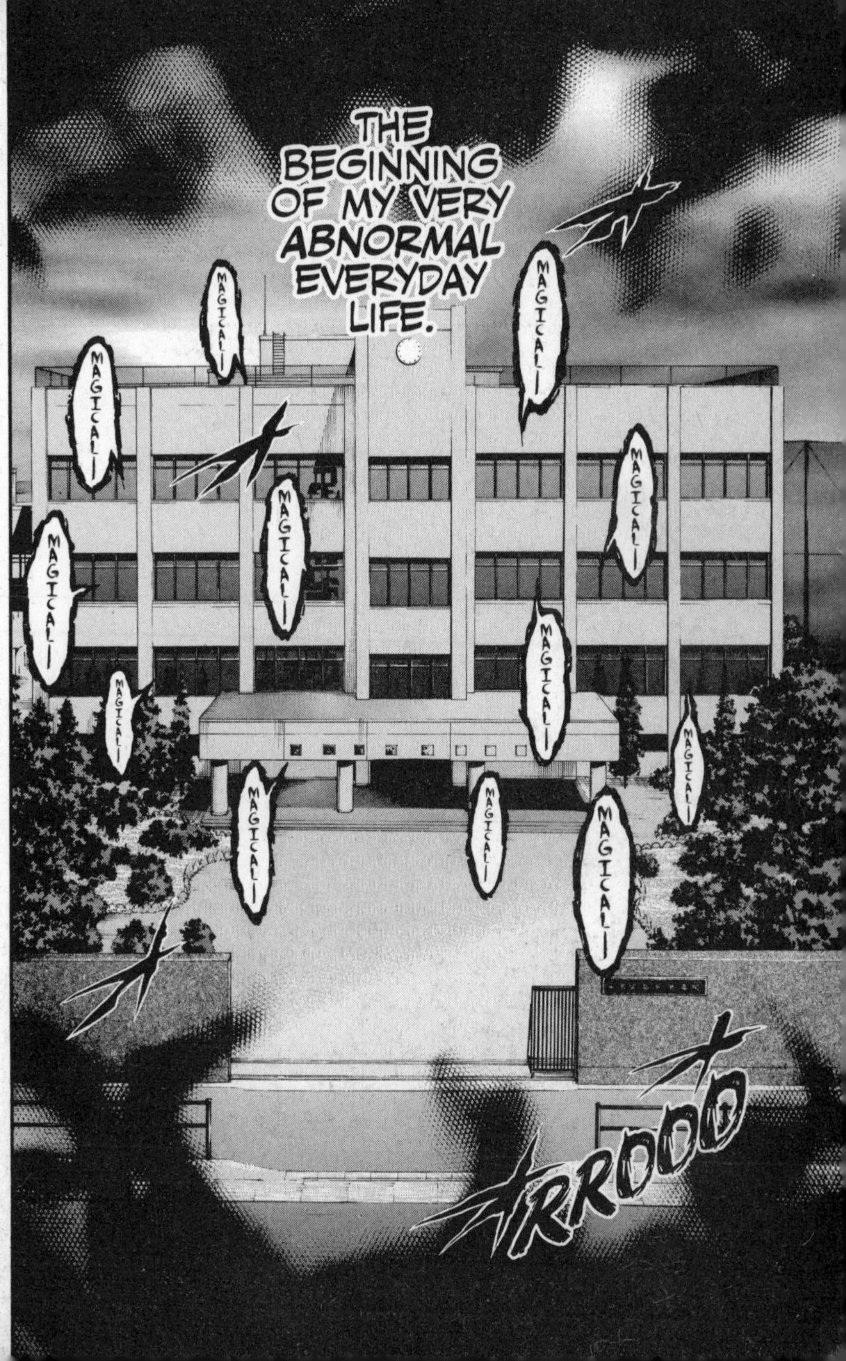
THE BEGINNING OF MY VERY ABNORMAL EVERYDAY LIFE.
MAGICAL!
MAGICAL!
MAGICAL!
MAGICAL!
MAGICAL!
MAGICAL!
MAGICAL!
MAGICAL!
MAGICAL!
MAGICAL!
MAGICAL!
MAGICAL!
RRDDD

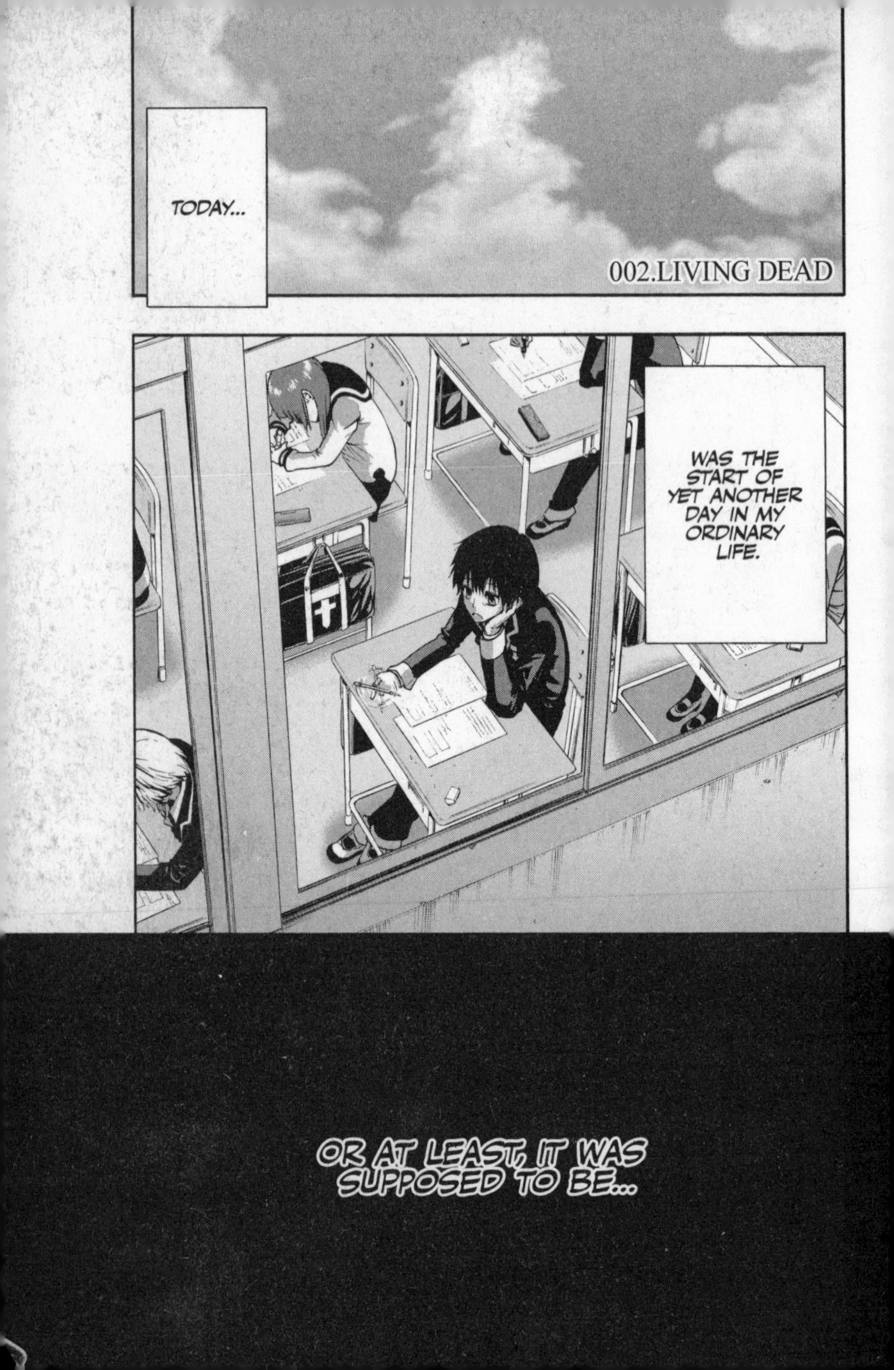
TODAY...
002.LIVING DEAD
WAS THE START OF YET ANOTHER DAY IN MY ORDINARY LIFE.
OR AT LEAST, IT WAS SUPPOSED TO BE...

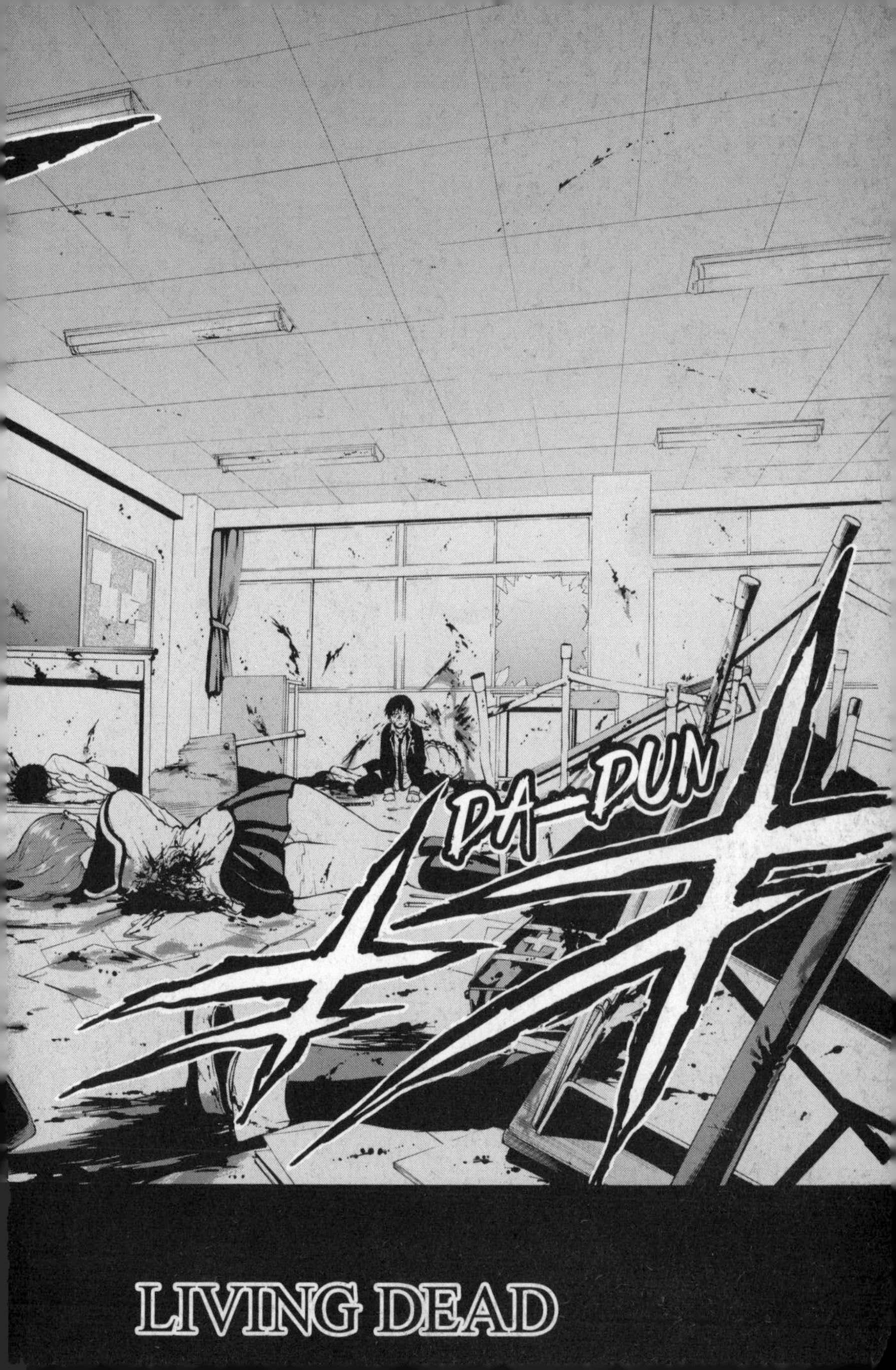
DA-DUN

LIVING DEAD

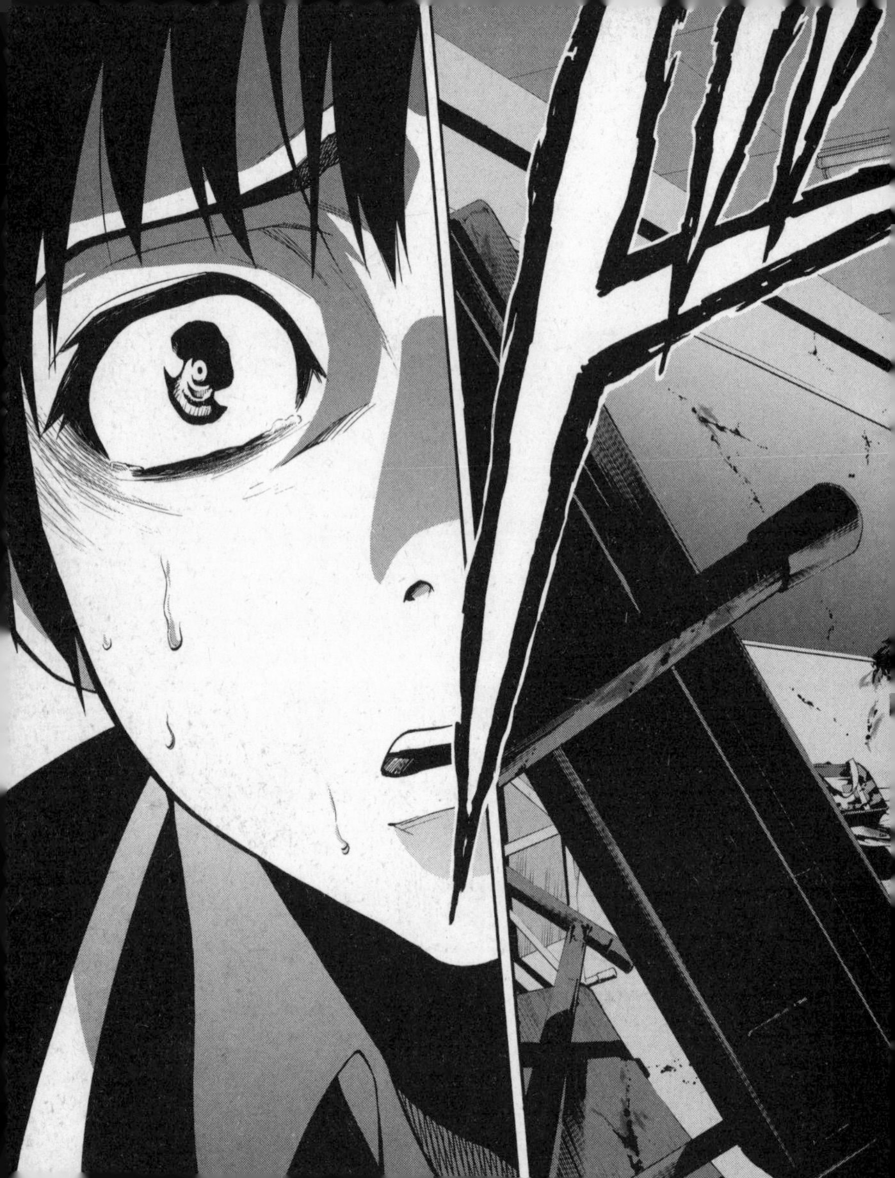

HELL NO.
MAYUYU
ALL THE
WAY!

H, THAT'S
OT WHAT

MAN,
TAKAMINA
REALLY

THIS
IS...

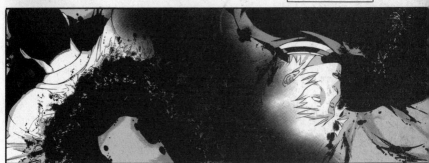

SO
MESSED
UP...

GOOD
MORNING!

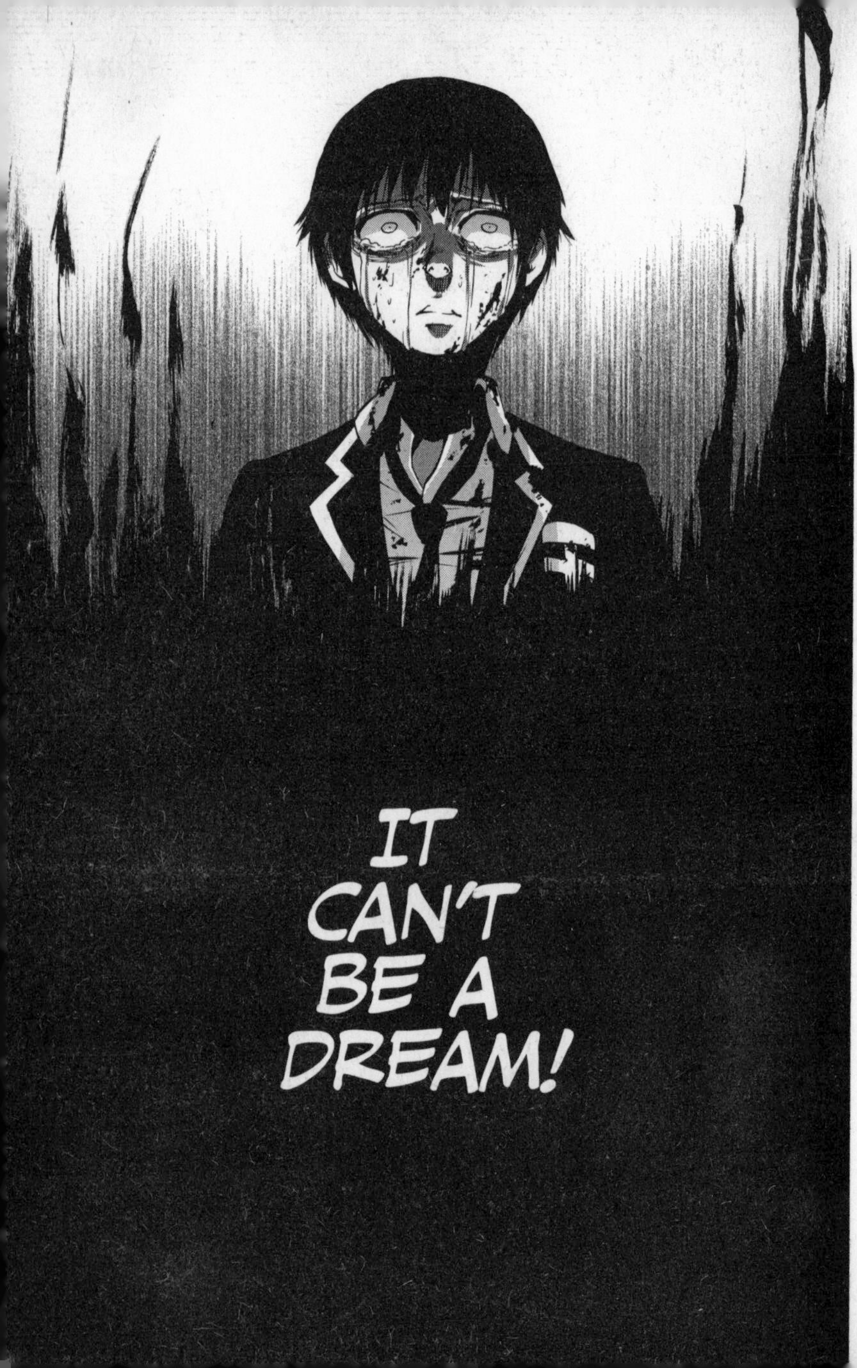
IT CAN'T BE A DREAM!

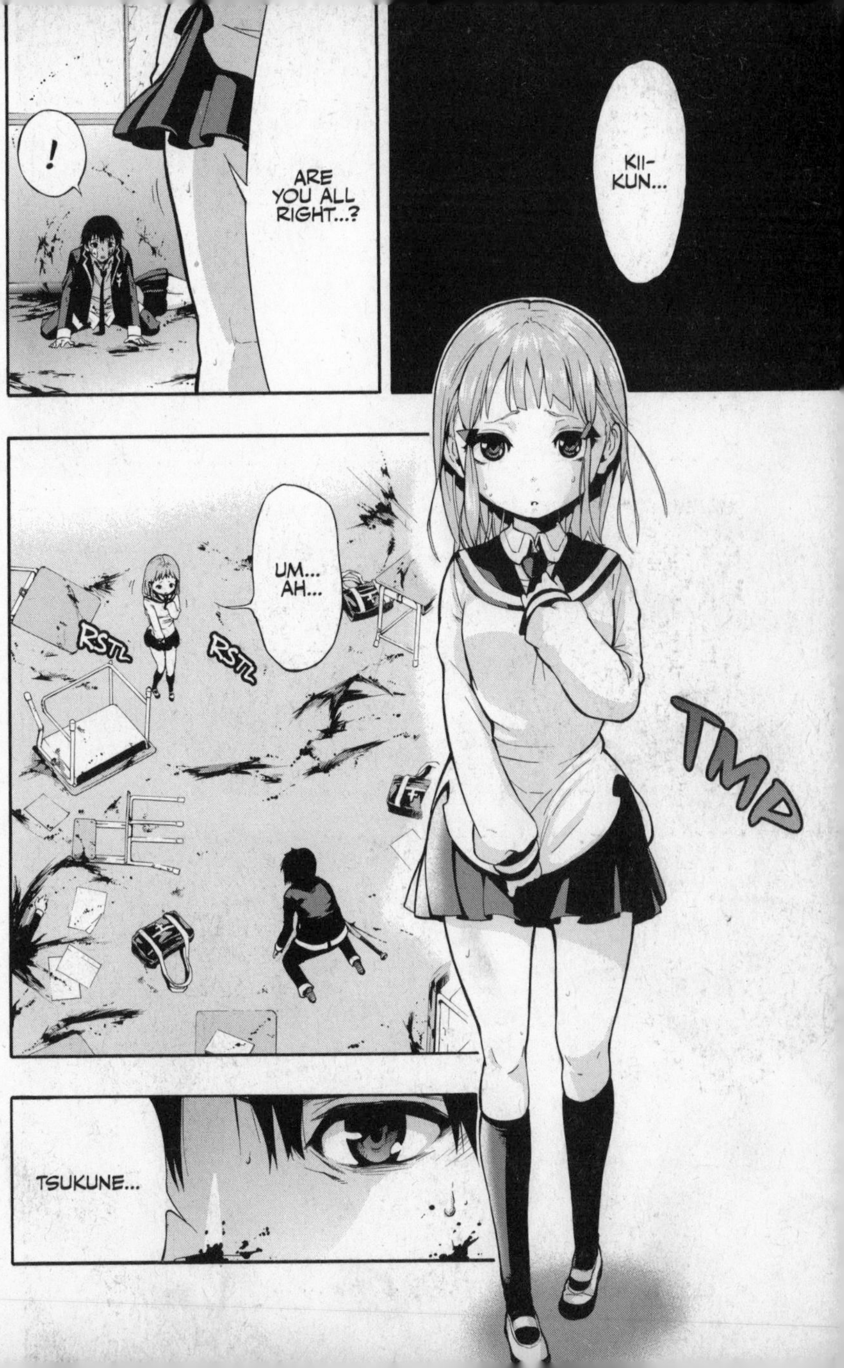
KII-KUN...
ARE YOU ALL RIGHT...?
!
UM... AH...
RSTL
RSTL
TMP
TSUKUNE...

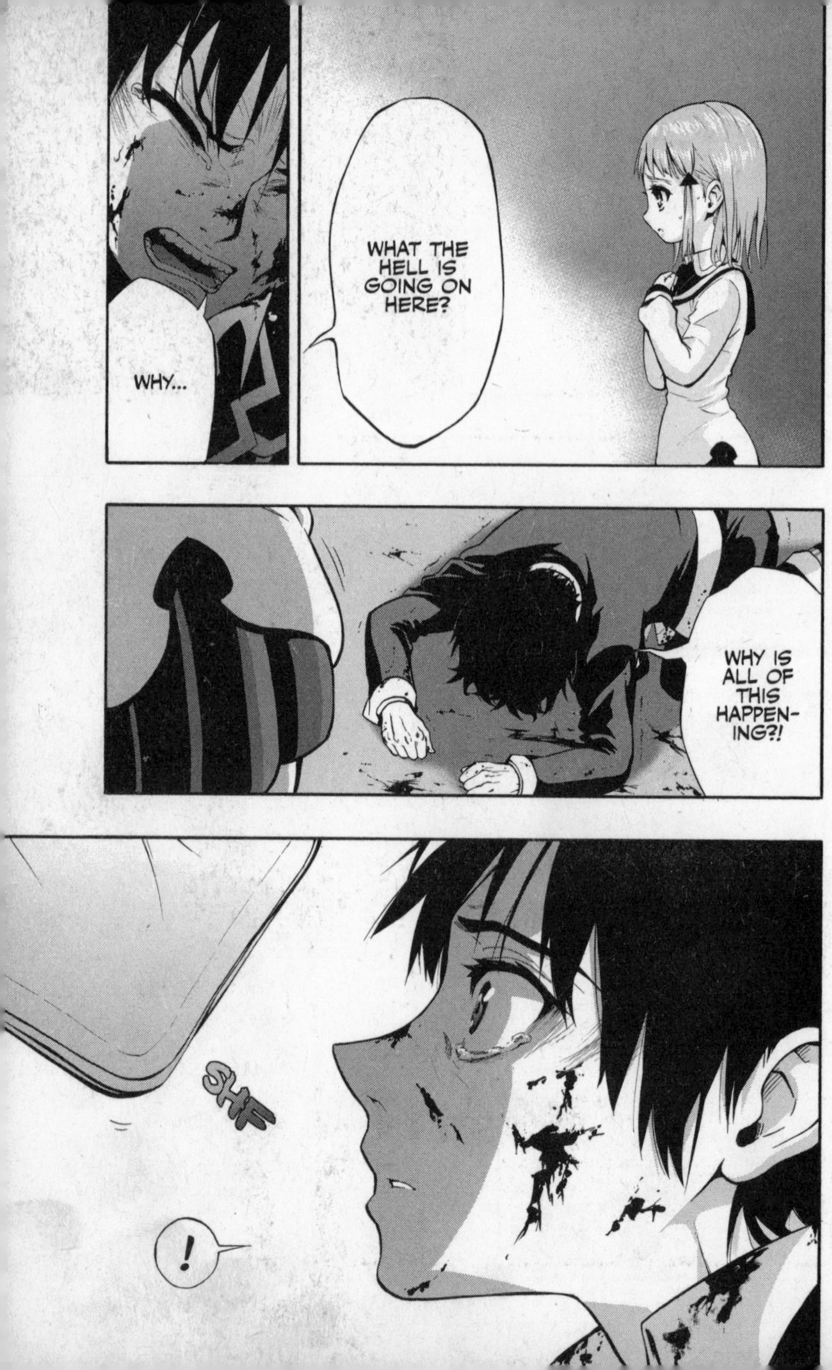
WHAT THE HELL IS GOING ON HERE?
WHY...
WHY IS ALL OF THIS HAPPEN-ING?!
SHF
!

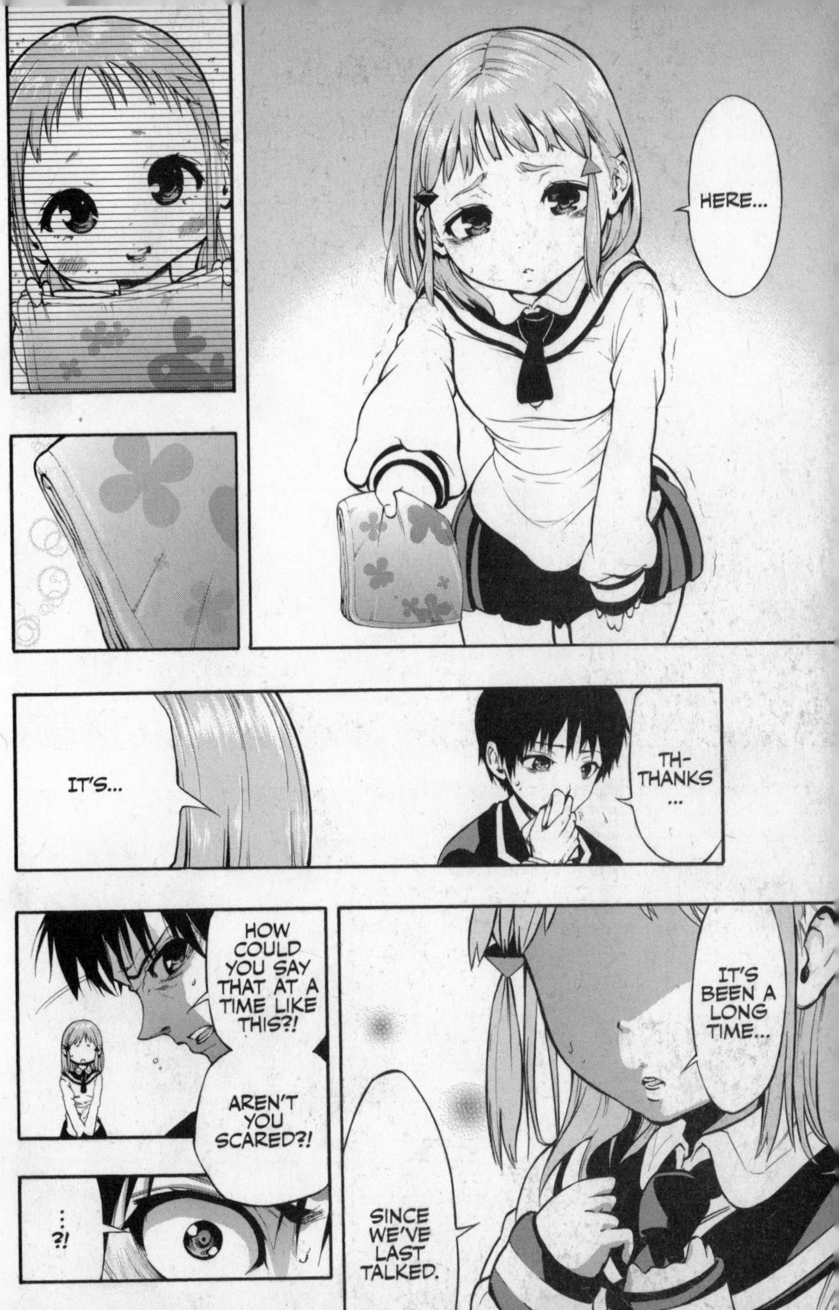
HERE...
TH- THANKS ...
IT'S...
IT'S BEEN A LONG TIME...
SINCE WE'VE LAST TALKED.
HOW COULD YOU SAY THAT AT A TIME LIKE THIS?!
AREN'T YOU SCARED?!
...?!

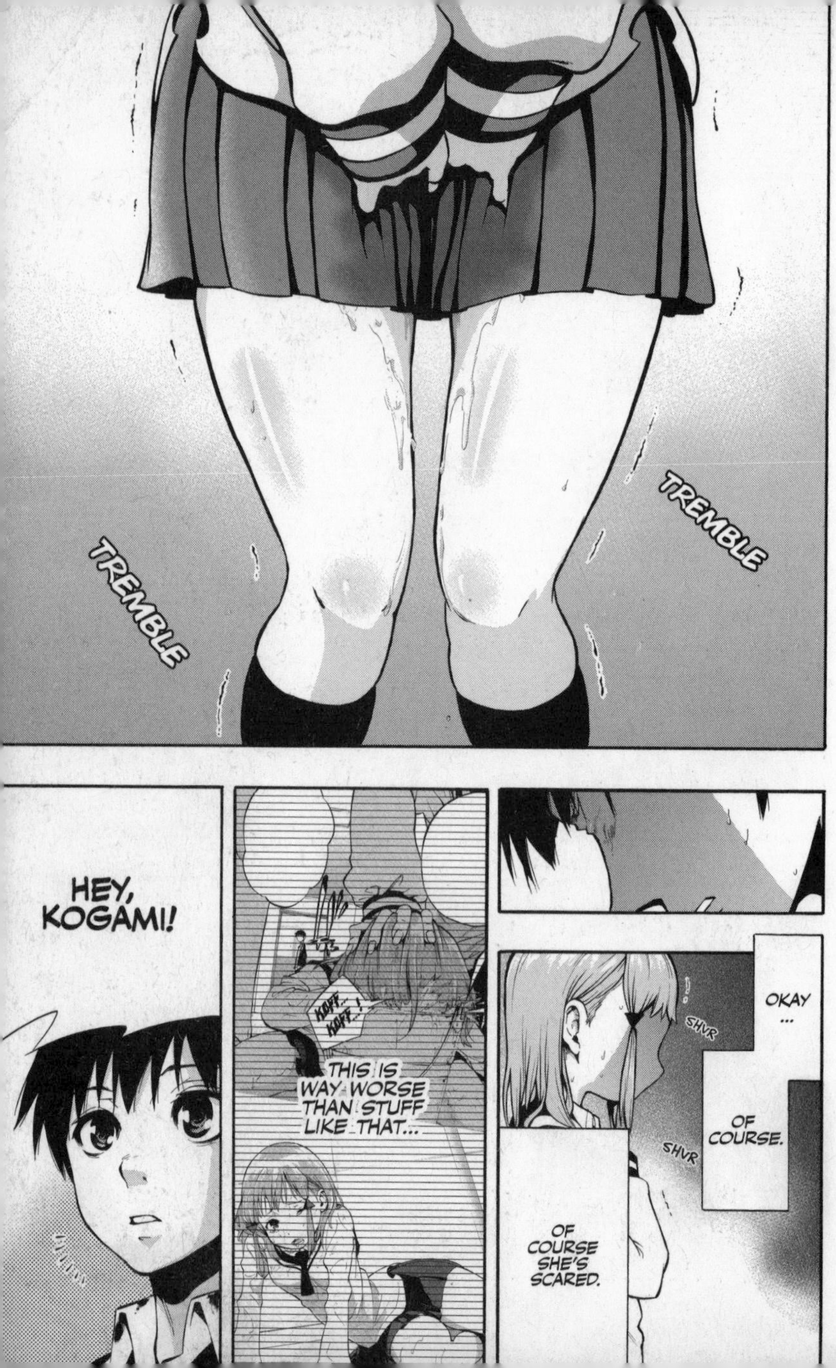
TREMBLE
TREMBLE
OKAY ...
SHVR
OF COURSE.
SHVR
OF COURSE SHE'S SCARED.
KOFF... KOFF...!
THIS IS WAY WORSE THAN STUFF LIKE THAT...
HEY, KOGAMI!

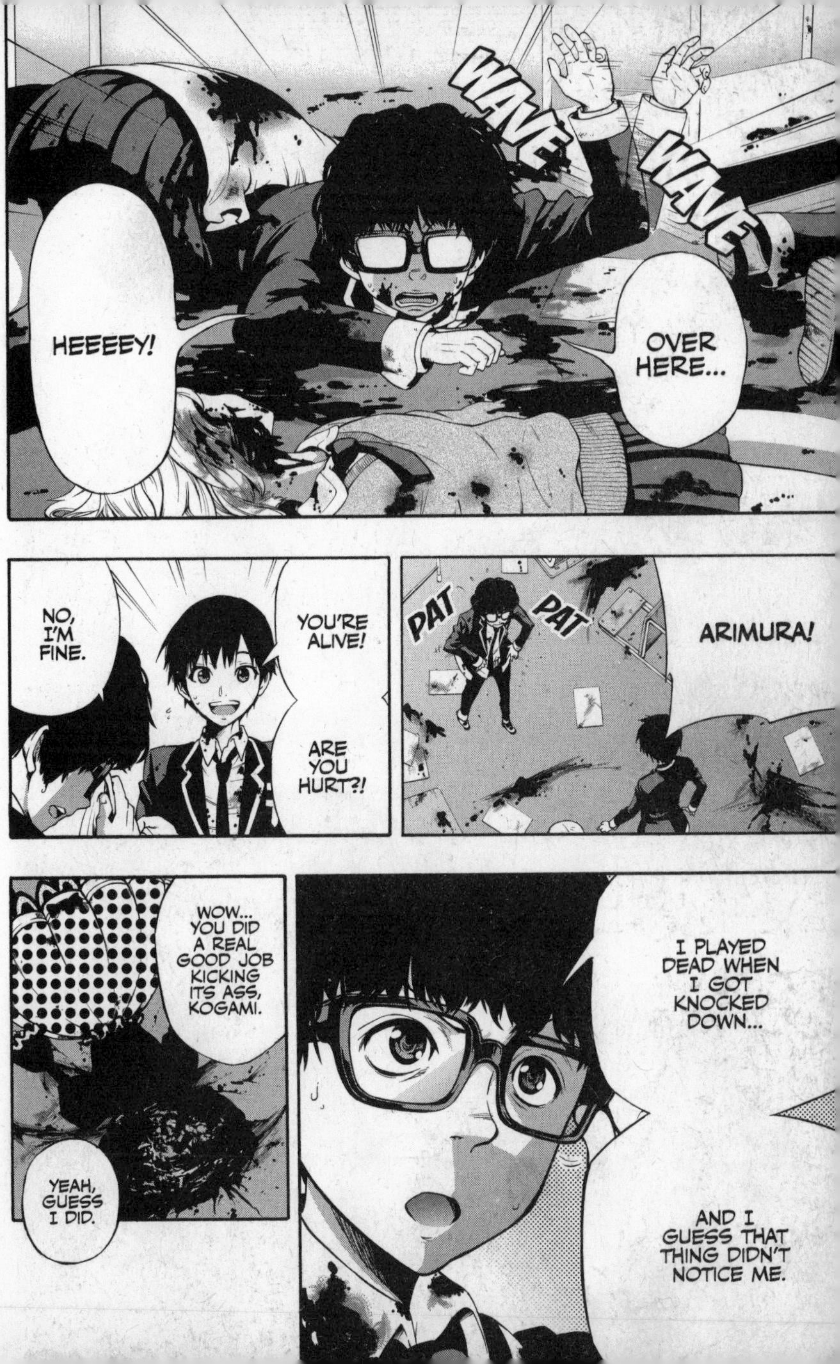
WAVE
WAVE
OVER HERE...
HEEEEY!
ARIMURA!
PAT
PAT
YOU'RE ALIVE!
ARE YOU HURT?!
NO, I'M FINE.
I PLAYED DEAD WHEN I GOT KNOCKED DOWN...
AND I GUESS THAT THING DIDN'T NOTICE ME.
WOW... YOU DID A REAL GOOD JOB KICKING ITS ASS, KOGAMI.
YEAH, GUESS I DID.

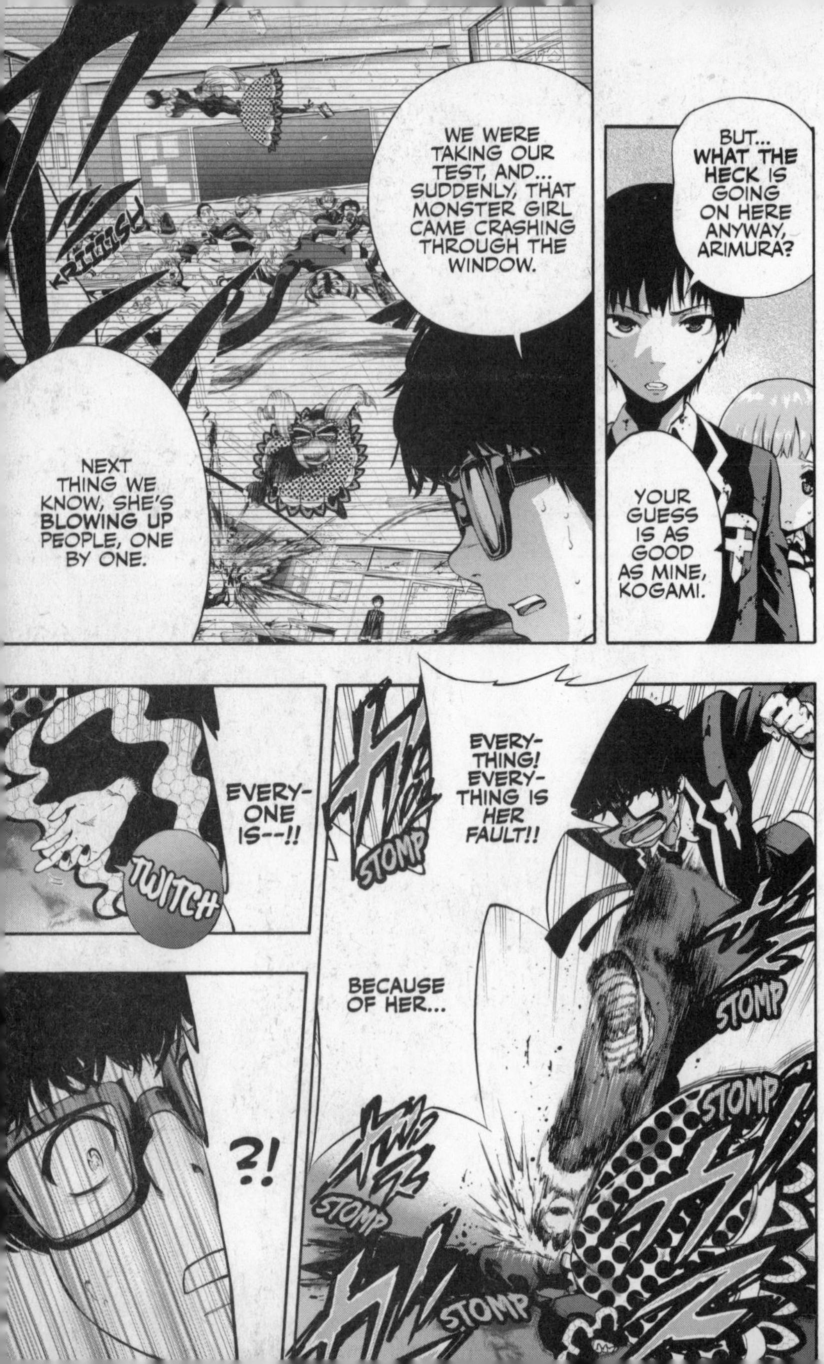

BUT... WHAT THE HECK IS GOING ON HERE ANYWAY, ARIMURA?
YOUR GUESS IS AS GOOD AS MINE, KOGAMI.
WE WERE TAKING OUR TEST, AND... SUDDENLY, THAT MONSTER GIRL CAME CRASHING THROUGH THE WINDOW.
KRIIIISH
NEXT THING WE KNOW, SHE'S BLOWING UP PEOPLE, ONE BY ONE.
EVERY-THING! EVERY-THING IS HER FAULT!!
STOMP
STOMP
BECAUSE OF HER...
STOMP
STOMP
STOMP
EVERY-ONE IS--!!
TWITCH
?!

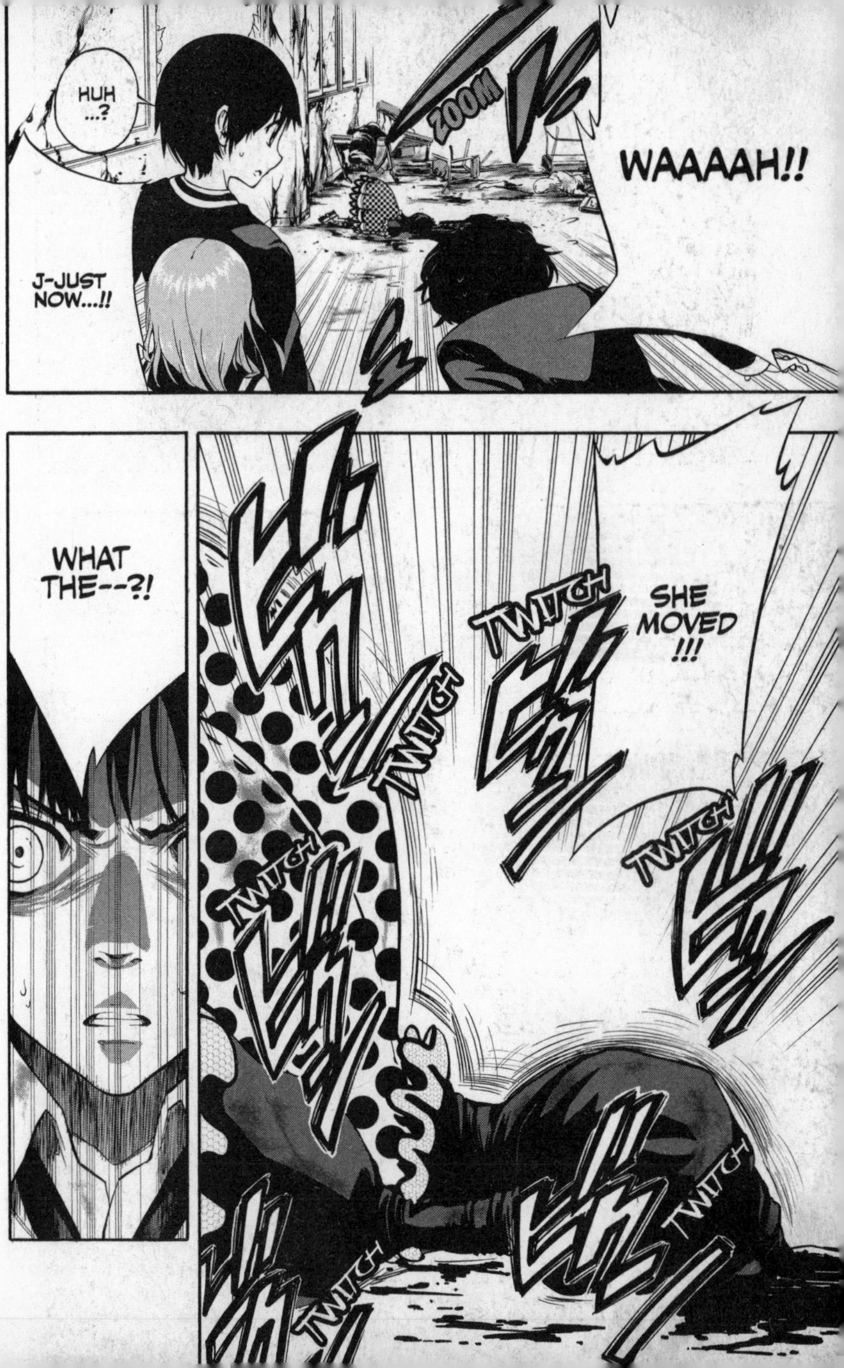

WAAAAH!!
ZOOM
HUH ...?
J-JUST NOW...!!
SHE MOVED !!!
TWITCH
TWITCH
TWITCH
TWITCH
TWITCH
TWITCH
WHAT THE--?!

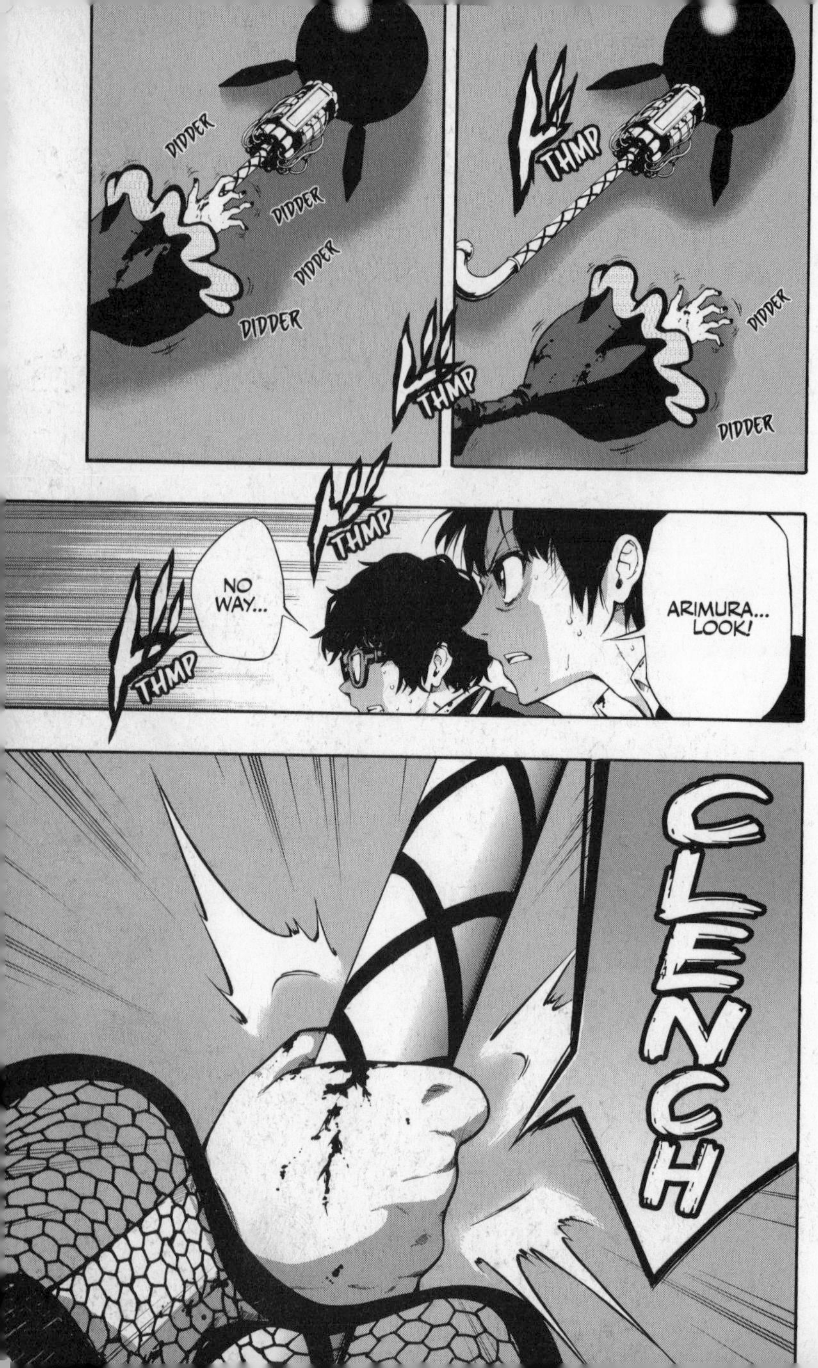
THMP
DIDDER
THMP
DIDDER
DIDDER
DIDDER
DIDDER
DIDDER
THMP
ARIMURA... LOOK!
NO WAY...
THMP
CLENCH

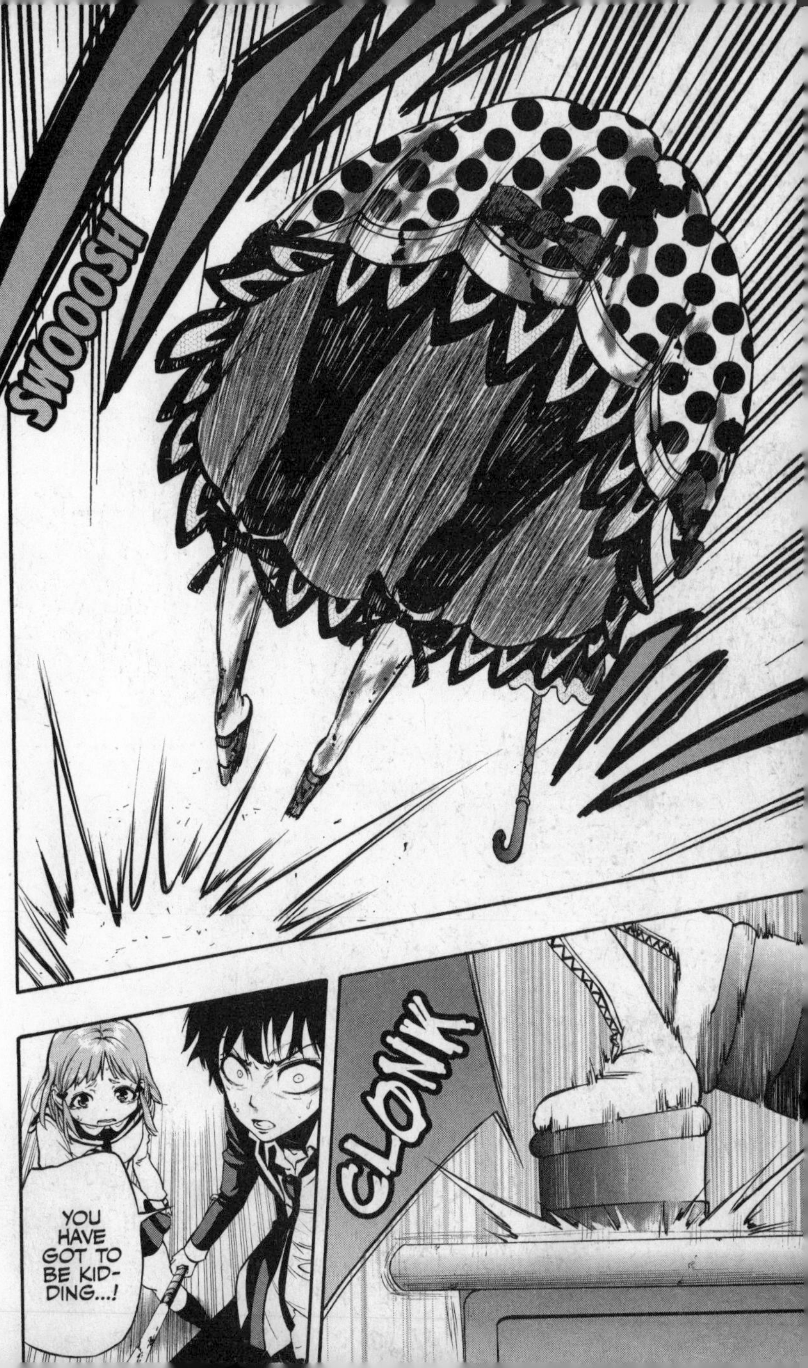
SWOOOSH
CLONK
YOU HAVE GOT TO BE KID-DING...!

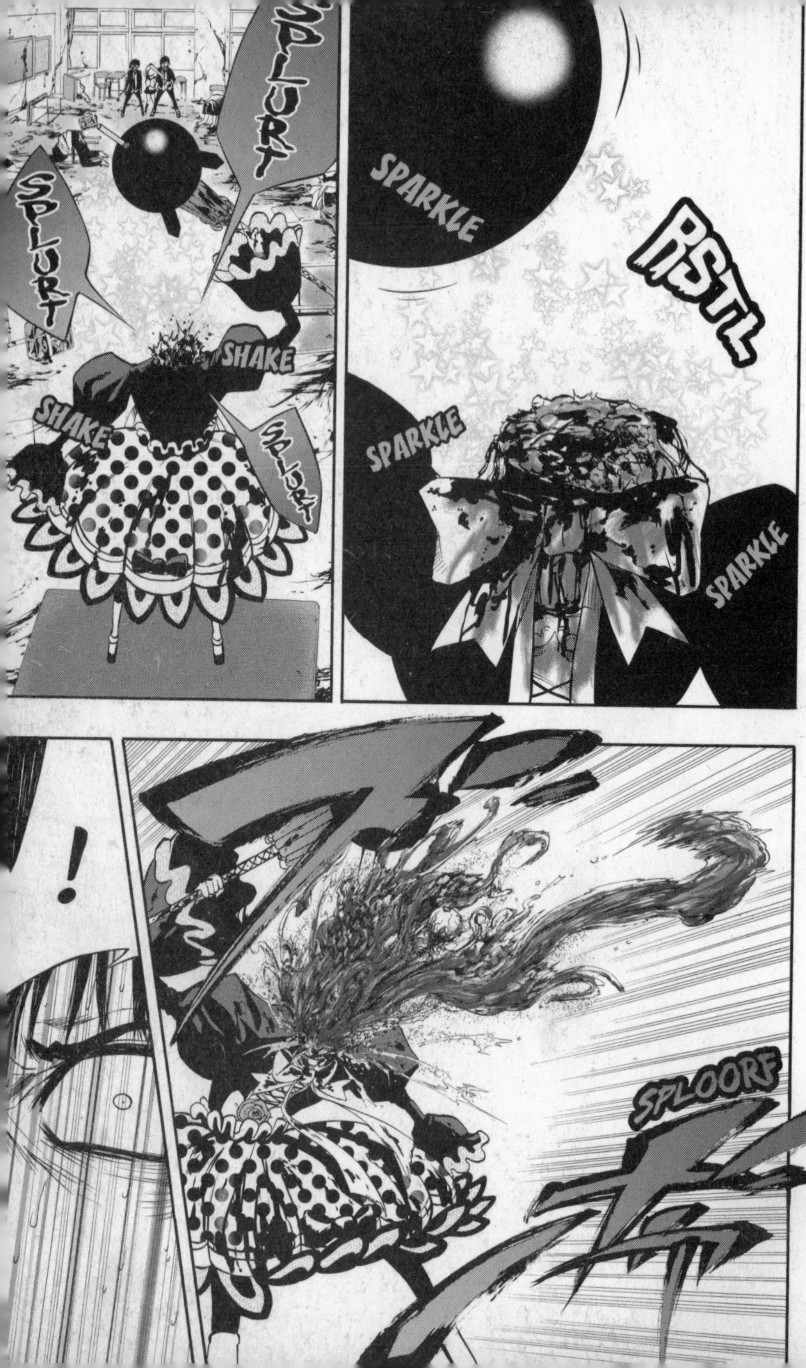
SPARKLE
RSTL
SPARKLE
SPARKLE
SPLURT
SPLURT
SHAKE
SHAKE
SPLURT
SPLOORF
!

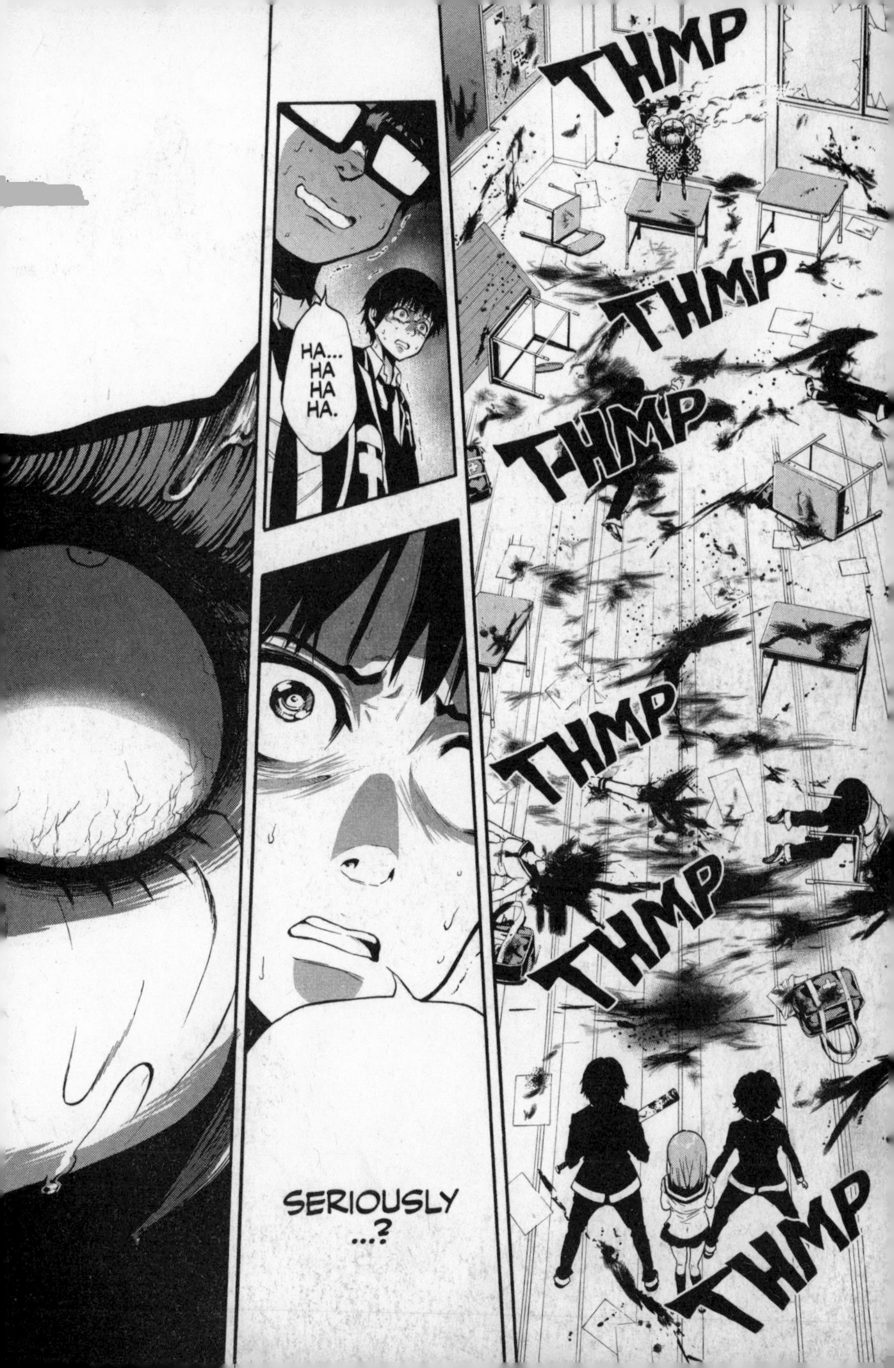
THMP
THMP
T-THMP
THMP
THMP
THMP
HA... HA HA HA.
SERIOUSLY ...?

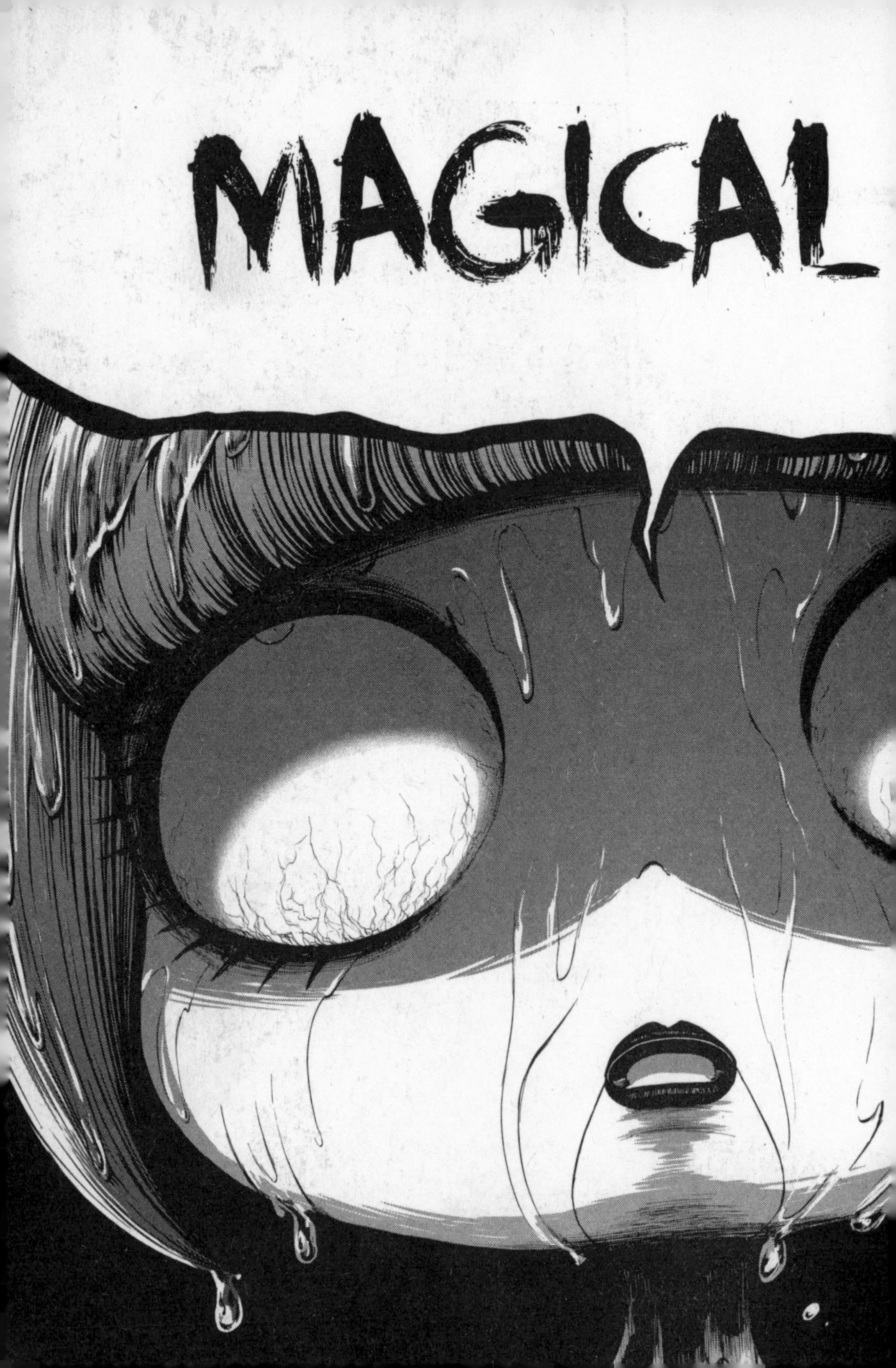
MAGICAL

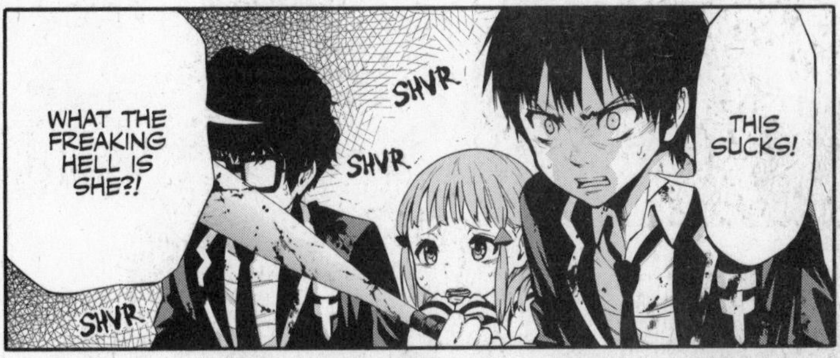
THIS SUCKS!
SHVR
WHAT THE FREAKING HELL IS SHE?!
SHVR
SHVR

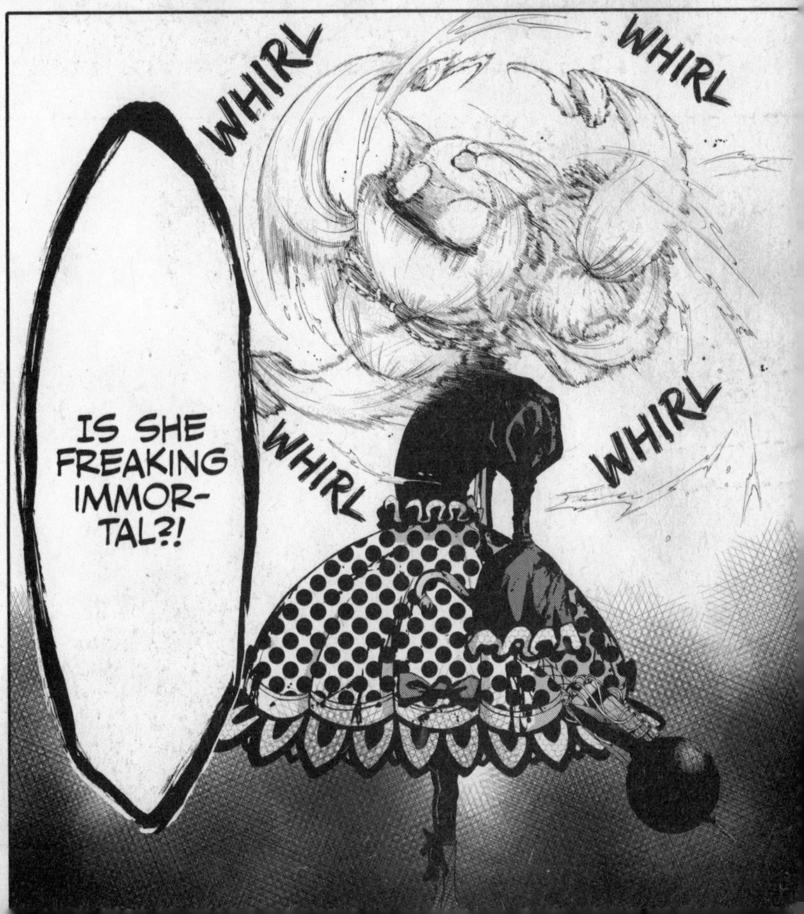
WHIRL
WHIRL
WHIRL
IS SHE FREAKING IMMOR-TAL?!
WHIRL

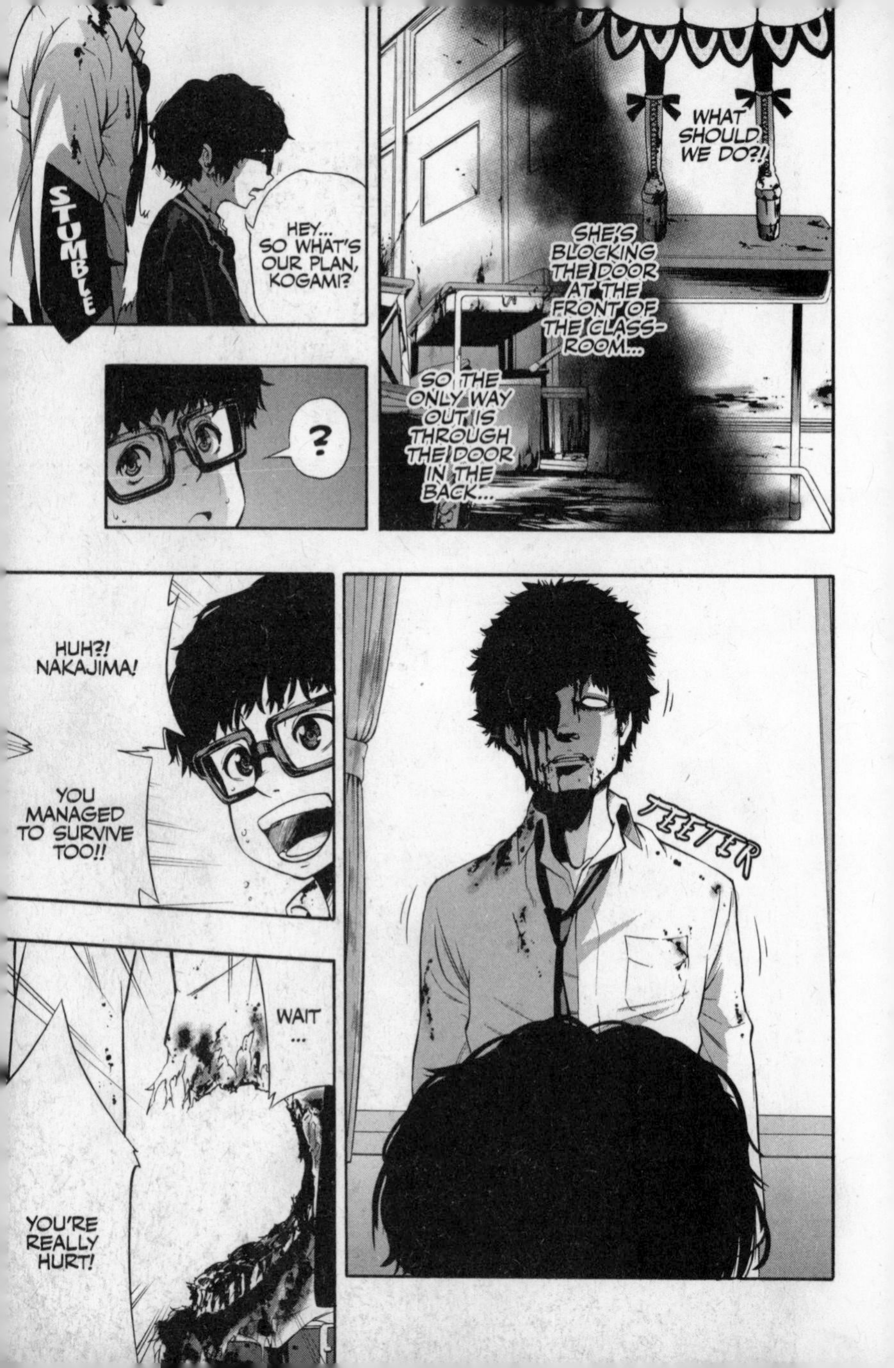
WHAT SHOULD WE DO?!
SHE'S BLOCKING THE DOOR AT THE FRONT OF THE CLASS-ROOM...
SO THE ONLY WAY OUT IS THROUGH THE DOOR IN THE BACK...
STUMBLE
HEY... SO WHAT'S OUR PLAN, KOGAMI?
?
TEETER
HUH?! NAKAJIMA!
YOU MANAGED TO SURVIVE TOO!!
WAIT ...
YOU'RE REALLY HURT!

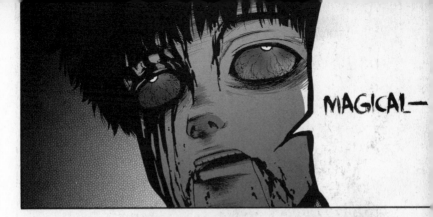

MAGICAL—

HUH?

SPLAT

GWOOF

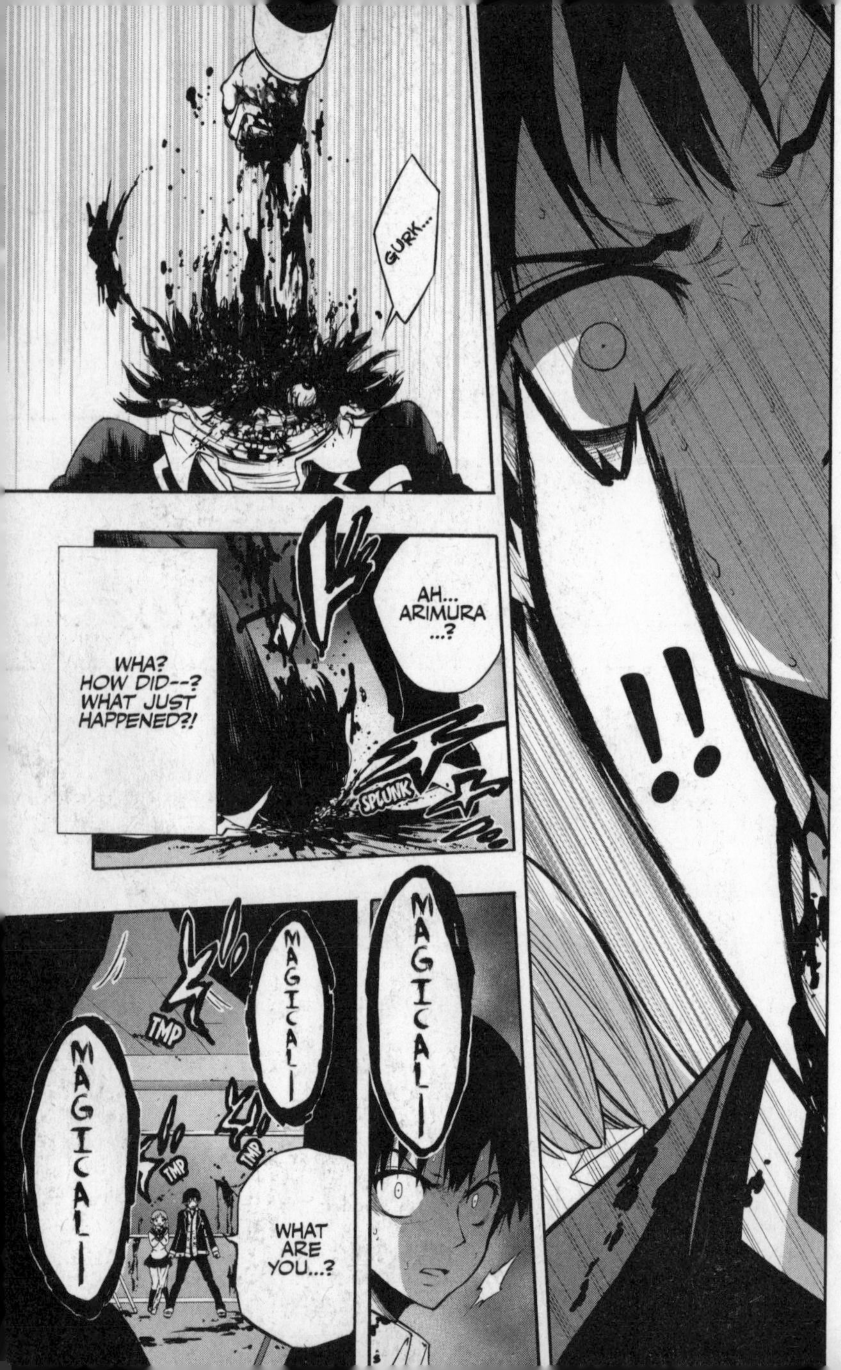
!!
GURK...
AH... ARIMURA ...?
SPLUNK
WHA? HOW DID--? WHAT JUST HAPPENED?!
MAGICAL!
MAGICAL!
TMP
MAGICAL!
TMP
TMP
WHAT ARE YOU...?

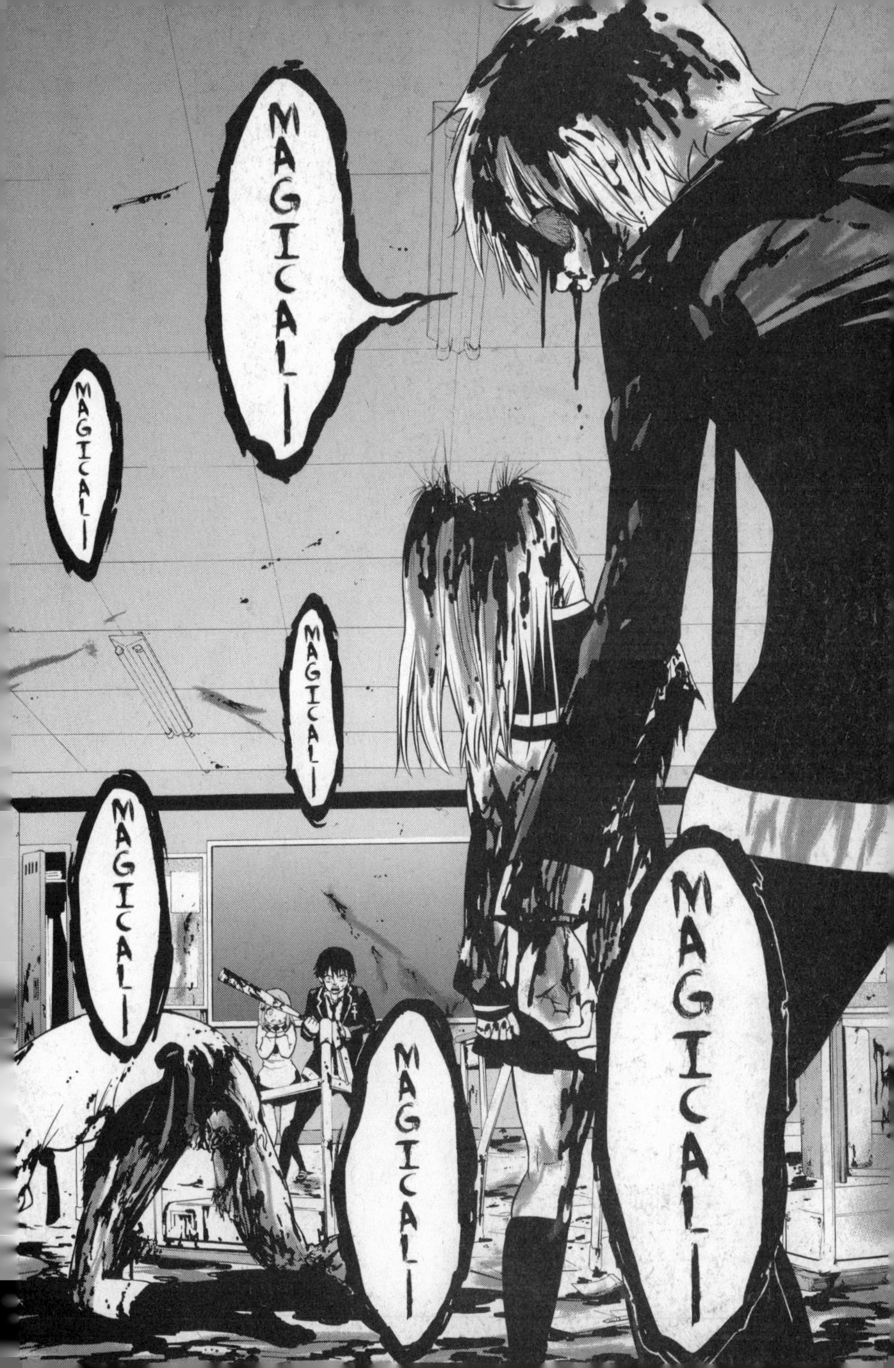
MAGICAL!
MAGICAL!
MAGICAL!
MAGICAL!
MAGICAL!
MAGICAL!

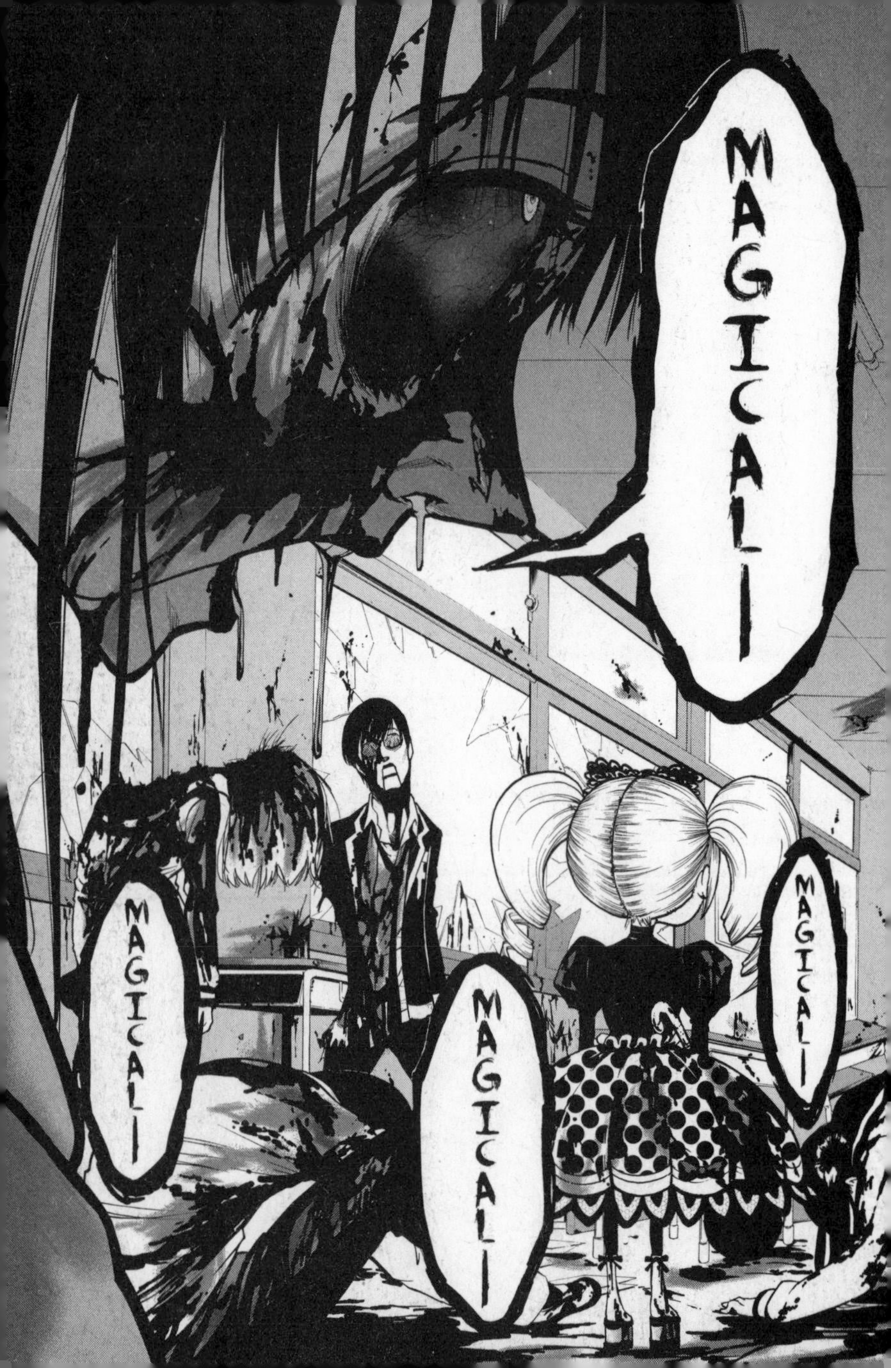
MAGICAL!
MAGICAL!
MAGICAL!
MAGICAL!

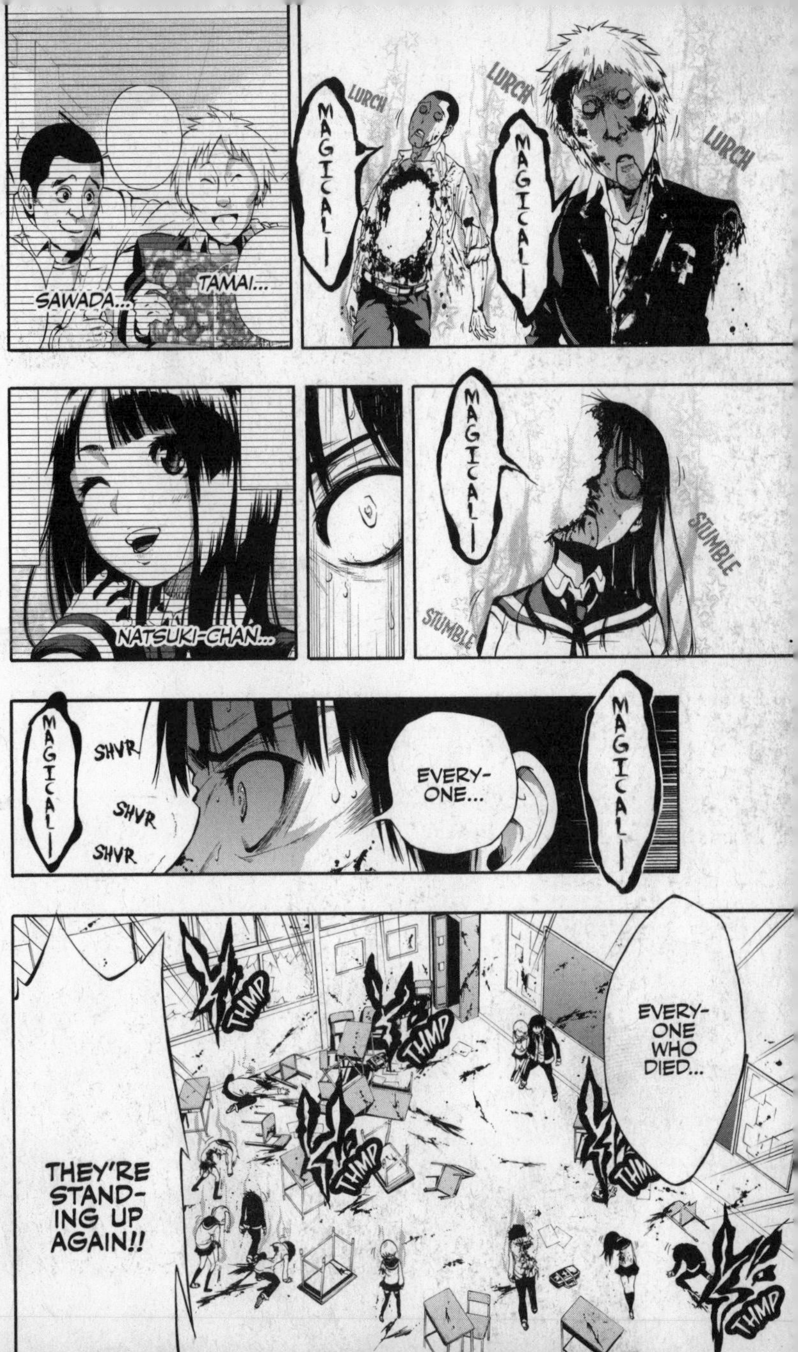
LURCH
LURCH
MAGICAL!
LURCH
MAGICAL!
TAMAI...
SAWADA...
MAGICAL!
STUMBLE
STUMBLE
NATSUKI-CHAN...
MAGICAL!
EVERY-ONE...
SHVR
SHVR
SHVR
MAGICAL!
EVERY-ONE WHO DIED...
THMP
THMP
THMP
THMP
THMP
THMP
THEY'RE STAND-ING UP AGAIN!!

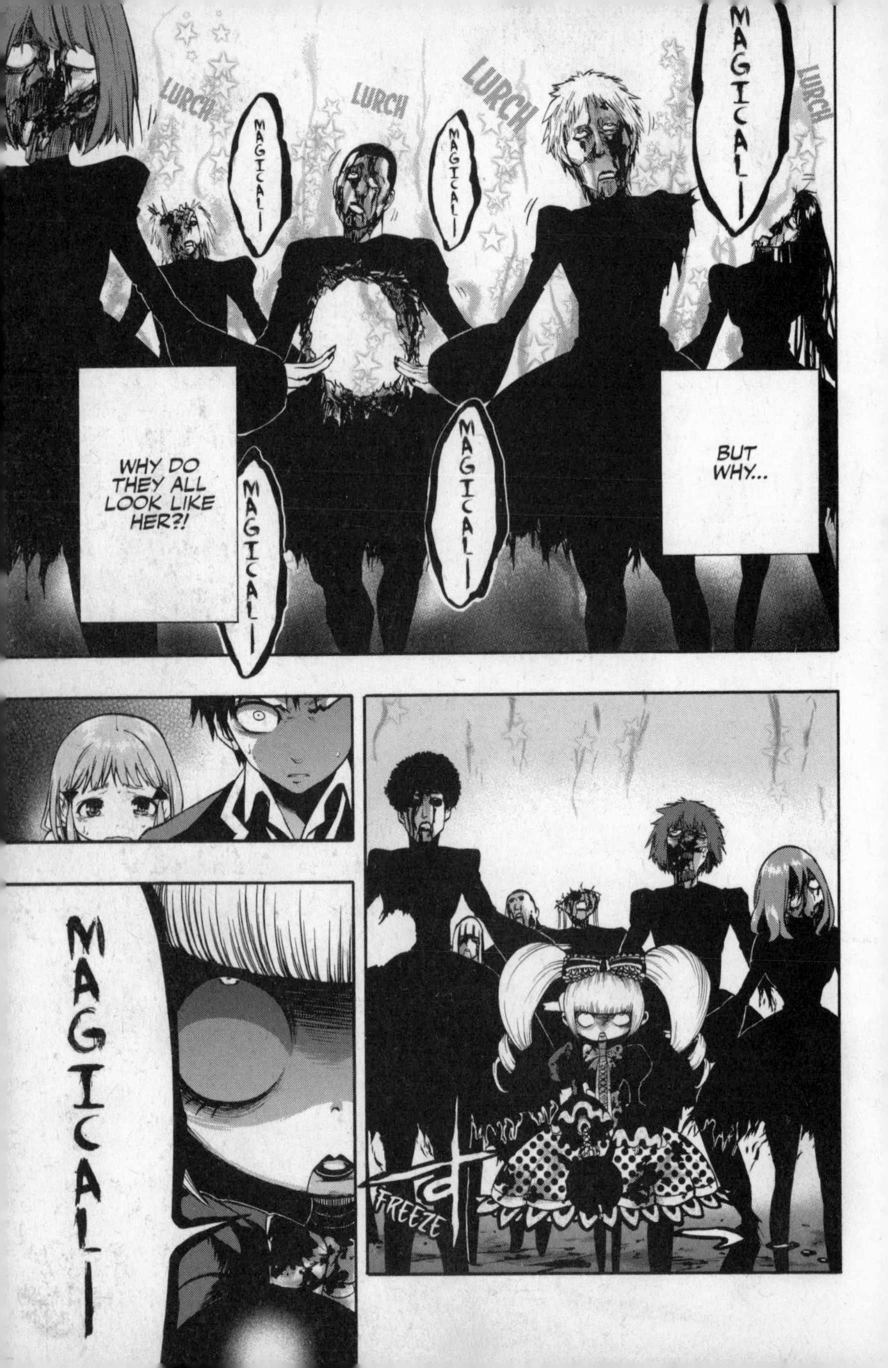
LURCH
MAGICALI
LURCH
MAGICALI
LURCH
MAGICALI
LURCH
MAGICALI
BUT WHY...
WHY DO THEY ALL LOOK LIKE HER?!
MAGICALI
MAGICALI
FREEZE
MAGICALI

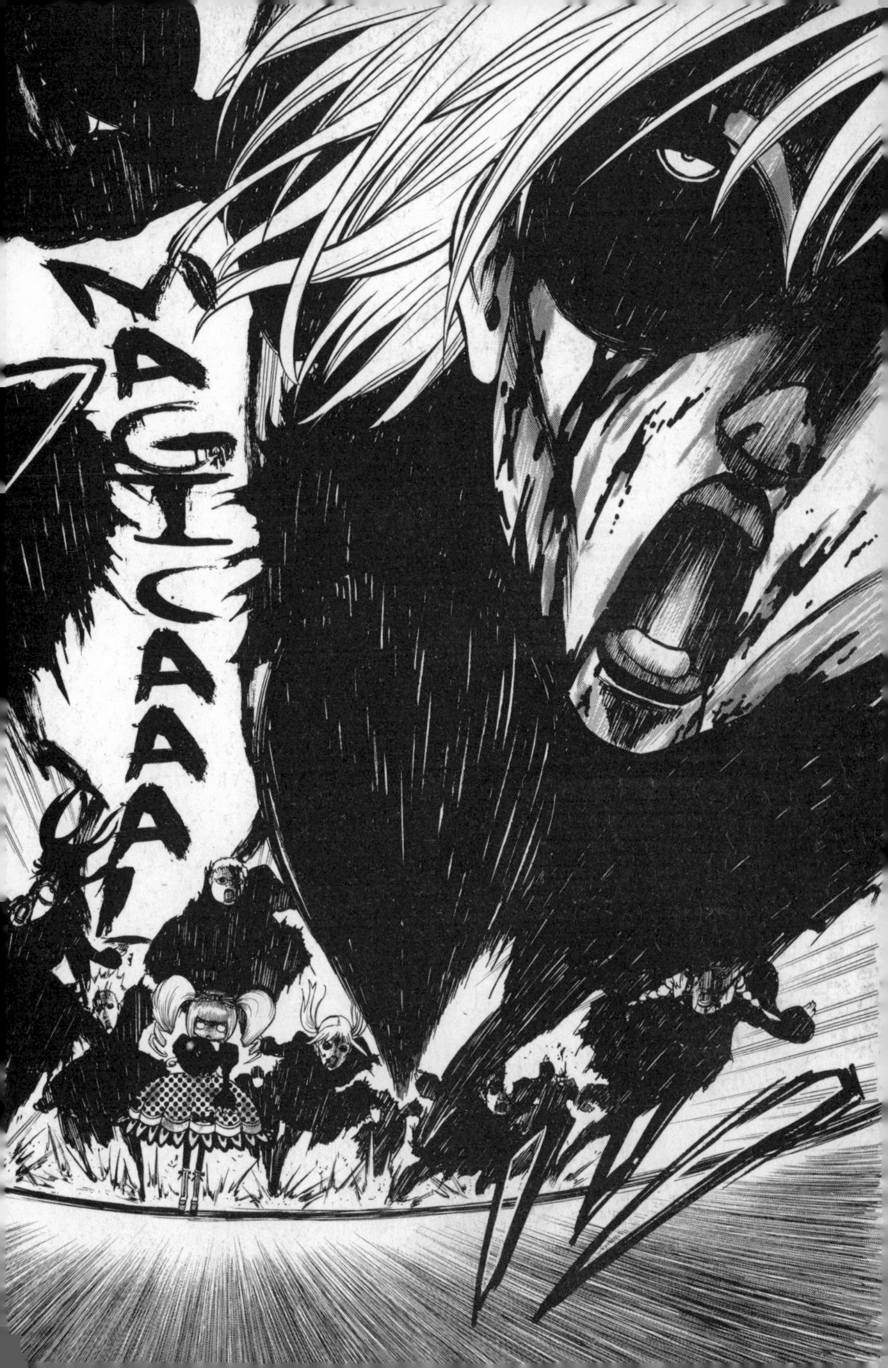
MAGHCAAA!

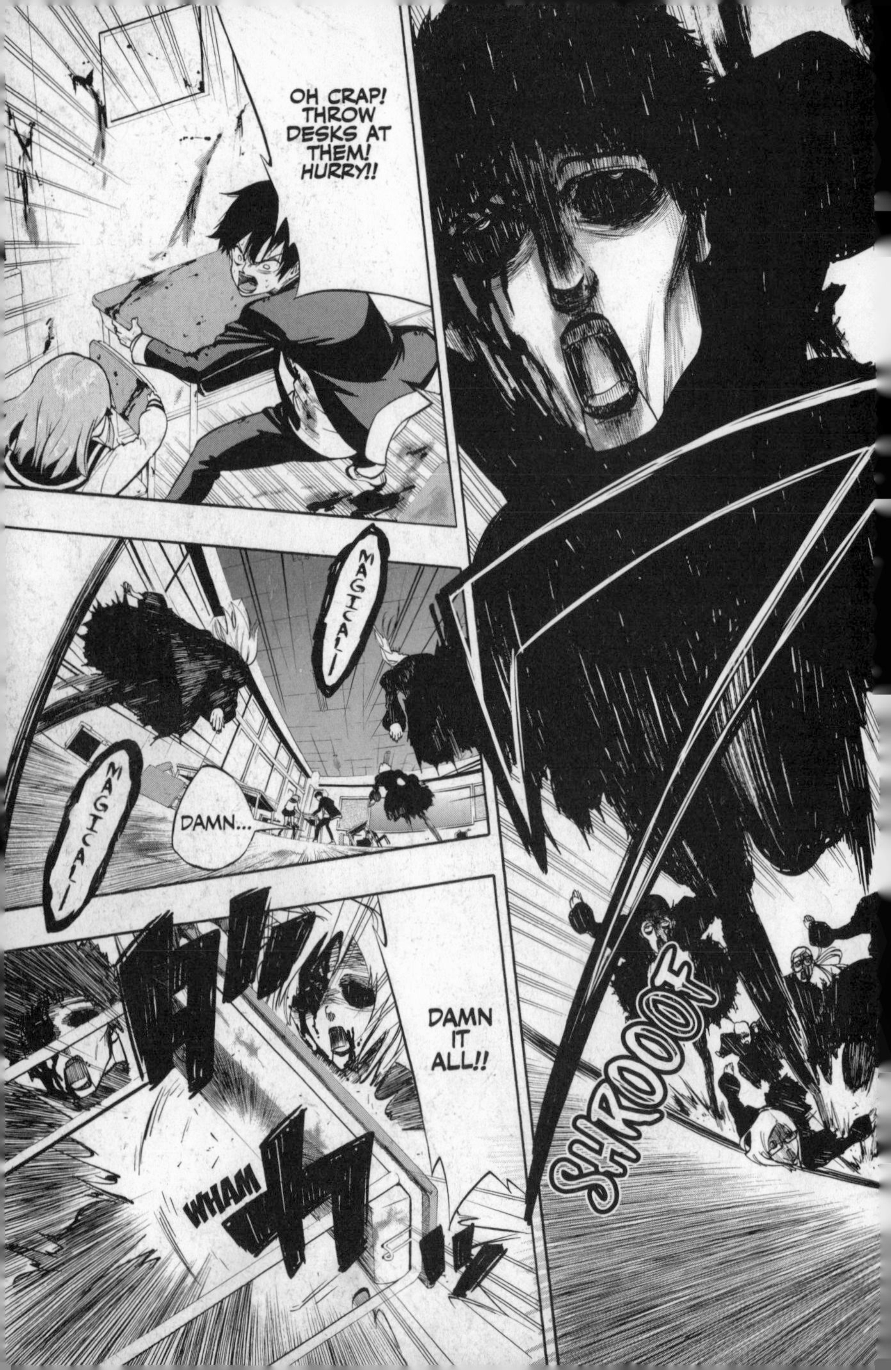
SHROOOF
OH CRAP! THROW DESKS AT THEM! HURRY!!
MAGICAL!
MAGICAL!
DAMN...
DAMN IT ALL!!
WHAM

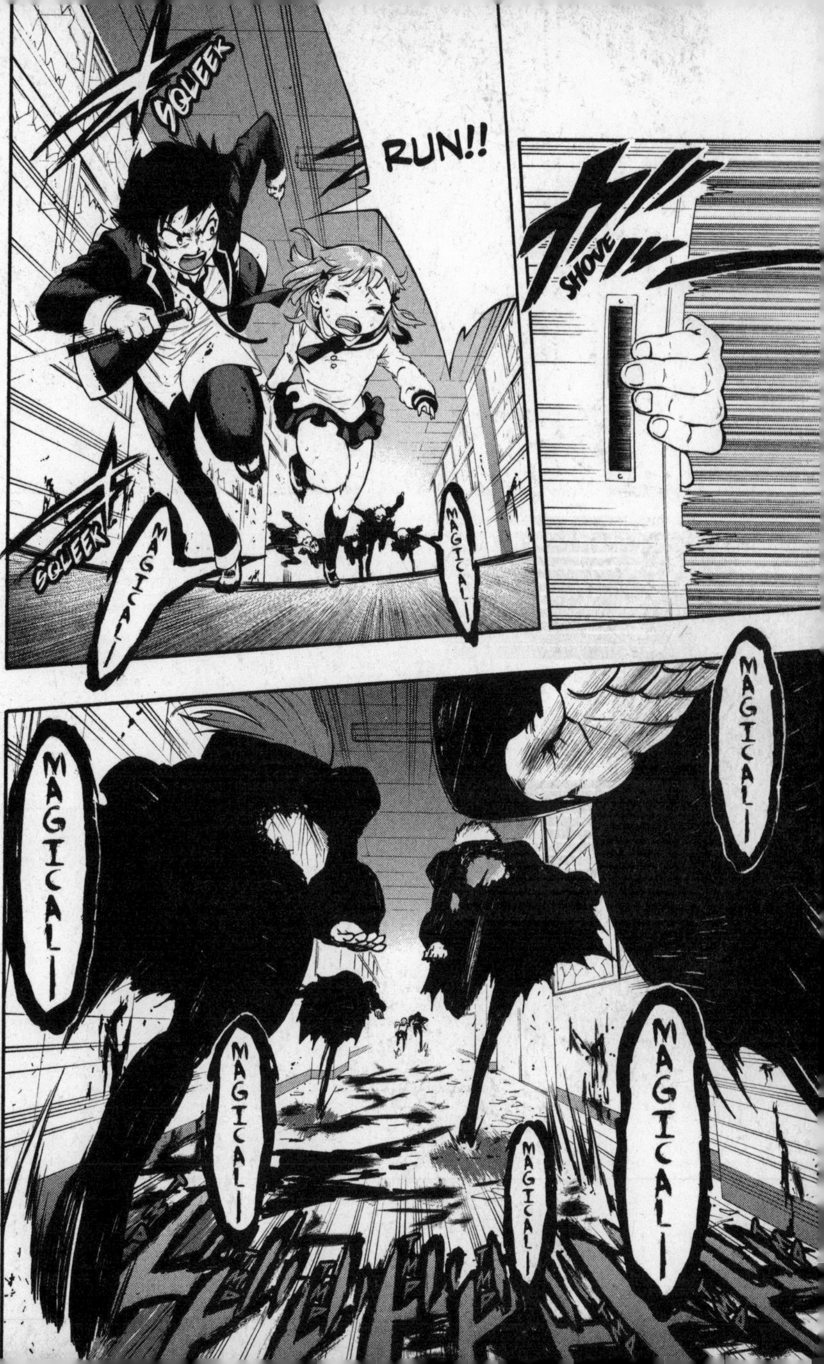
SHOVE
RUN!!
SQUEEK
MAGICALI
MAGICALI
SQUEEK
MAGICALI
MAGICALI
MAGICALI
MAGICALI
MAGICALI

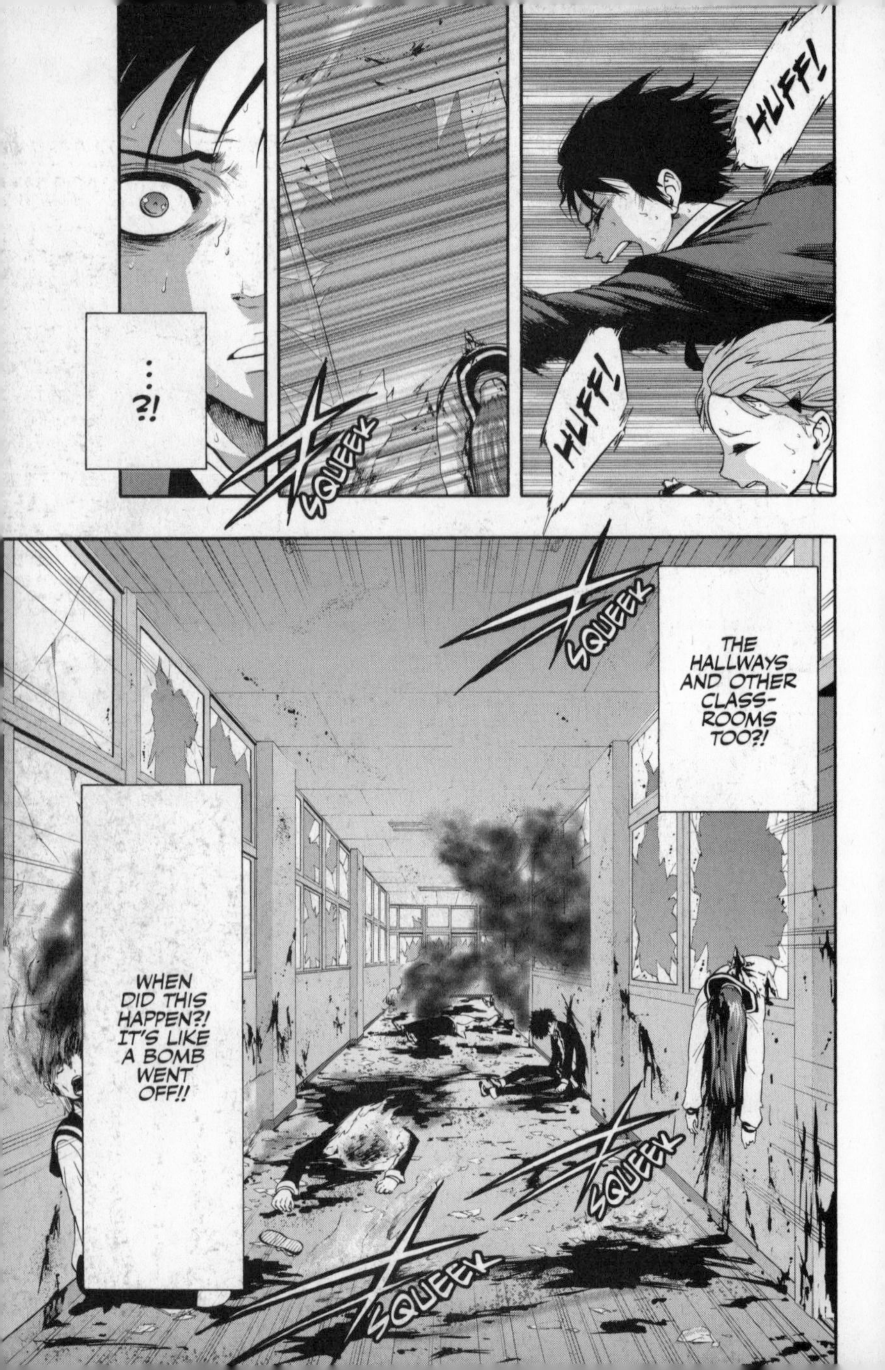
HUFF!
HUFF!
SQUEEK
...
?!
SQUEEK
THE HALLWAYS AND OTHER CLASS-ROOMS TOO?!
SQUEEK
WHEN DID THIS HAPPEN?! IT'S LIKE A BOMB WENT OFF!!
SQUEEK

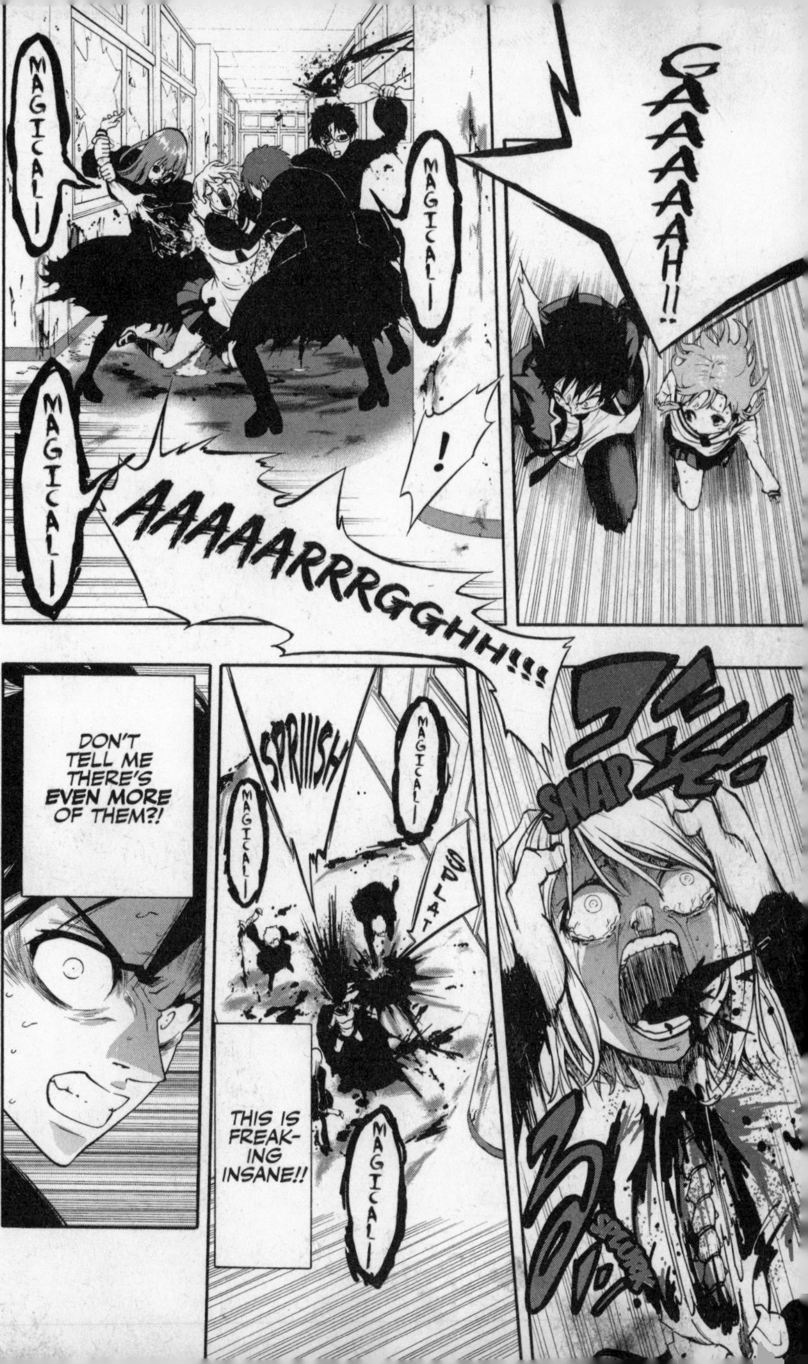
GAAAAAAH!!
MAGICAL!
MAGICAL!
!
MAGICAL!
AAAAAARRRRGGHH!!!
SNAP
SPRIIISH
MAGICAL!
MAGICAL!
SPLAT
MAGICAL!
THIS IS FREAK-ING INSANE!!
DON'T TELL ME THERE'S EVEN MORE OF THEM?!

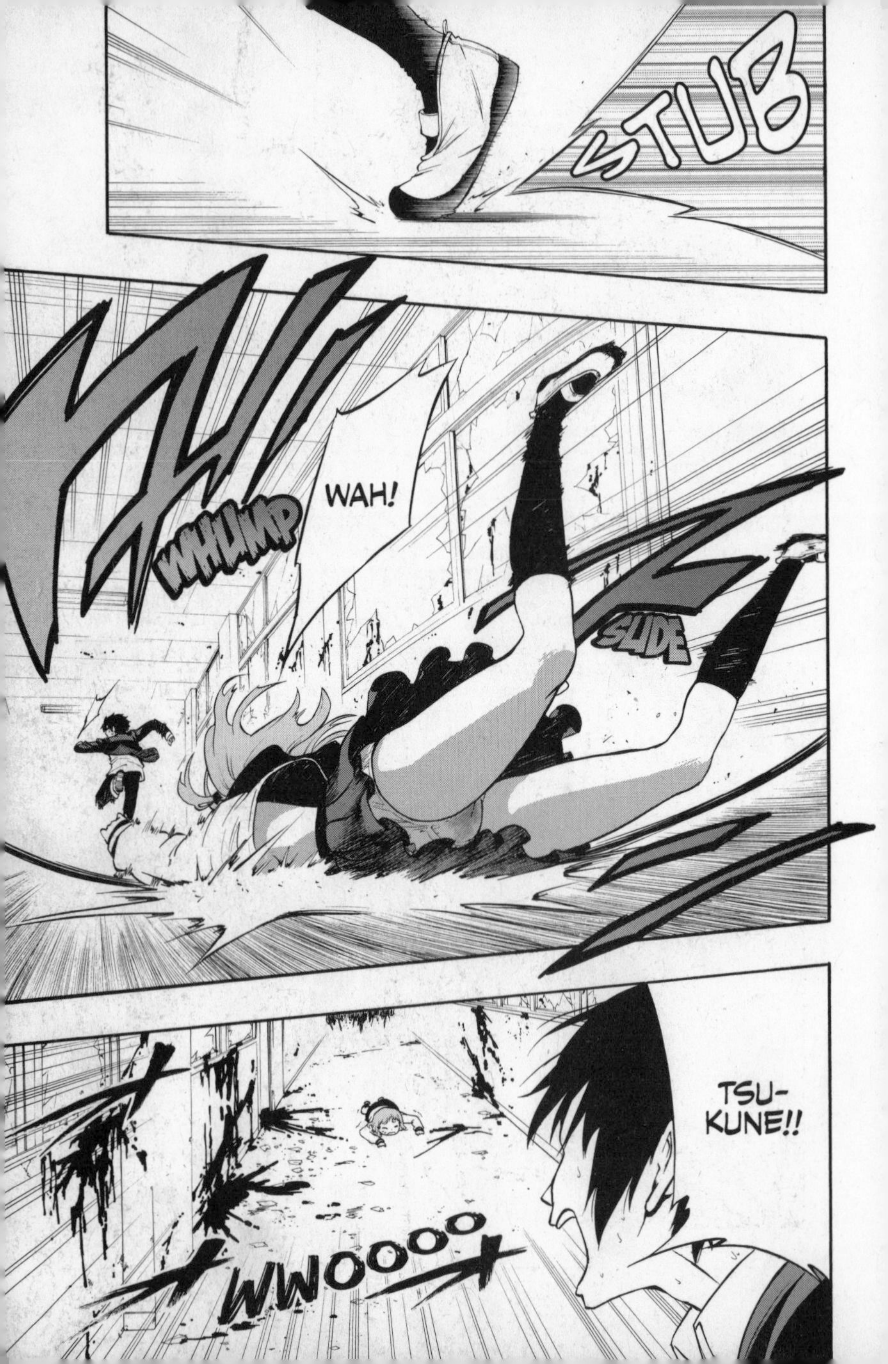
STUB
WAH!
WHUMP
SLIDE
TSU-KUNE!!
WWOOOO

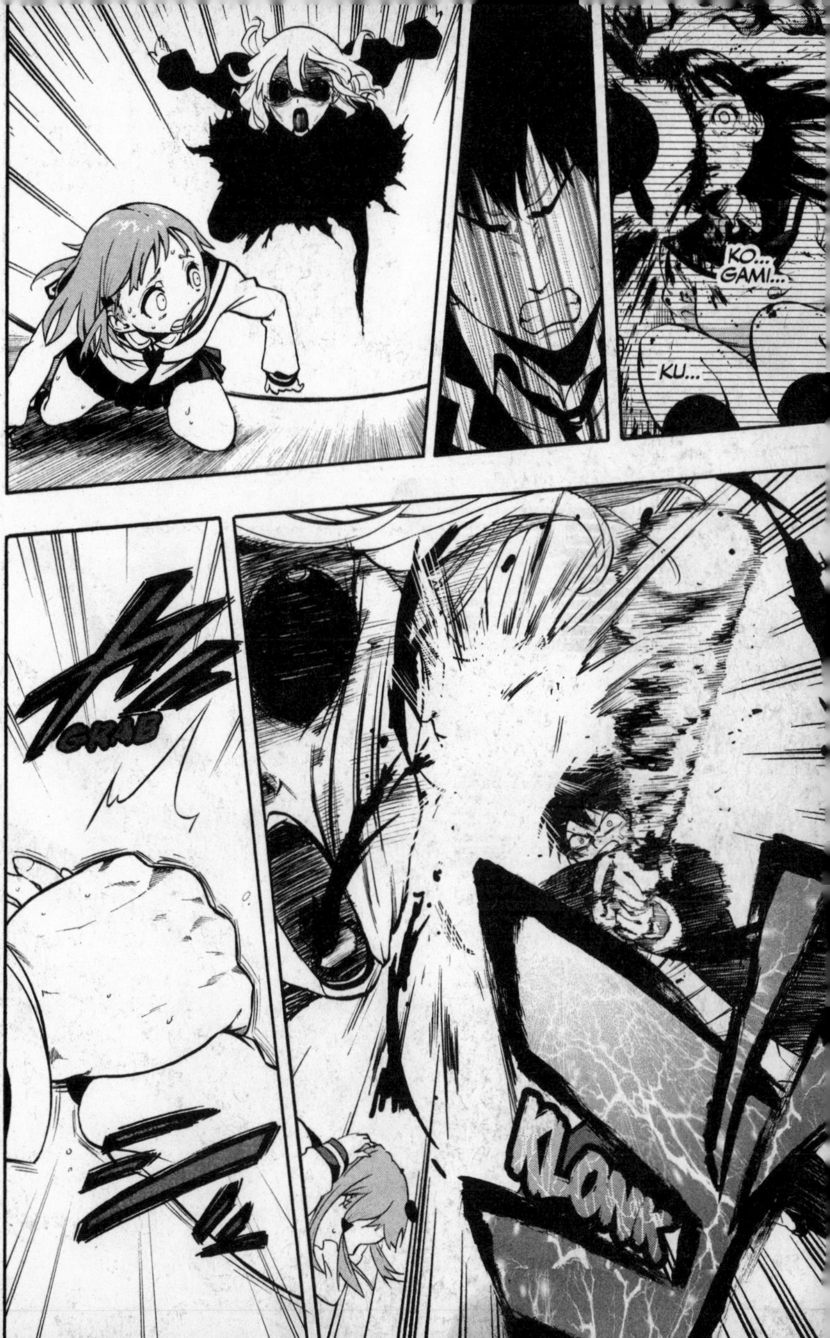
KO... GAMI...
KU...
KLONK
GRAB

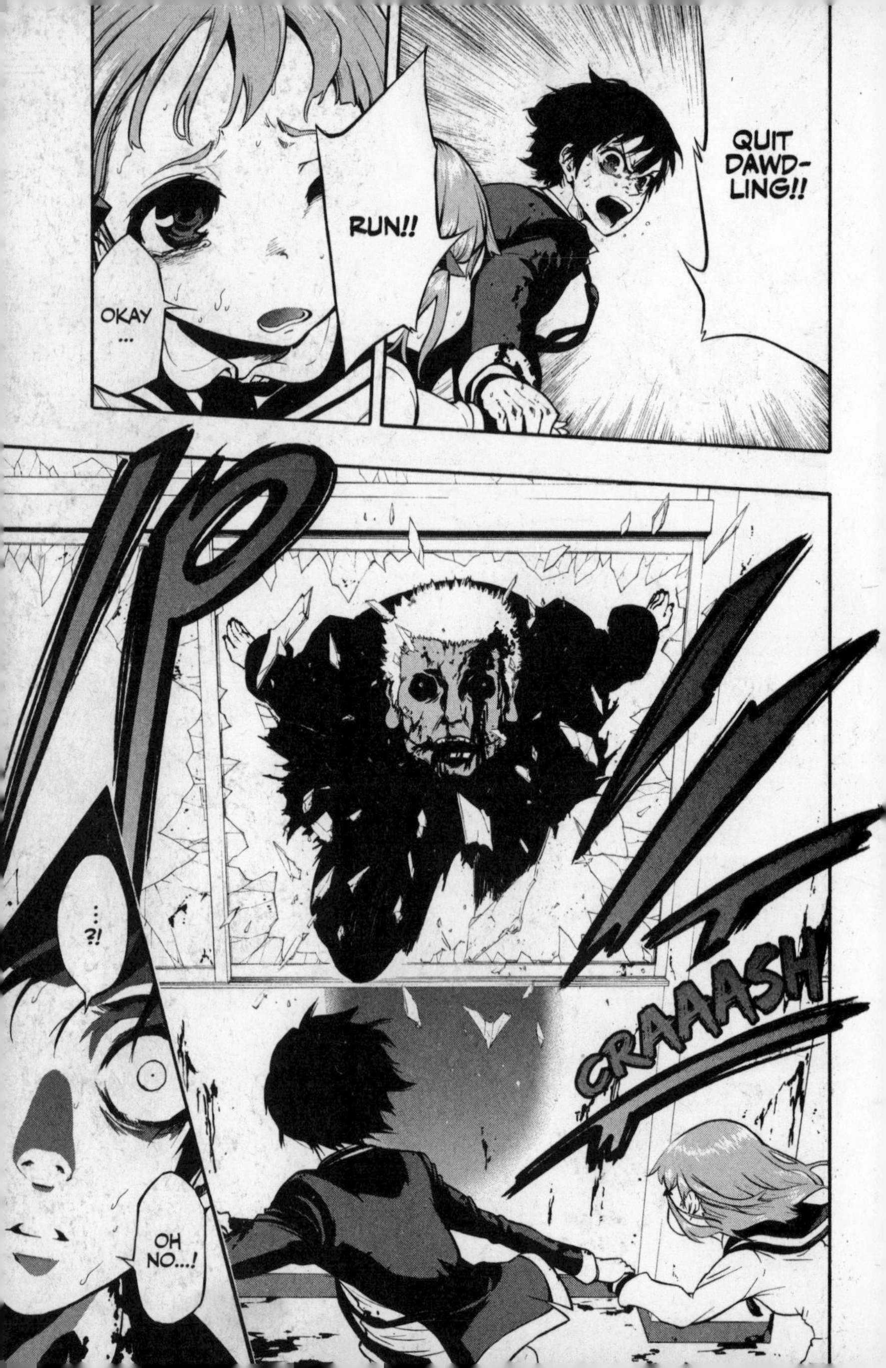
QUIT DAWD-LING!!
RUN!!
OKAY ...
CRAAASH
...?!
OH NO...!

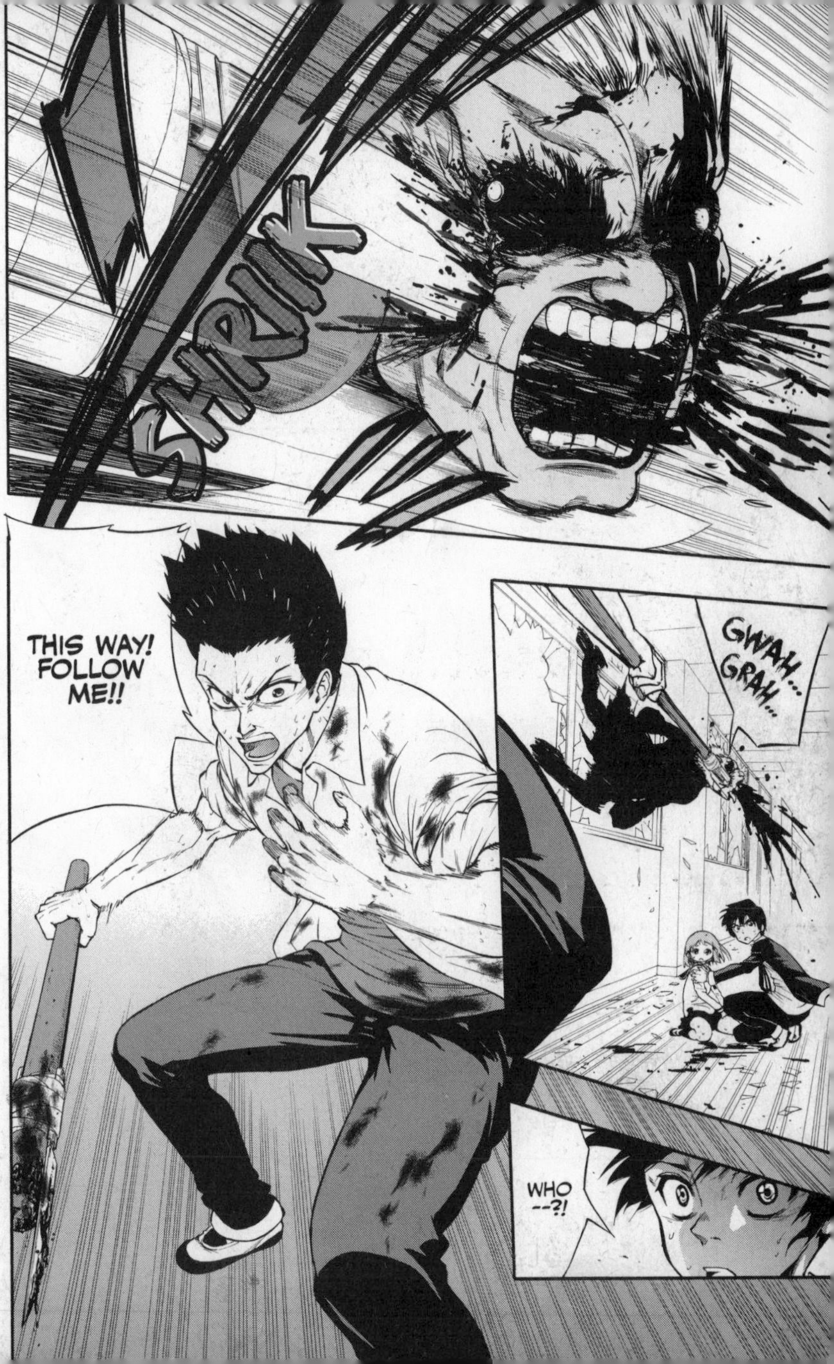
SHRIIK
GWAH GRAH...
WHO--?!
THIS WAY! FOLLOW ME!!

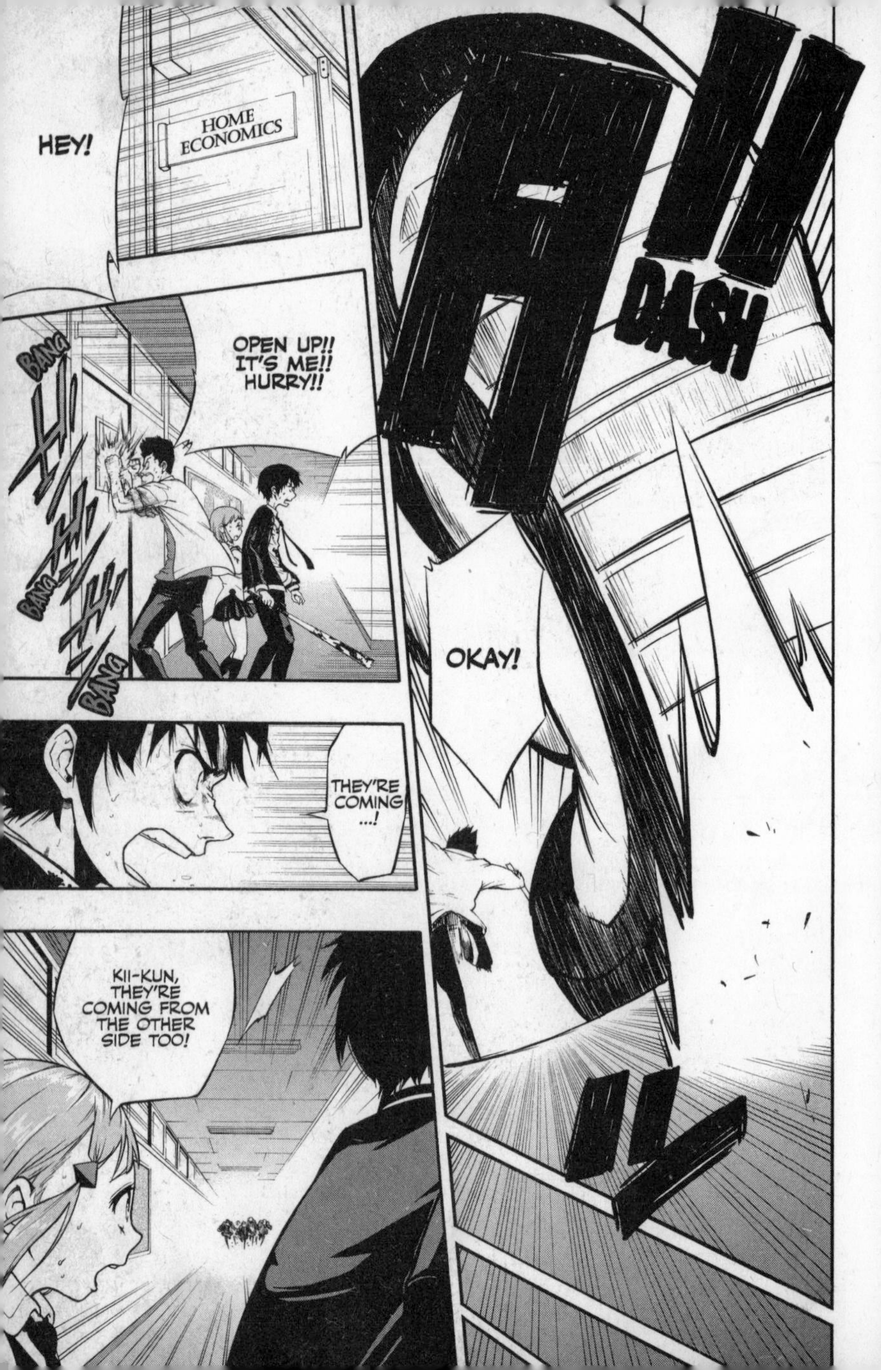
DASH
OKAY!
HOME ECONOMICS
HEY!
OPEN UP!! IT'S ME!! HURRY!!
BANG BANG BANG
THEY'RE COMING ...!
KII-KUN, THEY'RE COMING FROM THE OTHER SIDE TOO!

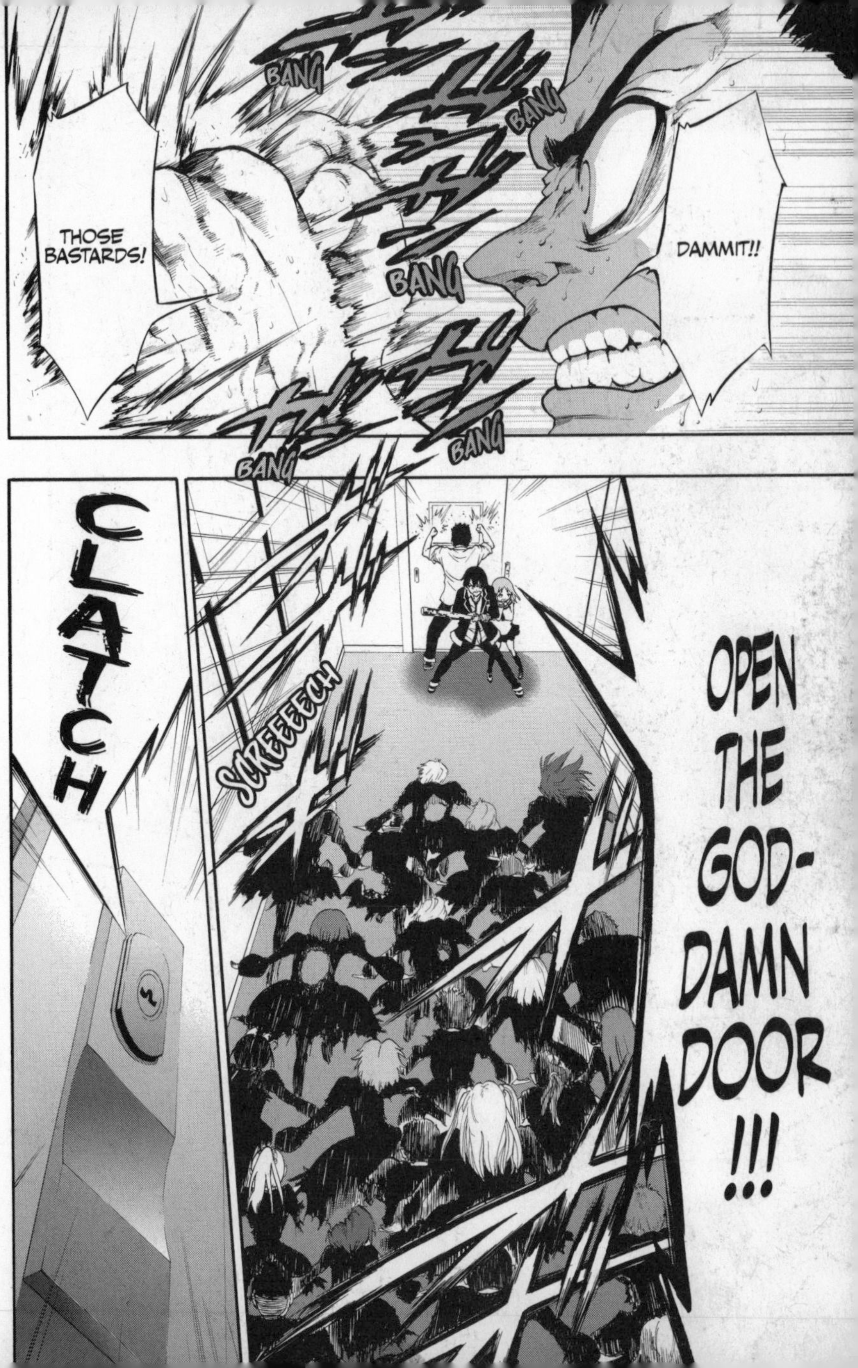
DAMMIT!!
BANG
BANG
BANG
BANG
BANG
THOSE BASTARDS!
OPEN THE GOD-DAMN DOOR!!!
SCREEEEECH
CLATCH

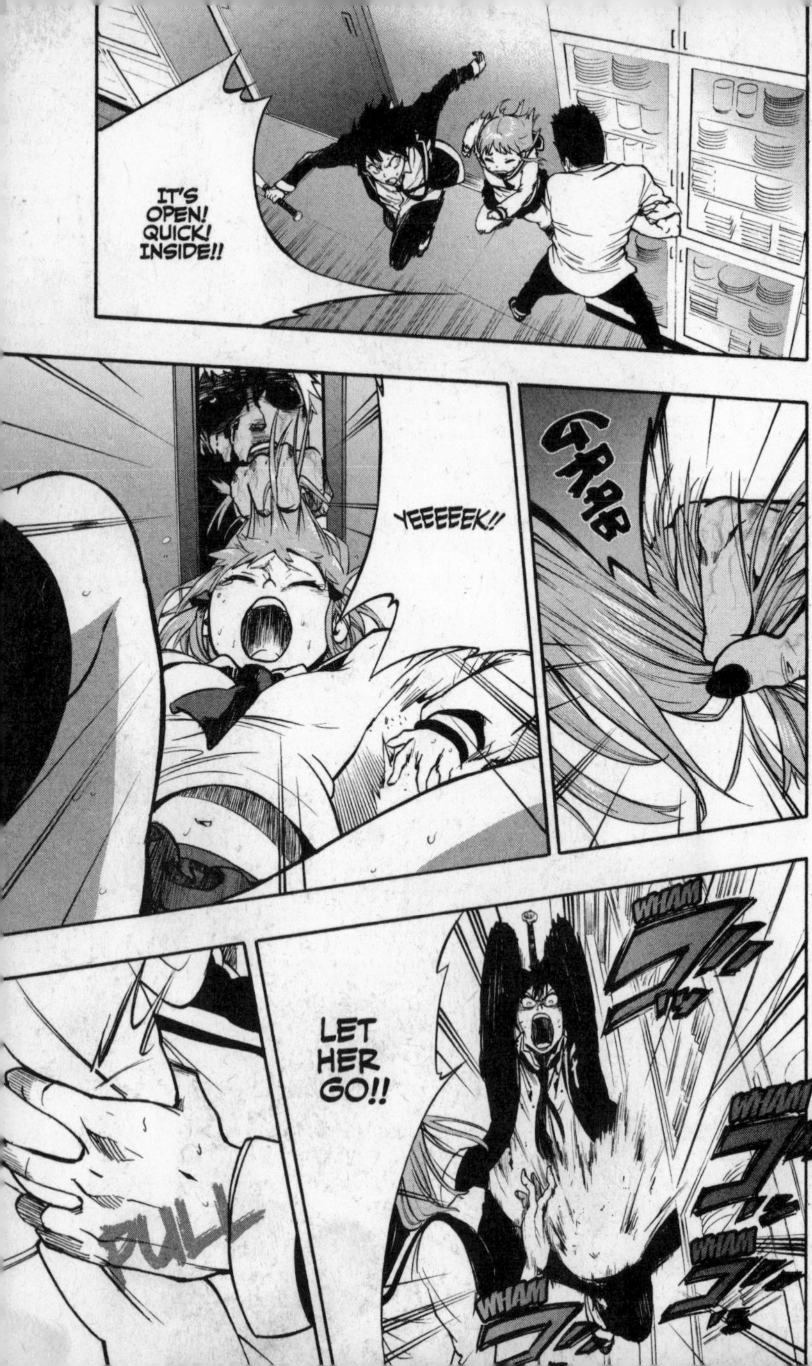
IT'S OPEN! QUICK! INSIDE!!
GRAB
YEEEEEK!!
WHAM
WHAM
LET HER GO!!
WHAM
WHAM
PULL

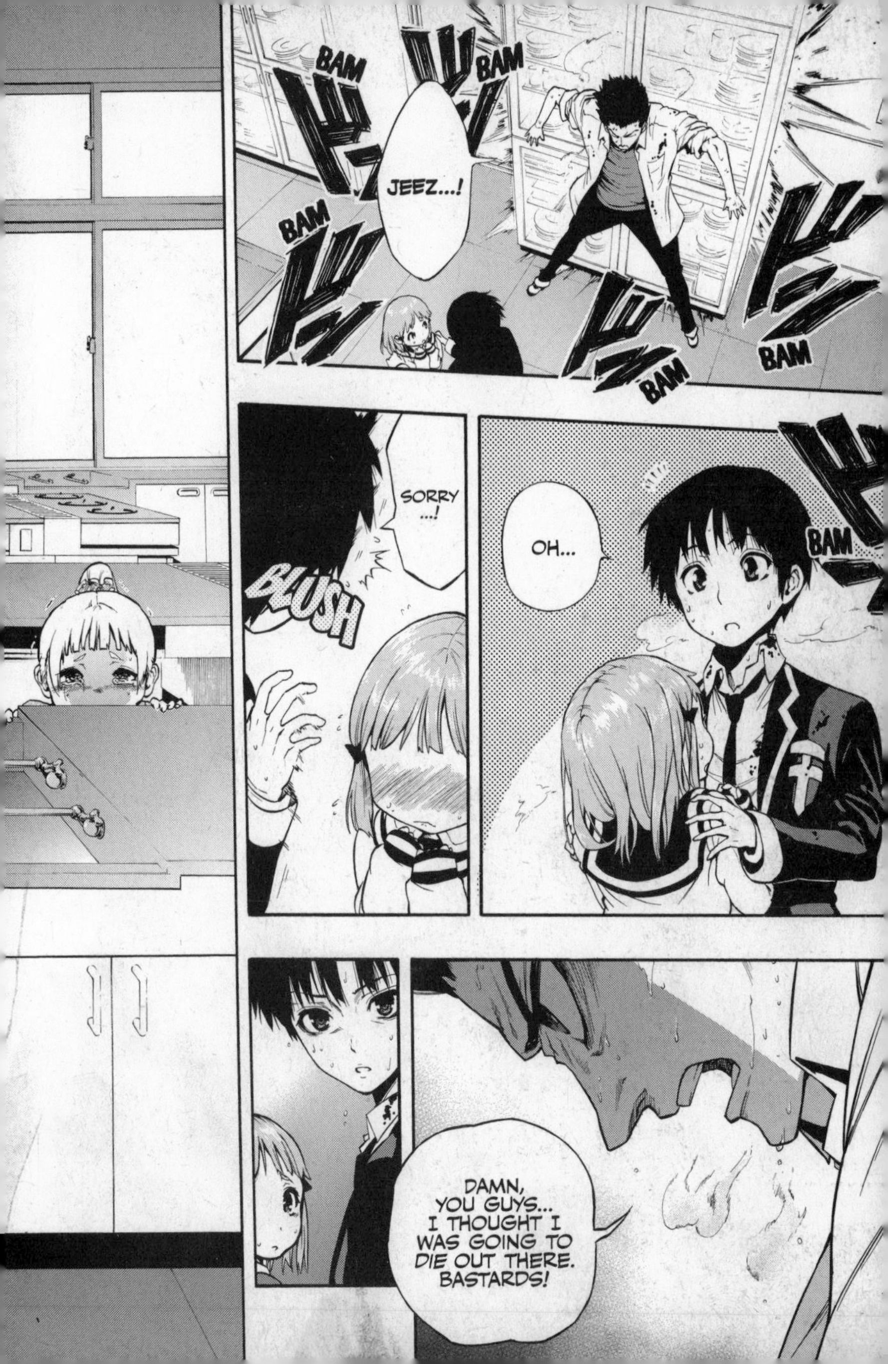
BAM
BAM
JEEZ...!
BAM
BAM
BAM
OH...
BAM
SORRY ...!
BLUSH
DAMN, YOU GUYS... I THOUGHT I WAS GOING TO DIE OUT THERE. BASTARDS!

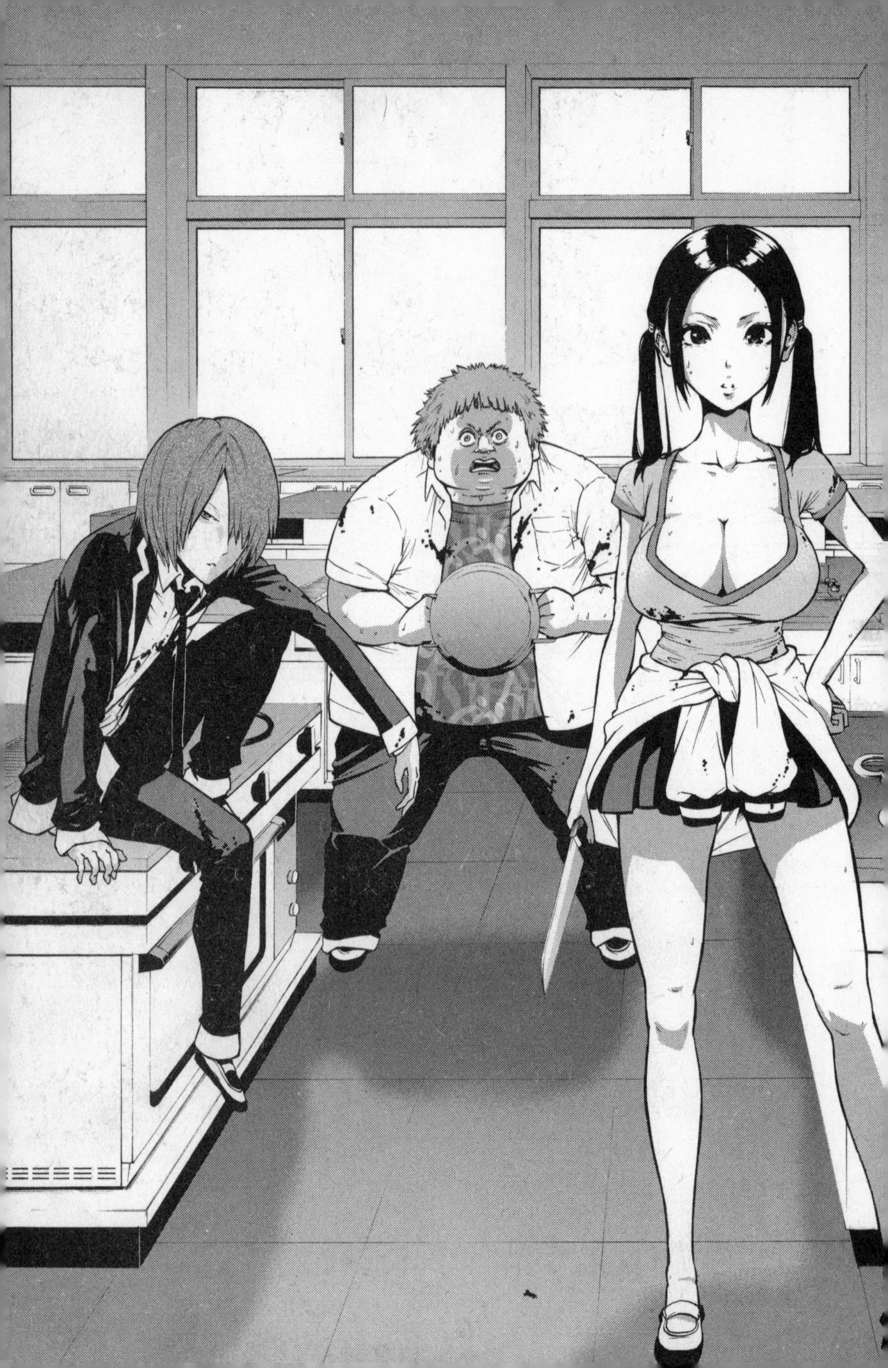

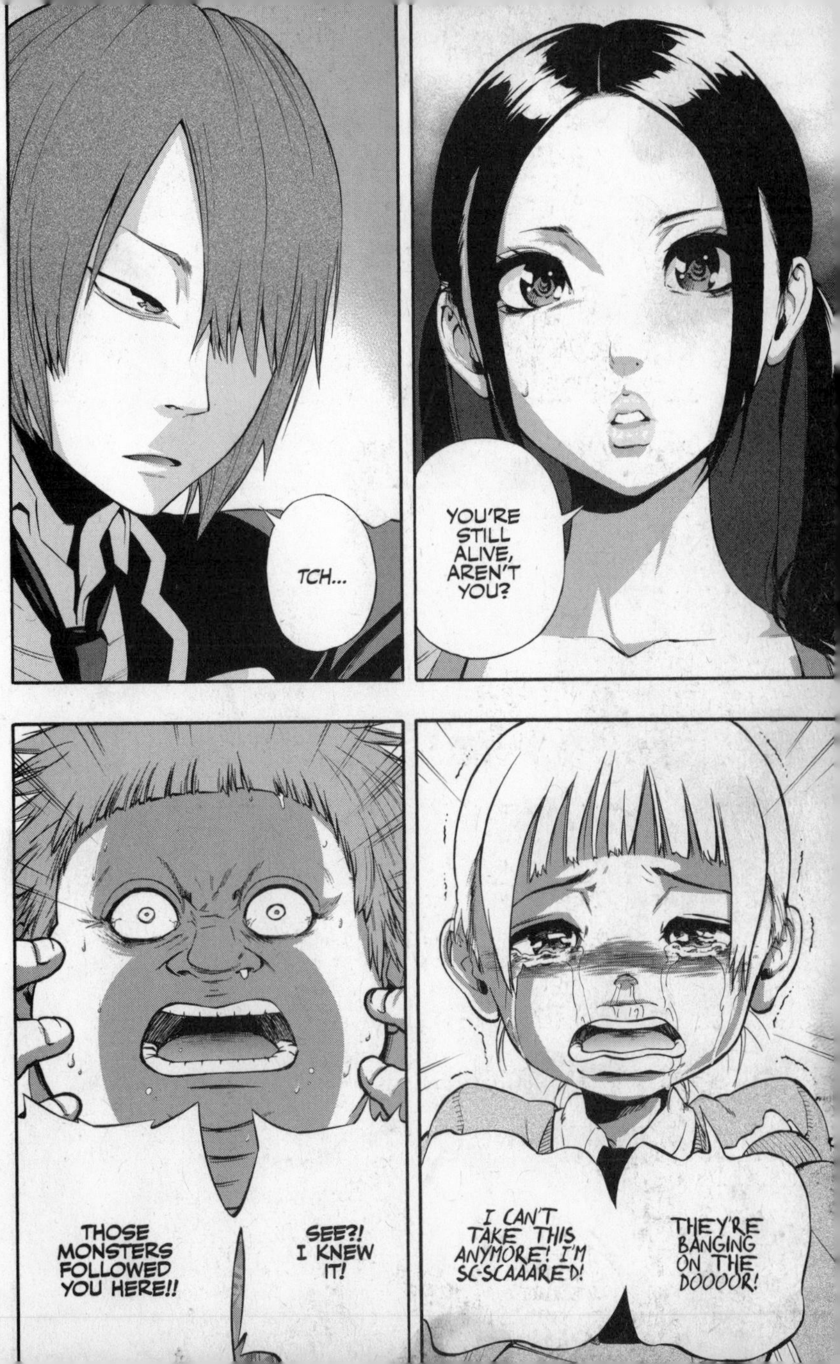
YOU'RE STILL ALIVE, AREN'T YOU?
TCH...
THEY'RE BANGING ON THE DOOOOR!
I CAN'T TAKE THIS ANYMORE! I'M SC-SCAAARED!
SEE?! I KNEW IT!
THOSE MONSTERS FOLLOWED YOU HERE!!

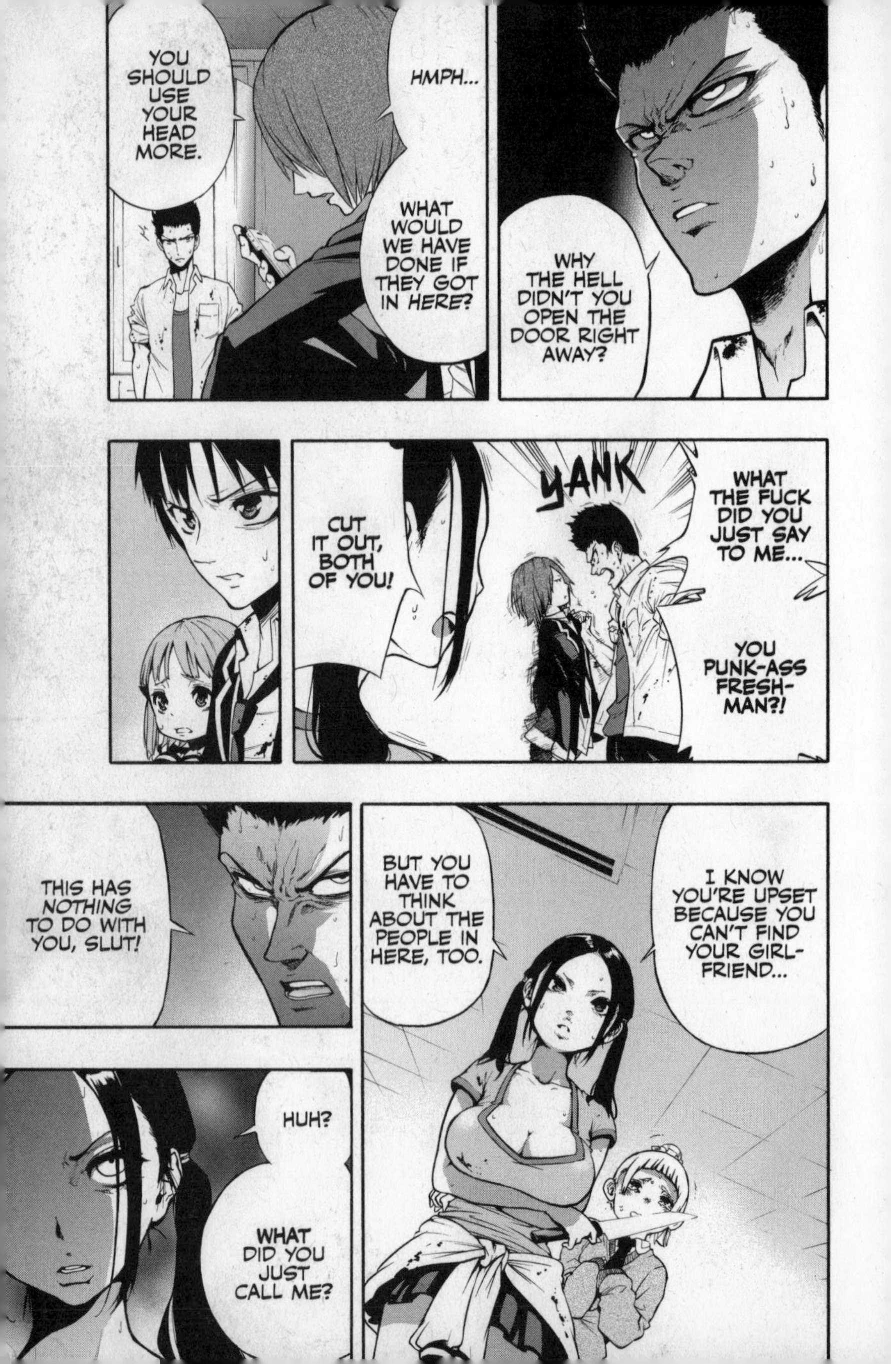
WHY THE HELL DIDN'T YOU OPEN THE DOOR RIGHT AWAY?
HMPH...
WHAT WOULD WE HAVE DONE IF THEY GOT IN *HERE*?
YOU SHOULD USE YOUR HEAD MORE.
WHAT THE FUCK DID YOU JUST SAY TO ME...
YANK
YOU PUNK-ASS FRESH-MAN?!
CUT IT OUT, BOTH OF YOU!
I KNOW YOU'RE UPSET BECAUSE YOU CAN'T FIND YOUR GIRL-FRIEND...
BUT YOU HAVE TO THINK ABOUT THE PEOPLE IN HERE, TOO.
THIS HAS *NOTHING* TO DO WITH YOU, SLUT!
HUH?
WHAT DID YOU JUST CALL ME?

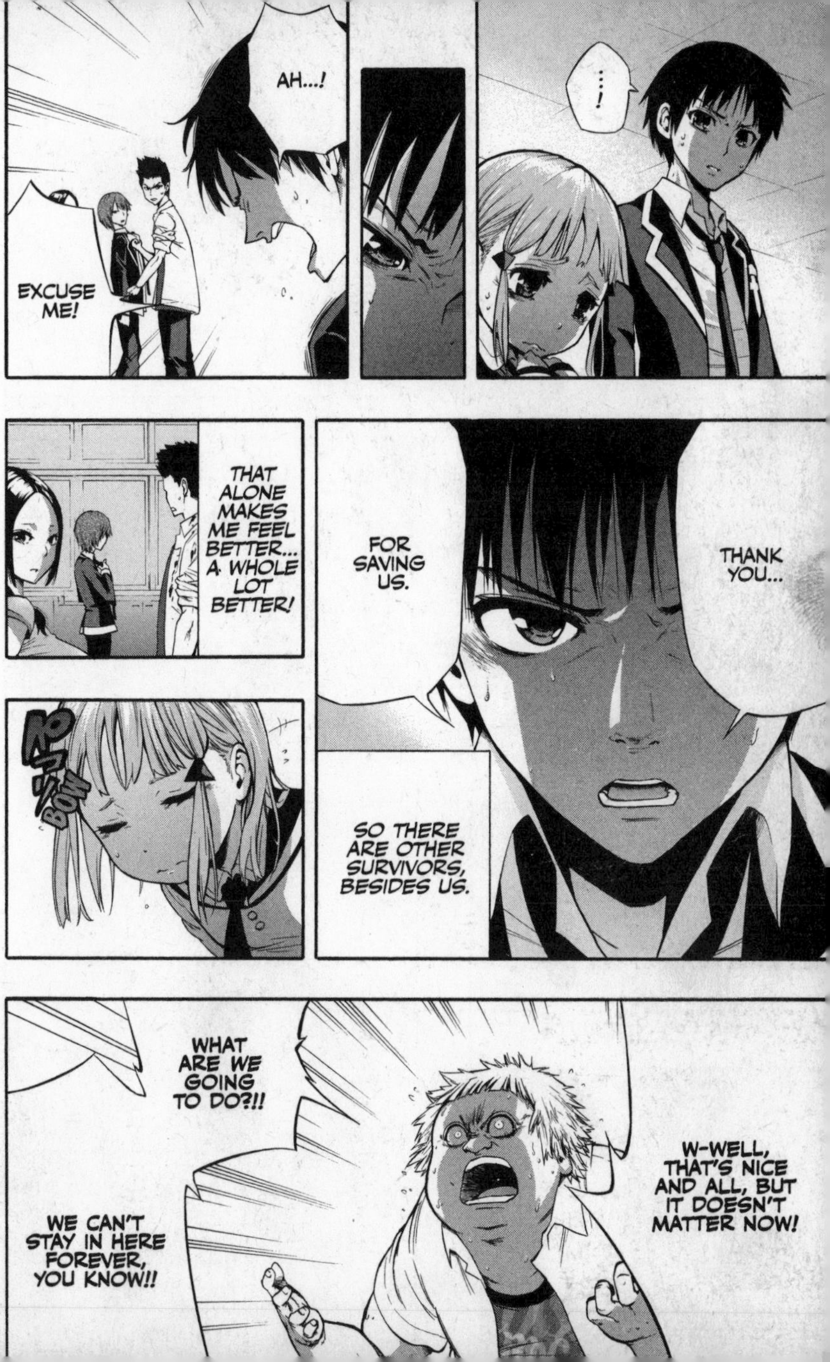
...!
AH...!
EXCUSE ME!
THANK YOU...
FOR SAVING US.
SO THERE ARE OTHER SURVIVORS, BESIDES US.
THAT ALONE MAKES ME FEEL BETTER... A WHOLE LOT BETTER!
BOW
W-WELL, THAT'S NICE AND ALL, BUT IT DOESN'T MATTER NOW!
WHAT ARE WE GOING TO DO?!!
WE CAN'T STAY IN HERE FOREVER, YOU KNOW!!

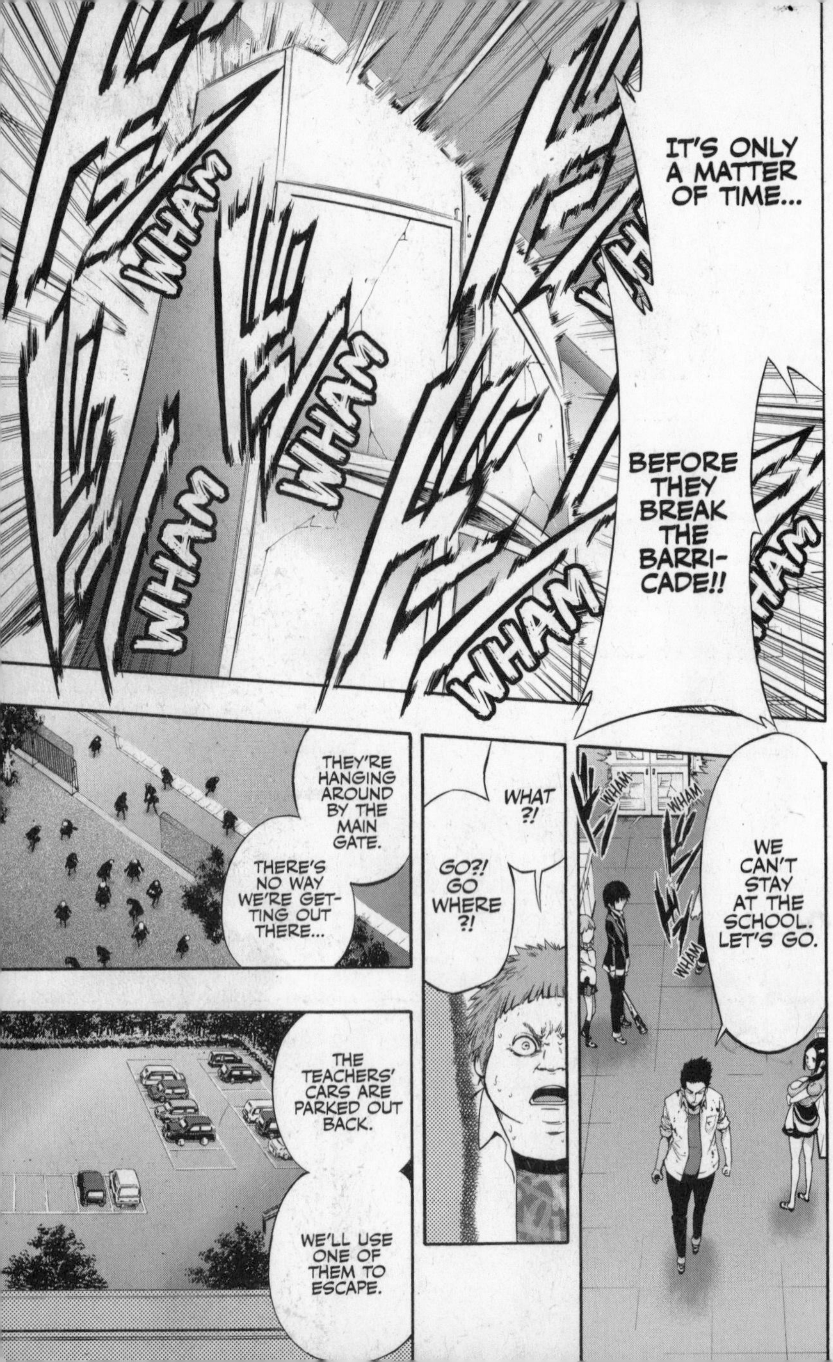
IT'S ONLY A MATTER OF TIME...
BEFORE THEY BREAK THE BARRICADE!!
WHAM
WHAM
WHAM
WHAM
WHAM
WHAM
WHAM
WE CAN'T STAY AT THE SCHOOL. LET'S GO.
WHAM
WHAM
WHAM
WHAT?!
GO?! GO WHERE?!
THEY'RE HANGING AROUND BY THE MAIN GATE.
THERE'S NO WAY WE'RE GETTING OUT THERE...
THE TEACHERS' CARS ARE PARKED OUT BACK.
WE'LL USE ONE OF THEM TO ESCAPE.

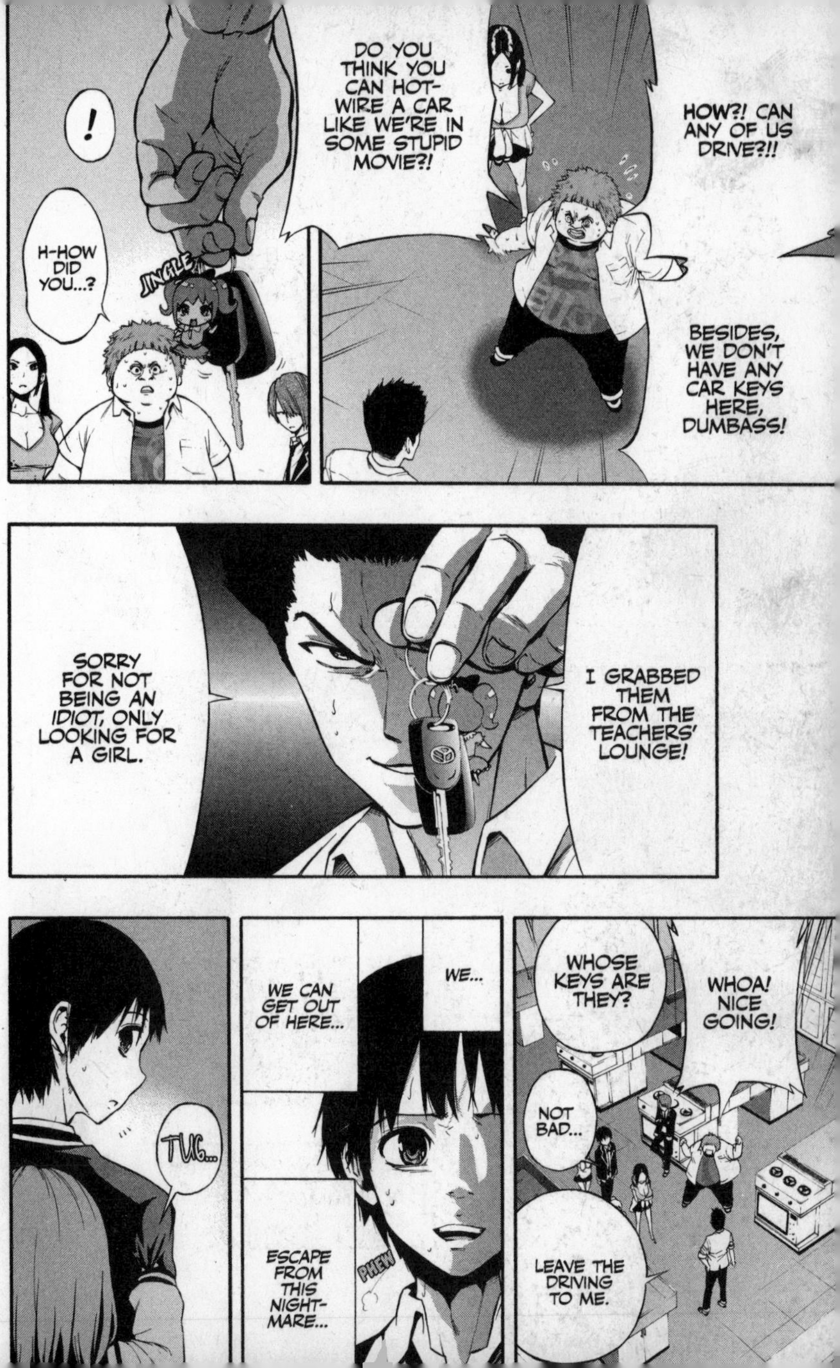
DO YOU THINK YOU CAN HOT-WIRE A CAR LIKE WE'RE IN SOME STUPID MOVIE?!
HOW?! CAN ANY OF US DRIVE?!!
BESIDES, WE DON'T HAVE ANY CAR KEYS HERE, DUMBASS!
!
JINGLE
H-HOW DID YOU...?
I GRABBED THEM FROM THE TEACHERS' LOUNGE!
SORRY FOR NOT BEING AN IDIOT, ONLY LOOKING FOR A GIRL.
WHOA! NICE GOING!
WHOSE KEYS ARE THEY?
NOT BAD...
LEAVE THE DRIVING TO ME.
WE...
WE CAN GET OUT OF HERE...
ESCAPE FROM THIS NIGHT-MARE...
PHEW
TUG...

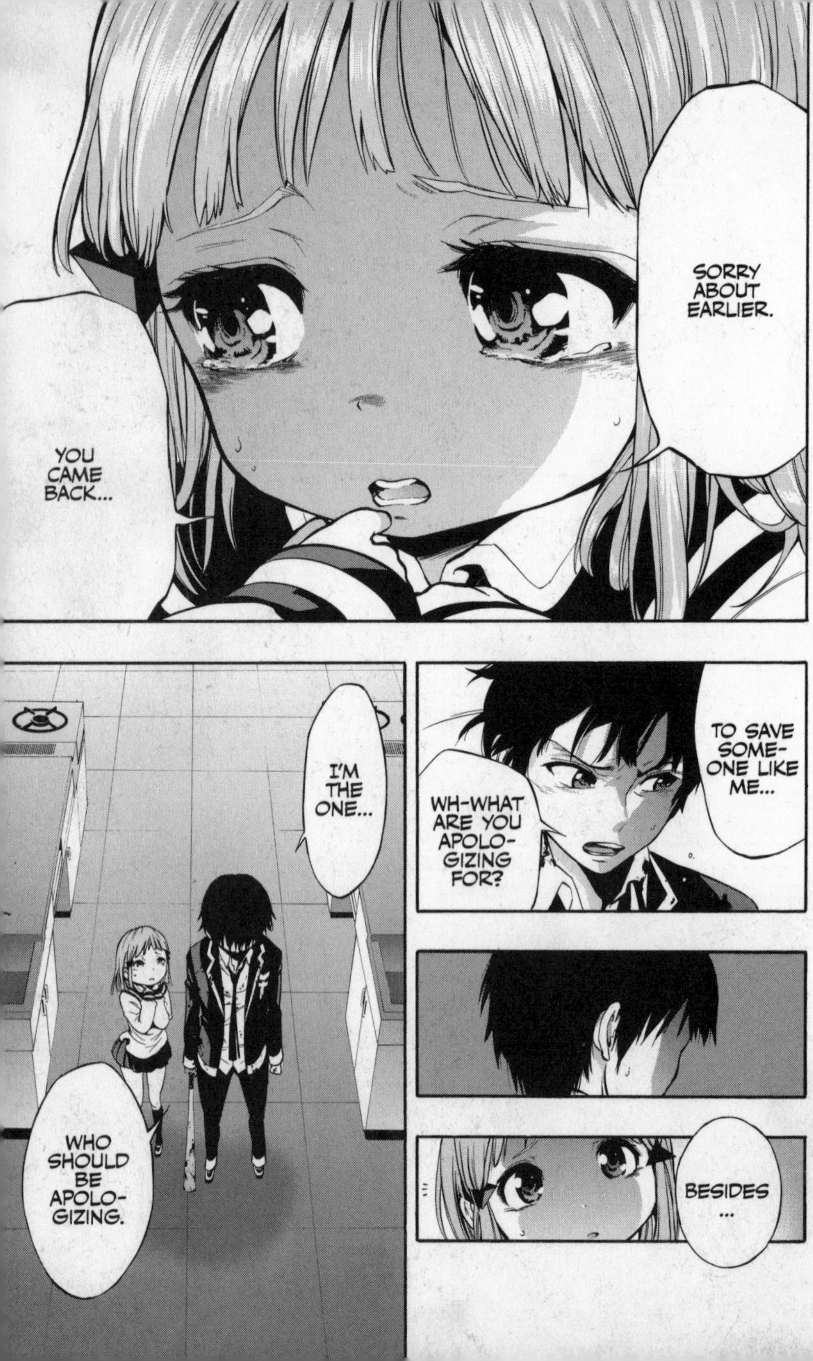
SORRY ABOUT EARLIER.
YOU CAME BACK...
TO SAVE SOME-ONE LIKE ME...
WH-WHAT ARE YOU APOLO-GIZING FOR?
BESIDES ...
I'M THE ONE...
WHO SHOULD BE APOLO-GIZING.

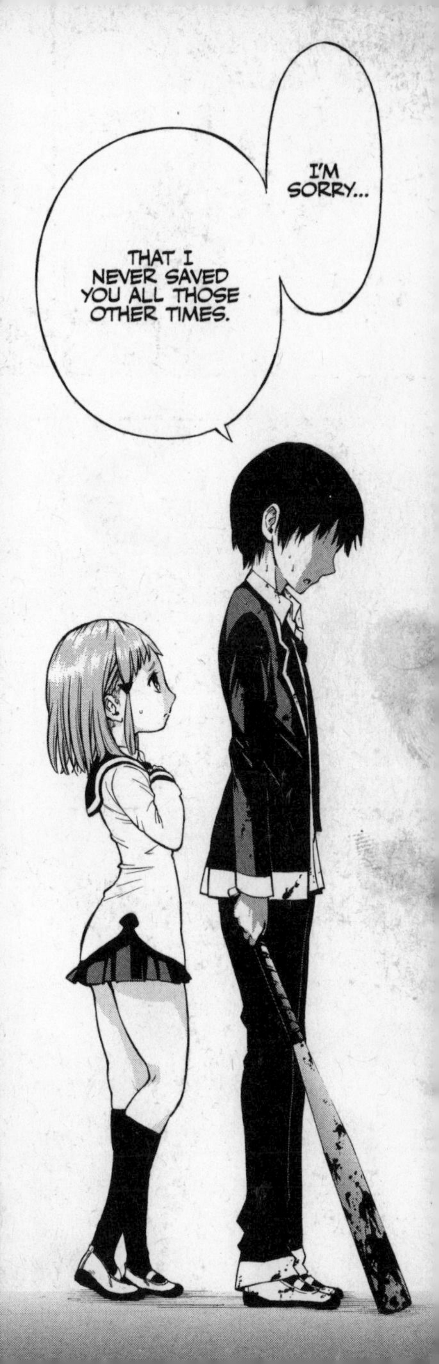
I'M SORRY...
THAT I NEVER SAVED YOU ALL THOSE OTHER TIMES.
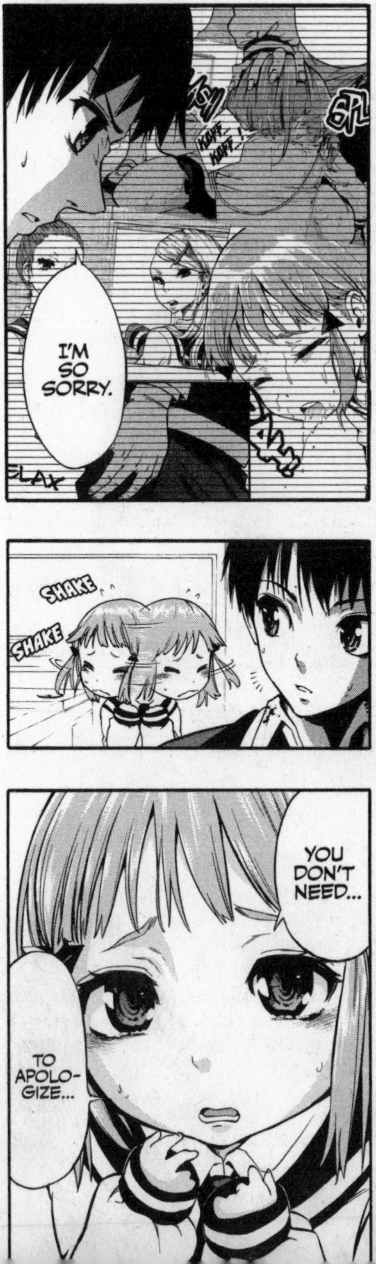
I'M SO SORRY.
SHAKE
SHAKE
YOU DON'T NEED...
TO APOLOGIZE...

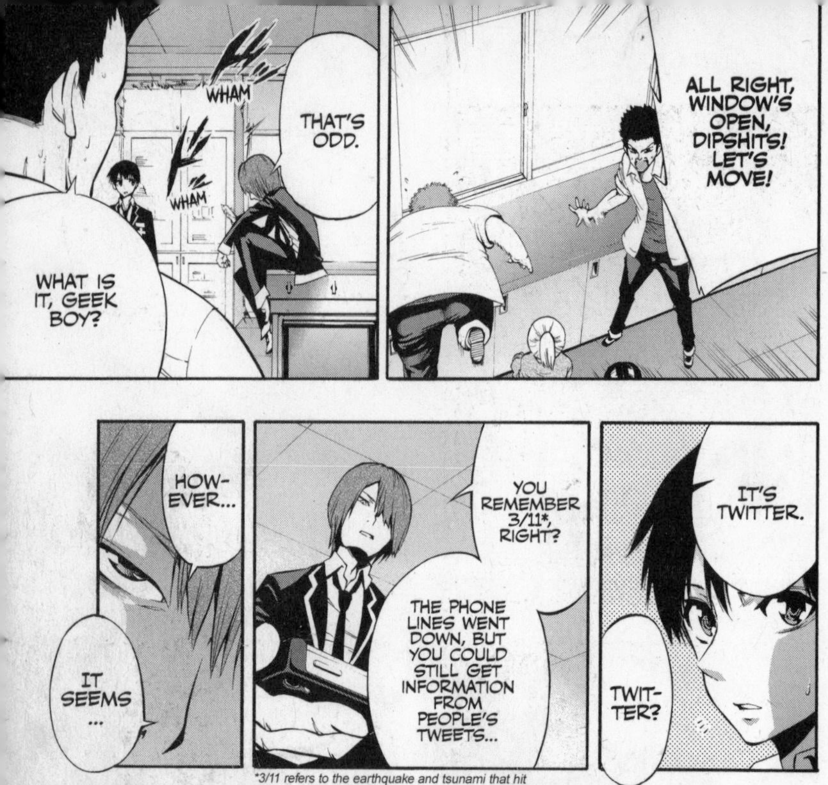
ALL RIGHT, WINDOW'S OPEN, DIPSHITS! LET'S MOVE!
THAT'S ODD.
WHAM
WHAM
WHAT IS IT, GEEK BOY?
IT'S TWITTER.
TWIT-TER?
YOU REMEMBER 3/11*, RIGHT?
THE PHONE LINES WENT DOWN, BUT YOU COULD STILL GET INFORMATION FROM PEOPLE'S TWEETS...
HOW-EVER...
IT SEEMS ...

*3/11 refers to the earthquake and tsunami that hit Japan on March 11, 2011.

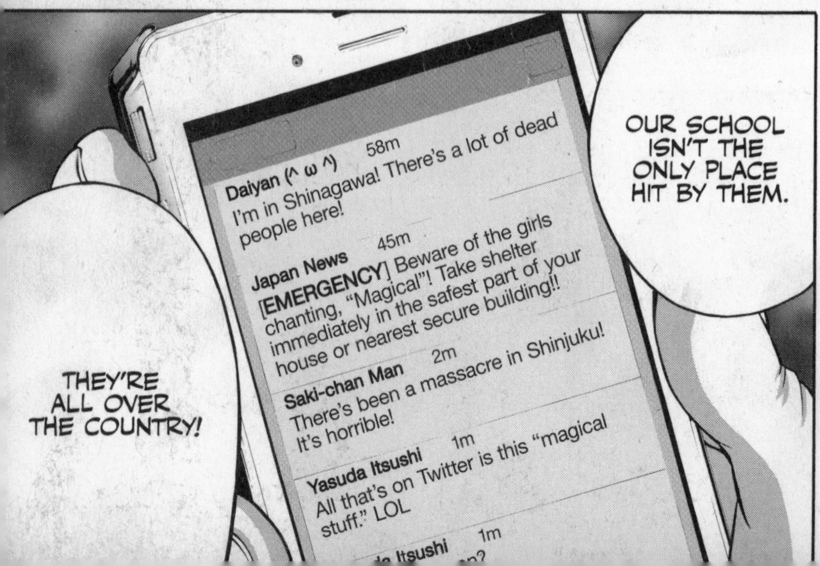
OUR SCHOOL ISN'T THE ONLY PLACE HIT BY THEM.
Daiyan (^ ω ^) 58m
I'm in Shinagawa! There's a lot of dead people here!
Japan News 45m
[EMERGENCY] Beware of the girls chanting, "Magical"! Take shelter immediately in the safest part of your house or nearest secure building!!
Saki-chan Man 2m
There's been a massacre in Shinjuku! It's horrible!
Yasuda Itsushi 1m
All that's on Twitter is this "magical stuff." LOL
1m
THEY'RE ALL OVER THE COUNTRY!

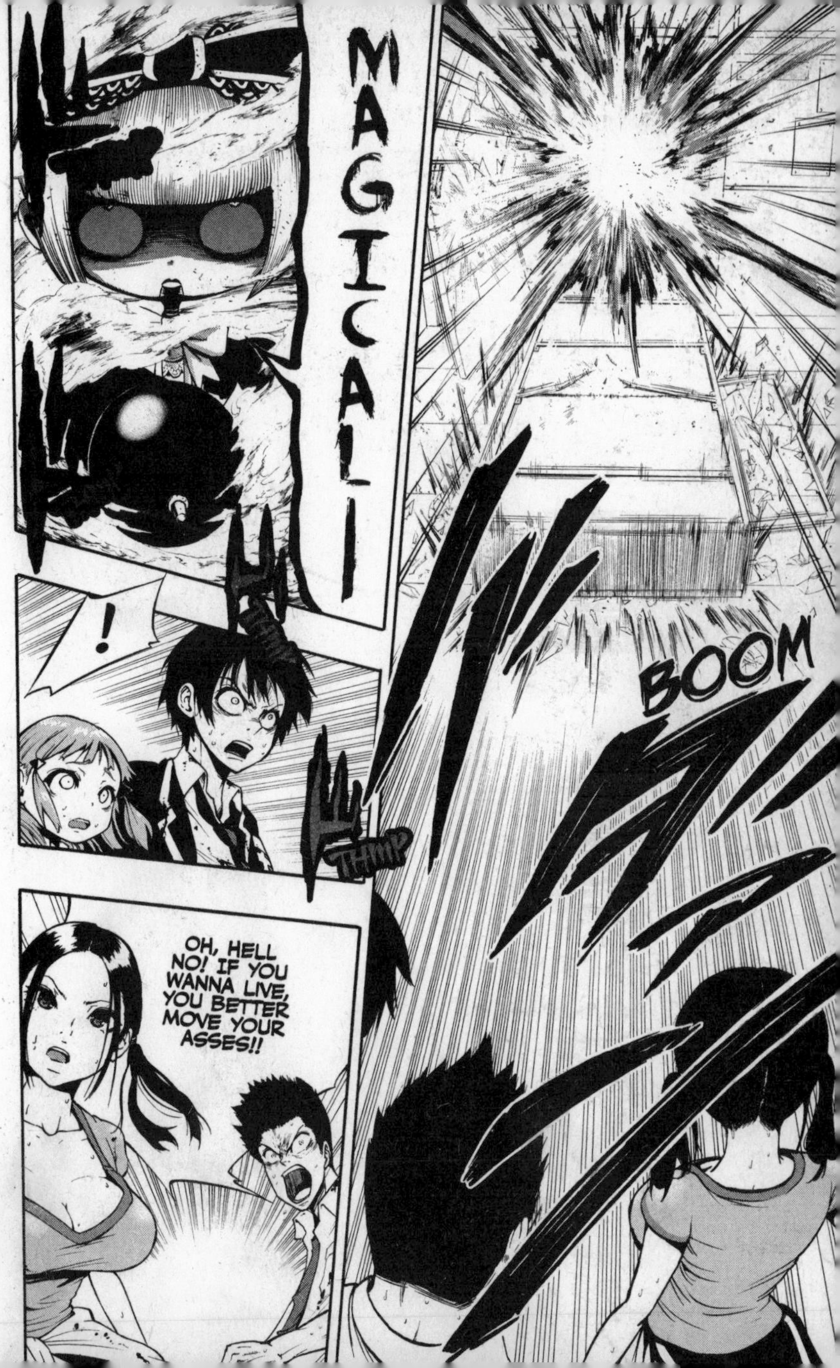
BOOM
MAGICAL!
!
THMP
OH, HELL NO! IF YOU WANNA LIVE, YOU BETTER MOVE YOUR ASSES!!

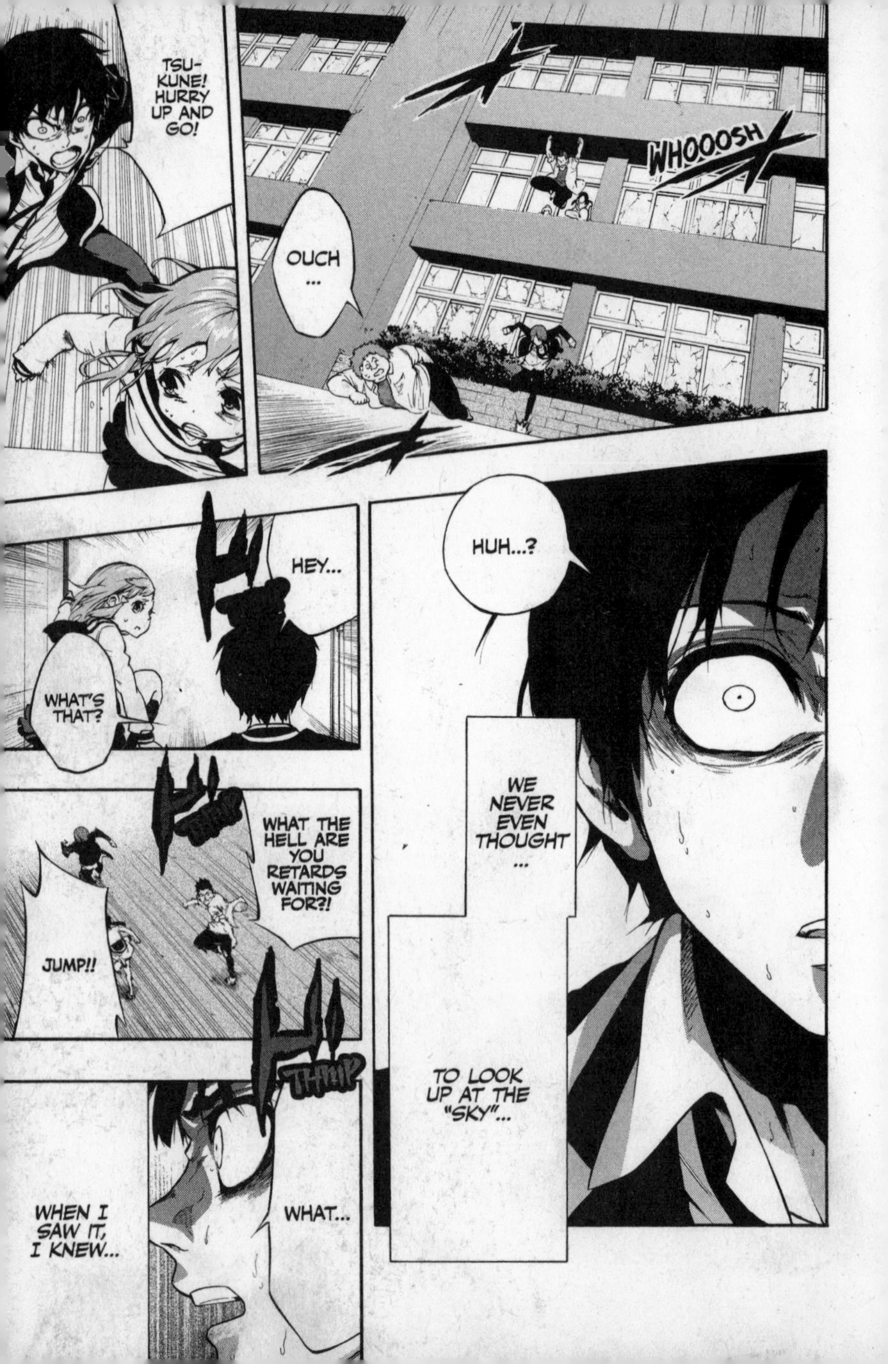
WHOOOSH
OUCH ...
TSU-KUNE! HURRY UP AND GO!
HUH...?
WE NEVER EVEN THOUGHT ...
TO LOOK UP AT THE "SKY"...
HEY...
WHAT'S THAT?
WHAT THE HELL ARE YOU RETARDS WAITING FOR?!
JUMP!!
WHAT...
WHEN I SAW IT, I KNEW...

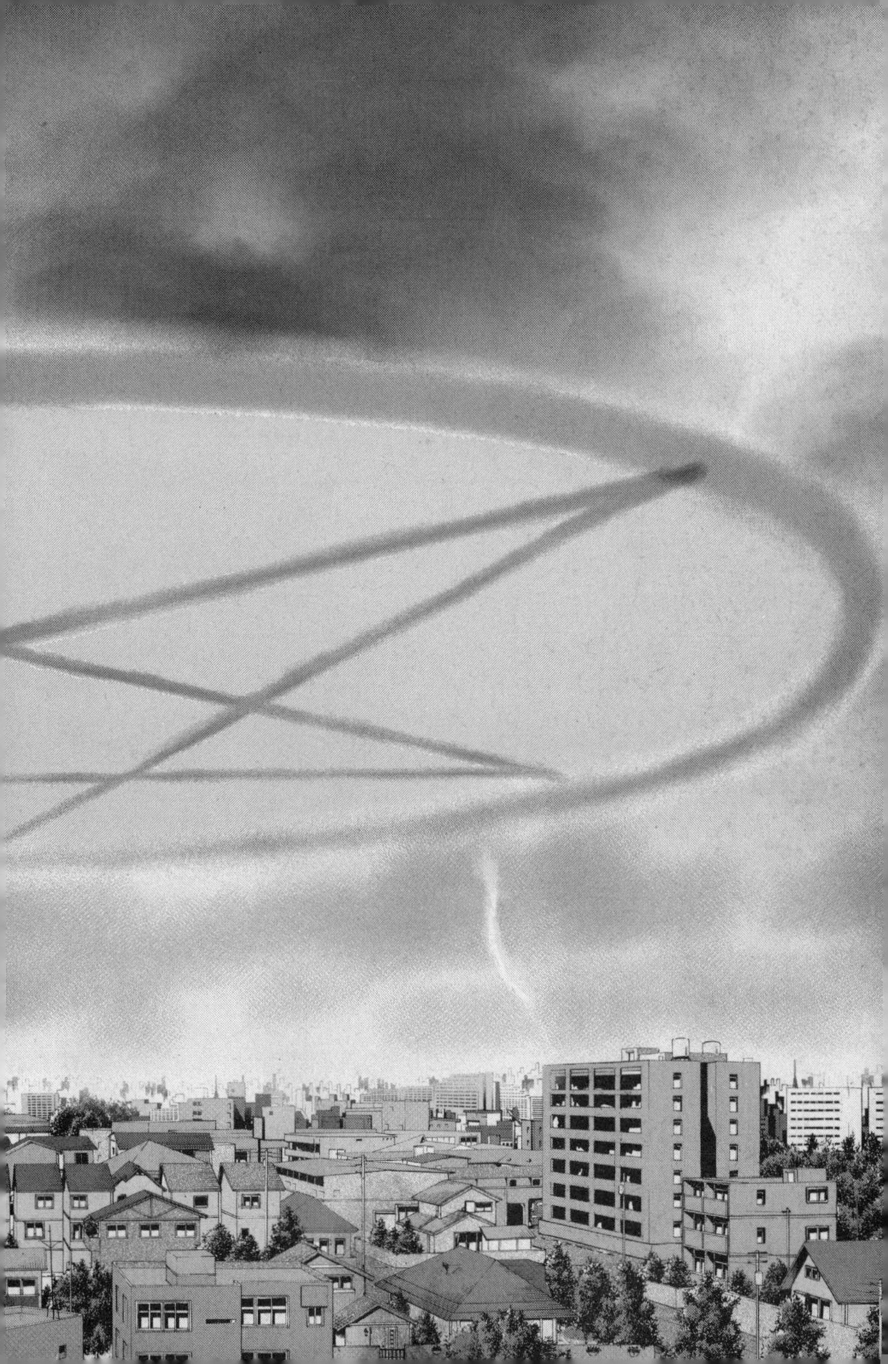

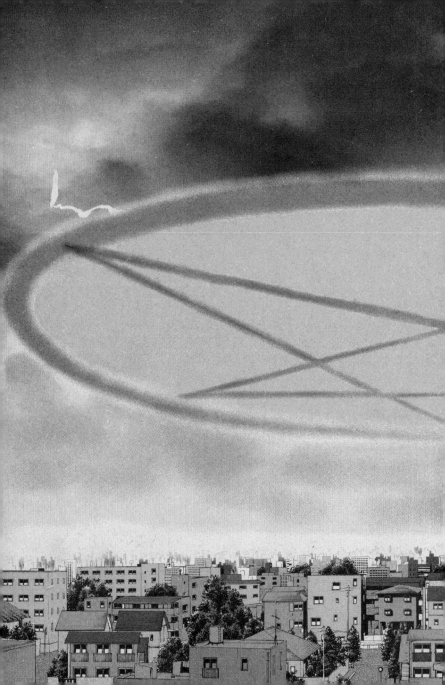

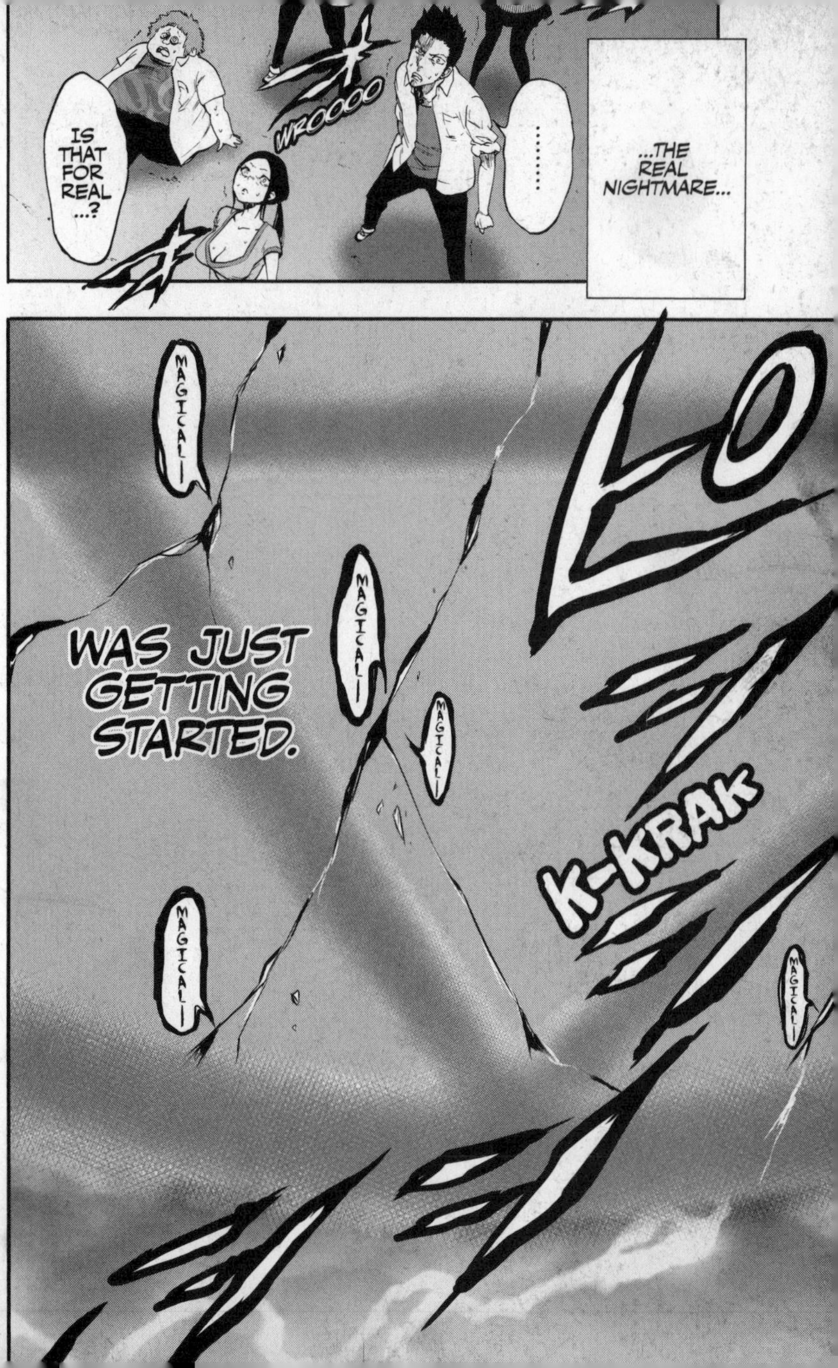
...THE REAL NIGHTMARE...
......
WROOOO
IS THAT FOR REAL ...?
K-KRAK
MAGICAL!
MAGICAL!
MAGICAL!
MAGICAL!
MAGICAL!
WAS JUST GETTING STARTED.

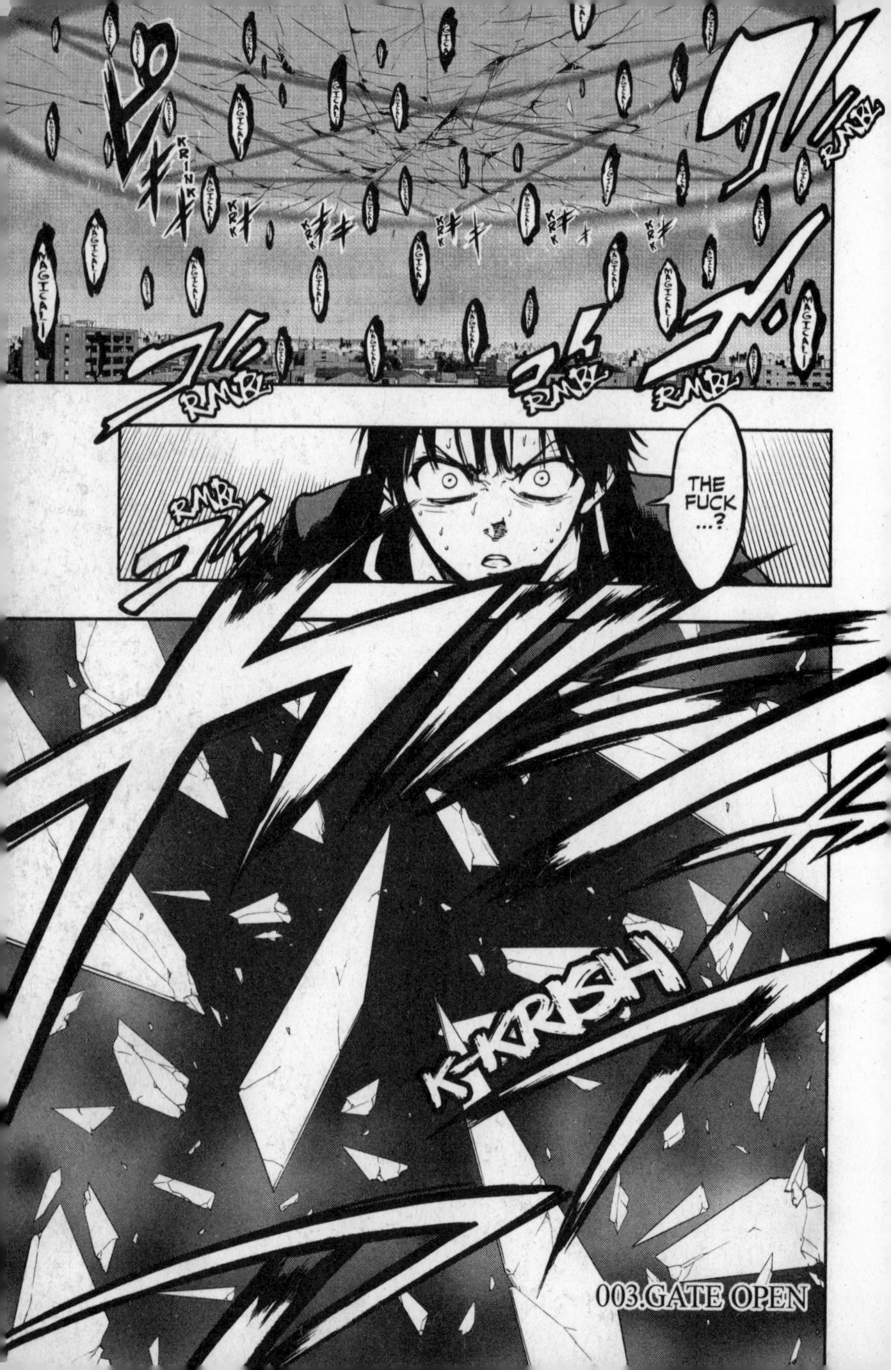
RMBL
MAGICAL!
KRINK
KRK
RMBL
RMBL
RMBL
THE FUCK ...?
RMBL
K-KRISH
003.GATE OPEN

003.GATE OPEN

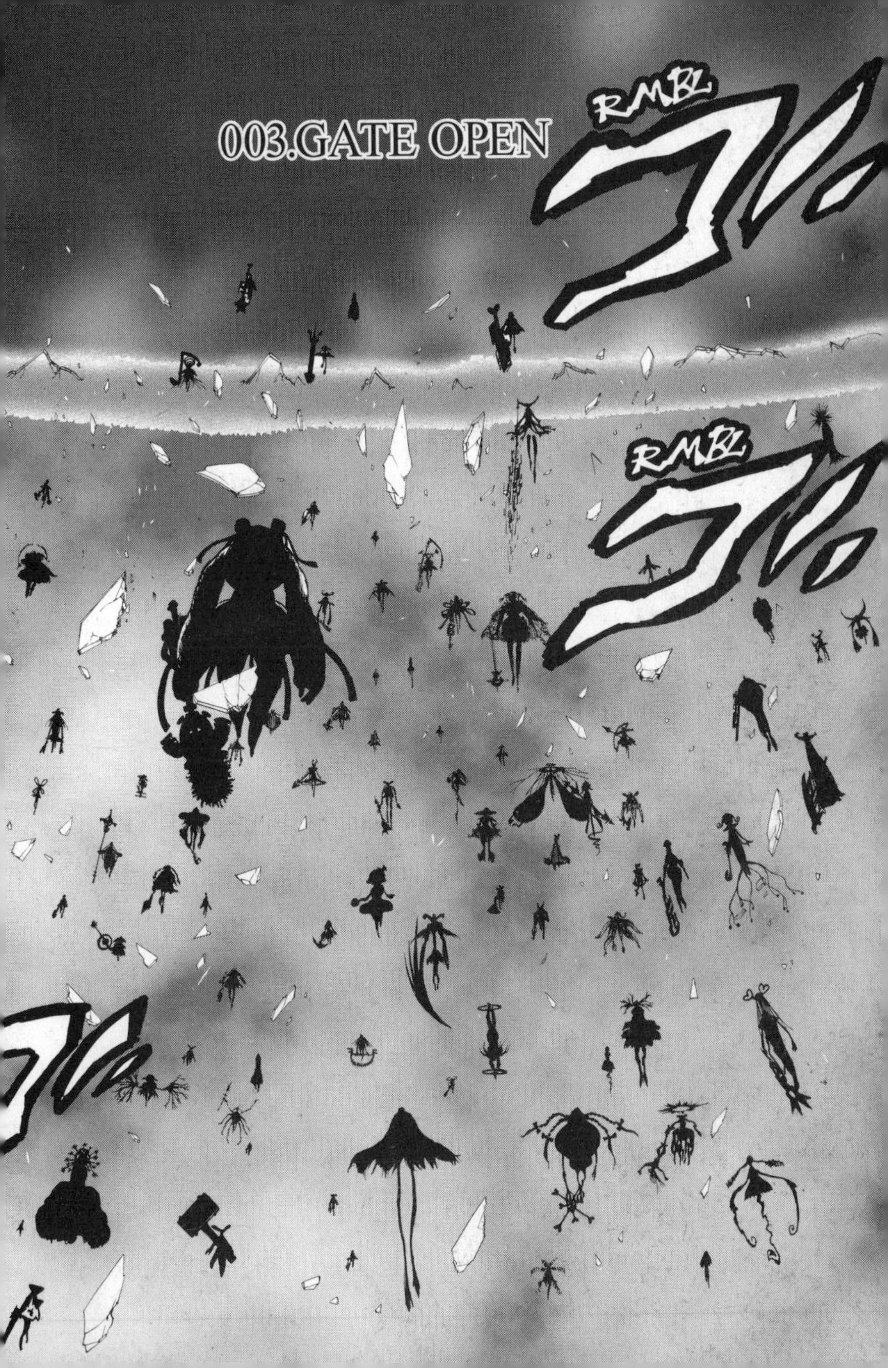
RMBL
RMBL

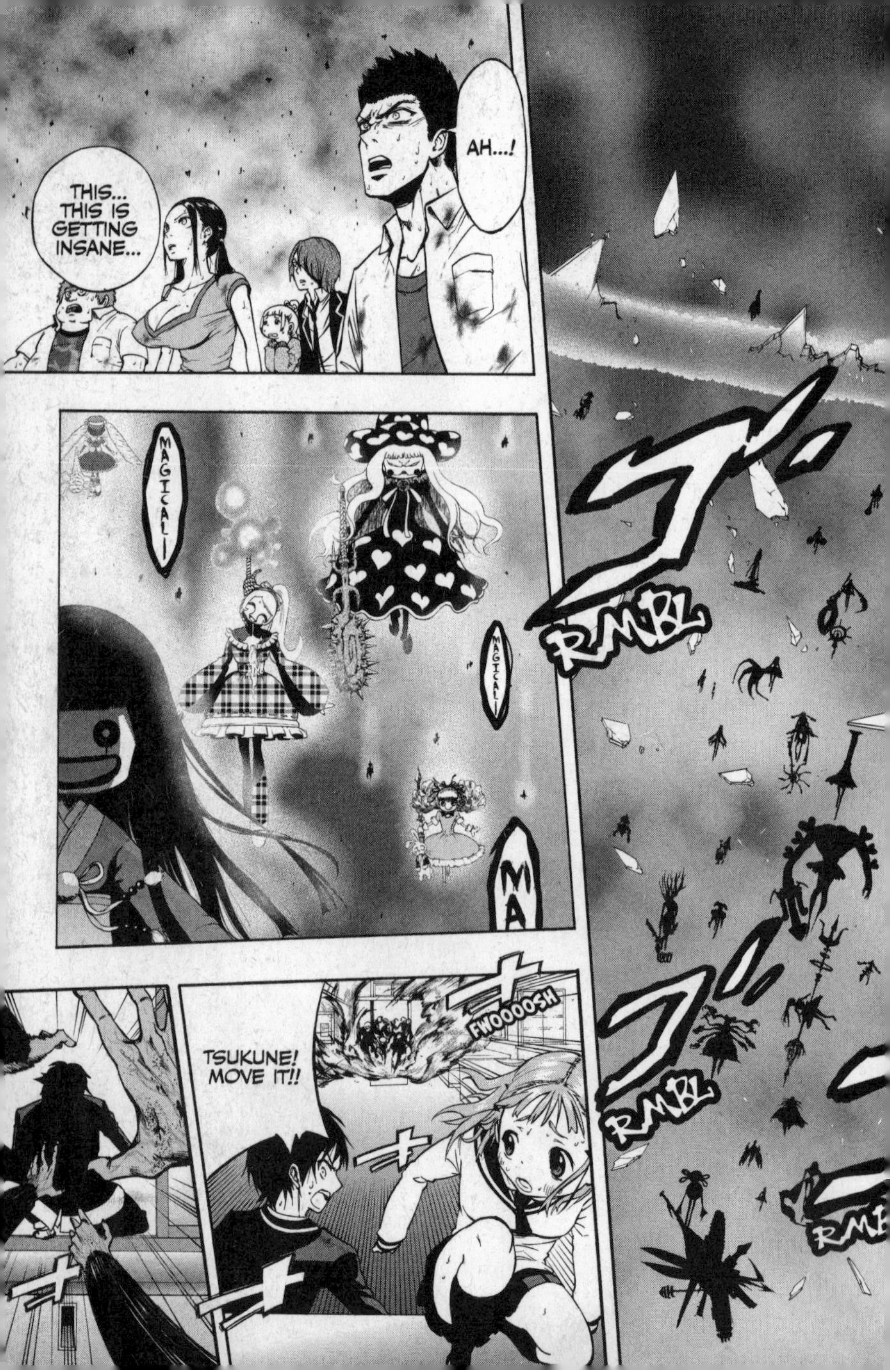
RMBL
RMBL
RMB
AH...!
THIS... THIS IS GETTING INSANE...
MAGICAL!
MAGICAL!
MA
FWOOOOSH
TSUKUNE! MOVE IT!!

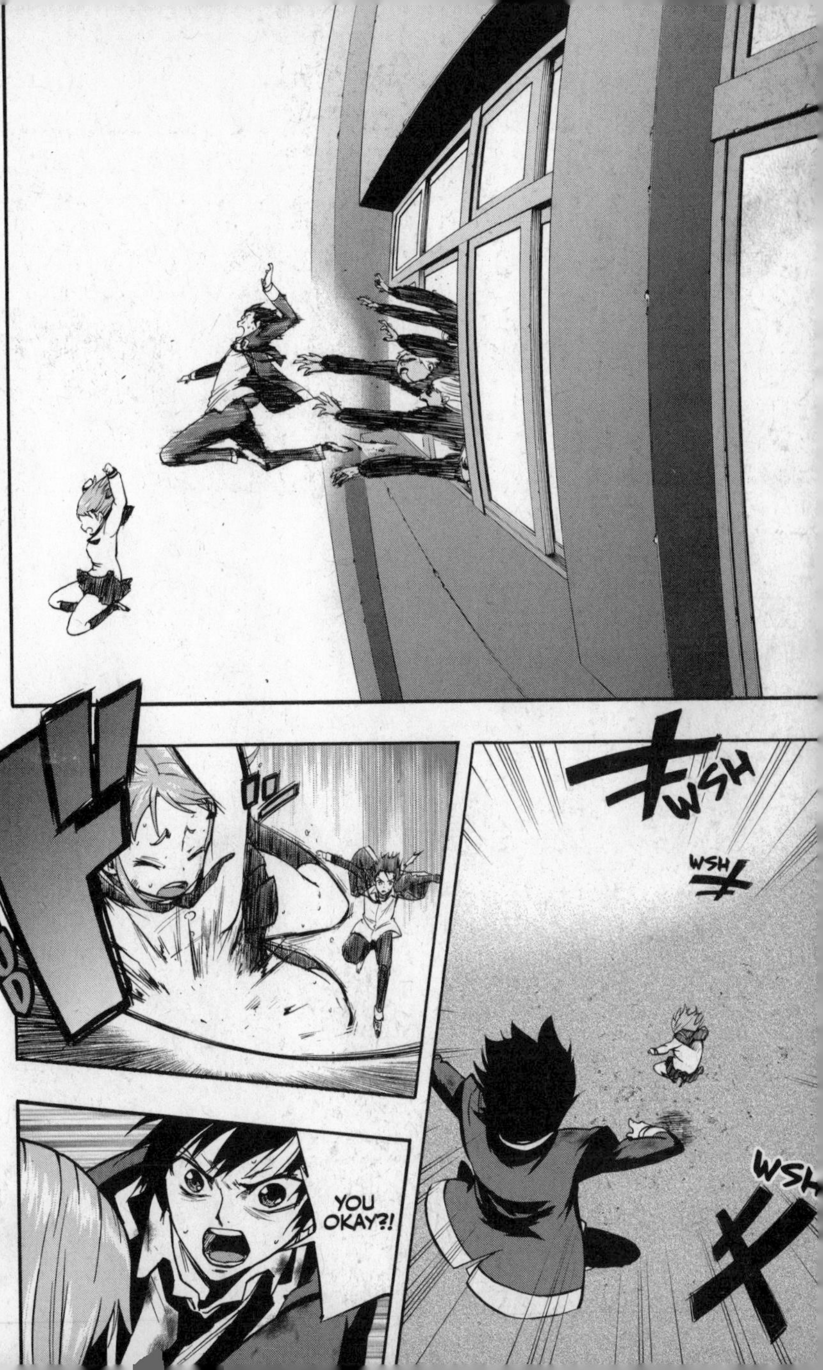
WSH
WSH
WSH
THUD
YOU OKAY?!

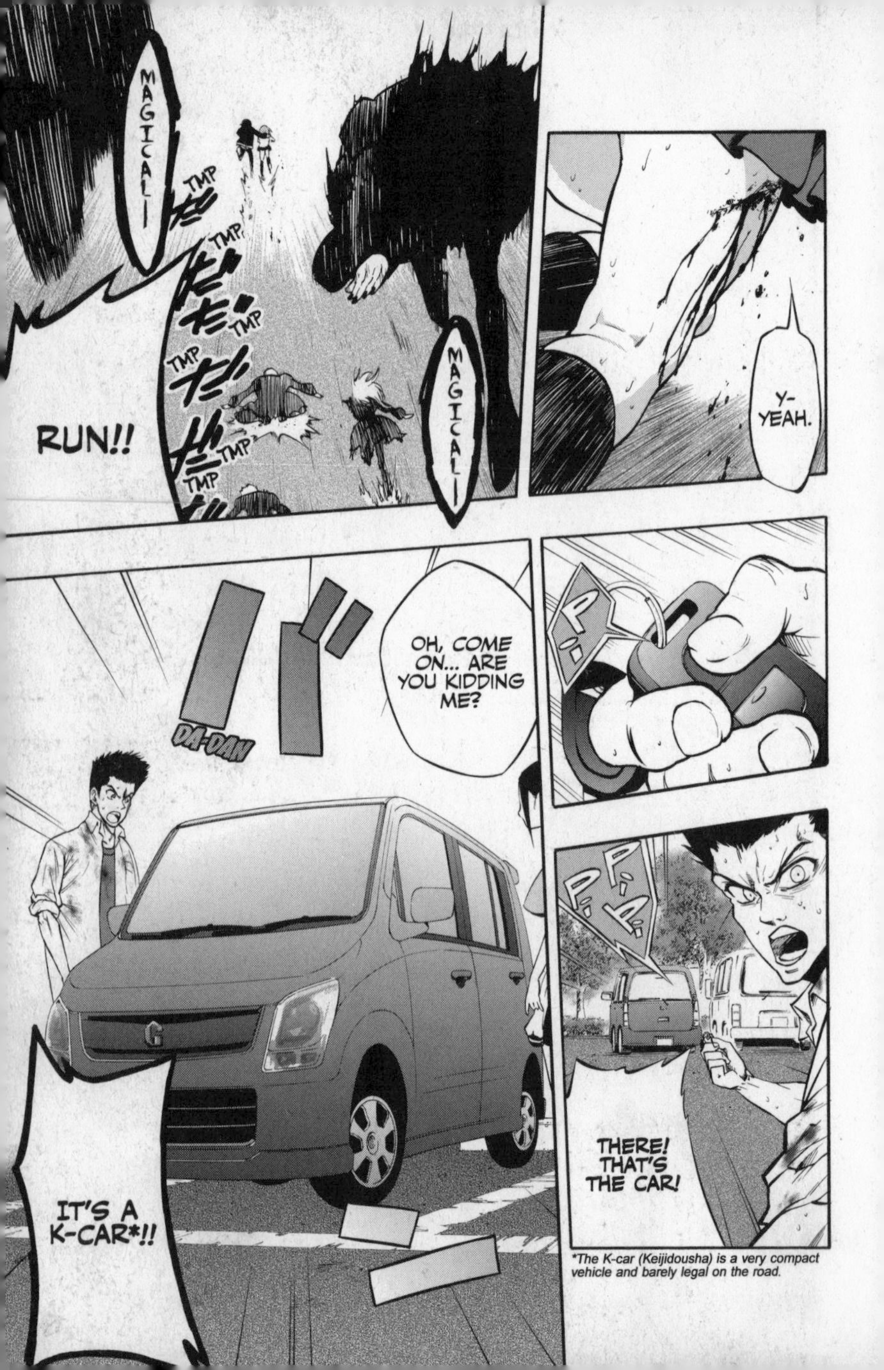
Y-YEAH.
MAGICAL I
MAGICAL I
TMP TMP TMP TMP TMP TMP
RUN!!
THERE! THAT'S THE CAR!
OH, COME ON... ARE YOU KIDDING ME?
DA-DAN
IT'S A K-CAR*!!
*The K-car (Keijidousha) is a very compact vehicle and barely legal on the road.

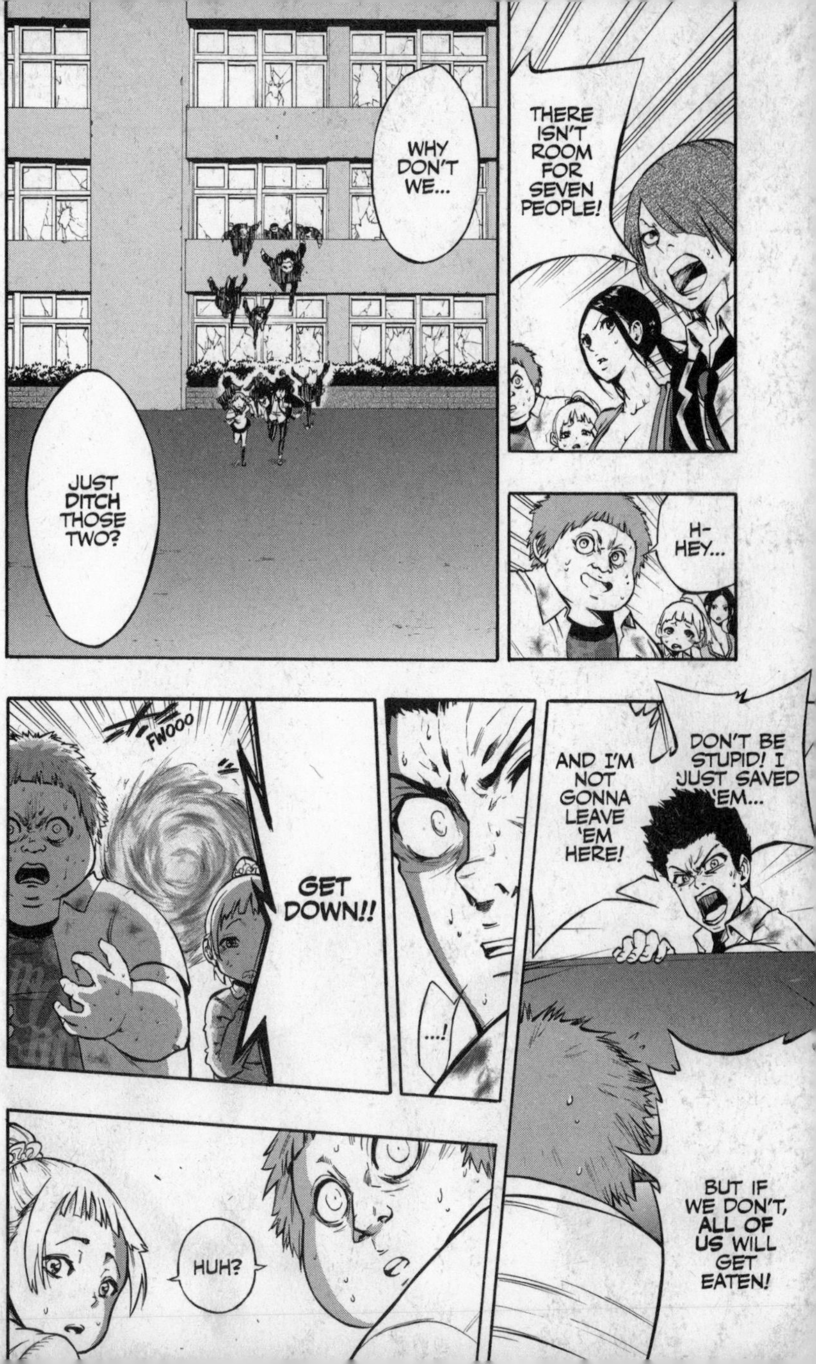
THERE ISN'T ROOM FOR SEVEN PEOPLE!
H-HEY...
WHY DON'T WE...
JUST DITCH THOSE TWO?
DON'T BE STUPID! I JUST SAVED 'EM...
AND I'M NOT GONNA LEAVE 'EM HERE!
...!
GET DOWN!!
FWOOO
BUT IF WE DON'T, ALL OF US WILL GET EATEN!
HUH?

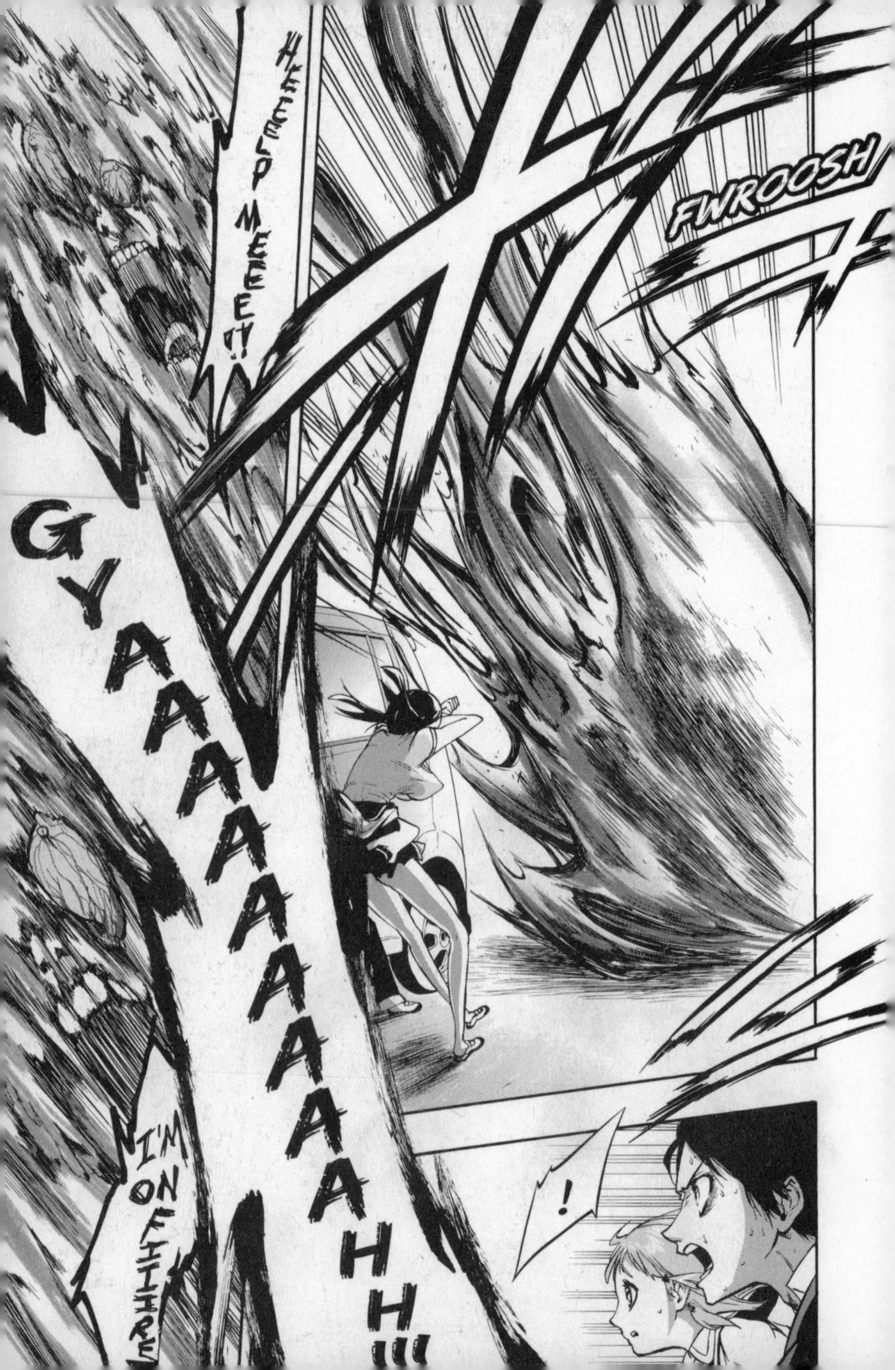
FWROOSH
HEEELP MEEEE!!
GYAAAAAAAAAAAHH!!
I'M ON FIIIRE
!

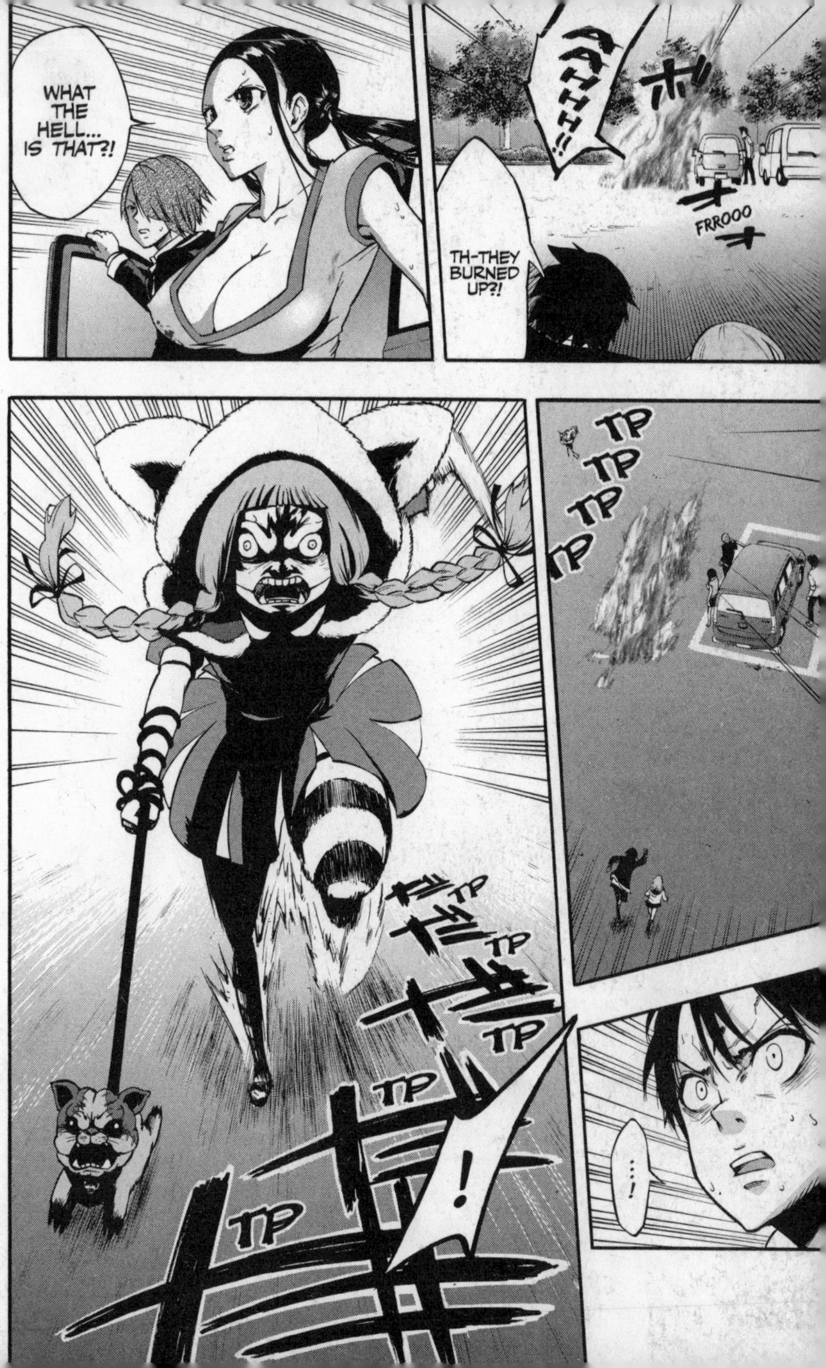
AAHHH!!
FRROOO
TH-THEY BURNED UP?!
WHAT THE HELL... IS THAT?!
TP TP TP TP
...!
TP TP TP TP TP
!

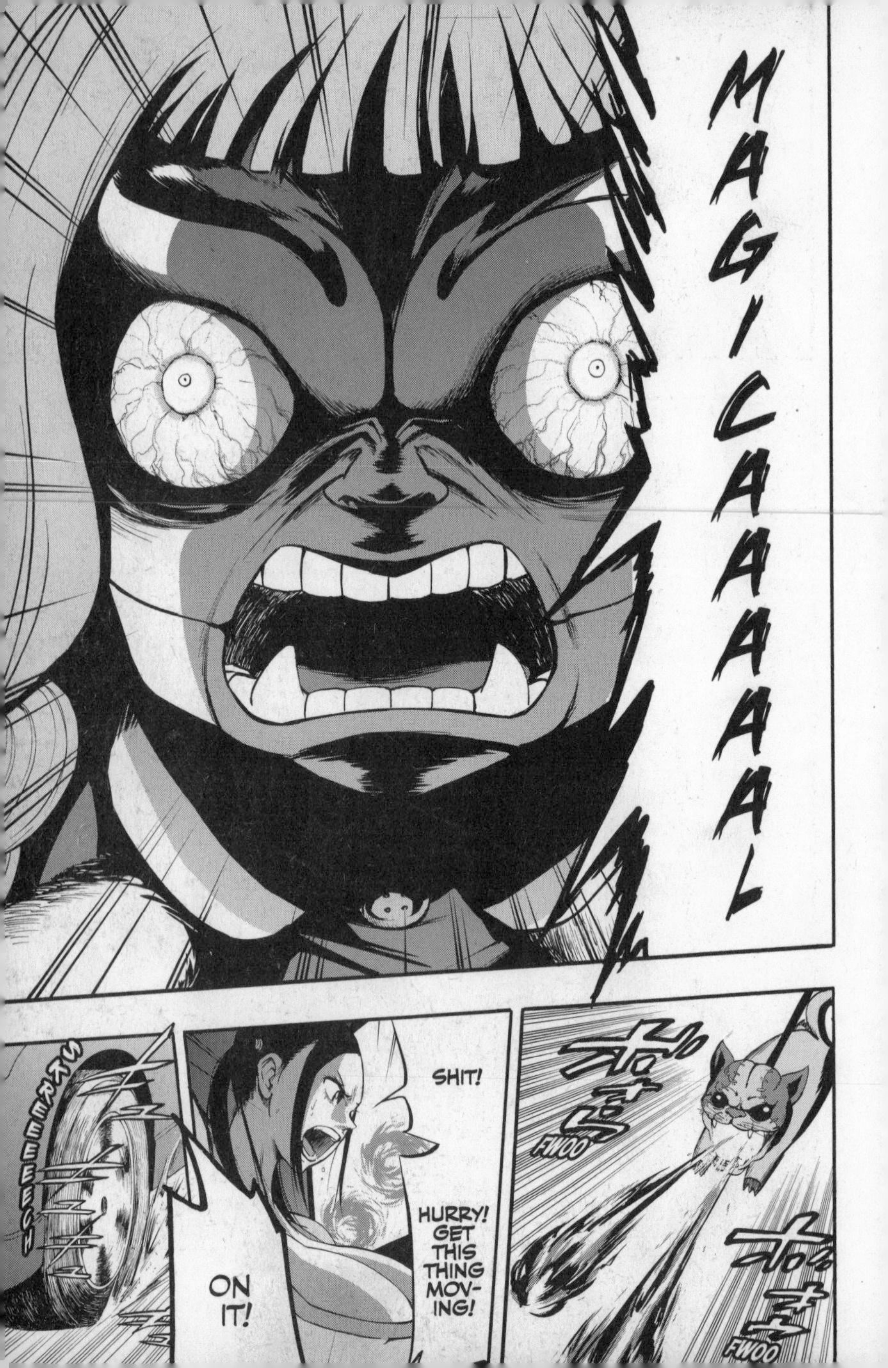
MAGICAAAAAAL
FWOO
FWOO
SHIT!
HURRY! GET THIS THING MOVING!
ON IT!
SKREEEEEECH

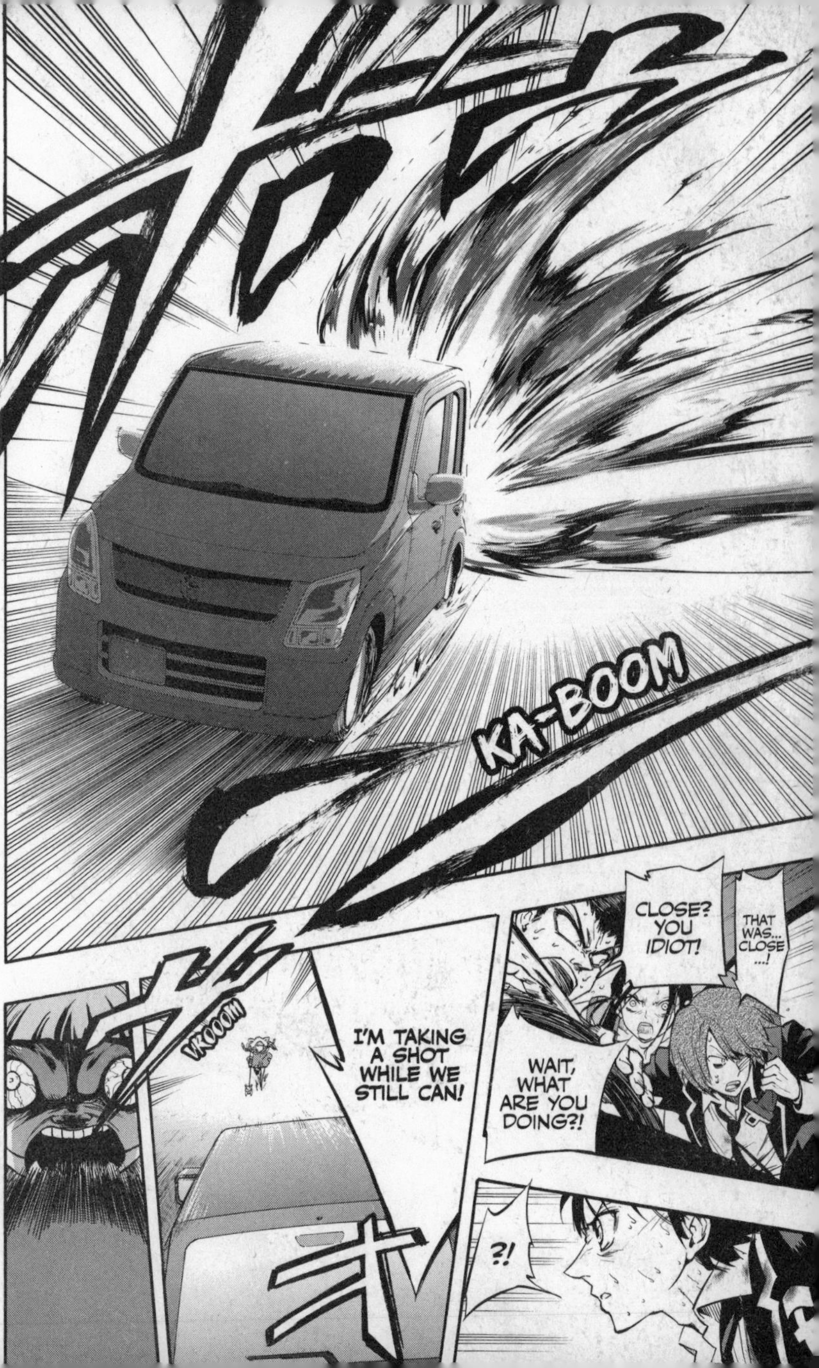
KA-BOOM
THAT WAS... CLOSE ...!
CLOSE? YOU IDIOT!
WAIT, WHAT ARE YOU DOING?!
?!
I'M TAKING A SHOT WHILE WE STILL CAN!
VROOOM

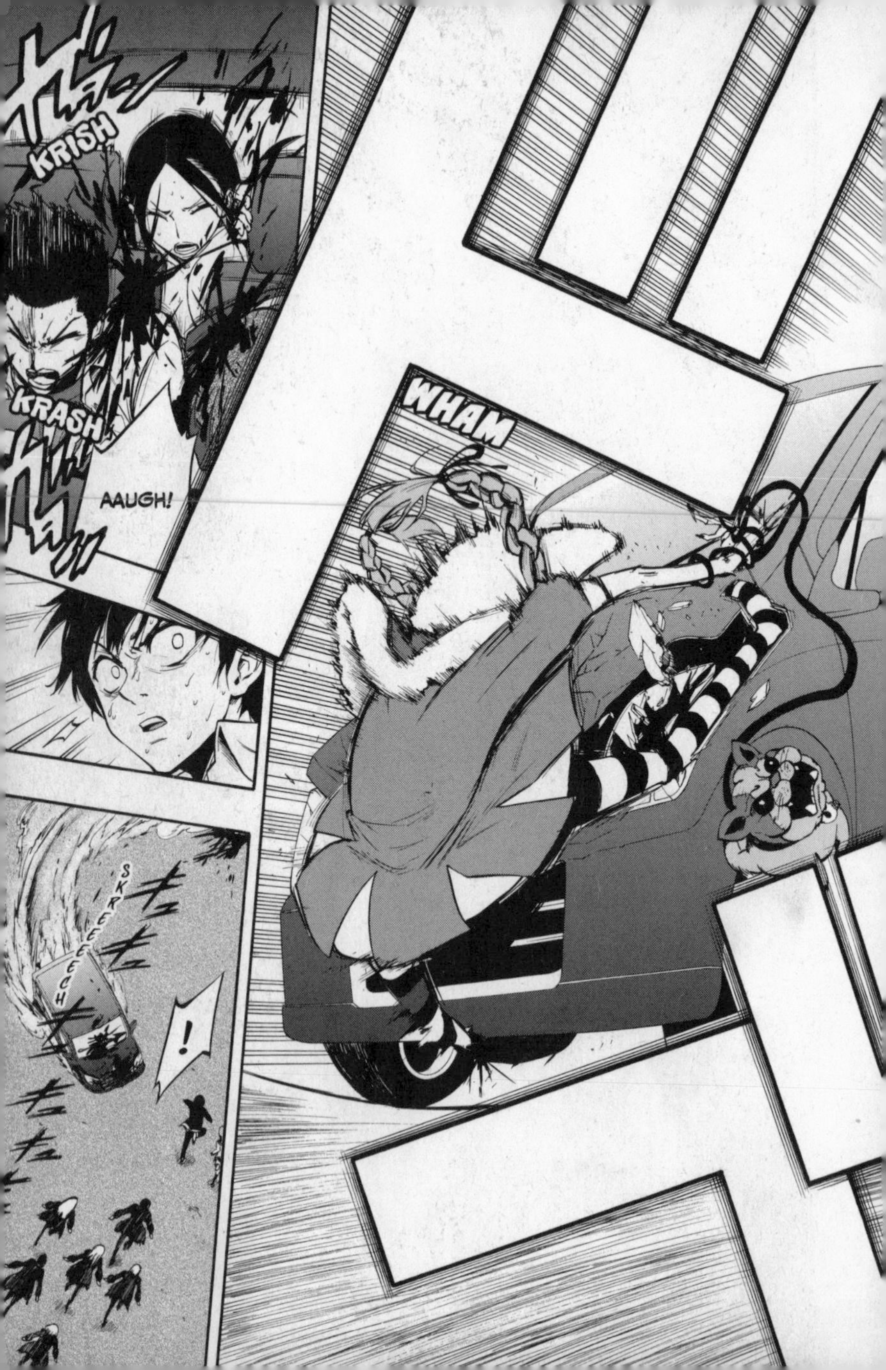
WHAM
KRISH
KRASH
AAUGH!
SKREEEECH
!

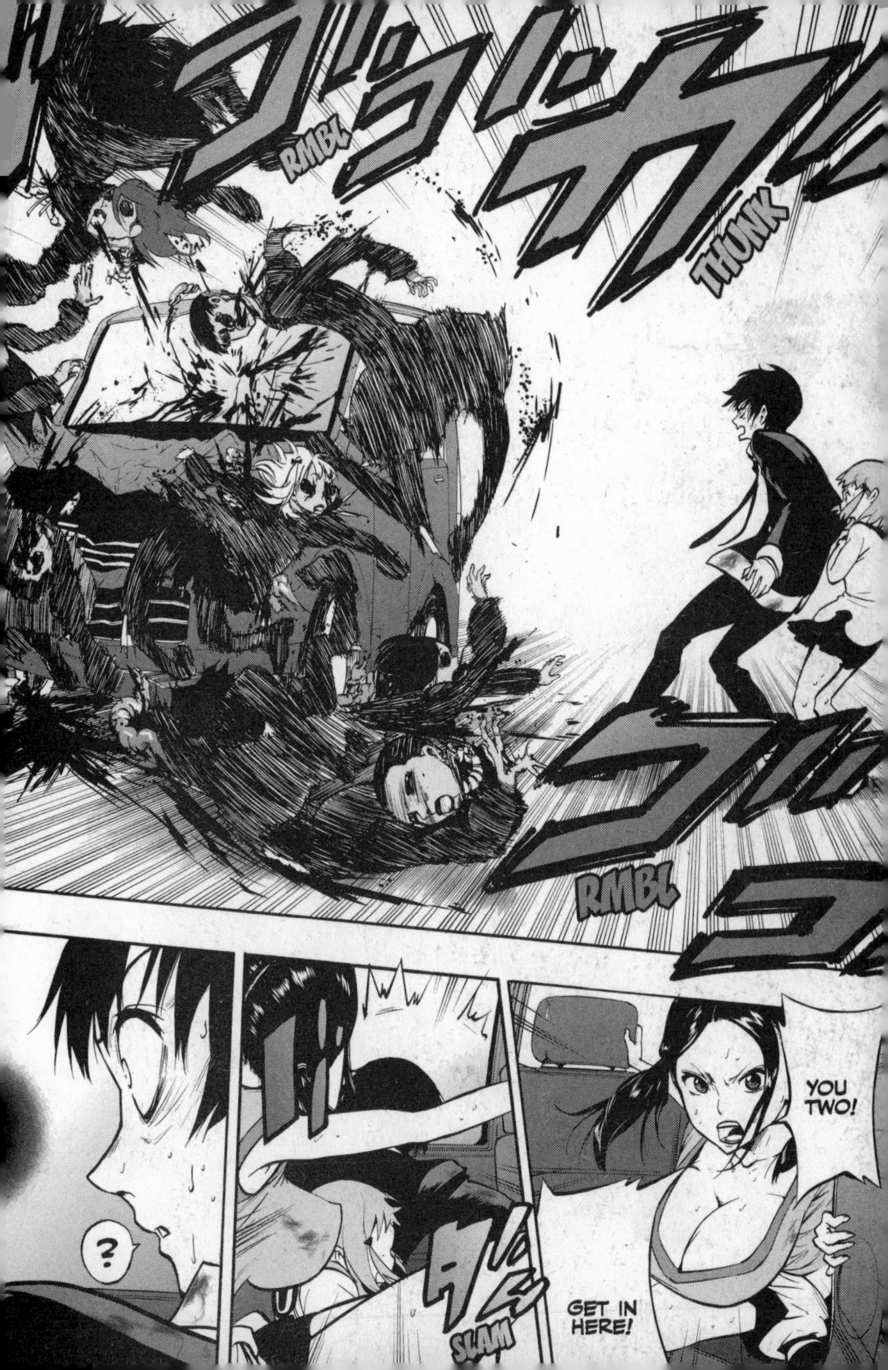
THUNK
RMBL
RMBL
YOU TWO!
GET IN HERE!
SLAM
?

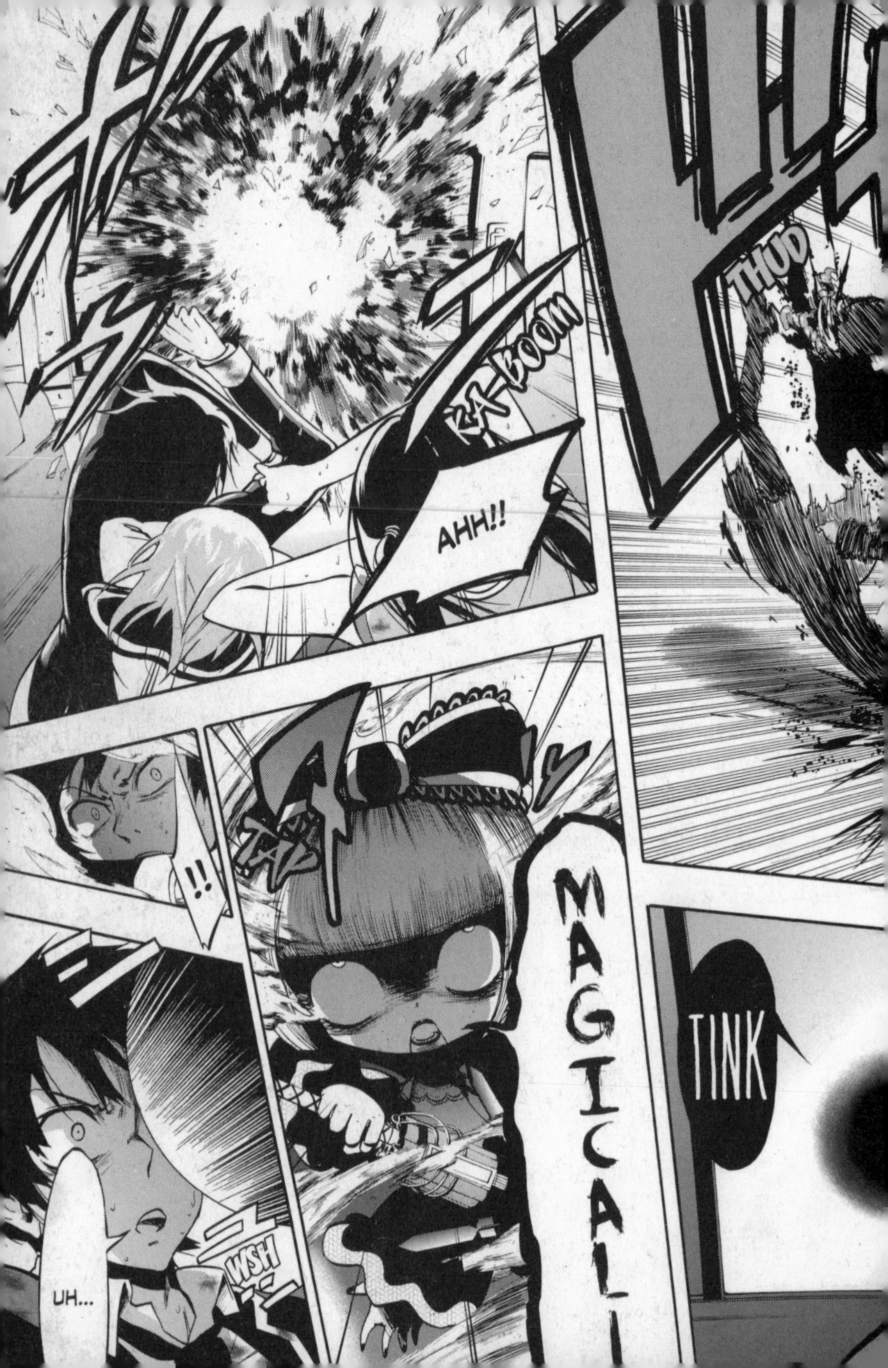
THUD
RA-BOOM
AHH!!
TINK
MAGICAL
!!
WSH
UH...

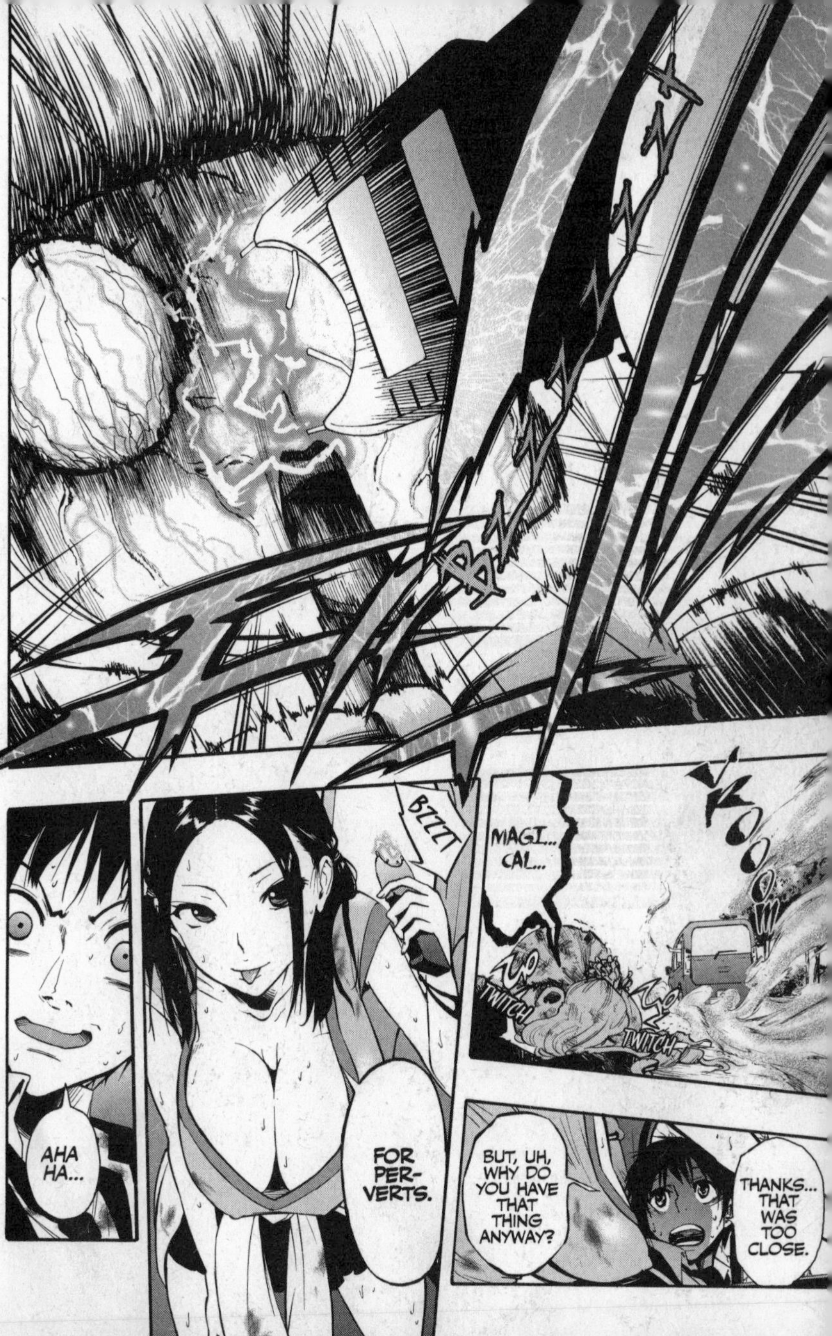
MAGI... CAL...
TWITCH
TWITCH
THANKS... THAT WAS TOO CLOSE.
BUT, UH, WHY DO YOU HAVE THAT THING ANYWAY?
BZZZT
FOR PER-VERTS.
AHA HA...

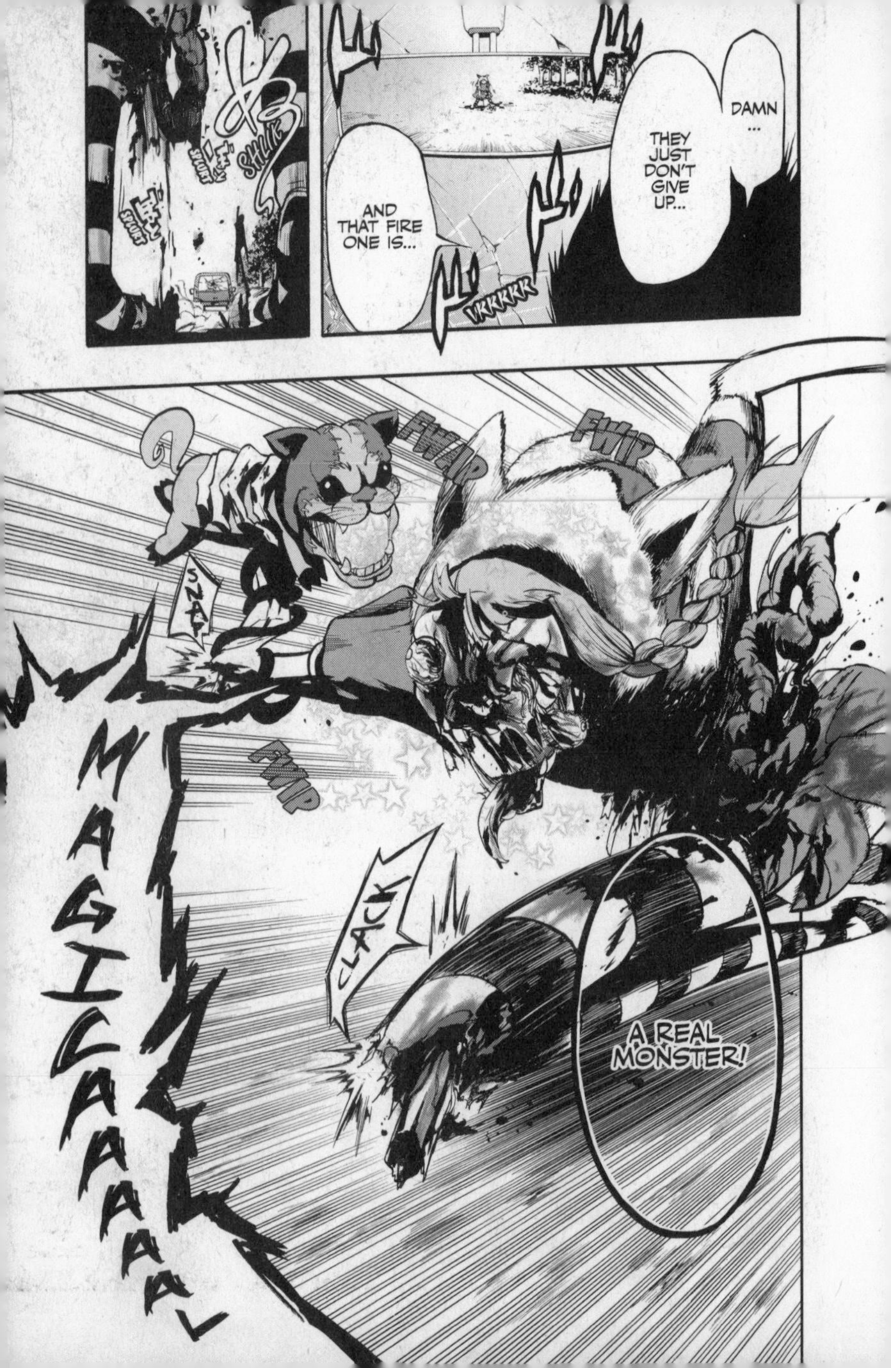
DAMN...
THEY JUST DON'T GIVE UP...
AND THAT FIRE ONE IS...
VRKKKR
SHLUK
SPLURT
SPLURT
FWIP
FWIP
SNAP
FWIP
A REAL MONSTER!
CLACK
MAGICAAAAAAL

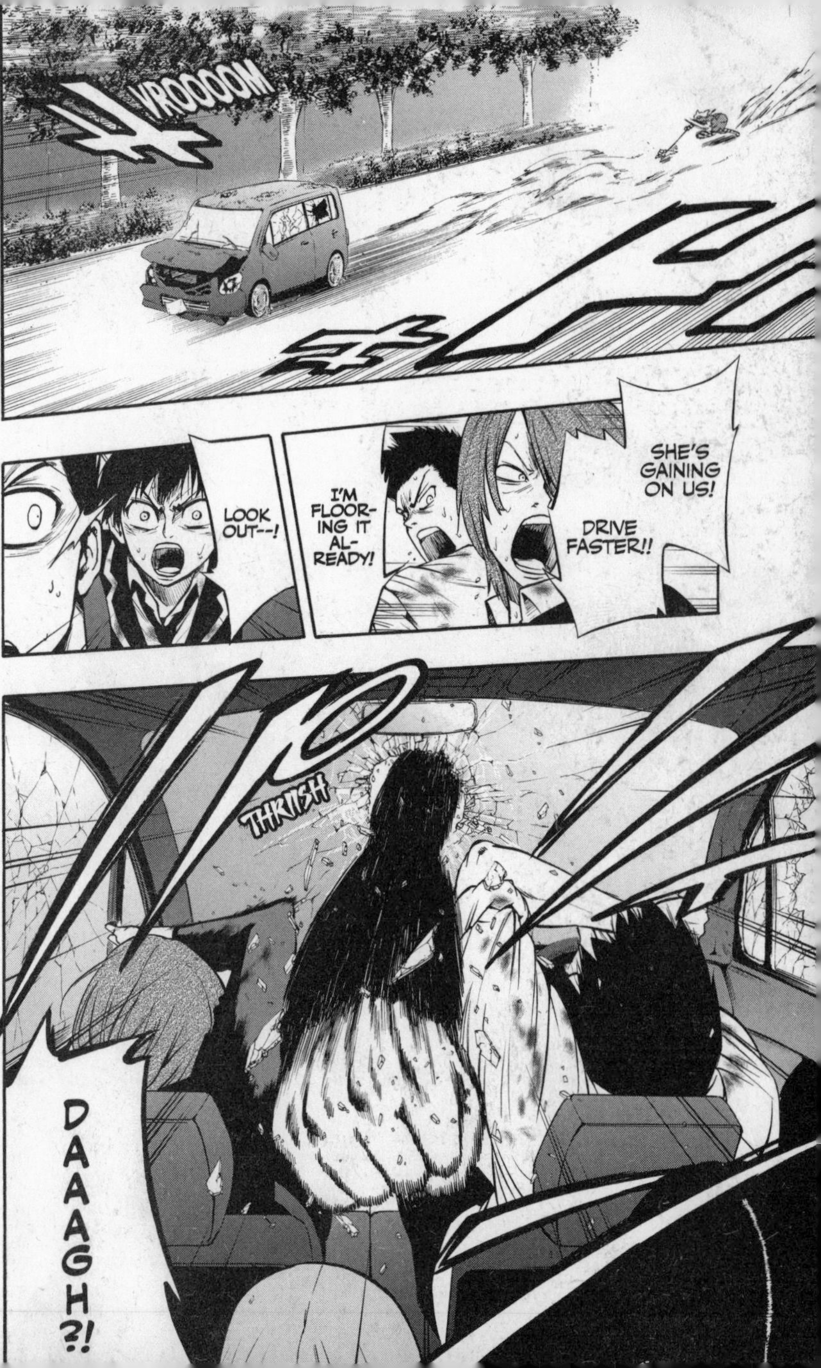
VROOOOM
SHE'S GAINING ON US!
DRIVE FASTER!!
I'M FLOORING IT AL-READY!
LOOK OUT--!
THRISH
DAAAAGH?!

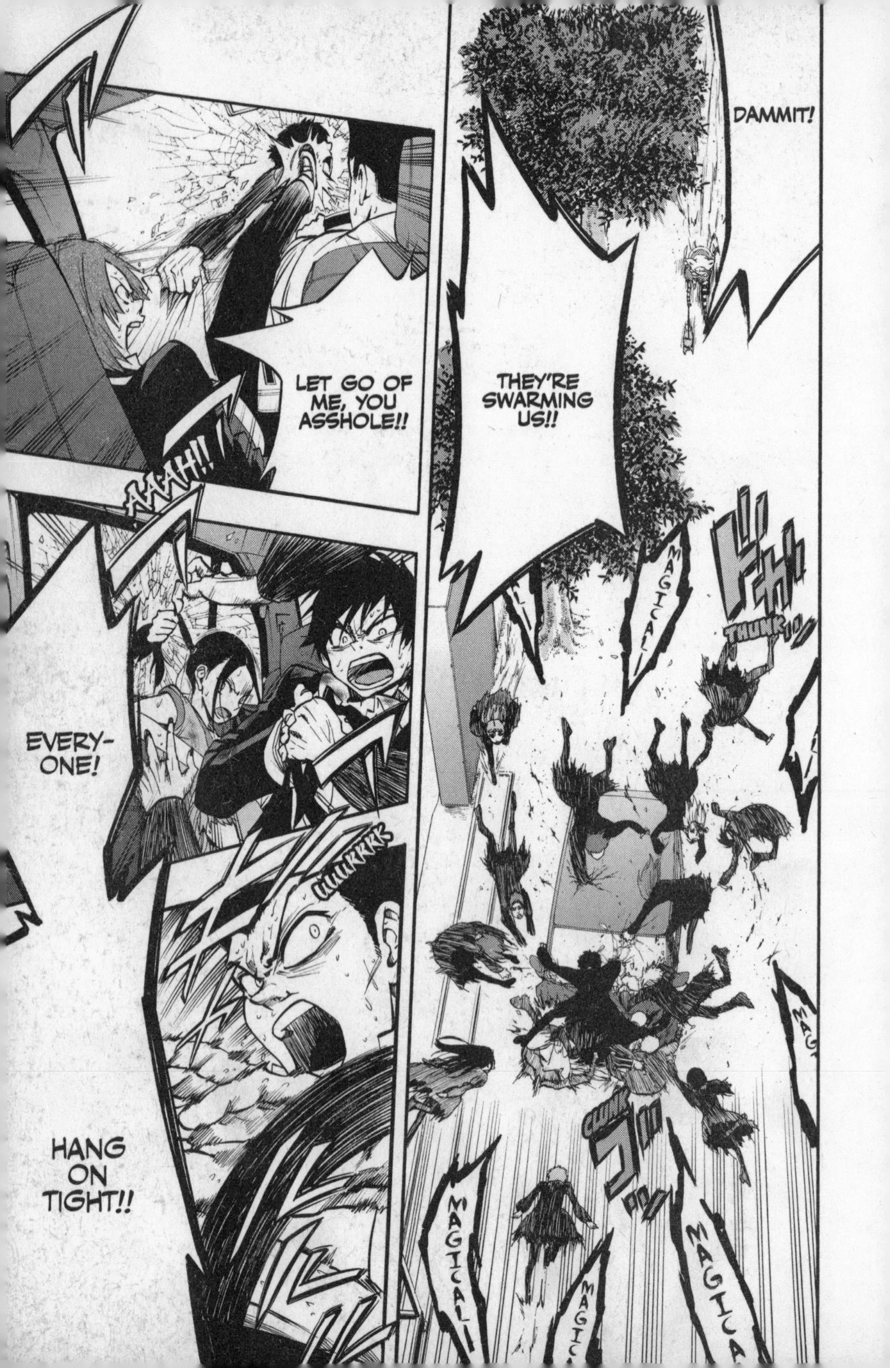
DAMMIT!
THEY'RE SWARMING US!!
MAGICAL!
THUNK!!
MAGICAL!
MAGICA
MAG
LET GO OF ME, YOU ASSHOLE!!
AAAAH!!
EVERY-ONE!
GUUURRRK
HANG ON TIGHT!!

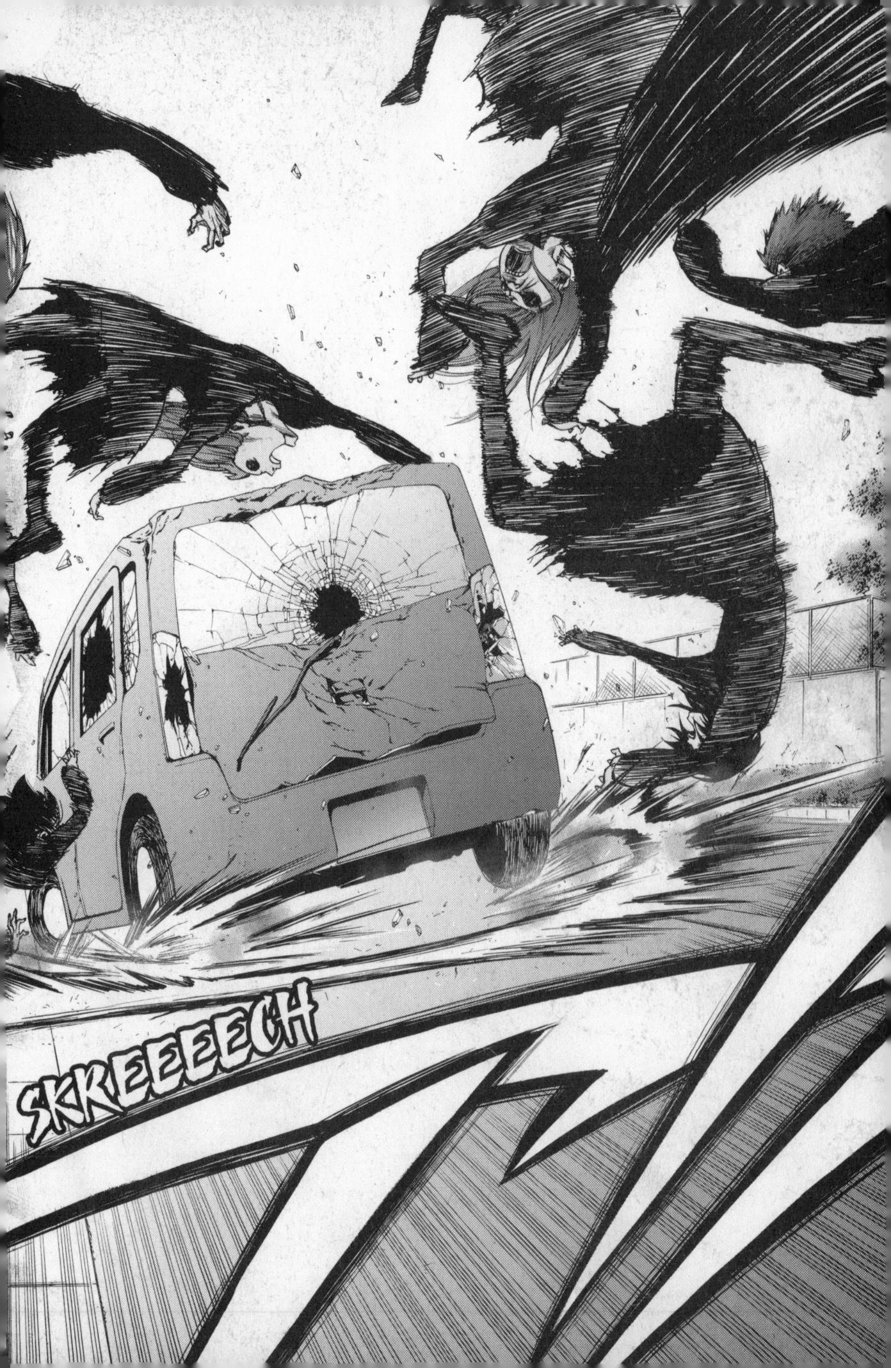
SKREEEEECH

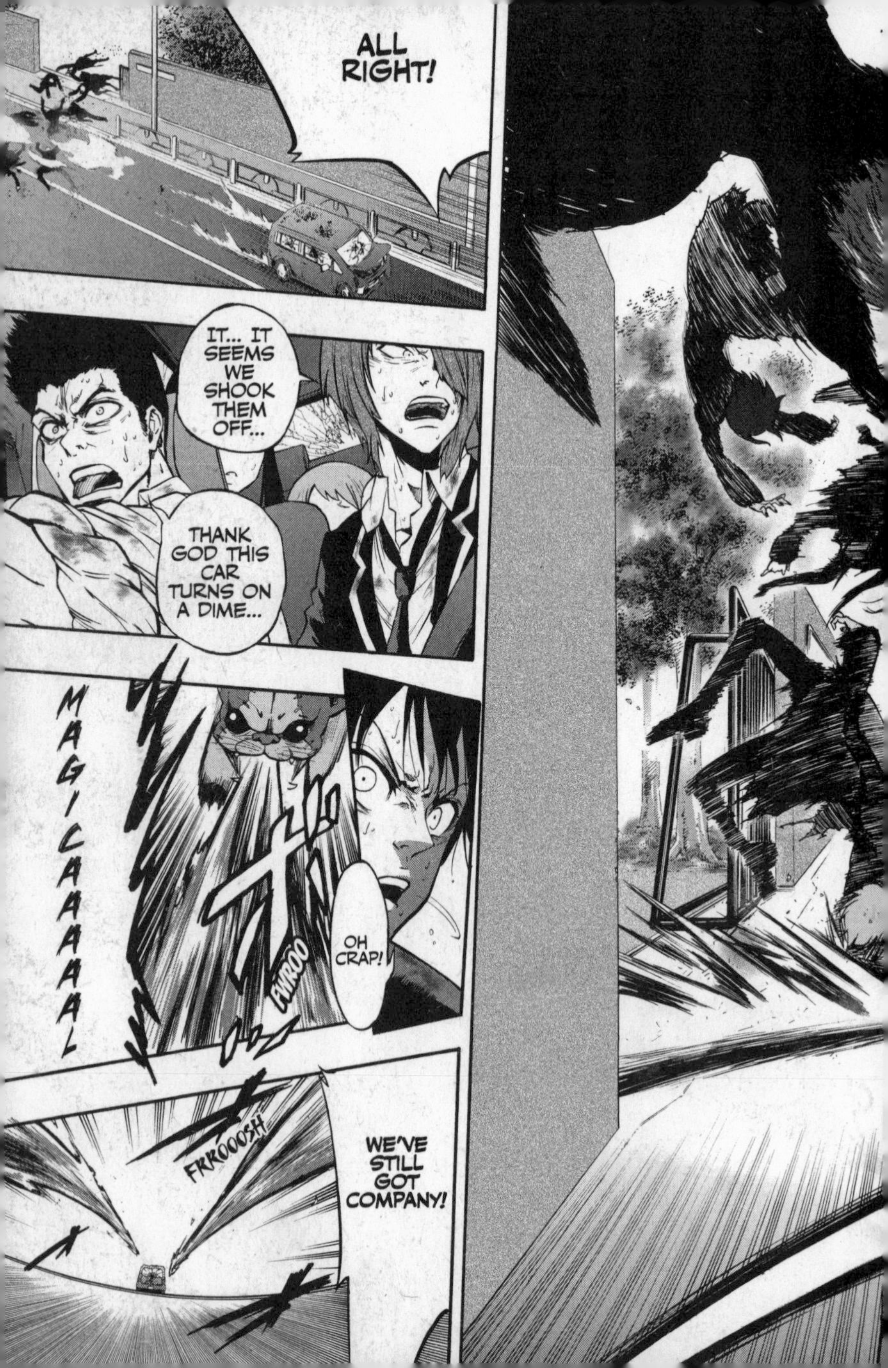
ALL RIGHT!
IT... IT SEEMS WE SHOOK THEM OFF...
THANK GOD THIS CAR TURNS ON A DIME...
MAGICAAAAAAAL
OH CRAP!
FWROO
FRROOOSH
WE'VE STILL GOT COMPANY!

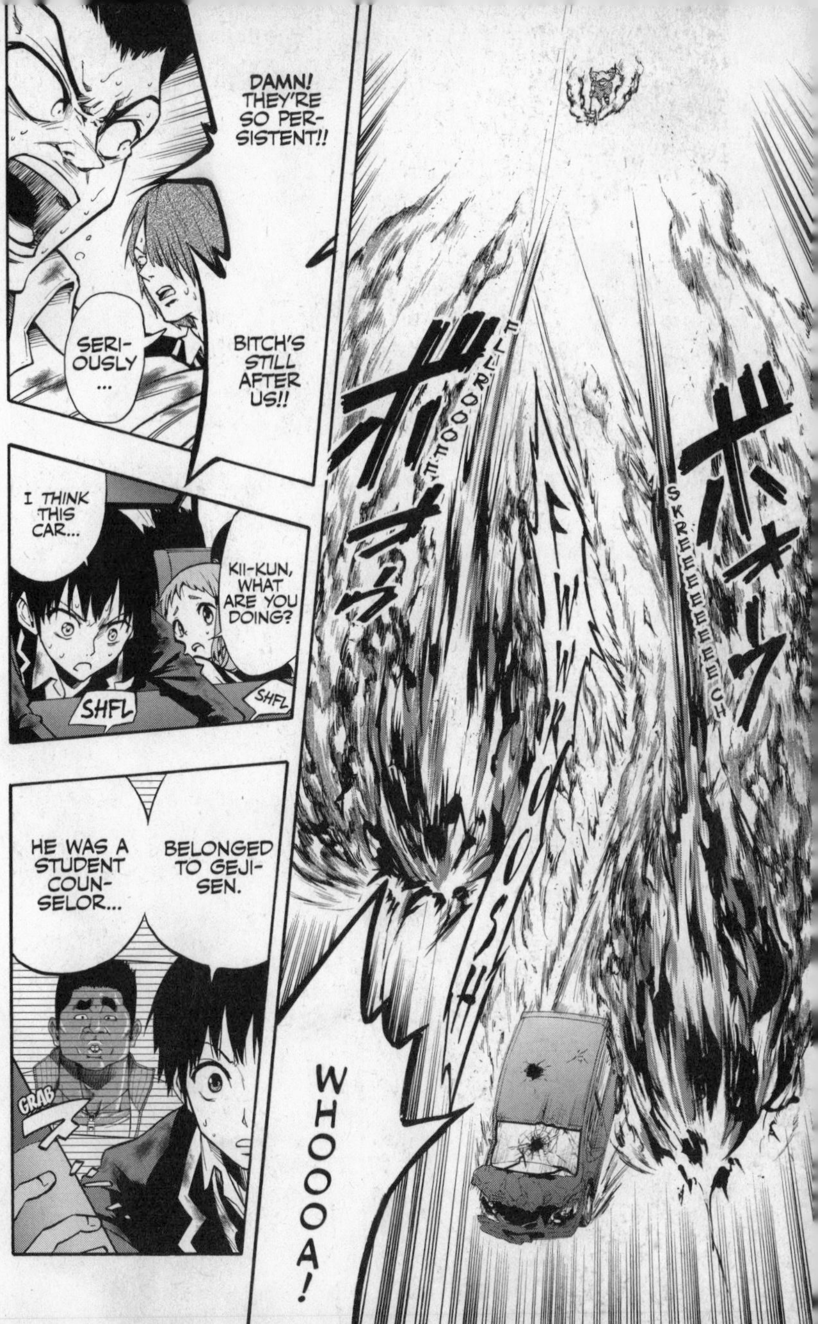
SKREEEEEEEECH
WHOOOA!
DAMN! THEY'RE SO PER-SISTENT!!
BITCH'S STILL AFTER US!!
SERI-OUSLY ...
KII-KUN, WHAT ARE YOU DOING?
I THINK THIS CAR...
SHFL
SHFL
BELONGED TO GEJI-SEN.
HE WAS A STUDENT COUN-SELOR...
GRAB

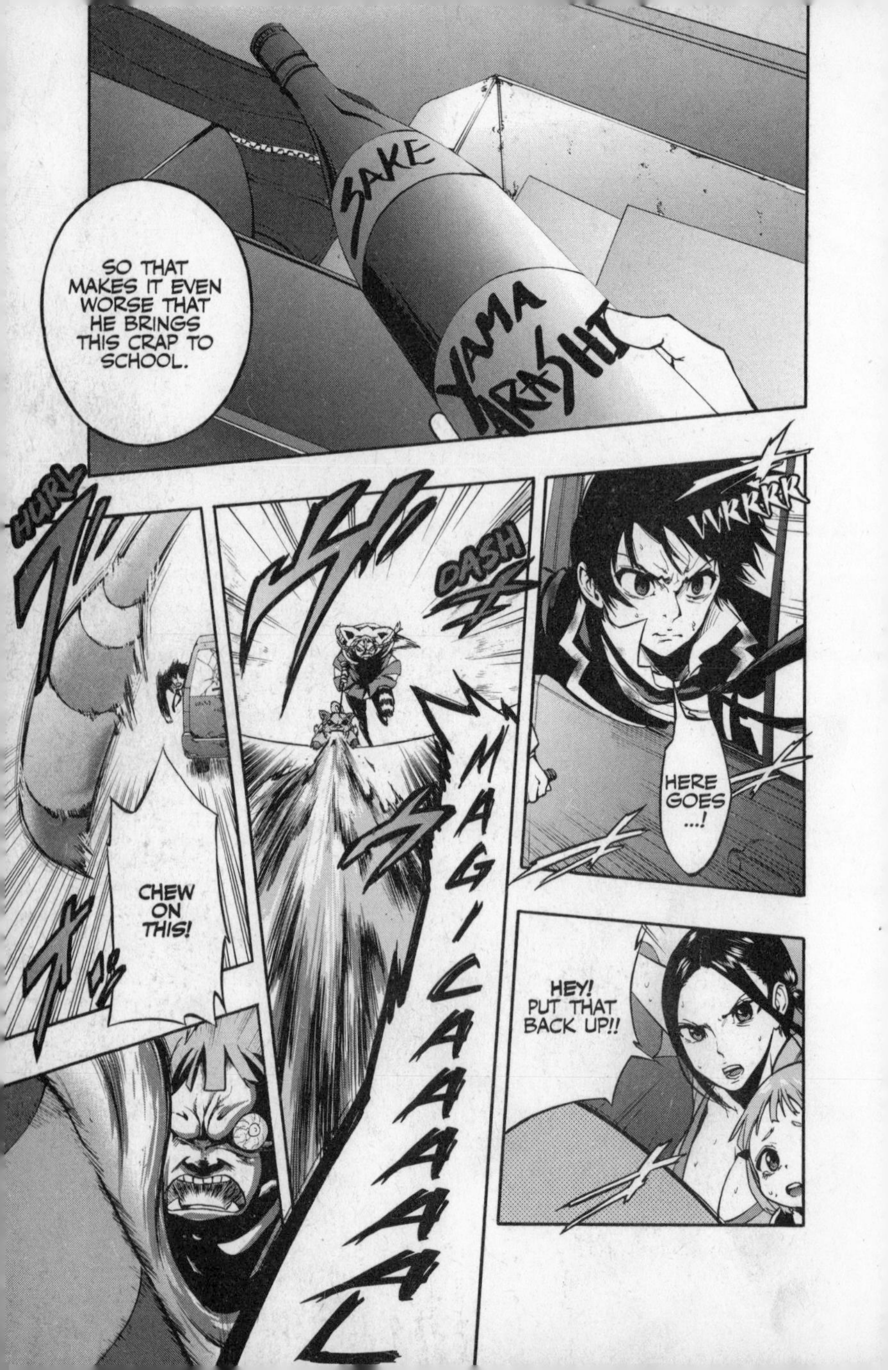
SAKE
YAMA
SO THAT MAKES IT EVEN WORSE THAT HE BRINGS THIS CRAP TO SCHOOL.
WRRRRR
HERE GOES ...!
HEY! PUT THAT BACK UP!!
DASH
MAGICAAAAAAL
HURL
CHEW ON THIS!

KRNISH

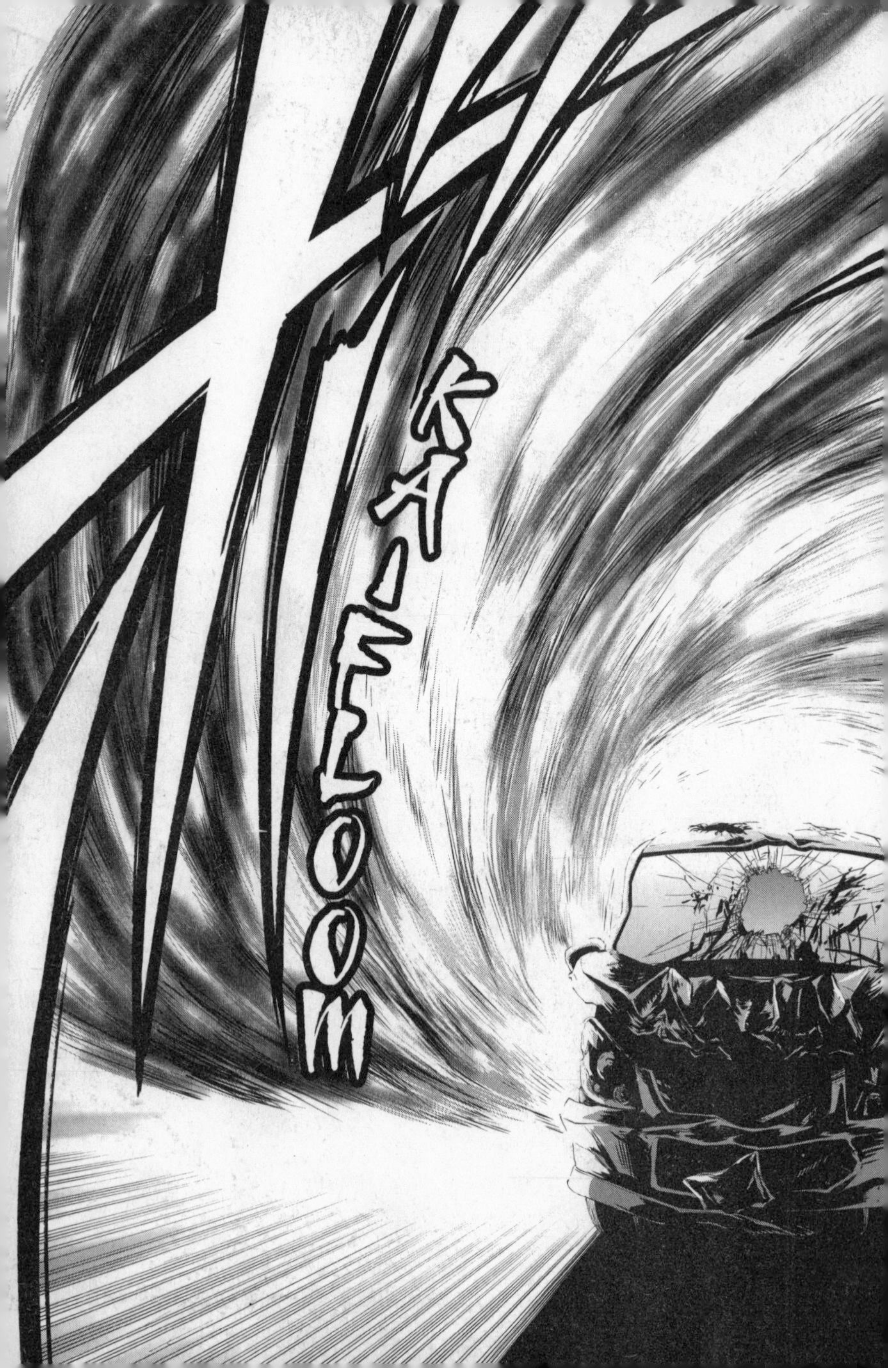
KABLOOM

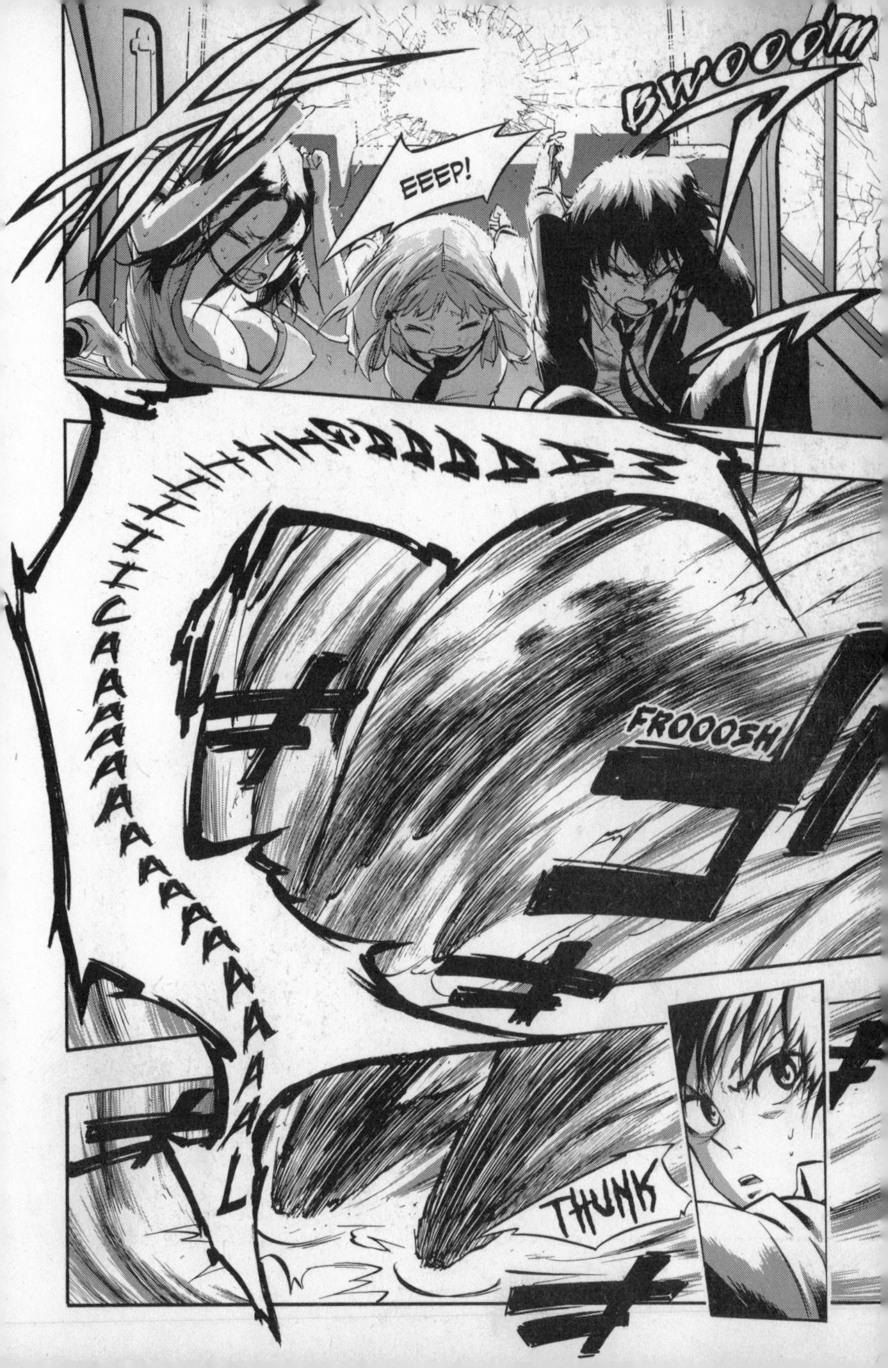
BWOOOOM
EEEP!
GRRRRAAAHHHHHHCAAAAAAAAAAAAAAAAL
FROOOSH
THUNK

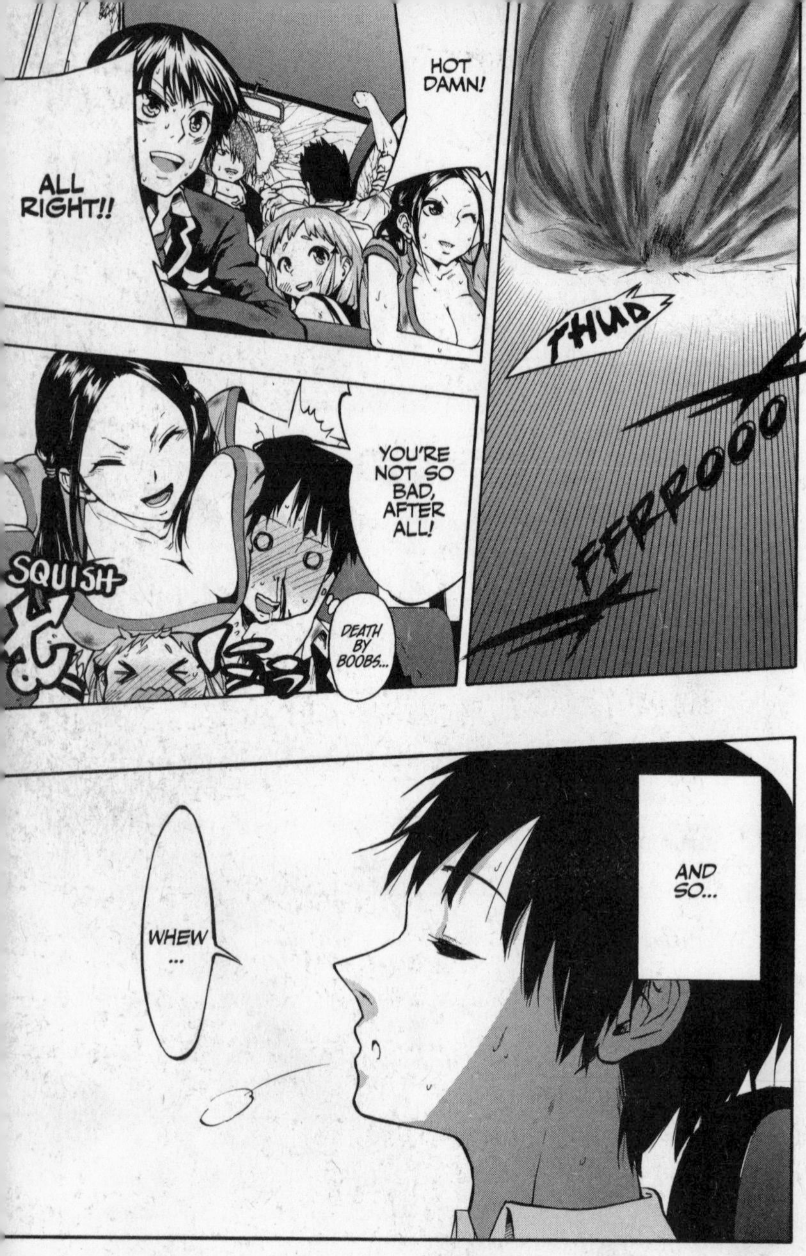
THUD
FFRROOO
HOT DAMN!
ALL RIGHT!!
YOU'RE NOT SO BAD, AFTER ALL!
DEATH BY BOOBS...
SQUISH
AND SO...
WHEW ...

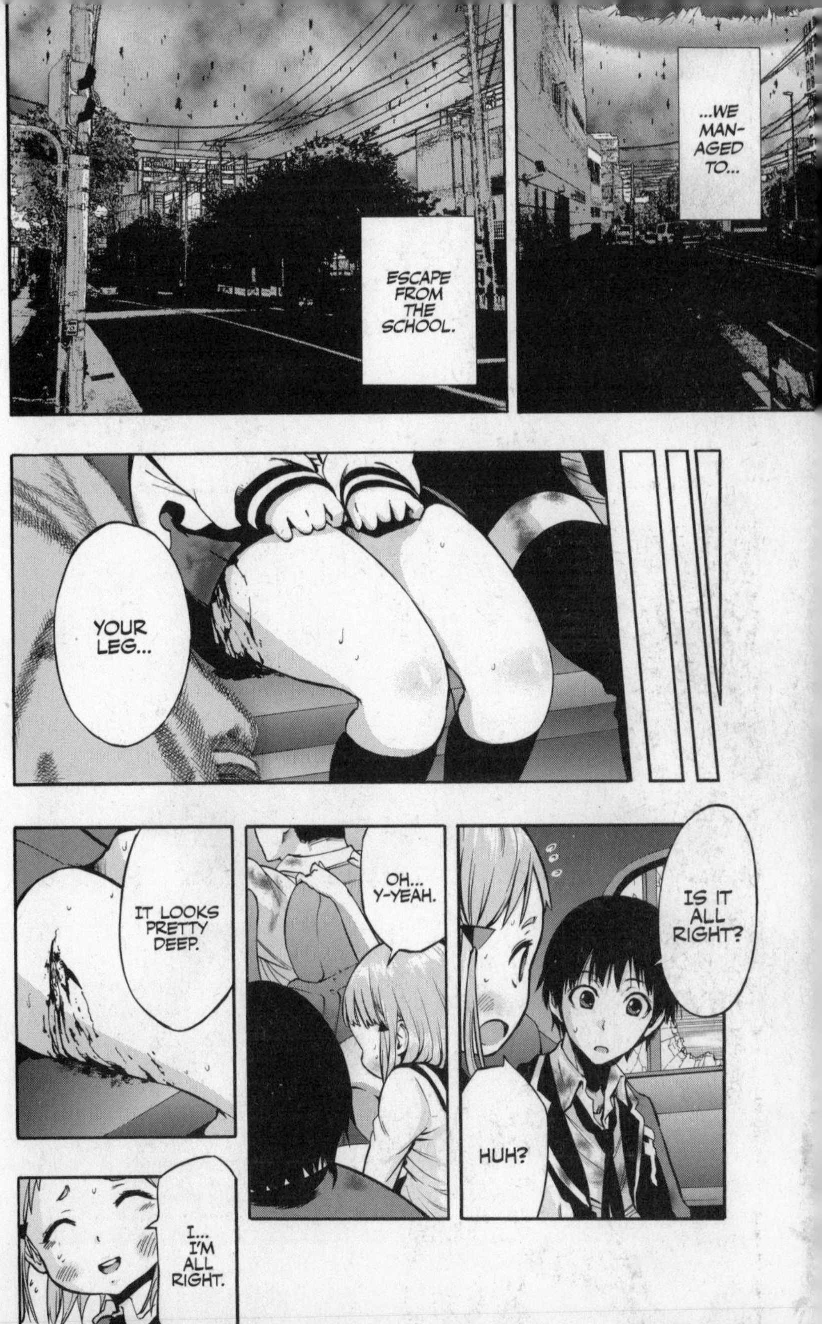
...WE MANAGED TO...
ESCAPE FROM THE SCHOOL.
YOUR LEG...
IS IT ALL RIGHT?
HUH?
OH... Y-YEAH.
IT LOOKS PRETTY DEEP.
I... I'M ALL RIGHT.

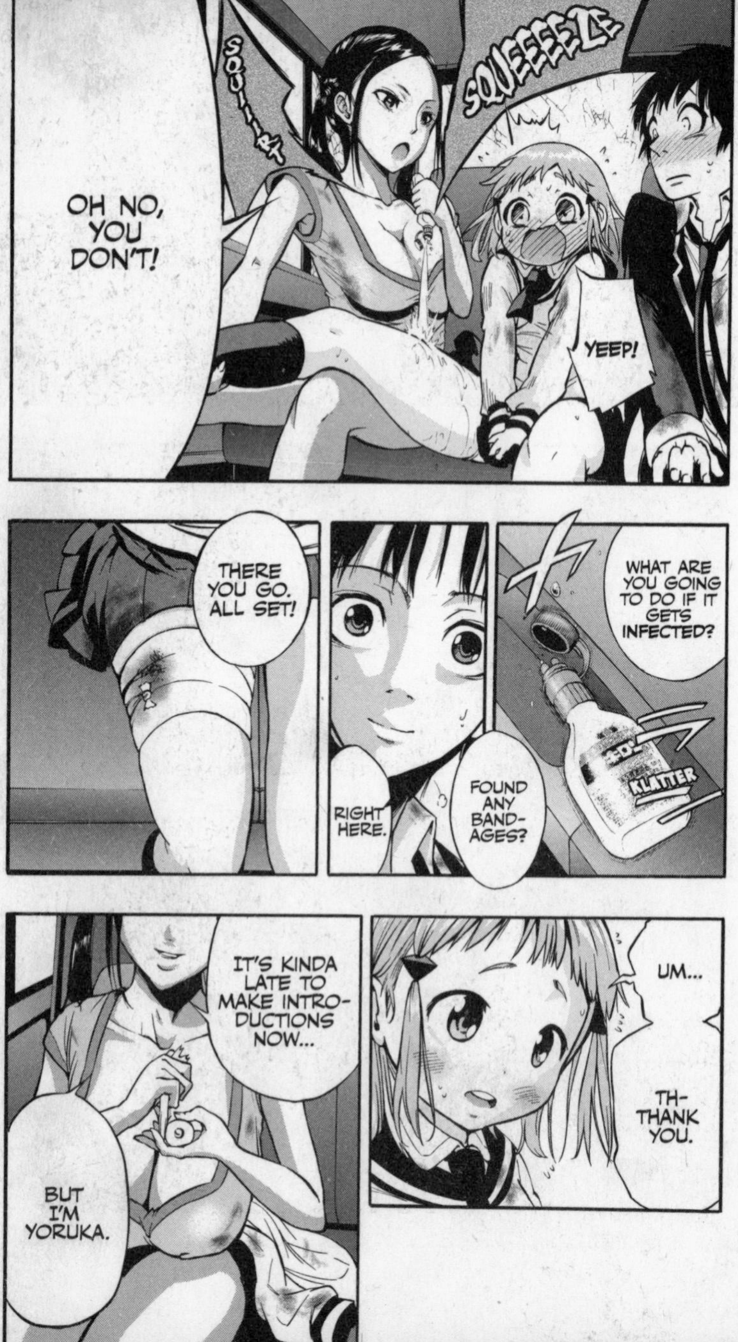
SQUEEEEEZE
OH NO, YOU DON'T!
YEEP!
WHAT ARE YOU GOING TO DO IF IT GETS INFECTED?
KLATTER
FOUND ANY BAND-AGES?
RIGHT HERE.
THERE YOU GO. ALL SET!
UM...
TH-THANK YOU.
IT'S KINDA LATE TO MAKE INTRO-DUCTIONS NOW...
BUT I'M YORUKA.

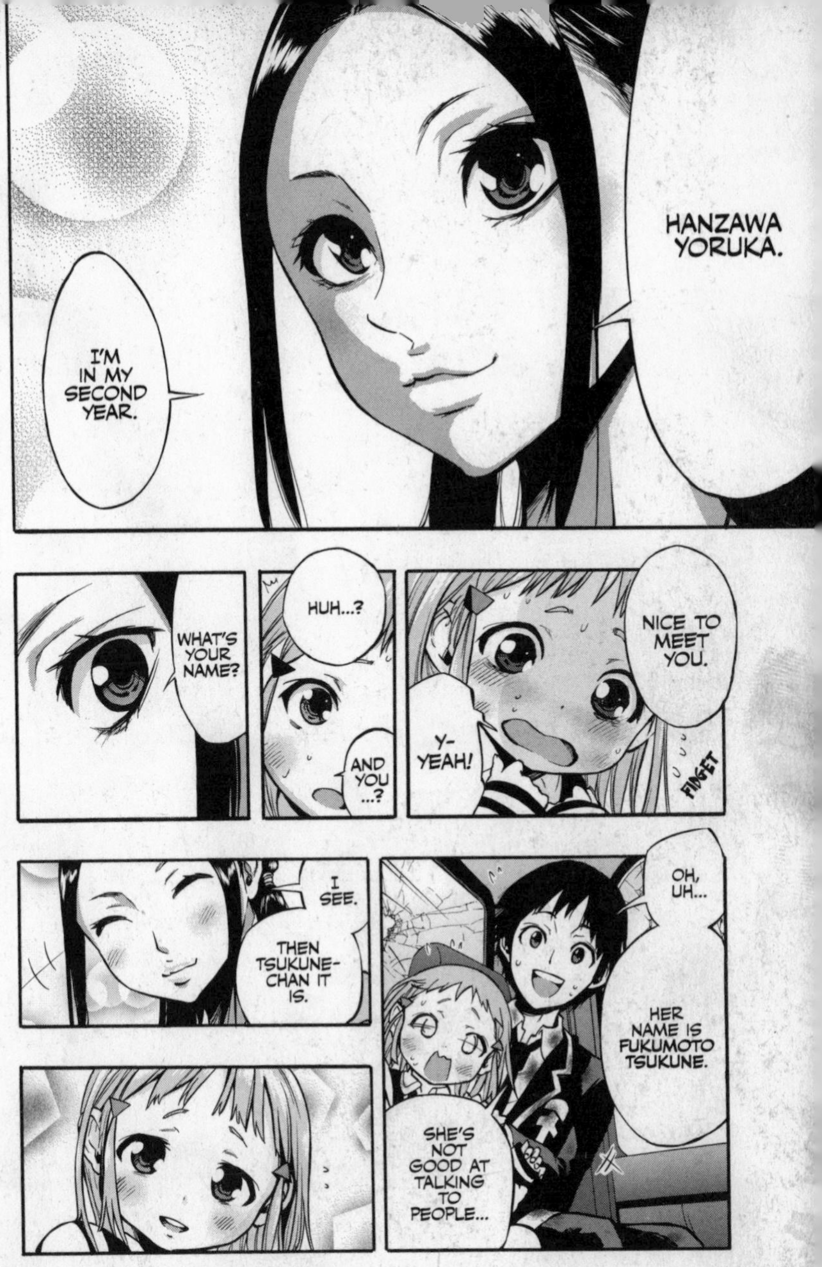
HANZAWA YORUKA.
I'M IN MY SECOND YEAR.
NICE TO MEET YOU.
Y-YEAH!
FIDGET
HUH...?
AND YOU ...?
WHAT'S YOUR NAME?
OH, UH...
HER NAME IS FUKUMOTO TSUKUNE.
SHE'S NOT GOOD AT TALKING TO PEOPLE...
I SEE.
THEN TSUKUNE-CHAN IT IS.

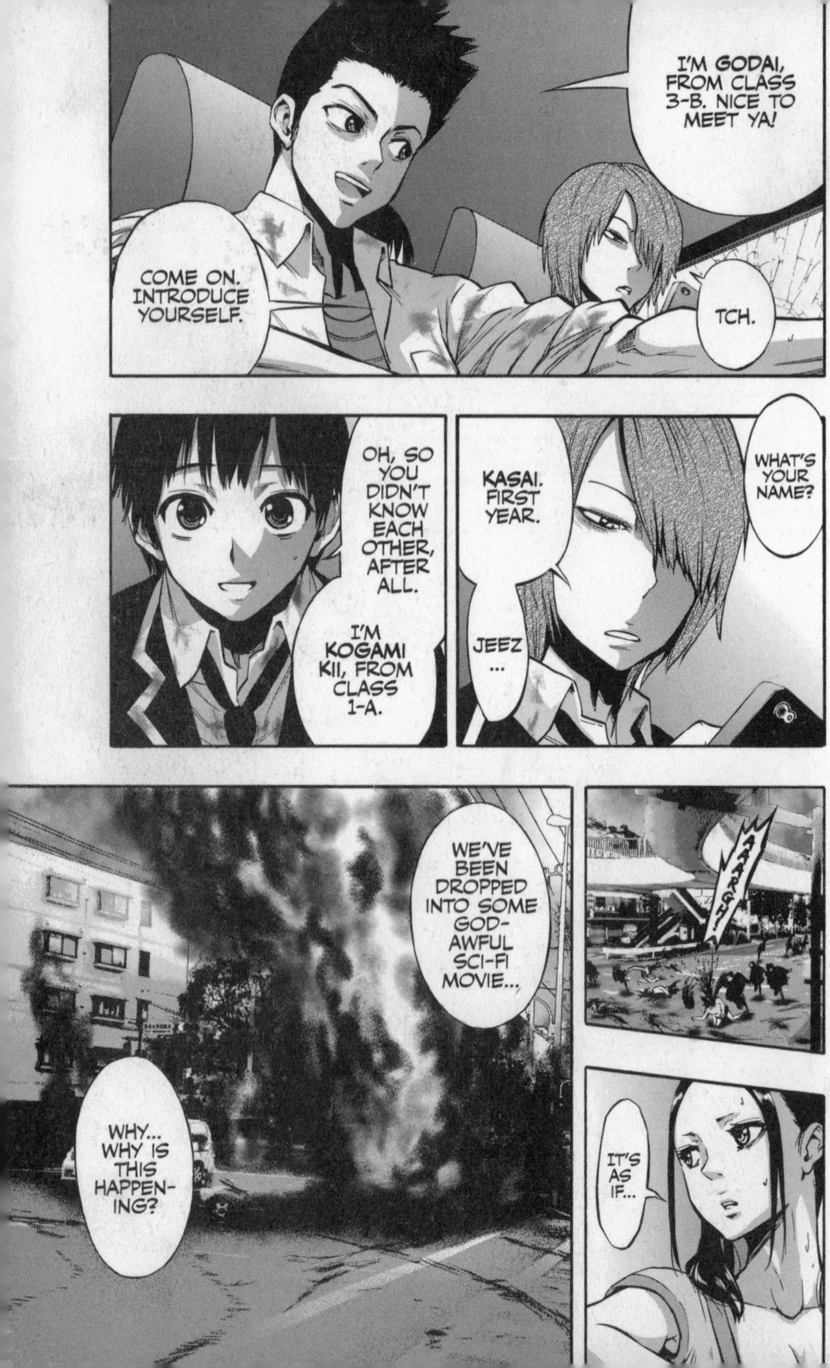
I'M GODAI, FROM CLASS 3-B. NICE TO MEET YA!
COME ON. INTRODUCE YOURSELF.
TCH.
WHAT'S YOUR NAME?
KASAI. FIRST YEAR.
JEEZ...
OH, SO YOU DIDN'T KNOW EACH OTHER, AFTER ALL.
I'M KOGAMI KII, FROM CLASS 1-A.
AAARGH!
IT'S AS IF...
WE'VE BEEN DROPPED INTO SOME GOD-AWFUL SCI-FI MOVIE...
WHY... WHY IS THIS HAPPENING?

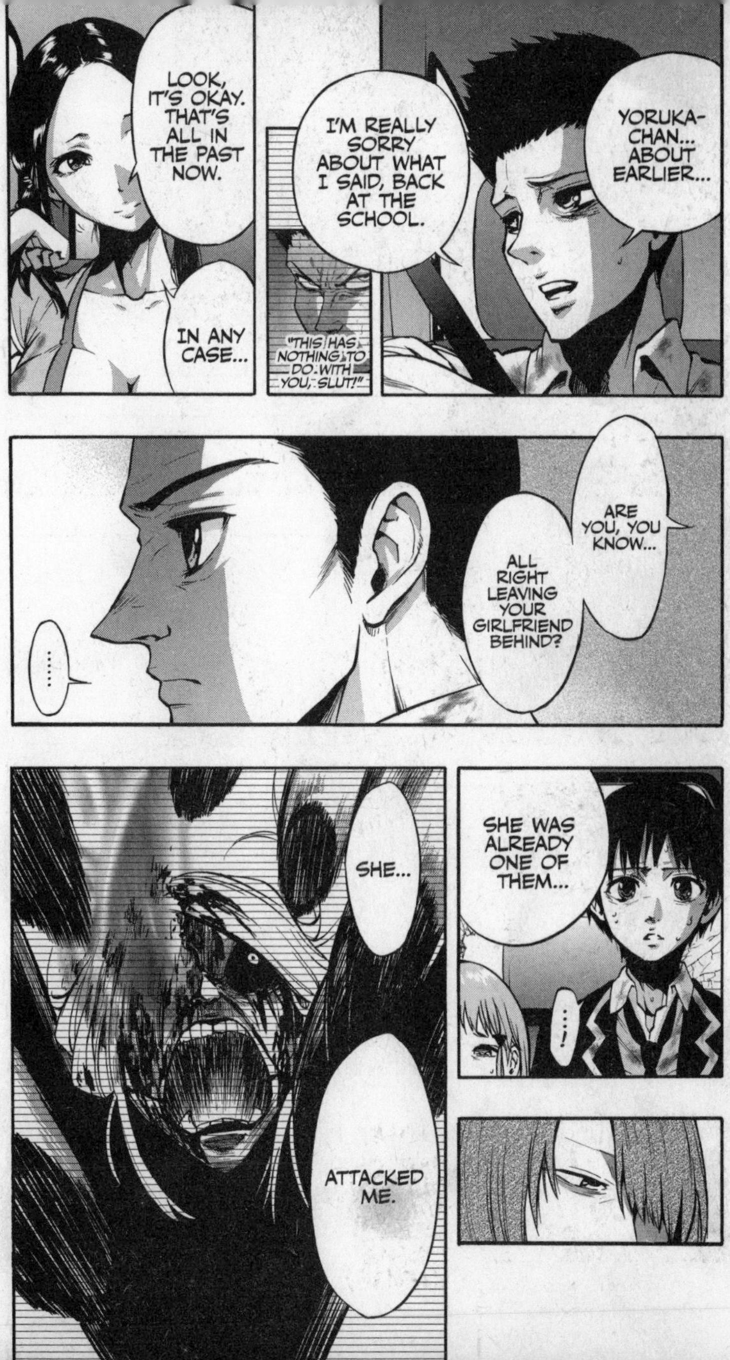
YORUKA-CHAN... ABOUT EARLIER...
I'M REALLY SORRY ABOUT WHAT I SAID, BACK AT THE SCHOOL.
"THIS HAS NOTHING TO DO WITH YOU, SLUT!"
LOOK, IT'S OKAY. THAT'S ALL IN THE PAST NOW.
IN ANY CASE...
ARE YOU, YOU KNOW...
ALL RIGHT LEAVING YOUR GIRLFRIEND BEHIND?
......
SHE WAS ALREADY ONE OF THEM...
...!
SHE...
ATTACKED ME.

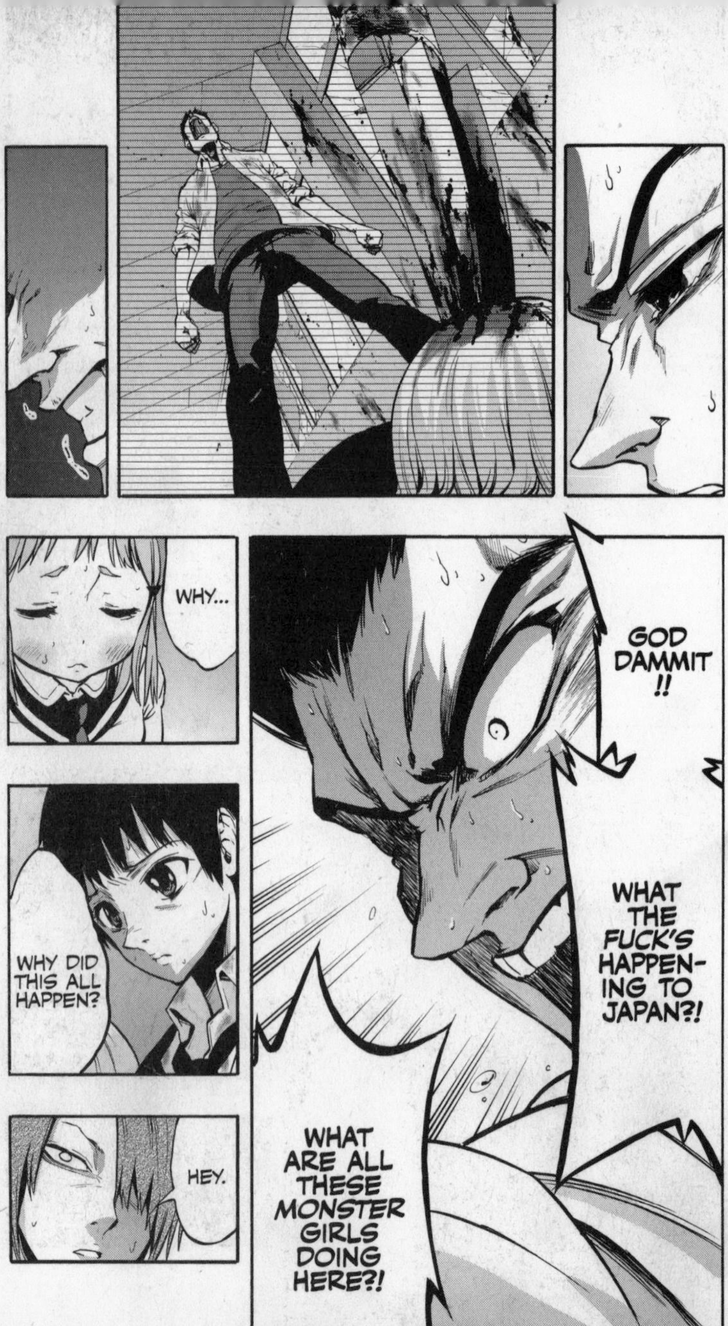
GOD DAMMIT !!
WHAT THE FUCK'S HAPPENING TO JAPAN?!
WHAT ARE ALL THESE MONSTER GIRLS DOING HERE?!
WHY...
WHY DID THIS ALL HAPPEN?
HEY.

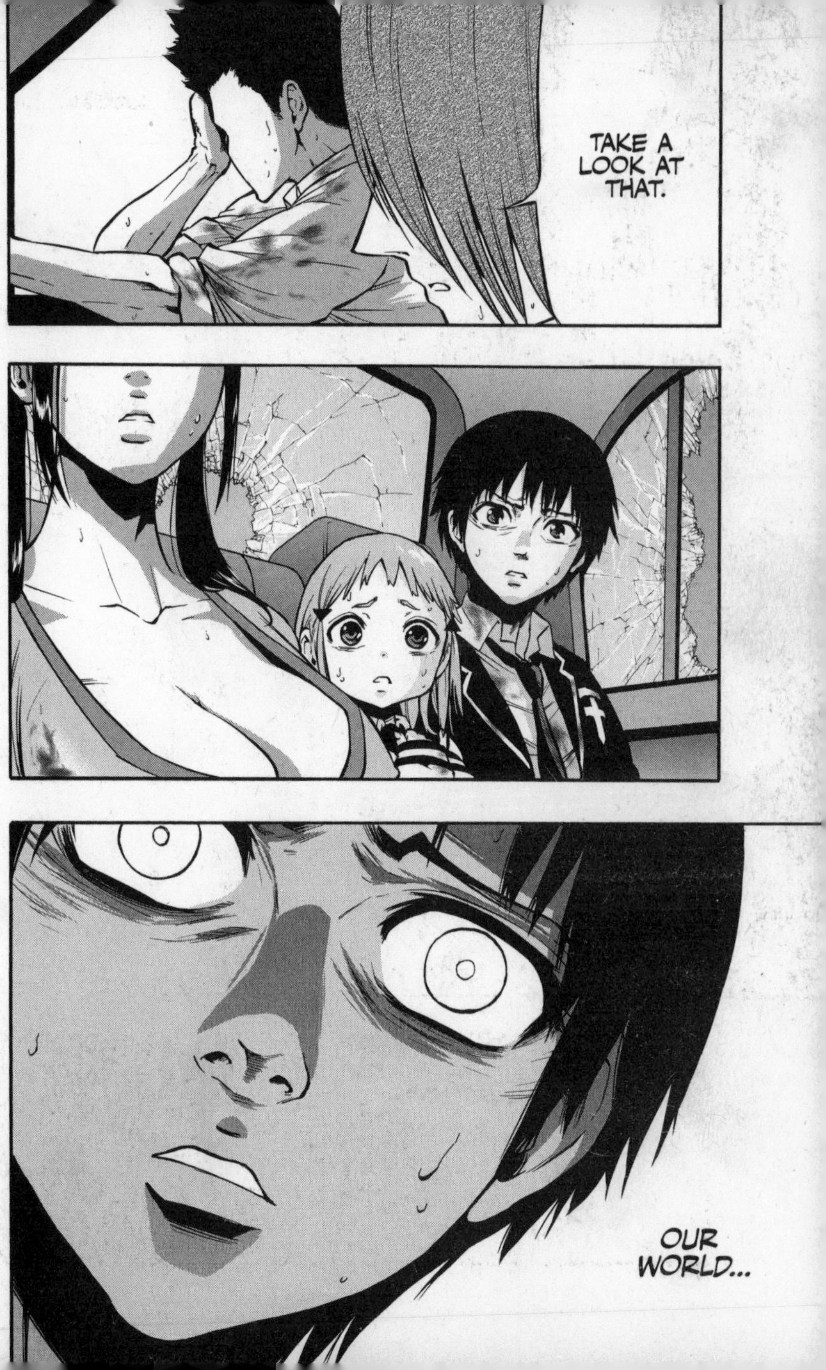
TAKE A LOOK AT THAT.
OUR WORLD...

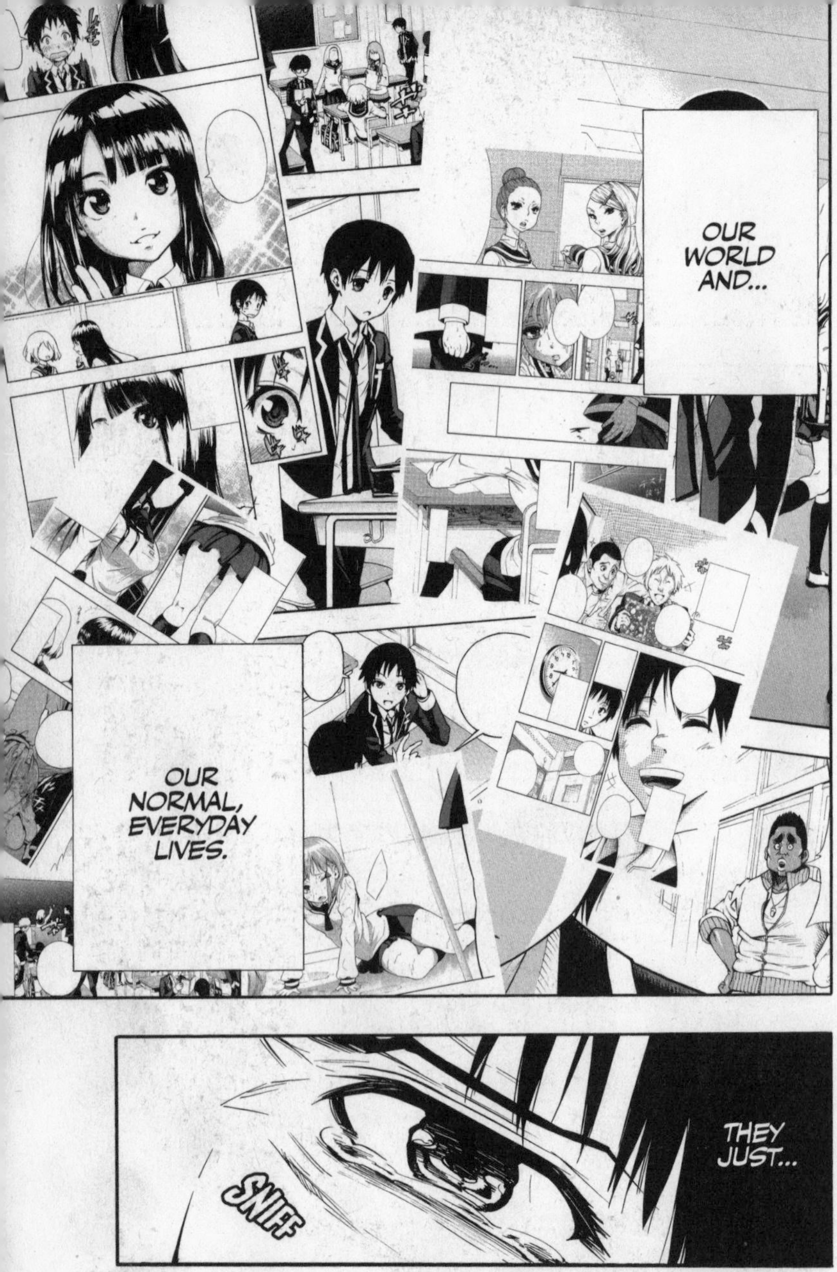
OUR WORLD AND...
OUR NORMAL, EVERYDAY LIVES.
THEY JUST...
SNIFF

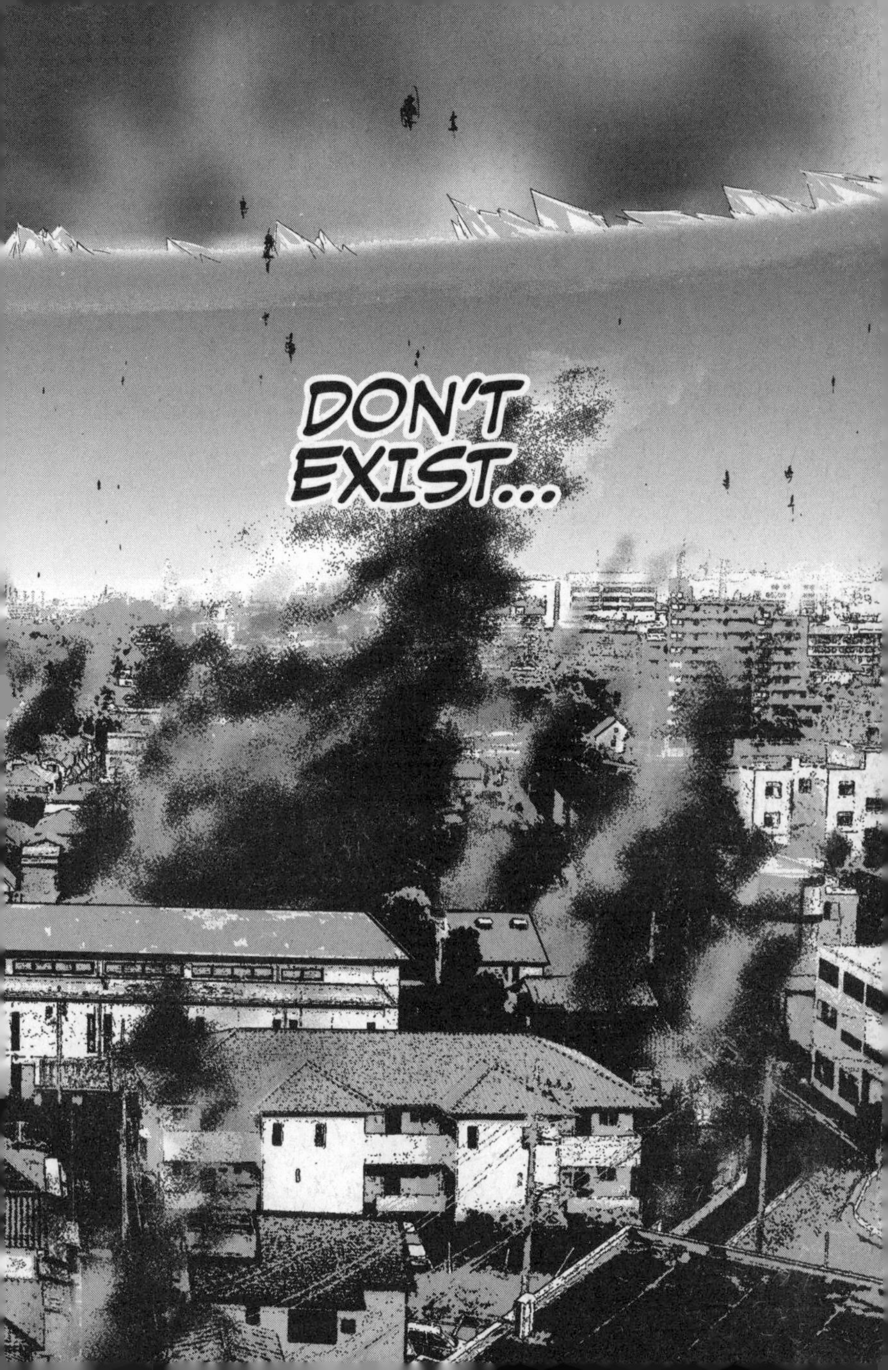
DON'T EXIST...

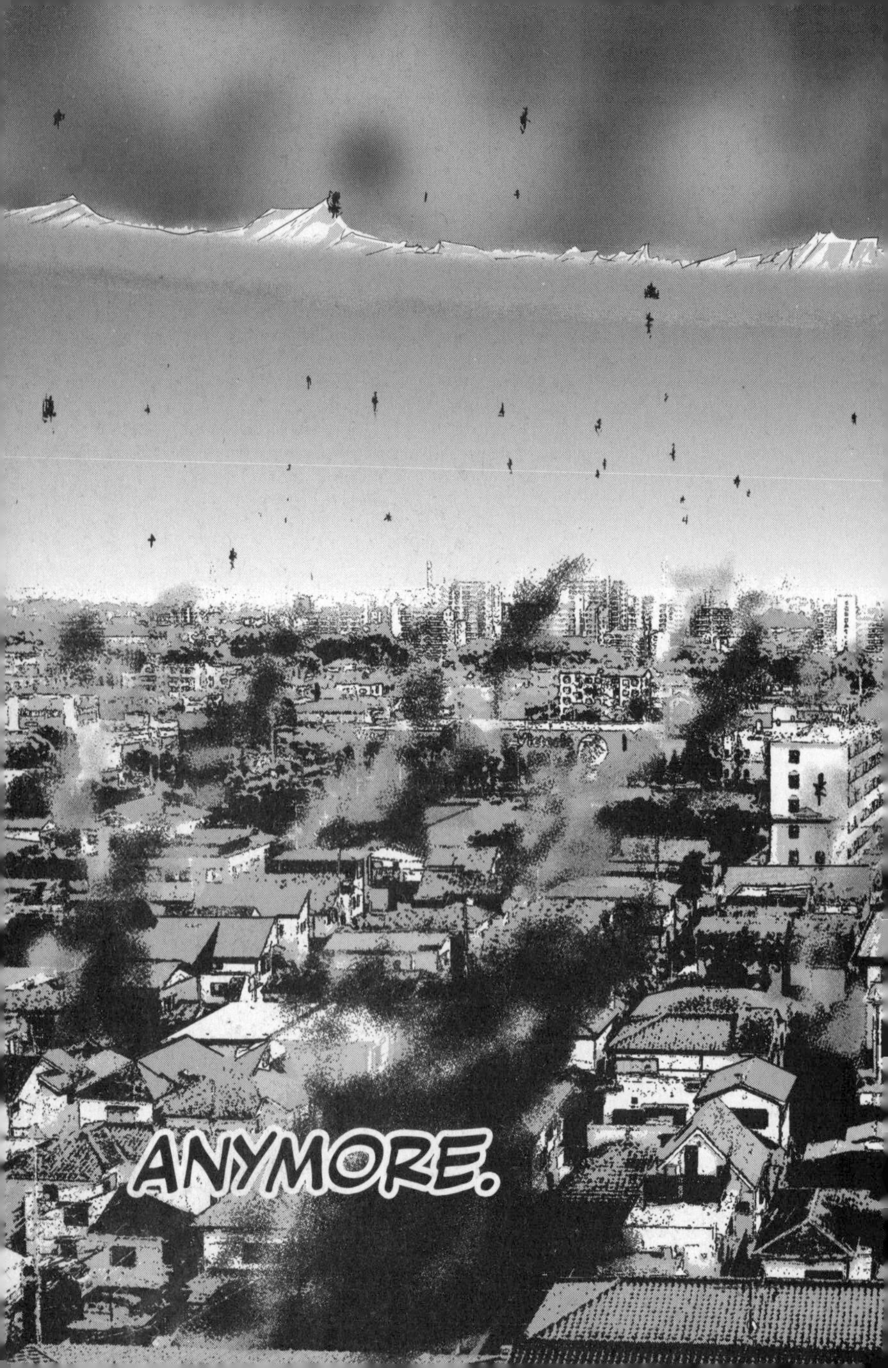
ANYMORE.

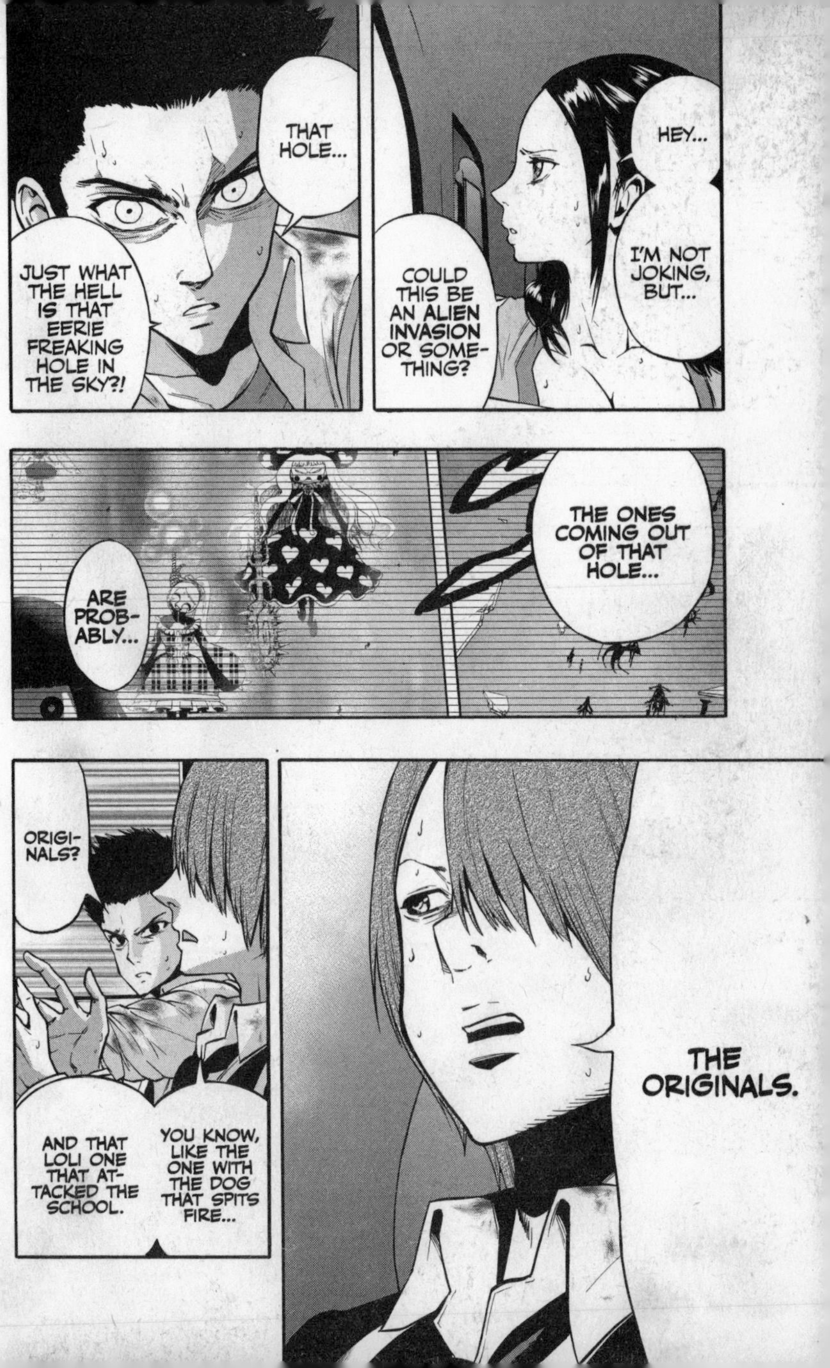
HEY...
I'M NOT JOKING, BUT...
COULD THIS BE AN ALIEN INVASION OR SOME-THING?
THAT HOLE...
JUST WHAT THE HELL IS THAT EERIE FREAKING HOLE IN THE SKY?!
THE ONES COMING OUT OF THAT HOLE...
ARE PROB-ABLY...
THE ORIGINALS.
ORIGI-NALS?
YOU KNOW, LIKE THE ONE WITH THE DOG THAT SPITS FIRE...
AND THAT LOLI ONE THAT AT-TACKED THE SCHOOL.

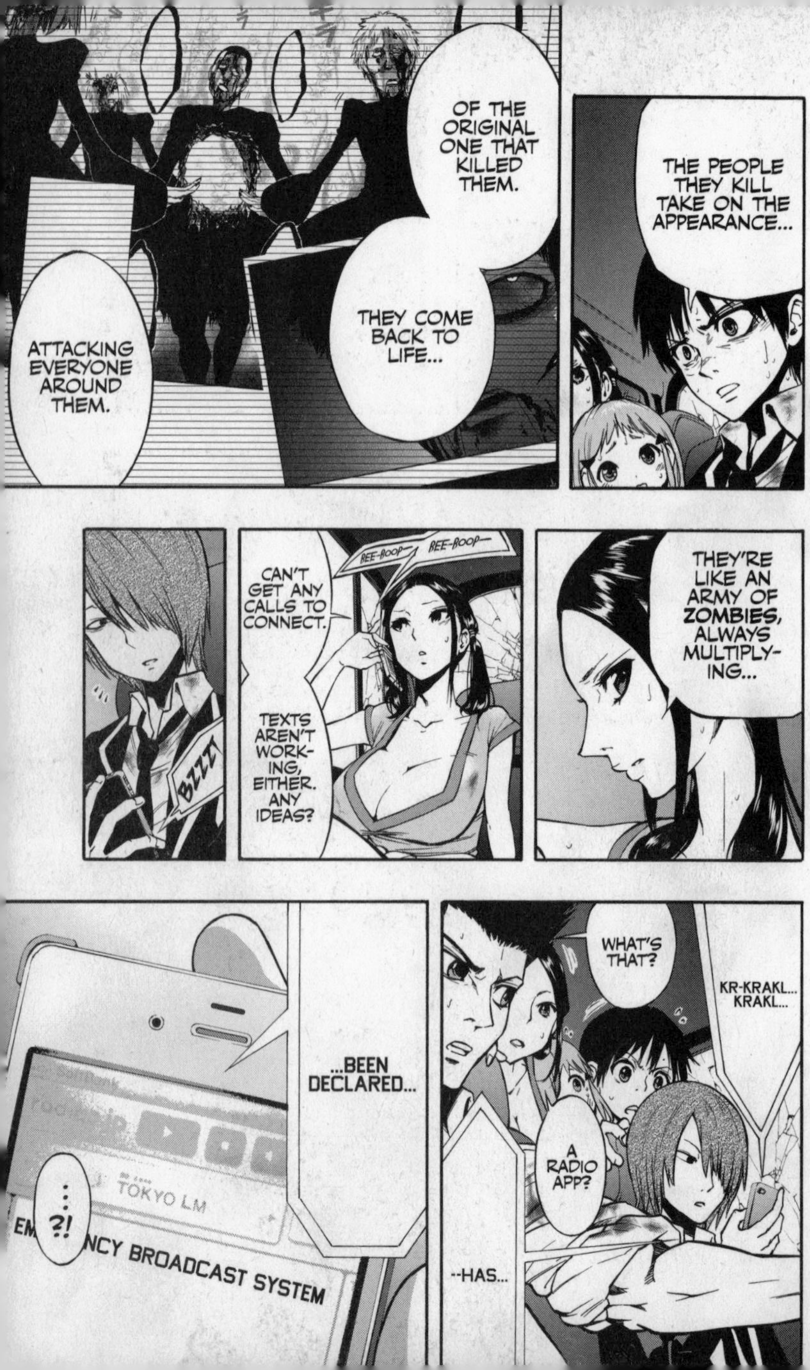
THE PEOPLE THEY KILL TAKE ON THE APPEARANCE...
OF THE ORIGINAL ONE THAT KILLED THEM.
THEY COME BACK TO LIFE...
ATTACKING EVERYONE AROUND THEM.
THEY'RE LIKE AN ARMY OF ZOMBIES, ALWAYS MULTIPLY-ING...
BEE-BOOP BEE-BOOP
CAN'T GET ANY CALLS TO CONNECT.
TEXTS AREN'T WORK-ING, EITHER. ANY IDEAS?
BZZZT
WHAT'S THAT?
KR-KRAKL... KRAKL...
A RADIO APP?
--HAS...
...BEEN DECLARED...
TOKYO LM
EM NCY BROADCAST SYSTEM
...?!

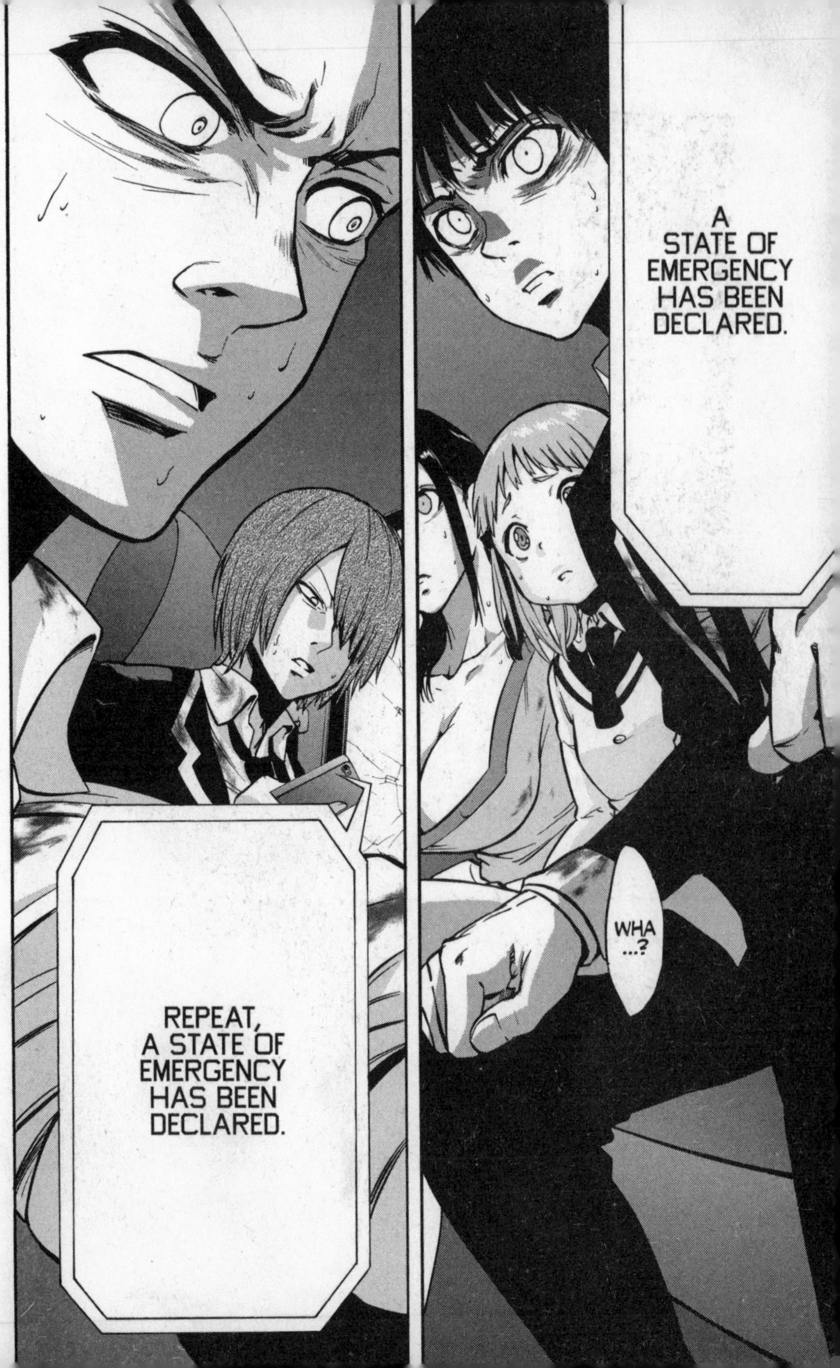
A STATE OF EMERGENCY HAS BEEN DECLARED.
WHA ...?
REPEAT, A STATE OF EMERGENCY HAS BEEN DECLARED.

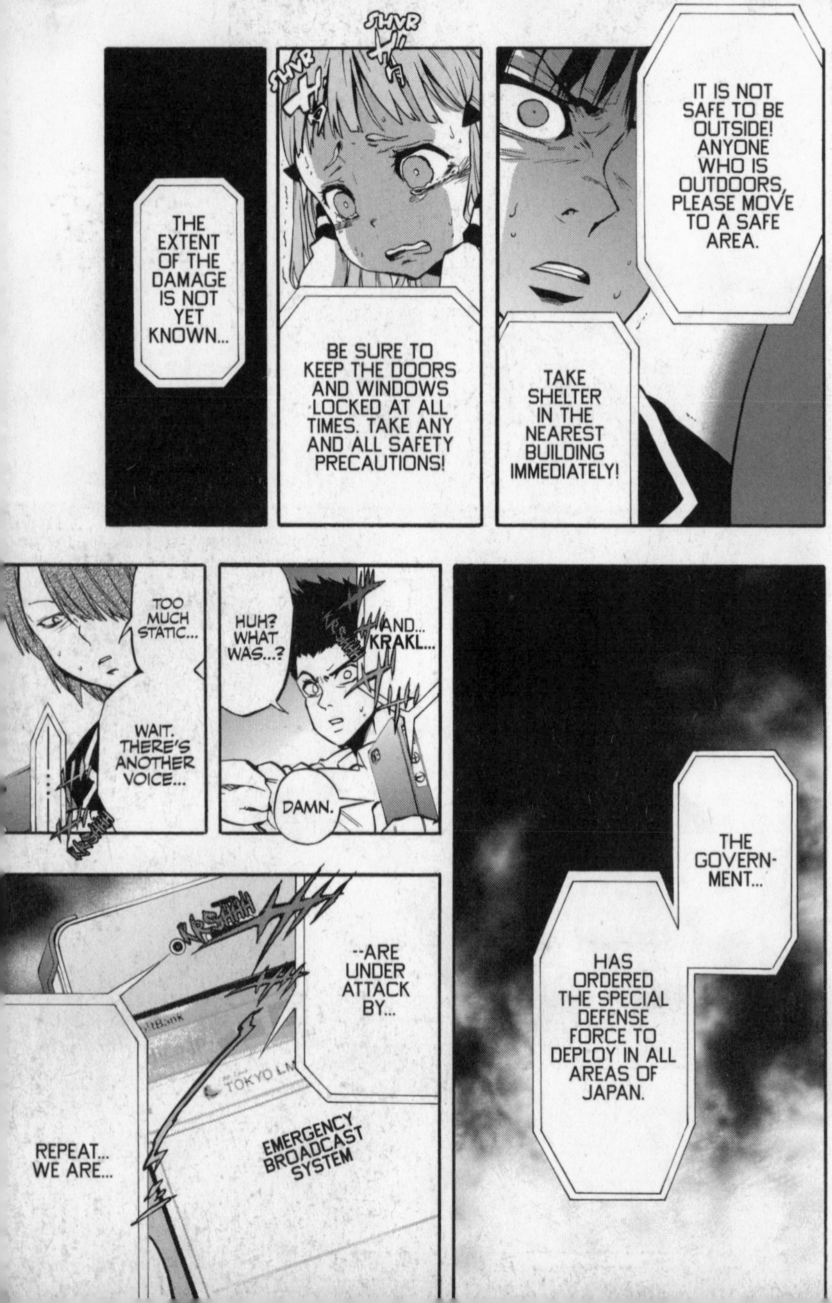
IT IS NOT SAFE TO BE OUTSIDE! ANYONE WHO IS OUTDOORS, PLEASE MOVE TO A SAFE AREA.
TAKE SHELTER IN THE NEAREST BUILDING IMMEDIATELY!
SHVR
SHVR
BE SURE TO KEEP THE DOORS AND WINDOWS LOCKED AT ALL TIMES. TAKE ANY AND ALL SAFETY PRECAUTIONS!
THE EXTENT OF THE DAMAGE IS NOT YET KNOWN...
THE GOVERNMENT...
HAS ORDERED THE SPECIAL DEFENSE FORCE TO DEPLOY IN ALL AREAS OF JAPAN.
...AND... KRAKL...
HUH? WHAT WAS...?
DAMN.
TOO MUCH STATIC...
WAIT. THERE'S ANOTHER VOICE...
...
--ARE UNDER ATTACK BY...
EMERGENCY BROADCAST SYSTEM
REPEAT... WE ARE...

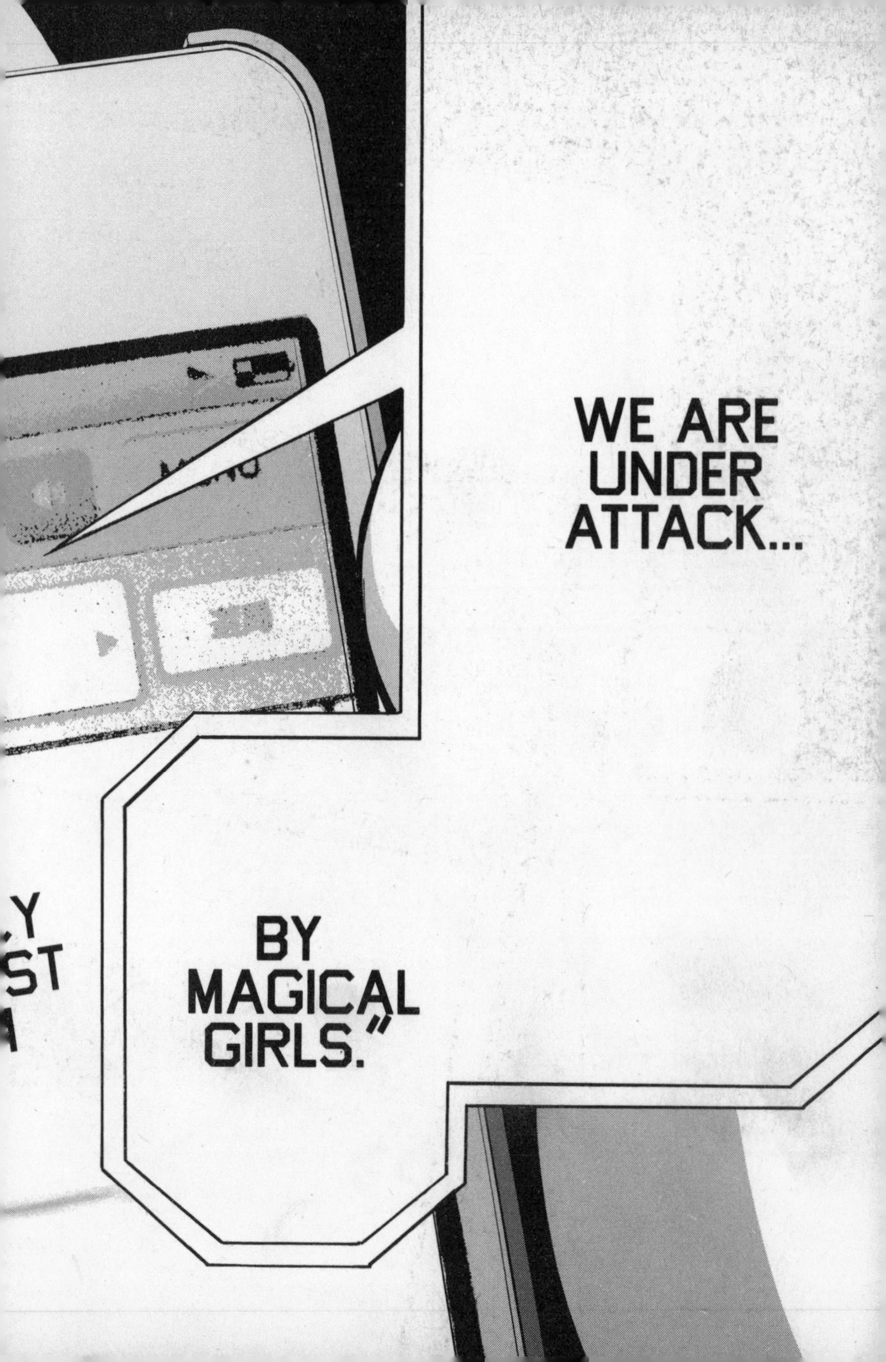
WE ARE UNDER ATTACK...
BY MAGICAL GIRLS.”

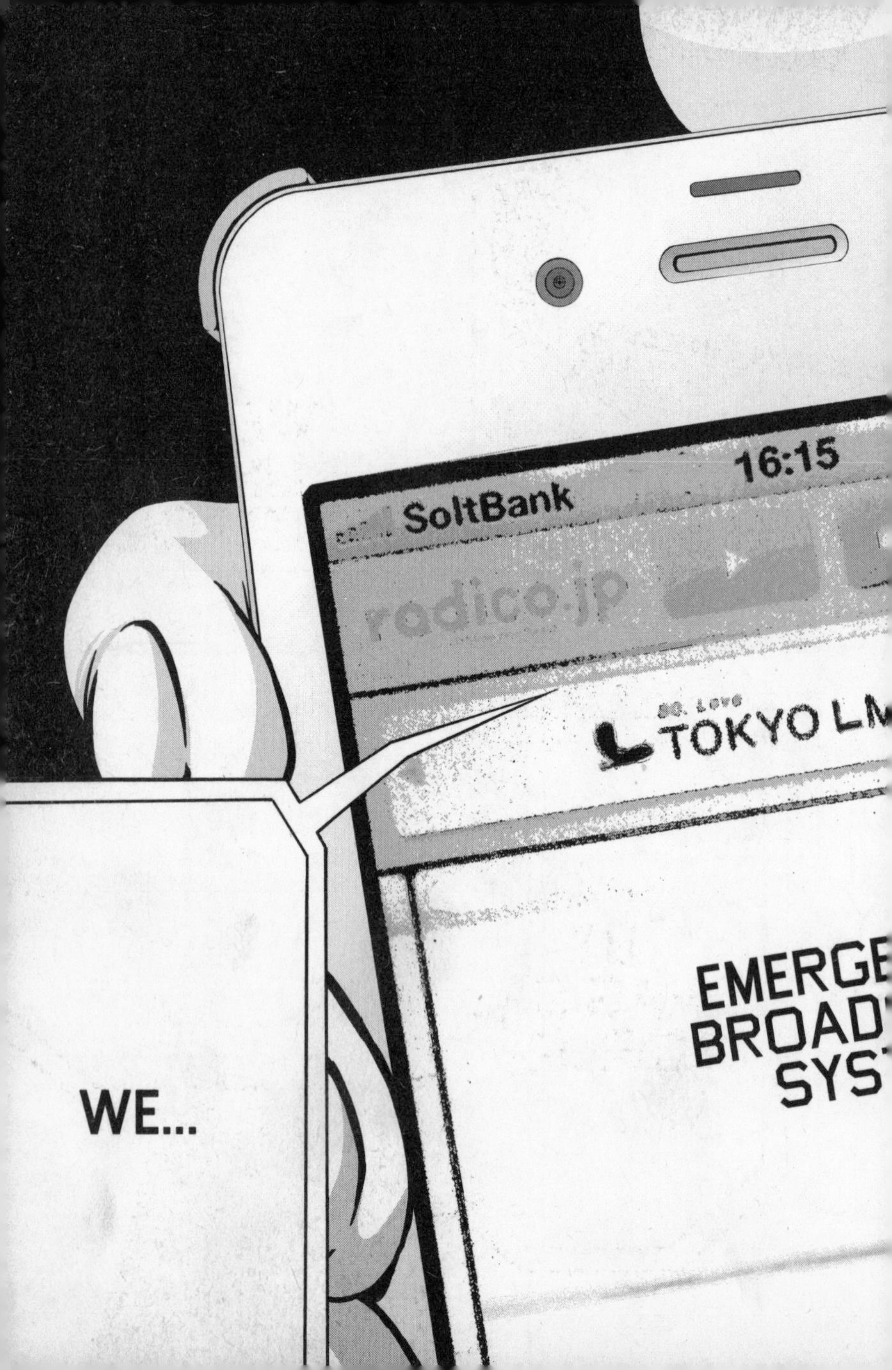
16:15
SoltBank
radico.jp
TOKYO LM
EMERGE
BROAD
SYST
WE...

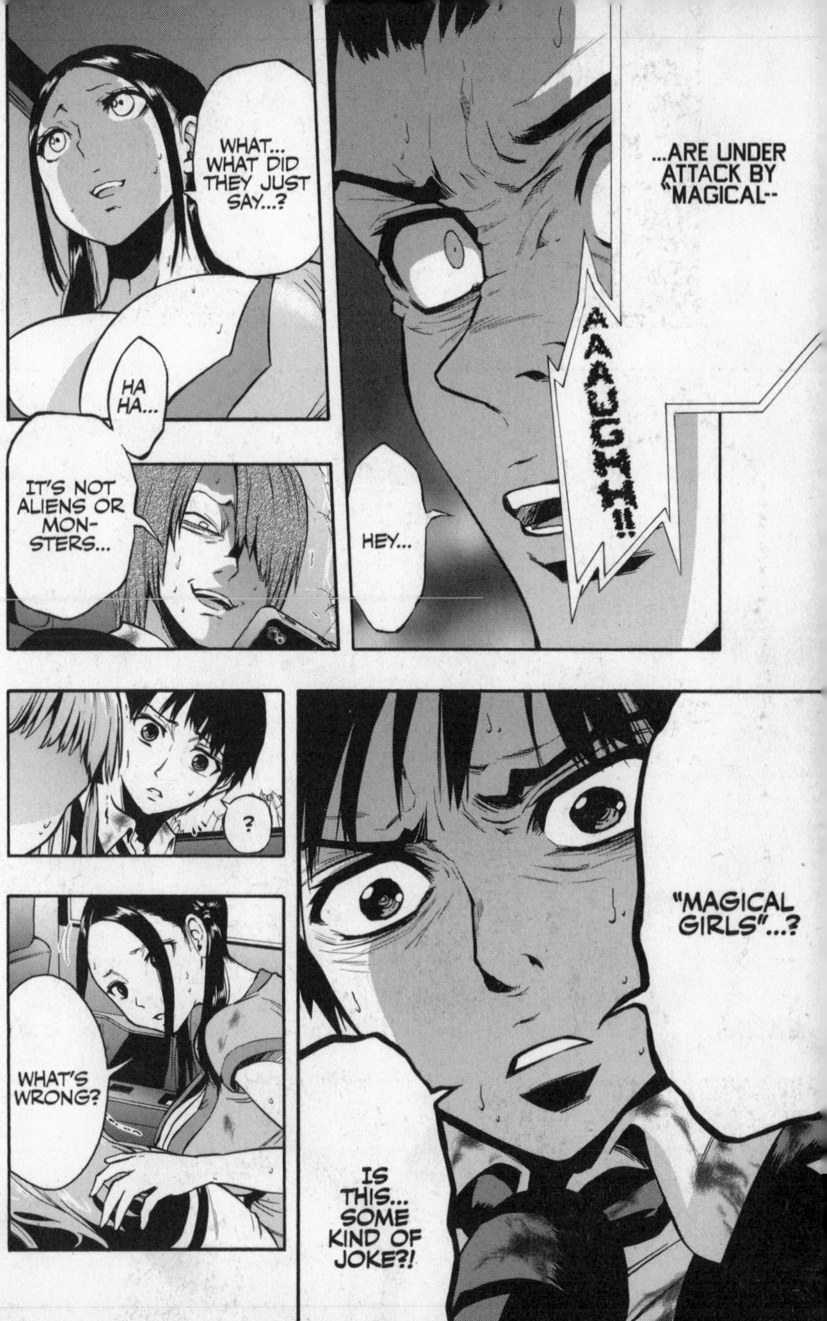
...ARE UNDER ATTACK BY "MAGICAL--
AAAUGHH!!
HEY...
WHAT... WHAT DID THEY JUST SAY...?
HA HA...
IT'S NOT ALIENS OR MON-STERS...
"MAGICAL GIRLS"...?
IS THIS... SOME KIND OF JOKE?!
?
WHAT'S WRONG?

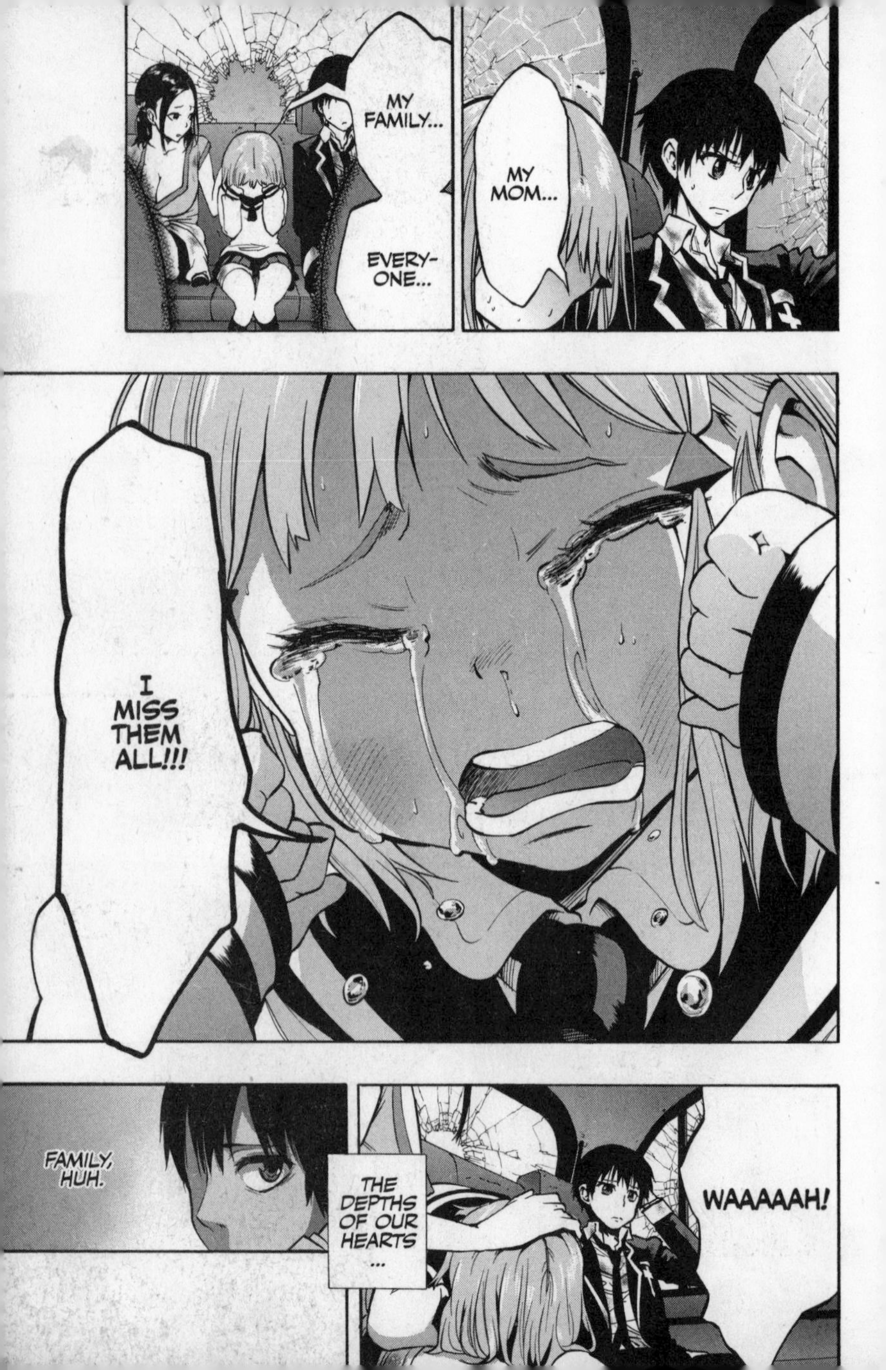
MY MOM...
MY FAMILY...
EVERY-ONE...
I MISS THEM ALL!!!
WAAAAAH!
THE DEPTHS OF OUR HEARTS ...
FAMILY, HUH.

...LIE SHROUDED
IN UNCERTAINTY.

FKROO

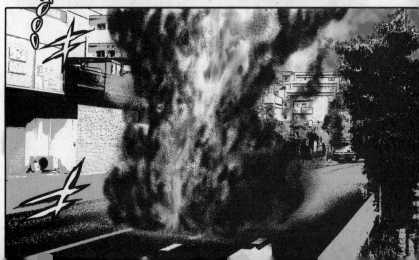

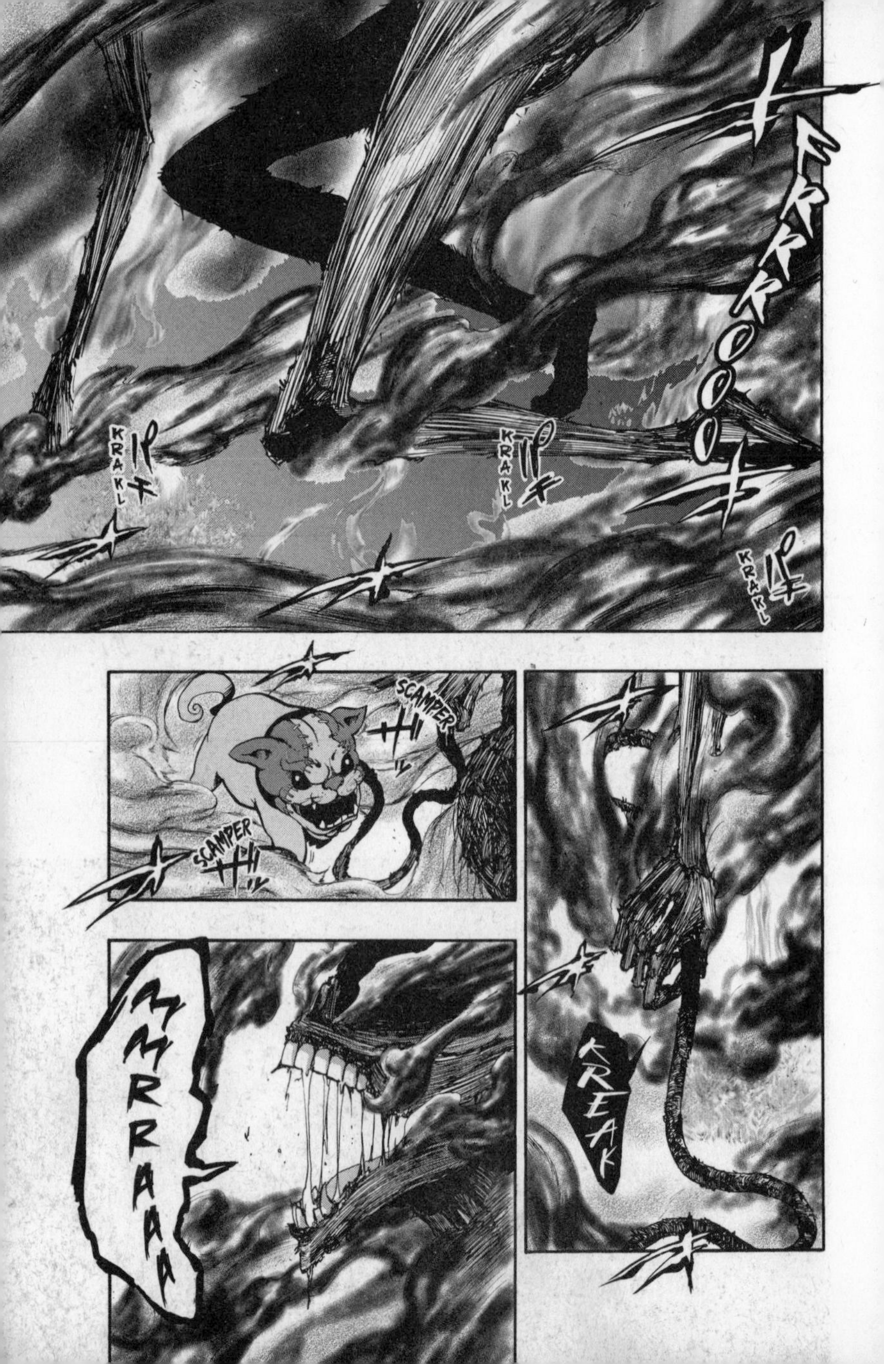
ERRROOO
KRAKL
KRAKL
KRAKL
KREAK
SCAMPER
SCAMPER
MMRRAAA

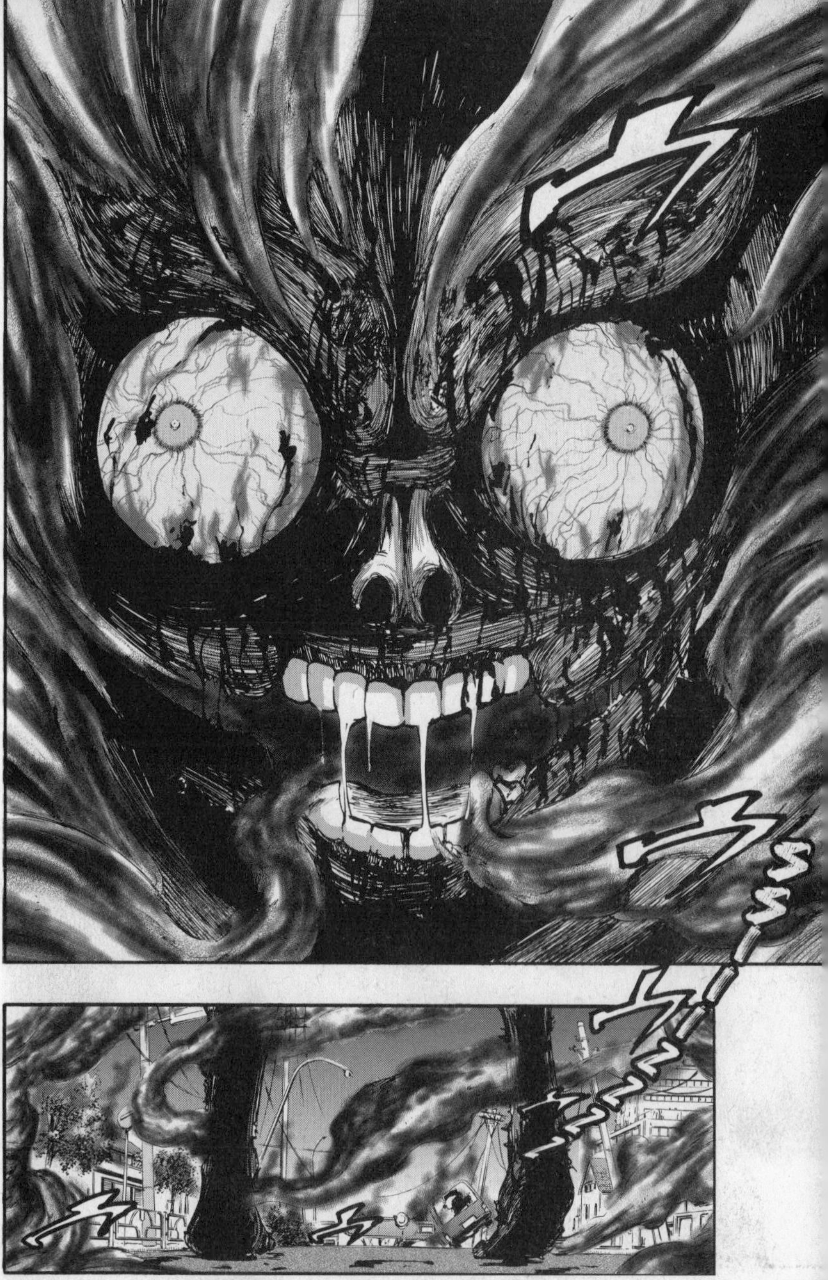
SS

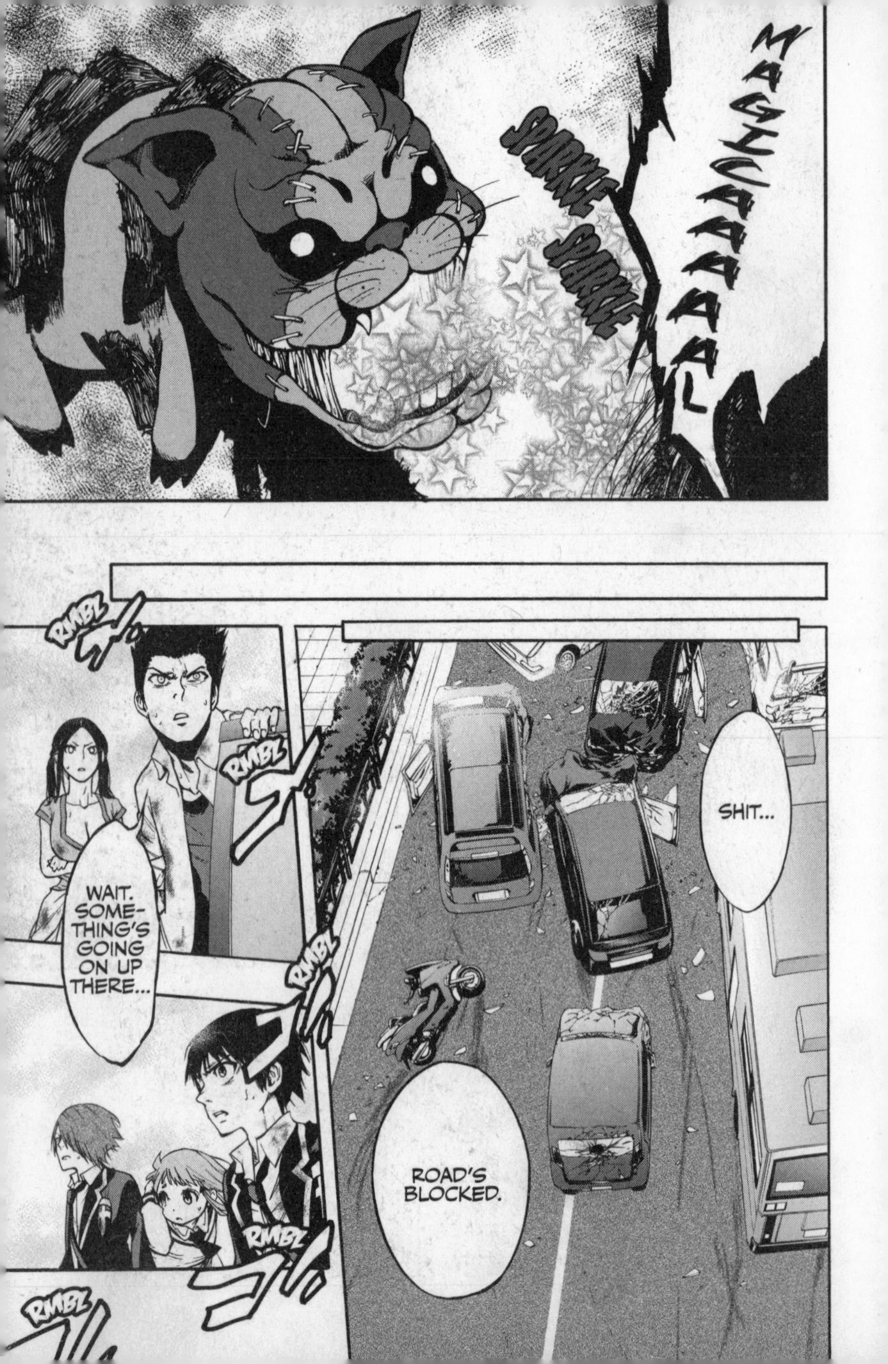
MAGICAAAAAAL
SPARKLE SPARKLE
SHIT...
ROAD'S BLOCKED.
RMBL
RMBL
WAIT. SOME-THING'S GOING ON UP THERE...
RMBL
RMBL
RMBL

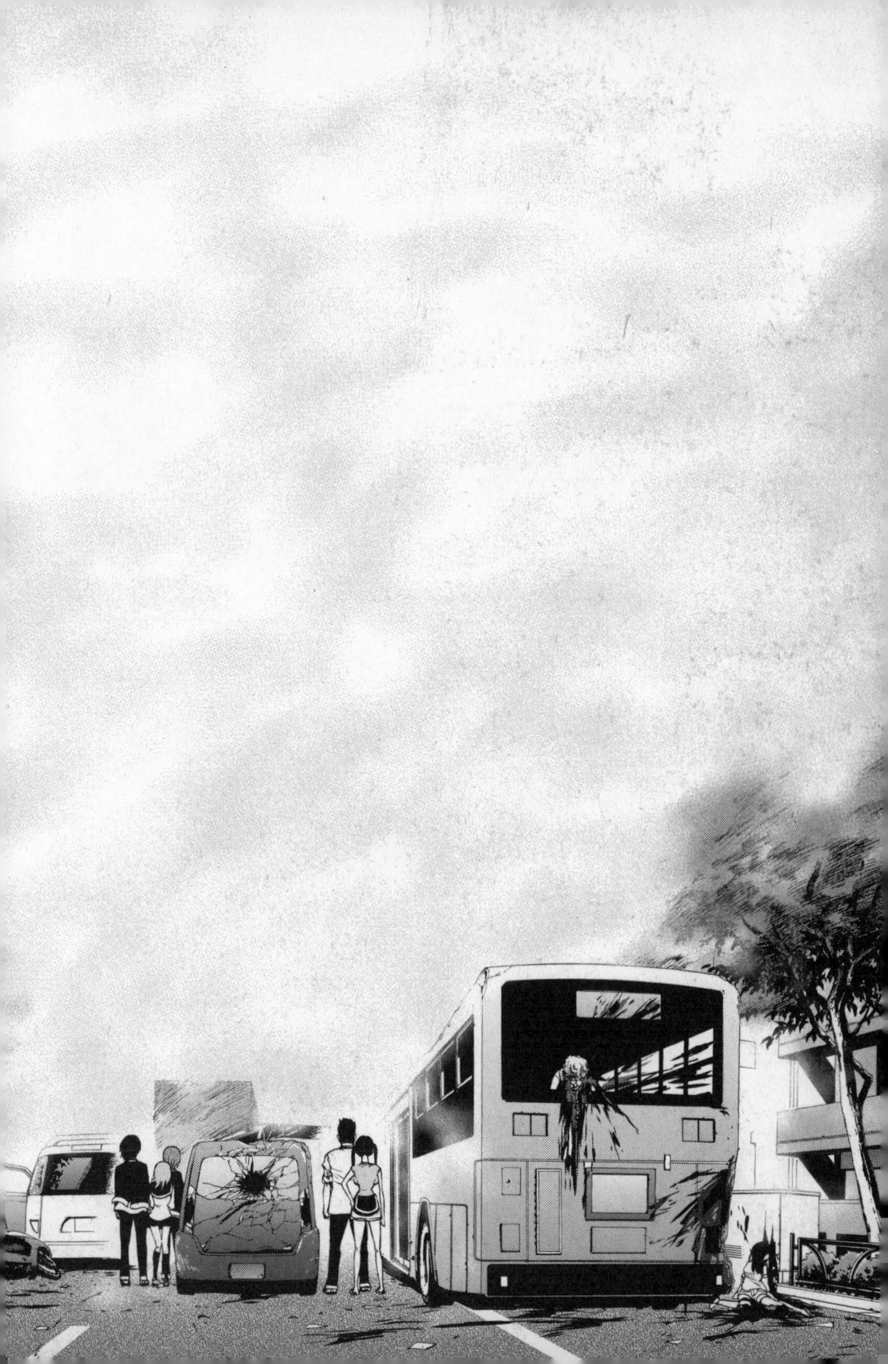

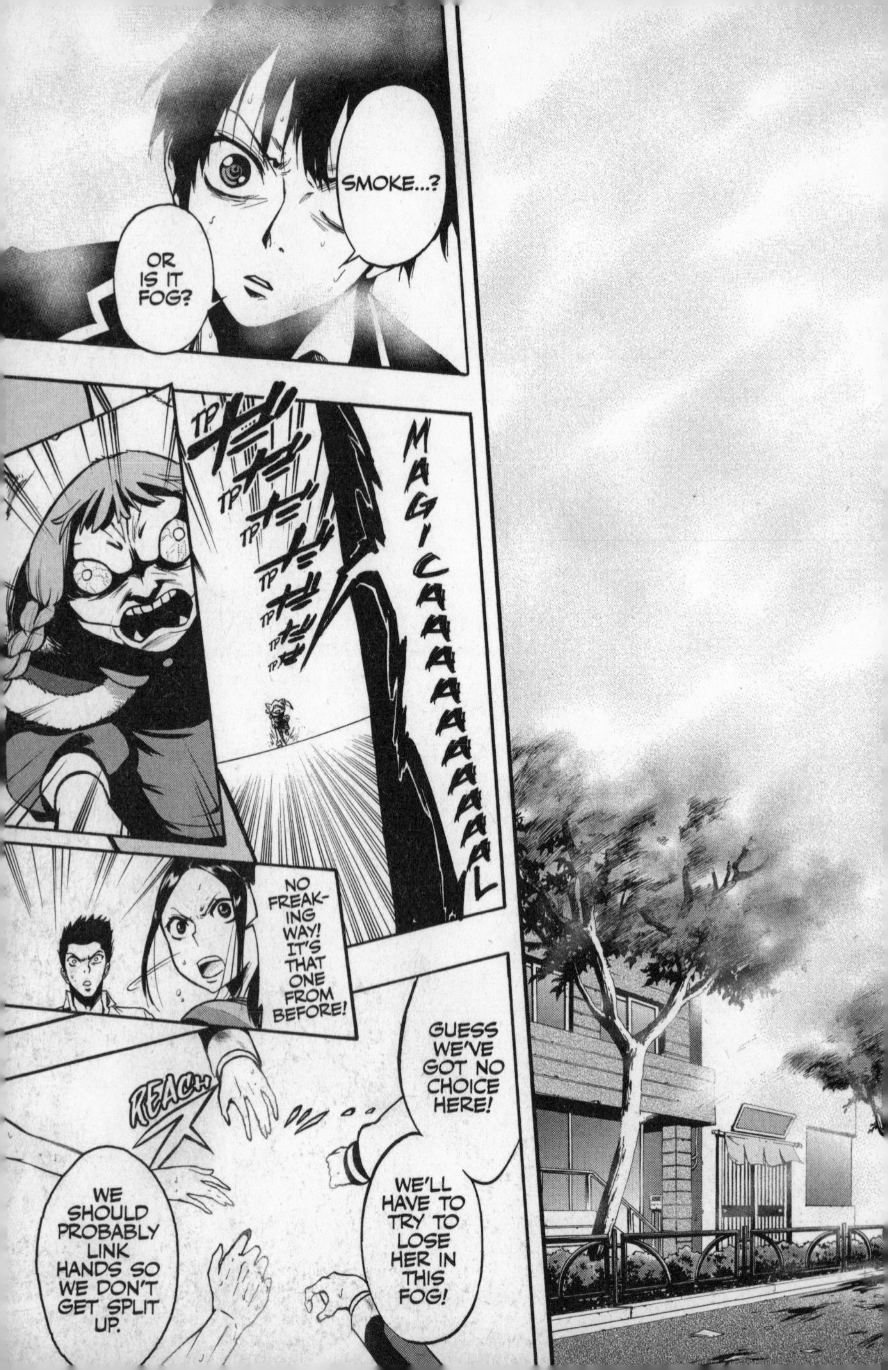
SMOKE...?
OR IS IT FOG?
MAGICAAAAAAAAAL
TP TP TP TP TP TP TP
NO FREAKING WAY! IT'S THAT ONE FROM BEFORE!
GUESS WE'VE GOT NO CHOICE HERE!
WE'LL HAVE TO TRY TO LOSE HER IN THIS FOG!
REACH
WE SHOULD PROBABLY LINK HANDS SO WE DON'T GET SPLIT UP.

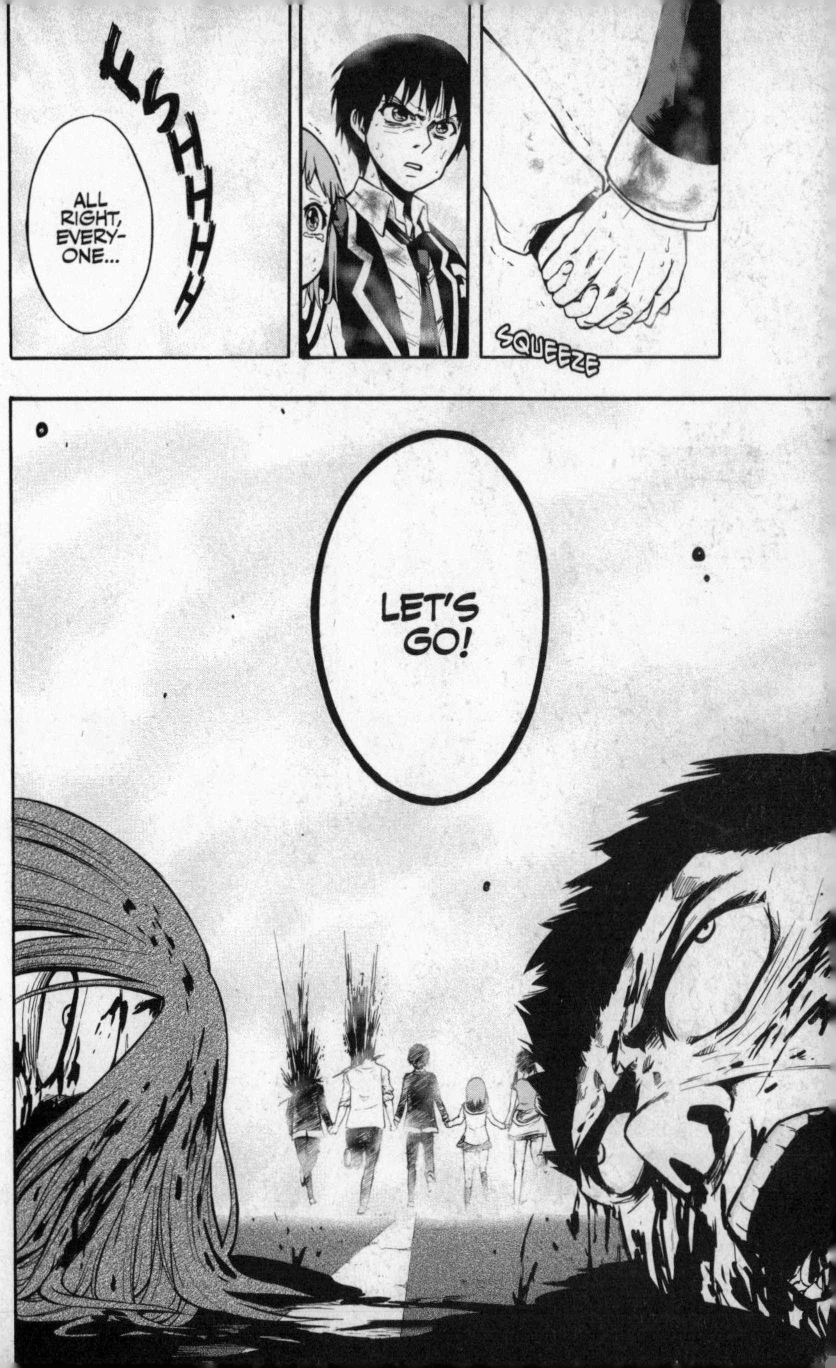
SQUEEZE
KSHHHHH
ALL RIGHT, EVERY-ONE...
LET'S GO!

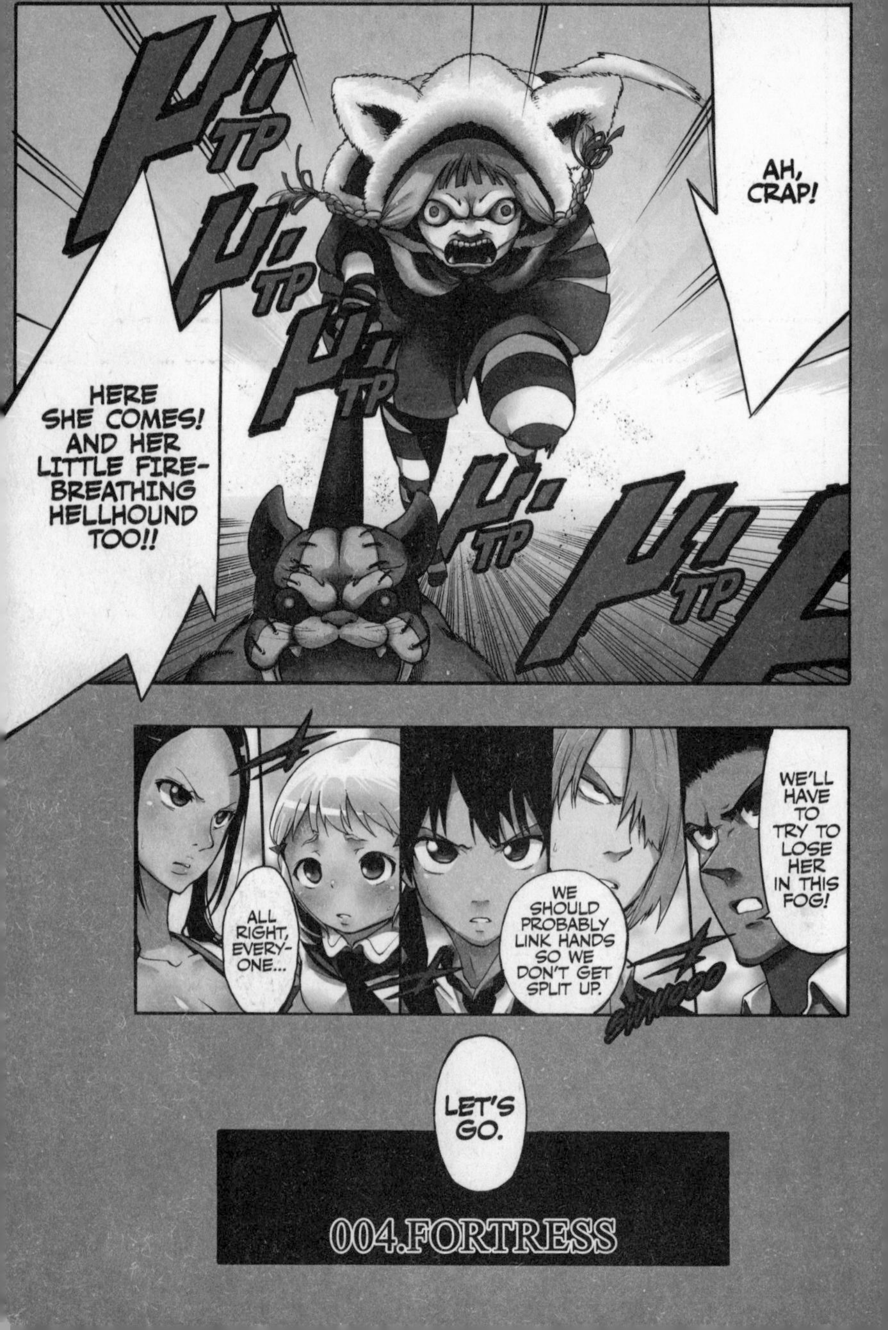
AH, CRAP!
TP
TP
TP
TP
TP
HERE SHE COMES! AND HER LITTLE FIRE-BREATHING HELLHOUND TOO!!
WE'LL HAVE TO TRY TO LOSE HER IN THIS FOG!
WE SHOULD PROBABLY LINK HANDS SO WE DON'T GET SPLIT UP.
ALL RIGHT, EVERY-ONE...
LET'S GO.
004.FORTRESS

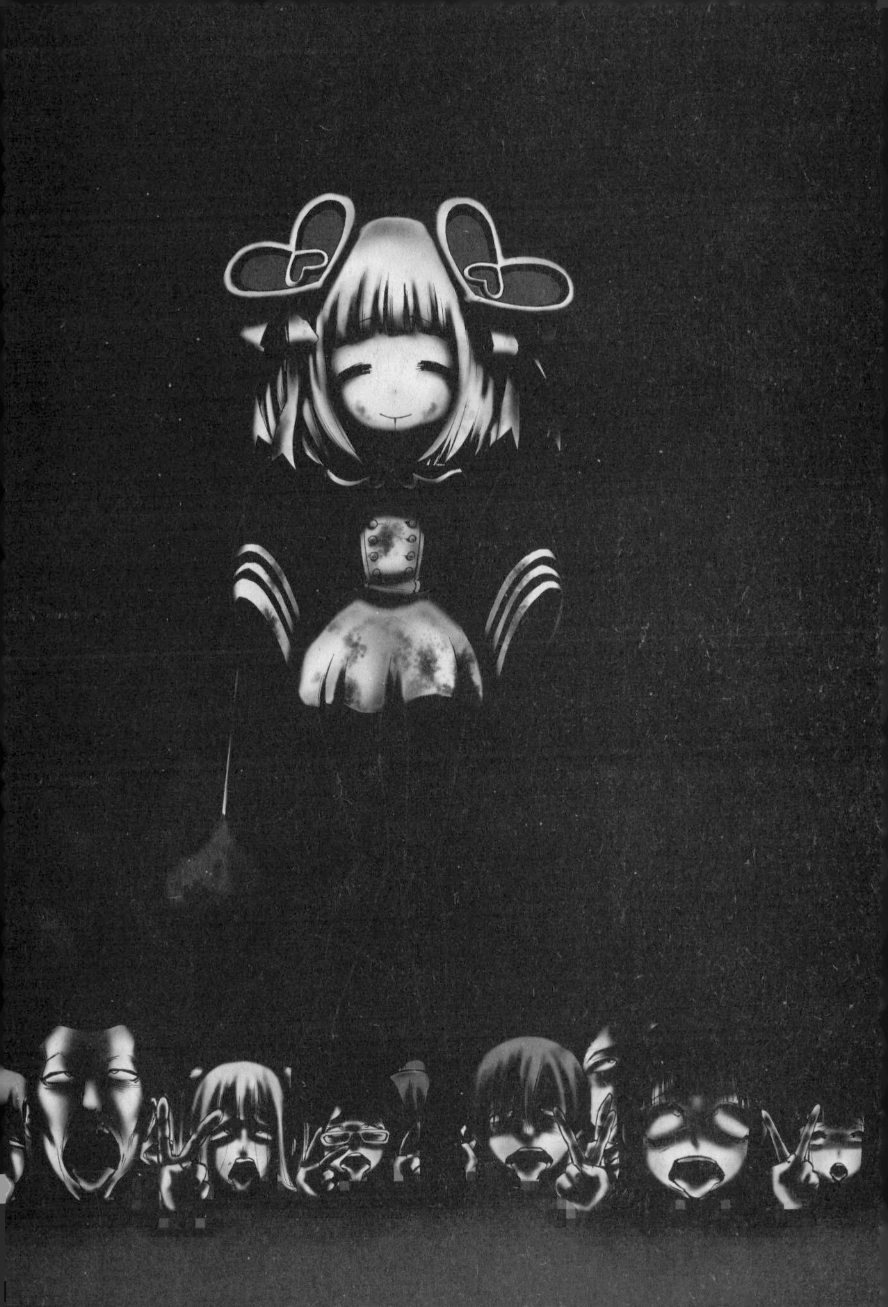

004.FORTRESS

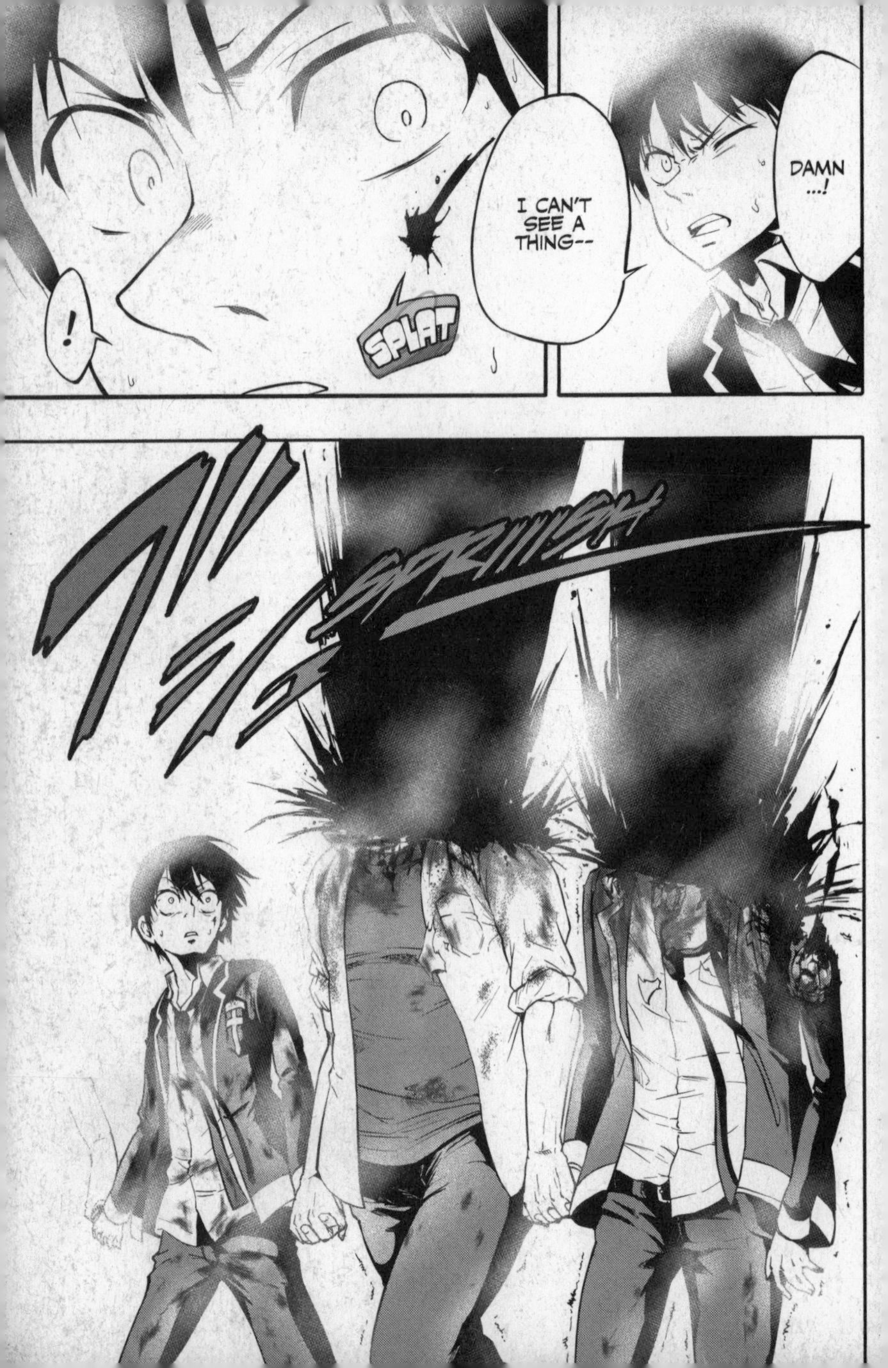
DAMN ...!
I CAN'T SEE A THING--
SPLAT
!

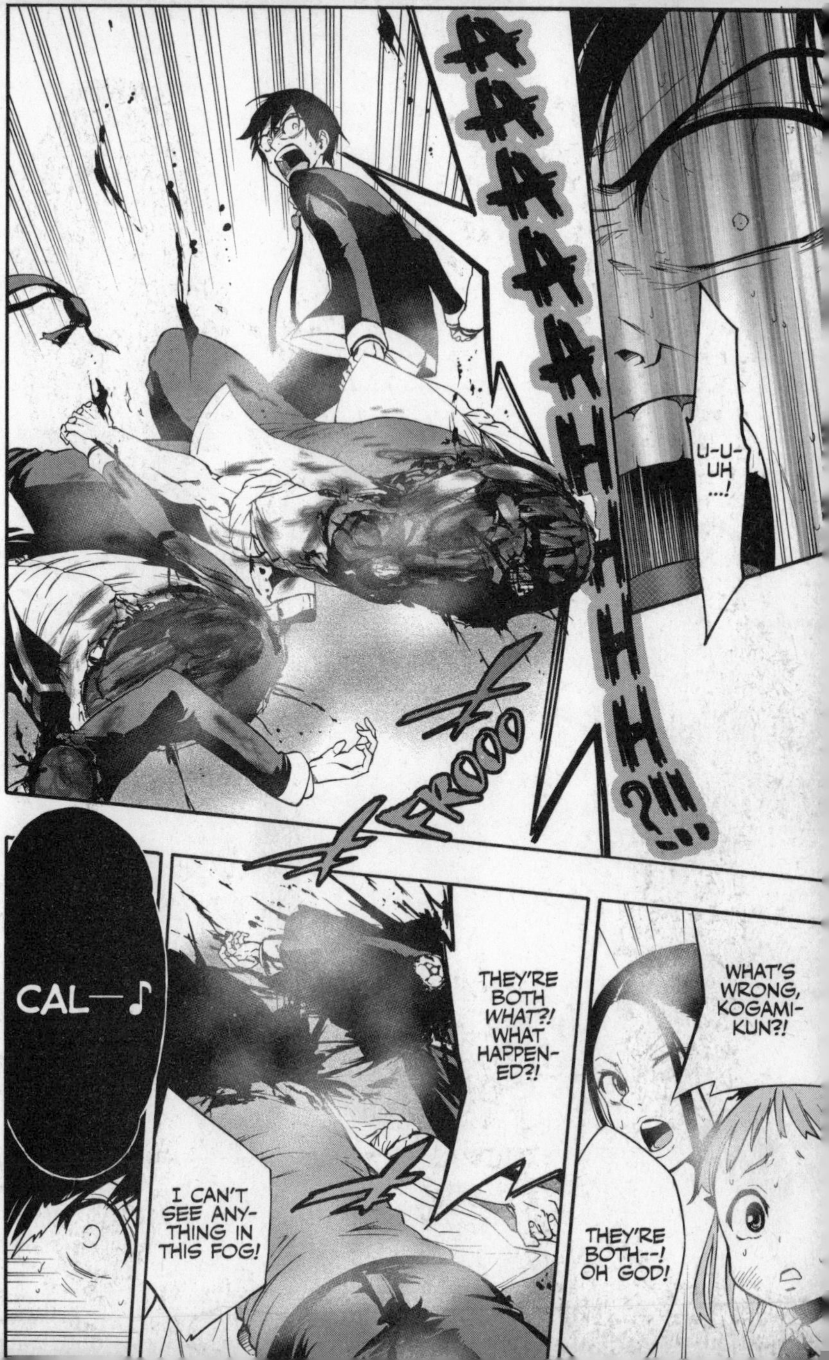
U-U-UH ...!
AAAAAHHHHHH?!!
FKOOO
WHAT'S WRONG, KOGAMI-KUN?!
THEY'RE BOTH--! OH GOD!
THEY'RE BOTH WHAT?! WHAT HAPPENED?!
I CAN'T SEE ANYTHING IN THIS FOG!
CAL—♪

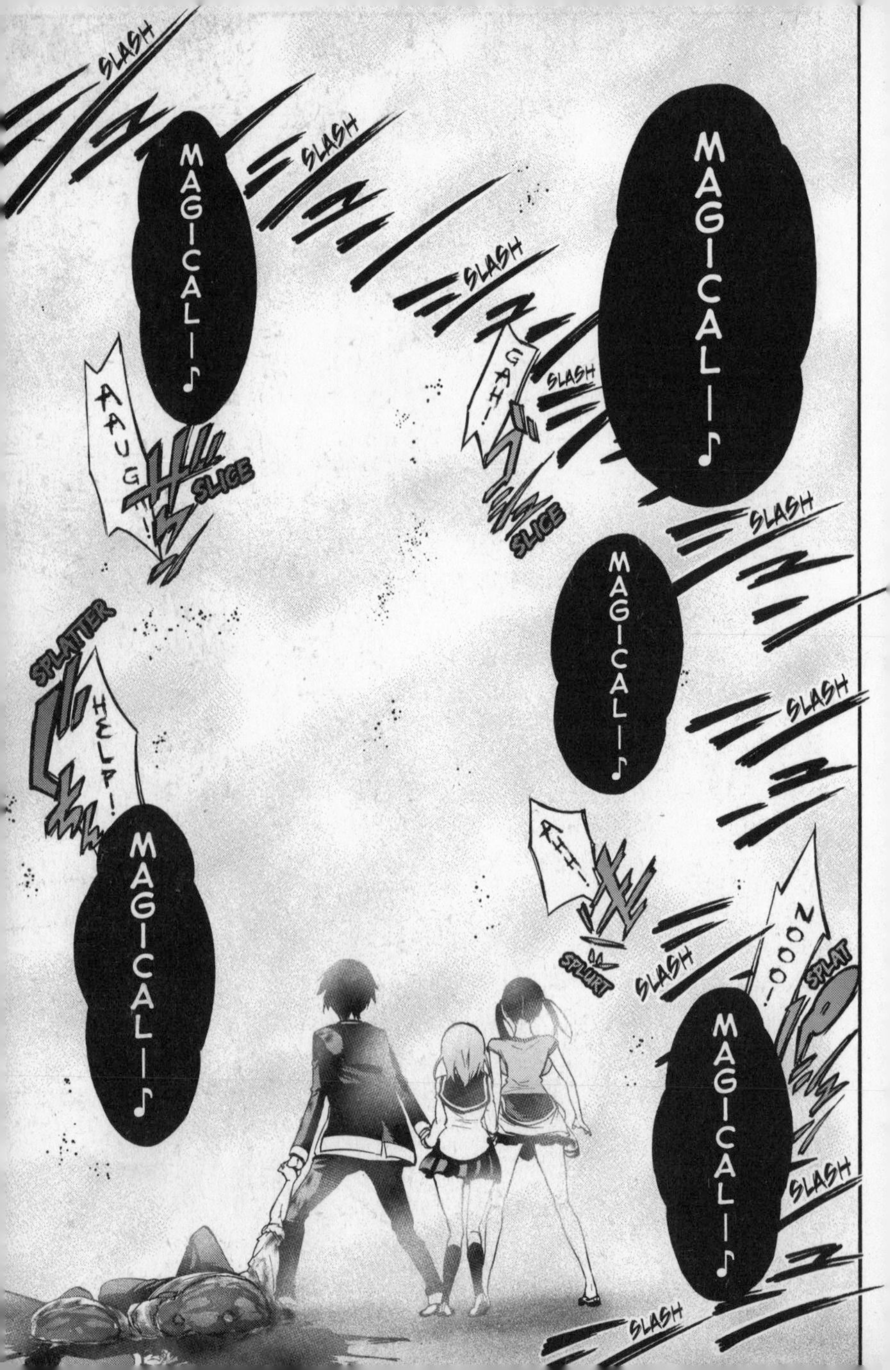

MAGICAL!♪
SLASH
SLASH
GAH!
SLICE
SLASH
SLASH
MAGICAL!♪
SLASH
AAUGH!
SLICE
MAGICAL!♪
SLASH
SLASH
HELP!
SPLATTER
MAGICAL!♪
AH!
SPLURT
SLASH
NOOOO!
SPLAT
MAGICAL!♪
SLASH
SLASH

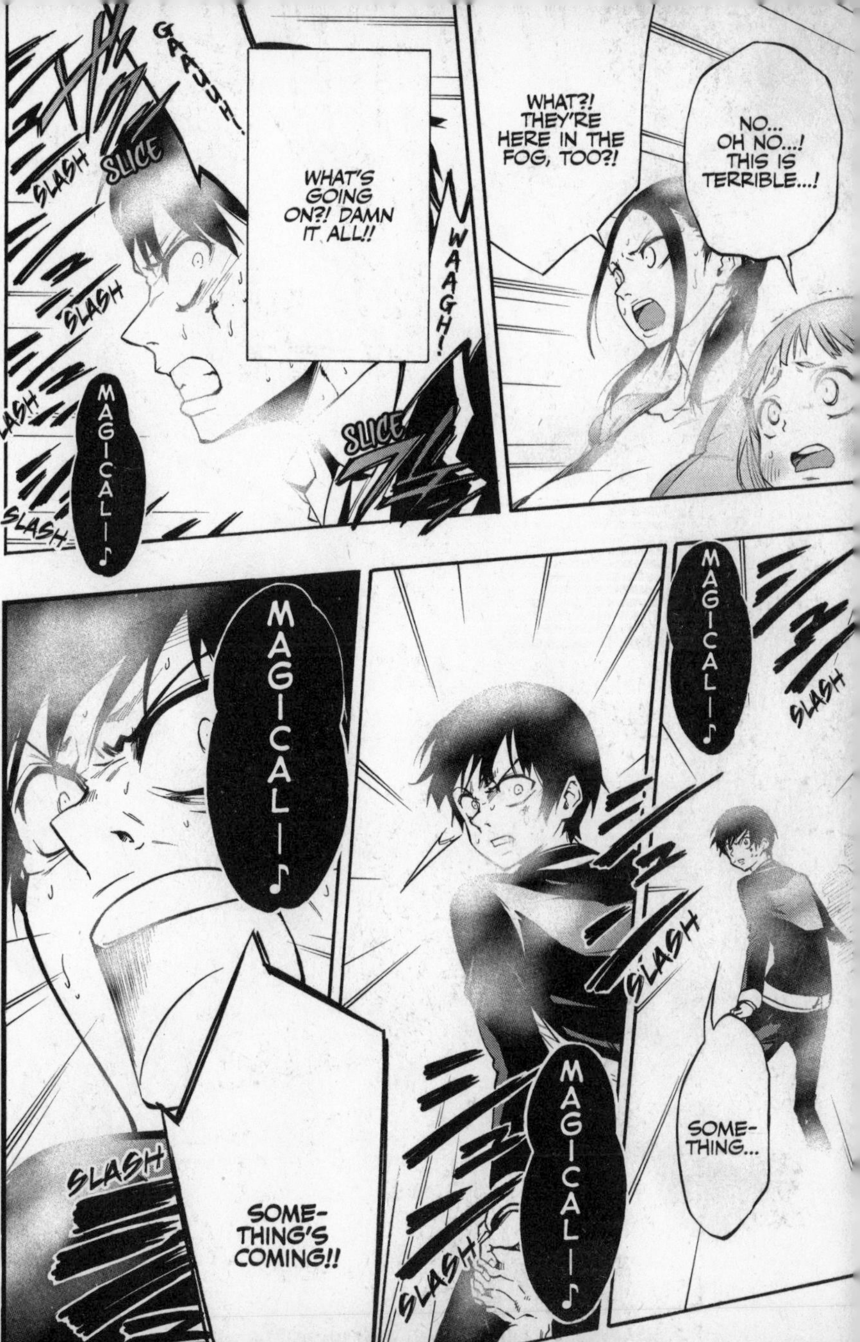
NO... OH NO...! THIS IS TERRIBLE...!
WHAT?! THEY'RE HERE IN THE FOG, TOO?!
WAAAGH!
SLICE
WHAT'S GOING ON?! DAMN IT ALL!!
GAAUUH!
SLICE
SLASH
SLASH
SLASH
SLASH
MAGICAL♪
MAGICAL♪
SLASH
SOME-THING...
SLASH
MAGICAL♪
SLASH
MAGICAL♪
SOME-THING'S COMING!!
SLASH

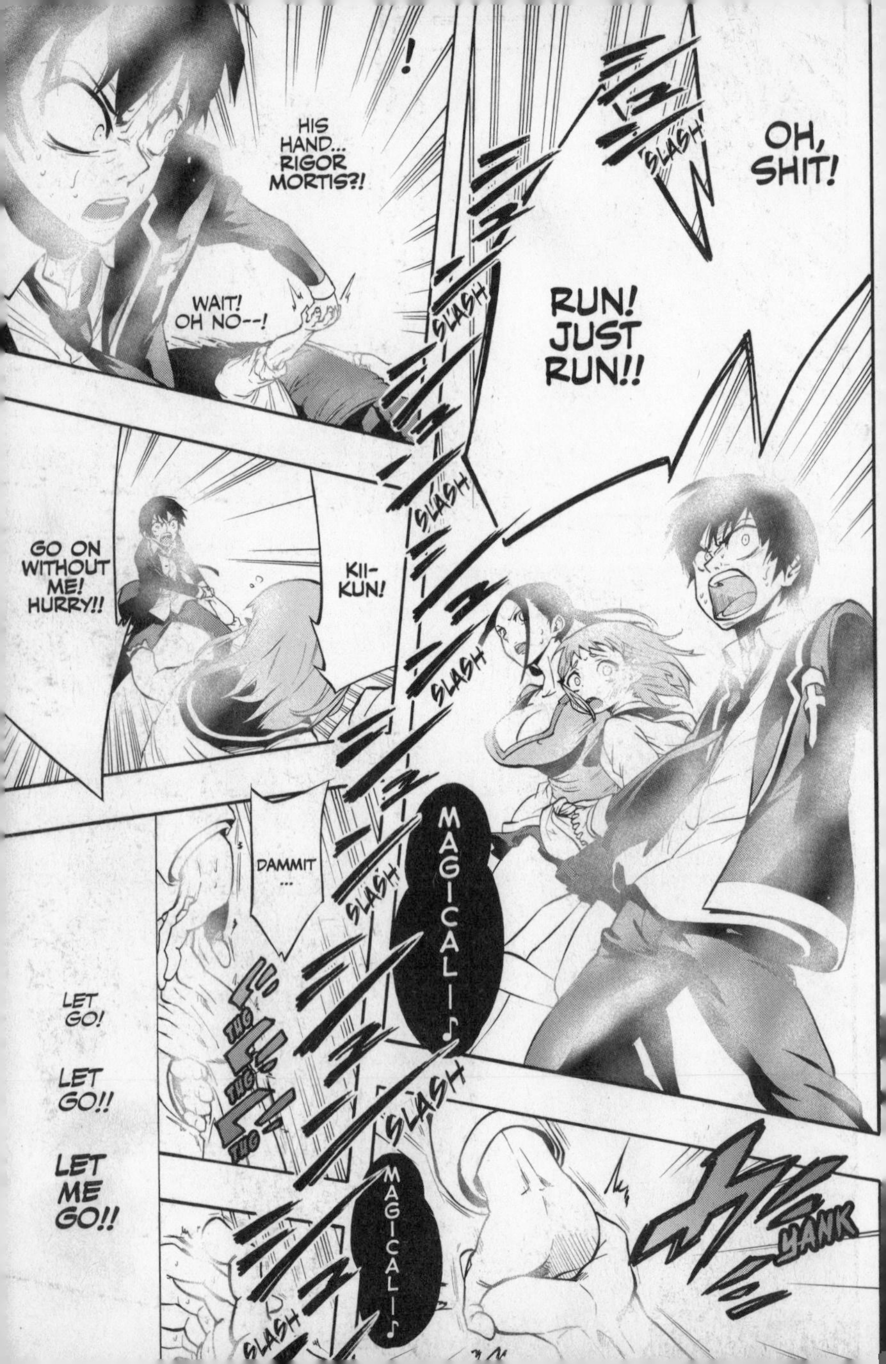

OH, SHIT!
SLASH
!
HIS HAND... RIGOR MORTIS?!
WAIT! OH NO--!
RUN! JUST RUN!!
SLASH
SLASH
SLASH
KII-KUN!
GO ON WITHOUT ME! HURRY!!
MAGICAL♪
SLASH
DAMMIT...
THG THG THG
LET GO!
LET GO!!
LET ME GO!!
YANK
SLASH
MAGICAL♪
SLASH

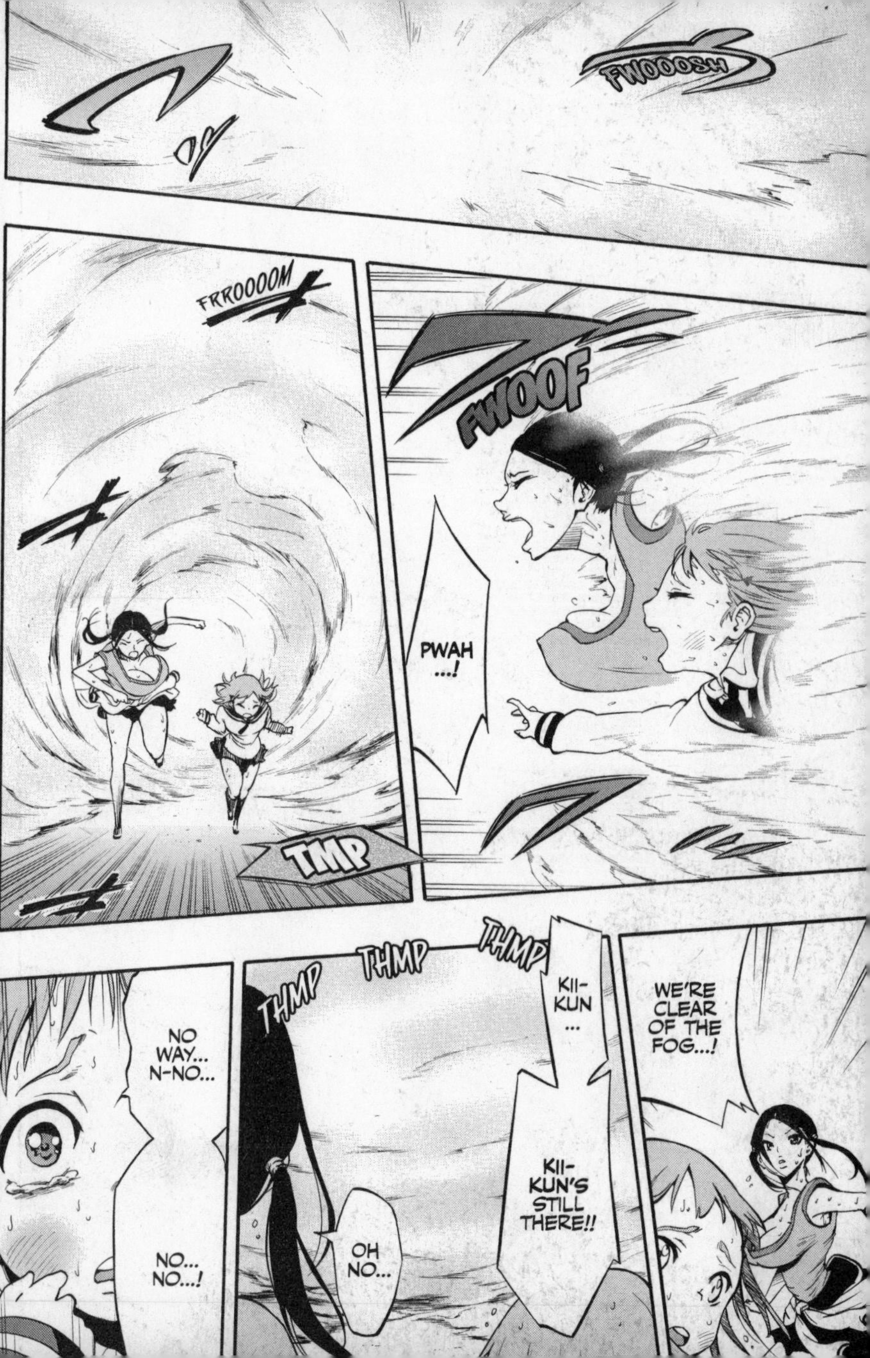
FWOOOSH
FWOOF
PWAH ...!
FRROOOOM
TMP
WE'RE CLEAR OF THE FOG...!
THMP
THMP
THMP
KII-KUN ...
KII-KUN'S STILL THERE!!
OH NO...
NO WAY... N-NO...
NO... NO...!

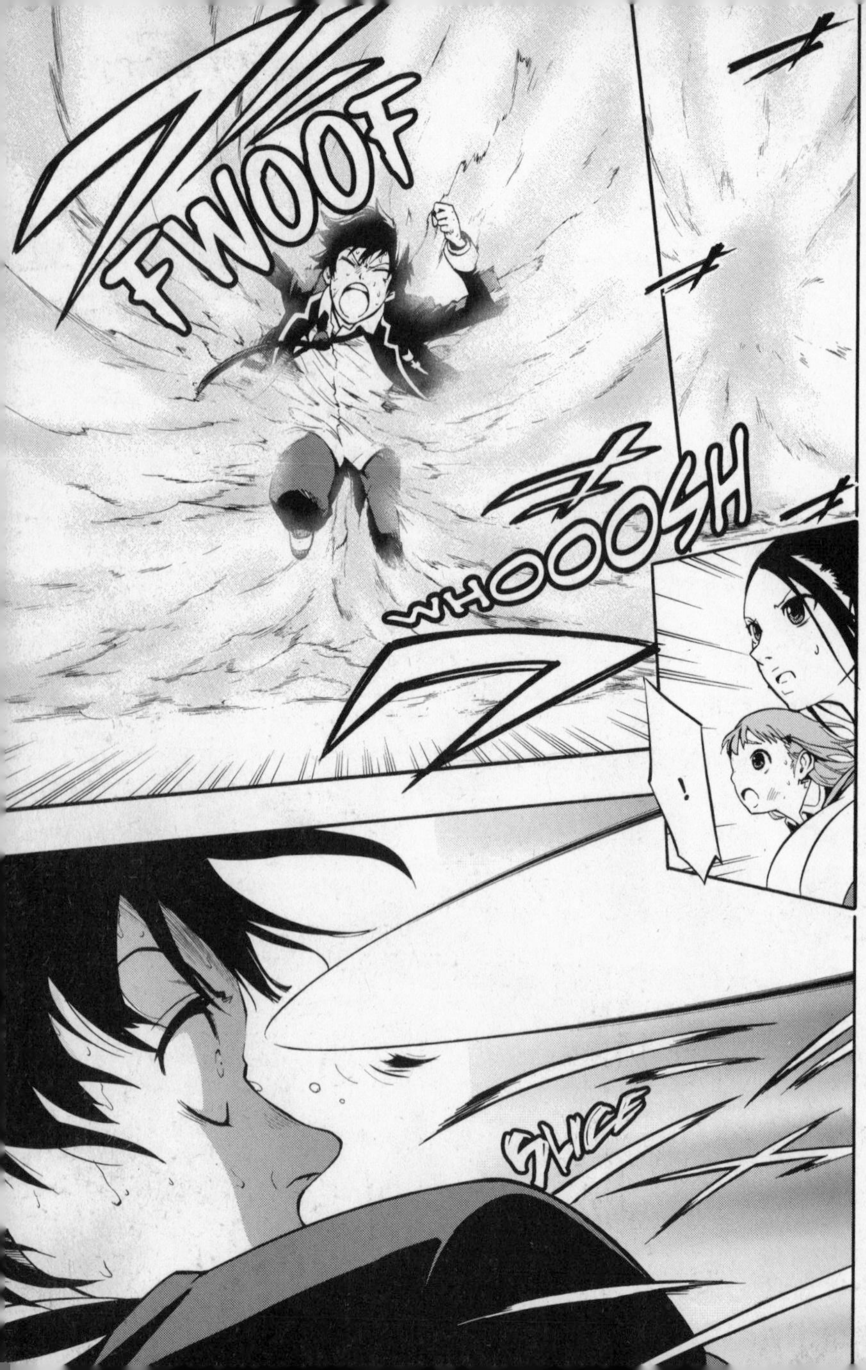
FWOOF
WHOOOOSH
!
SLICE

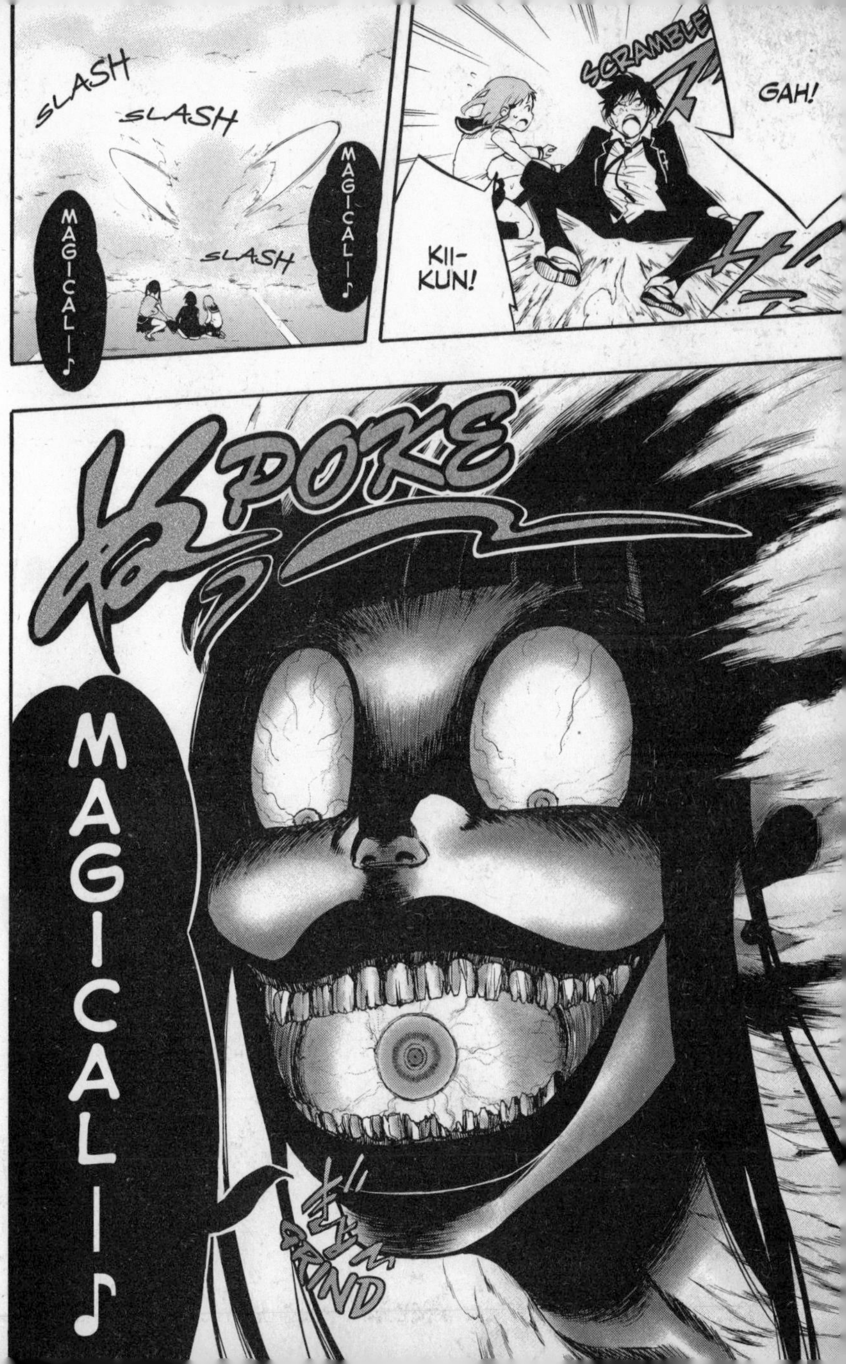
SCRAMBLE
GAH!
KII-KUN!
MAGICAL—♪
SLASH
SLASH
SLASH
MAGICAL—♪
POKE
MAGICAL—♪
GRIND

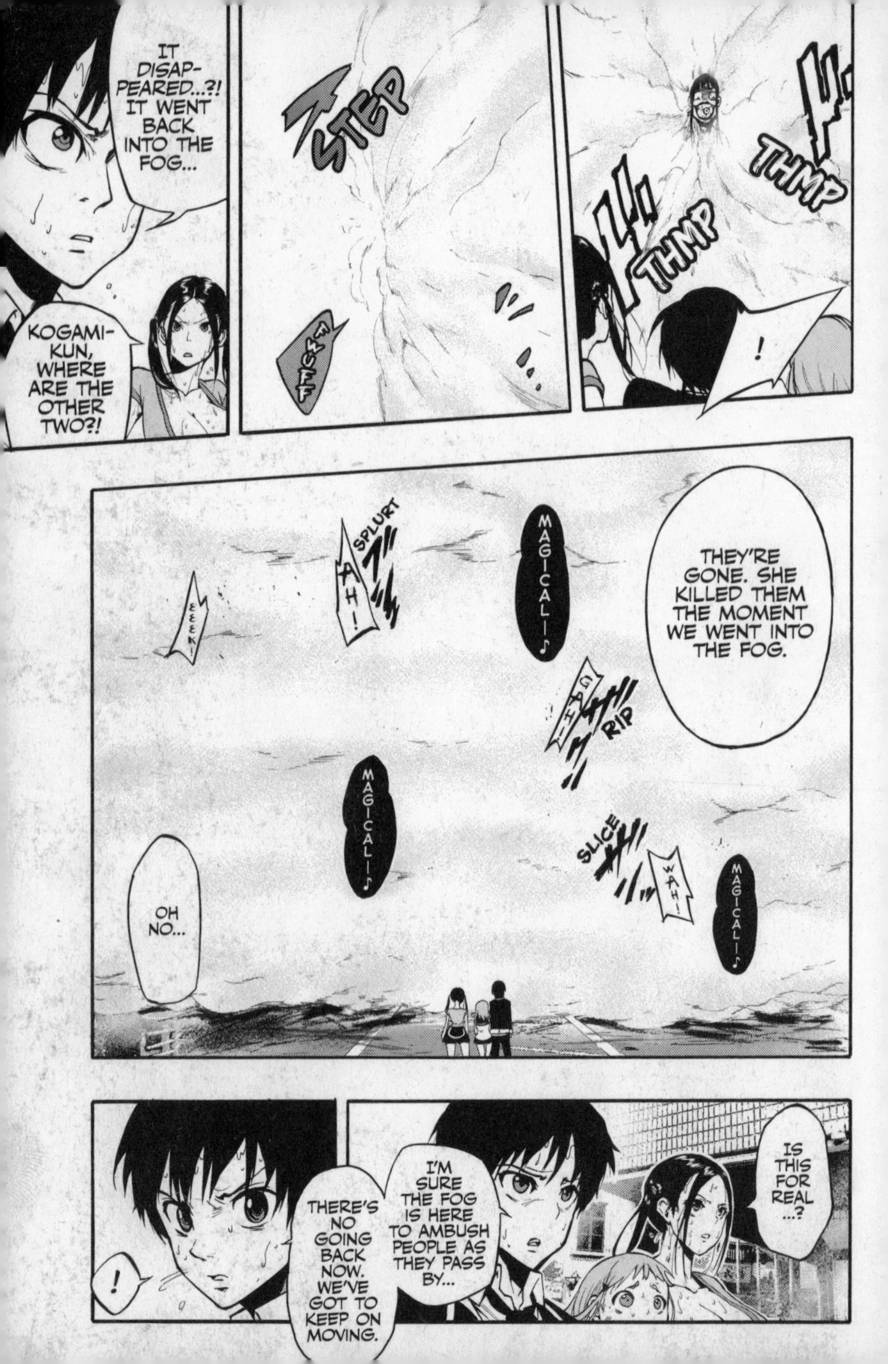
THMP
THMP
!
STEP
FWUFF
IT DISAPPEARED...?! IT WENT BACK INTO THE FOG...
KOGAMI-KUN, WHERE ARE THE OTHER TWO?!
THEY'RE GONE. SHE KILLED THEM THE MOMENT WE WENT INTO THE FOG.
MAGICAL!♪
SPLURT
AH!
EEEK!
GAH!
RIP
SLICE
WAH!
MAGICAL!♪
MAGICAL!♪
OH NO...
IS THIS FOR REAL...?
I'M SURE THE FOG IS HERE TO AMBUSH PEOPLE AS THEY PASS BY...
THERE'S NO GOING BACK NOW. WE'VE GOT TO KEEP ON MOVING.
!

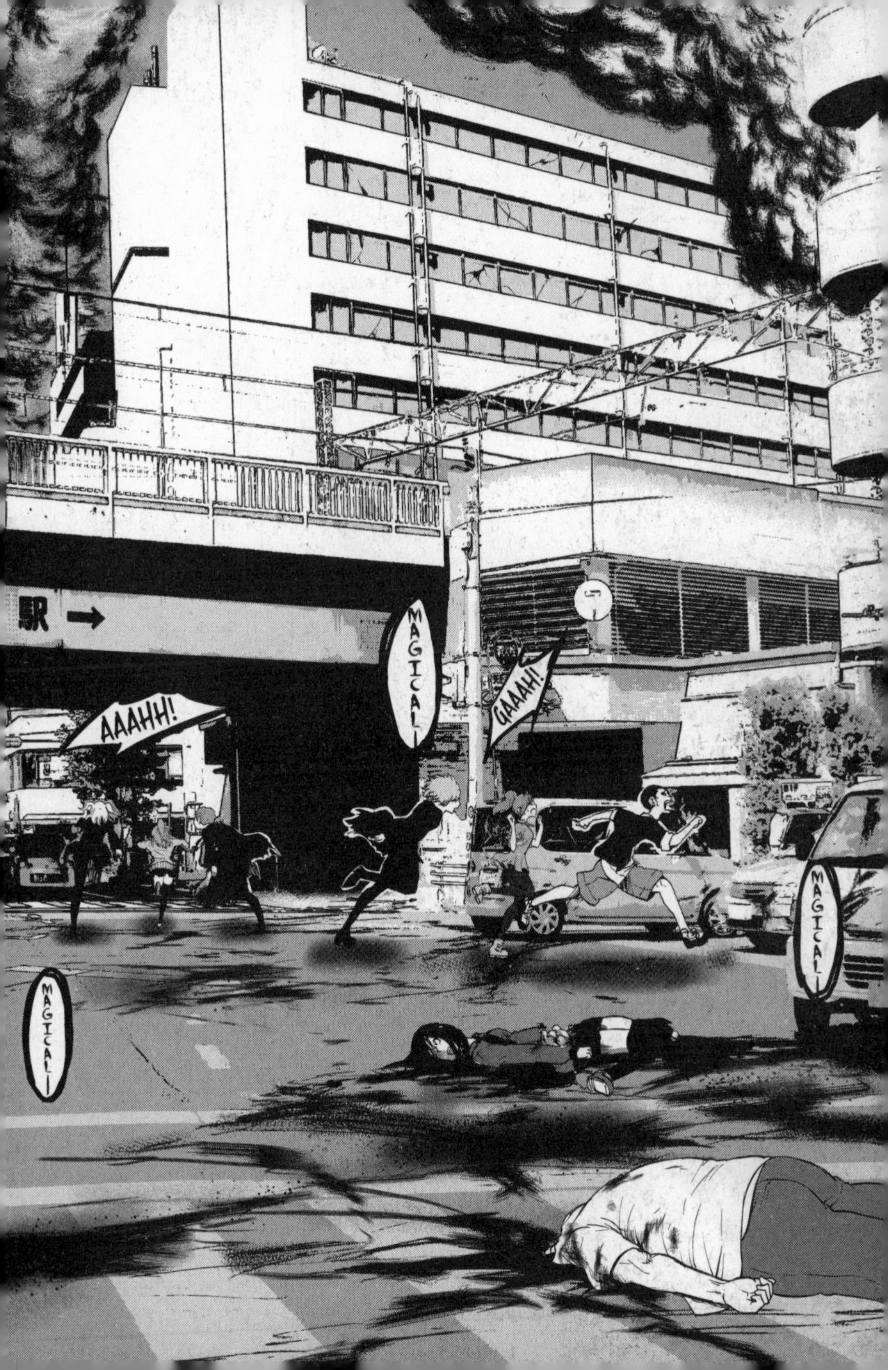

MAGICAL!
GAAAH!
駅
AAAHH!
MAGICAL!
MAGICAL!

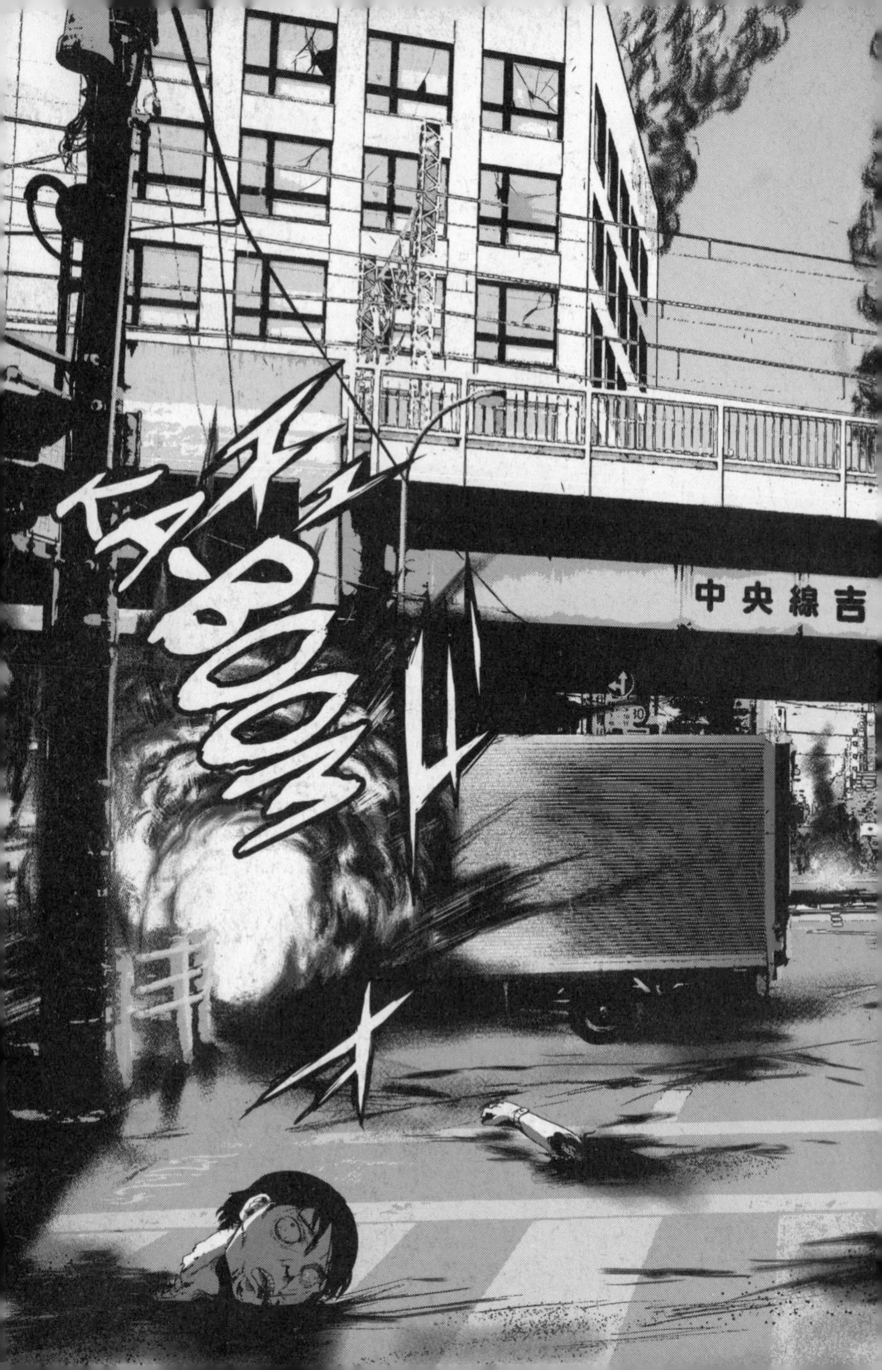
KA-BOOM!!
中央線吉

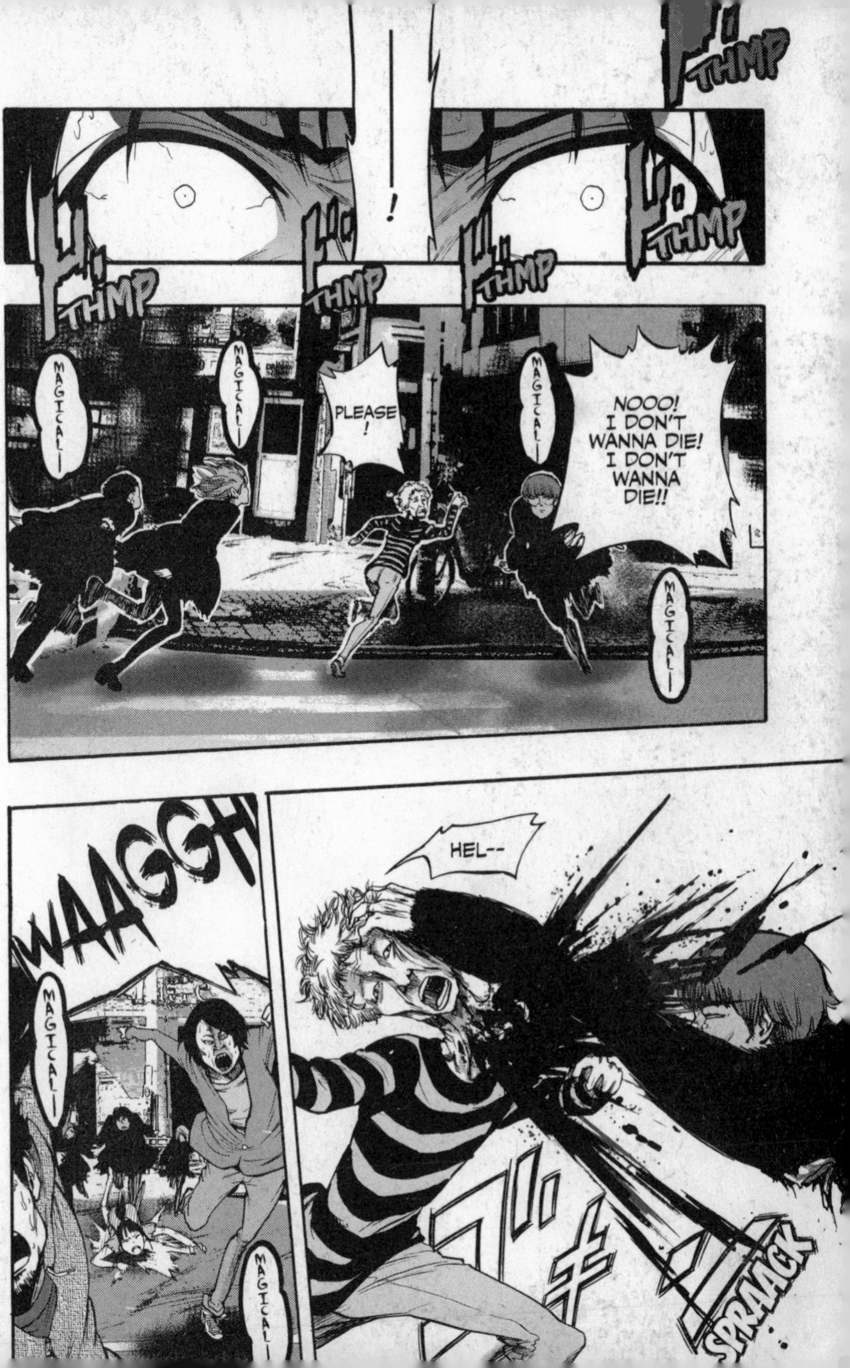
THMP
!
THMP
THMP
THMP
THMP
MAGICAL-I
NOOO! I DON'T WANNA DIE! I DON'T WANNA DIE!!
MAGICAL-I
PLEASE!
MAGICAL-I
MAGICAL-I
HEL--
SPRAACK
WAAGH
MAGICAL-I
MAGICAL-I

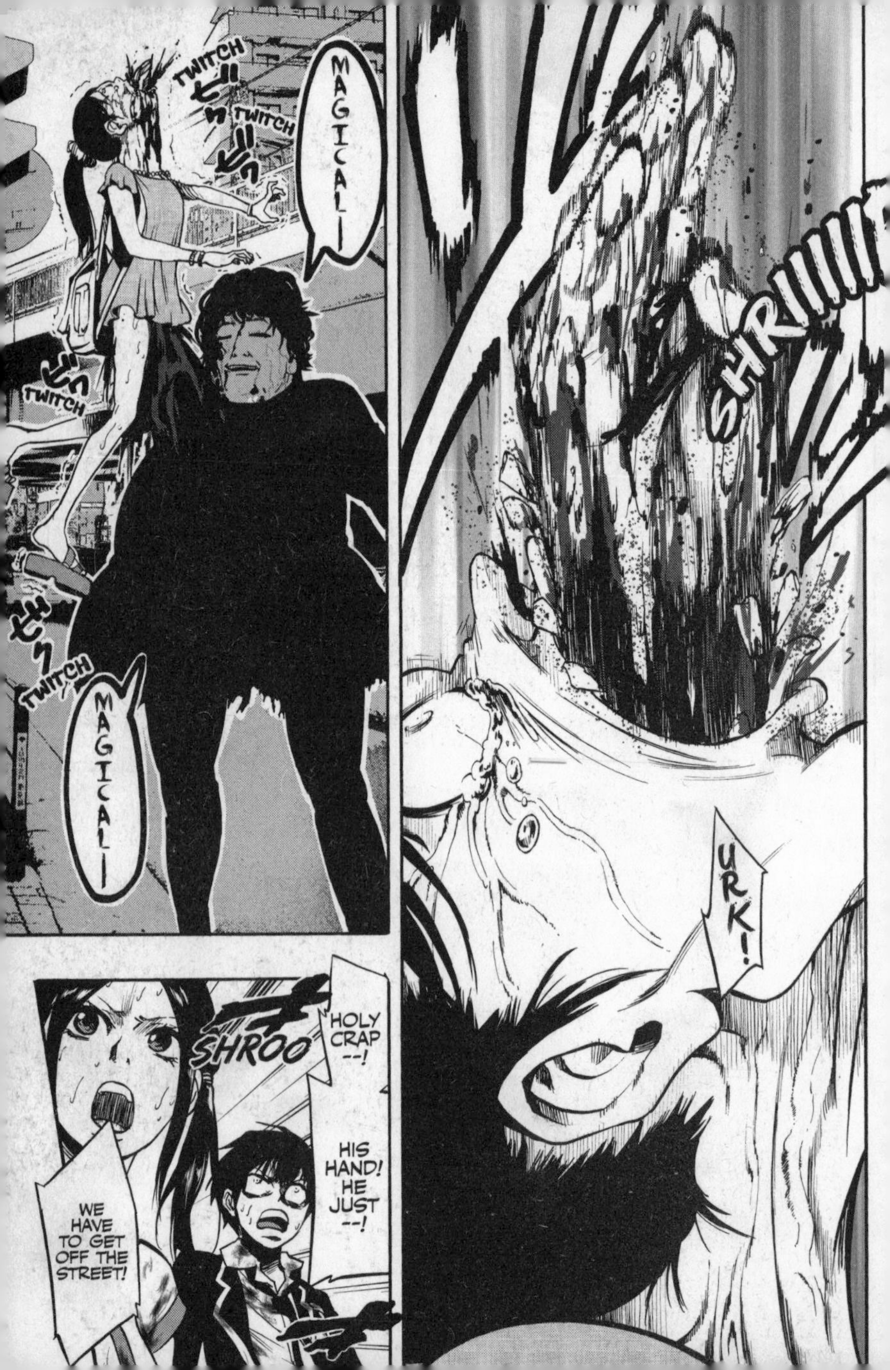
SHRIIIII
URK!
MAGICALI
TWITCH
TWITCH
TWITCH
MAGICALI
TWITCH
HOLY CRAP --!
SHROO
HIS HAND! HE JUST --!
WE HAVE TO GET OFF THE STREET!

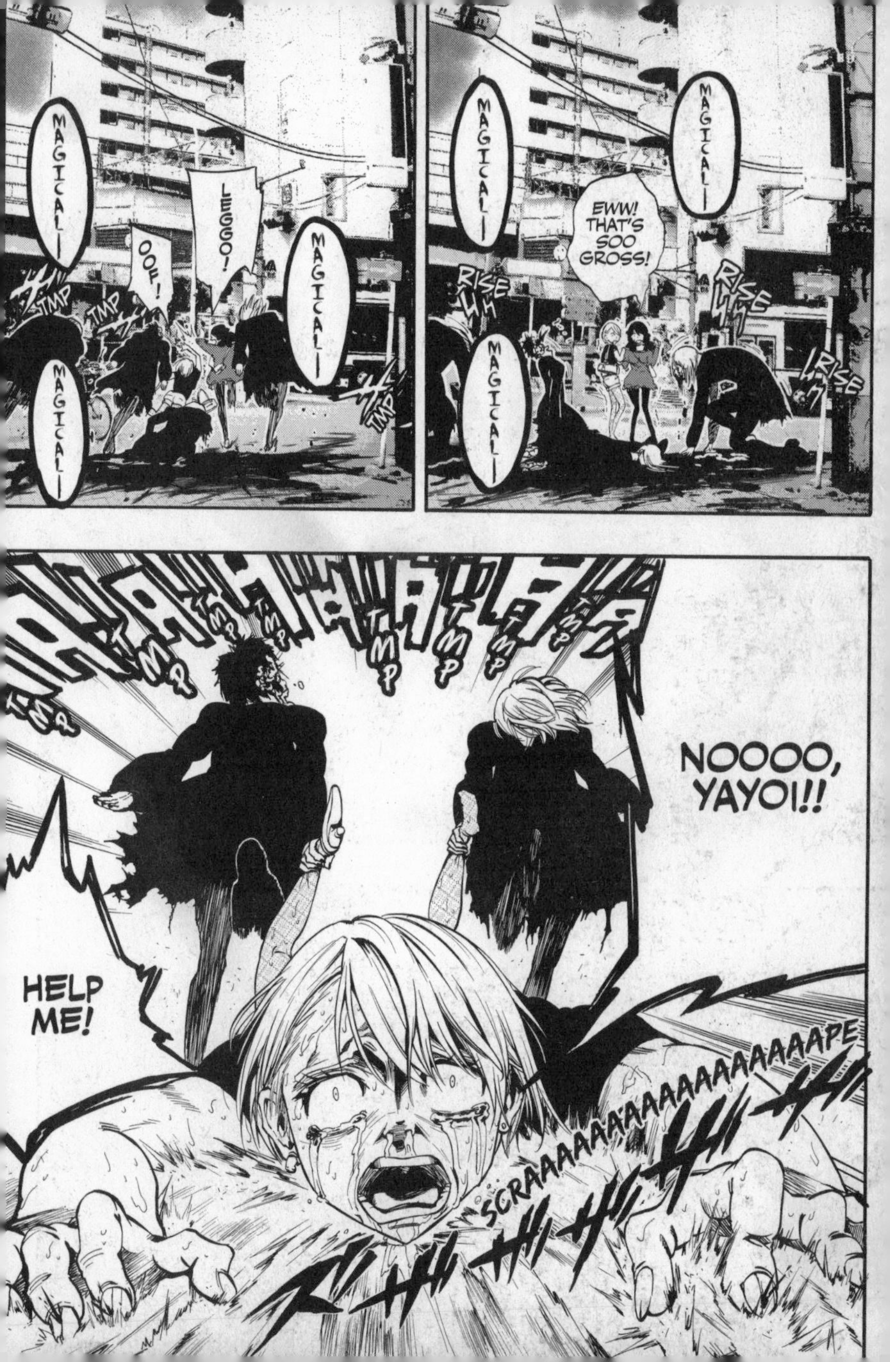
MAGICAL!
MAGICAL!
EWW! THAT'S SOO GROSS!
RISE
RISE
RISE
MAGICAL!
MAGICAL!
LEGGO!
OOF!
MAGICAL!
TMP
TMP
TMP
MAGICAL!
TMP TMP TMP TMP TMP TMP TMP
NOOOO, YAYOI!!
HELP ME!
SCRAAAAAAAAAAAAAAAPE

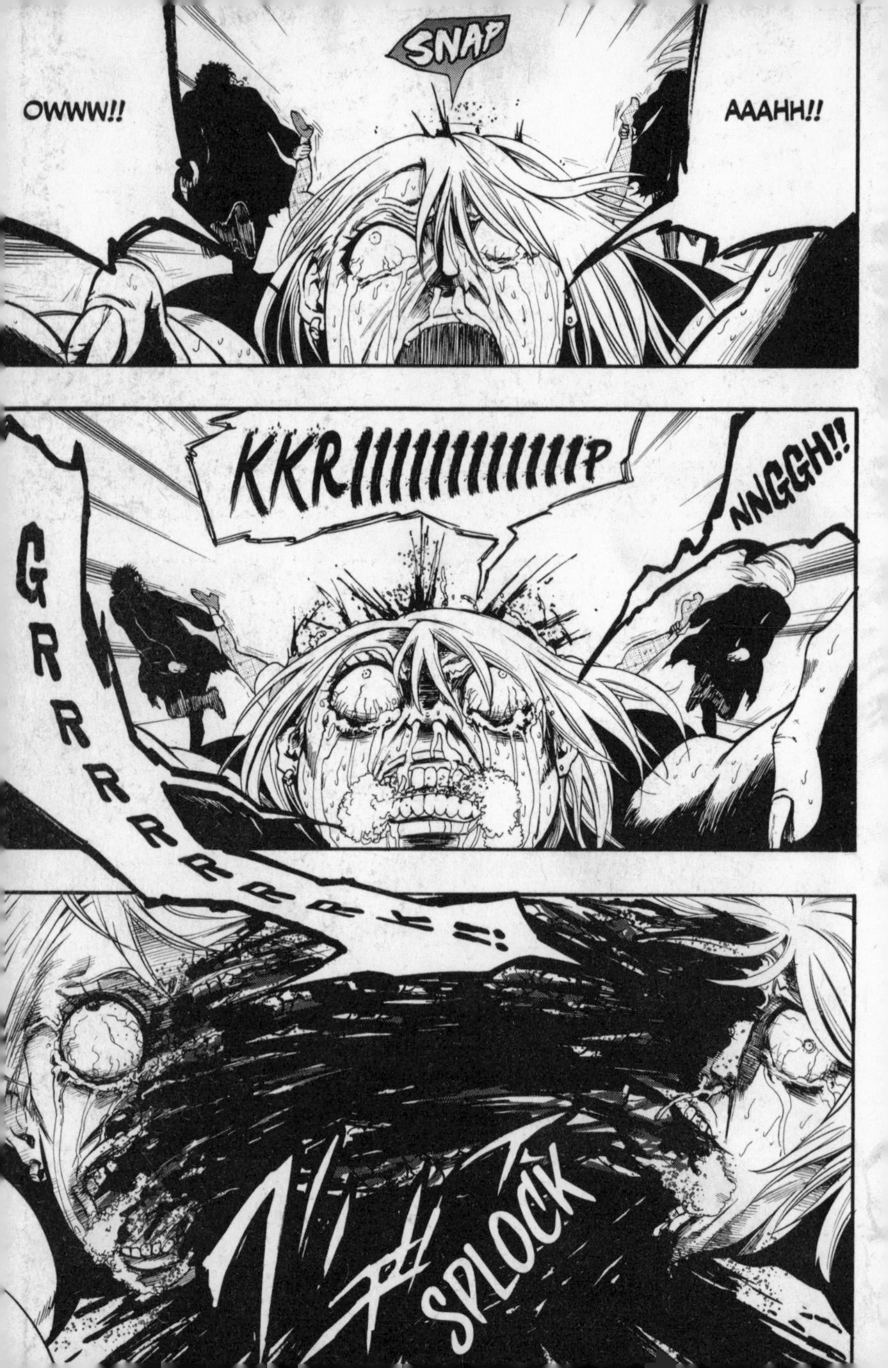

AAAHH!!
SNAP
OWWW!!
NNGGH!!
KKRIIIIIIIIIIIIP
GRRRRRRRRY!!
SPLOCK

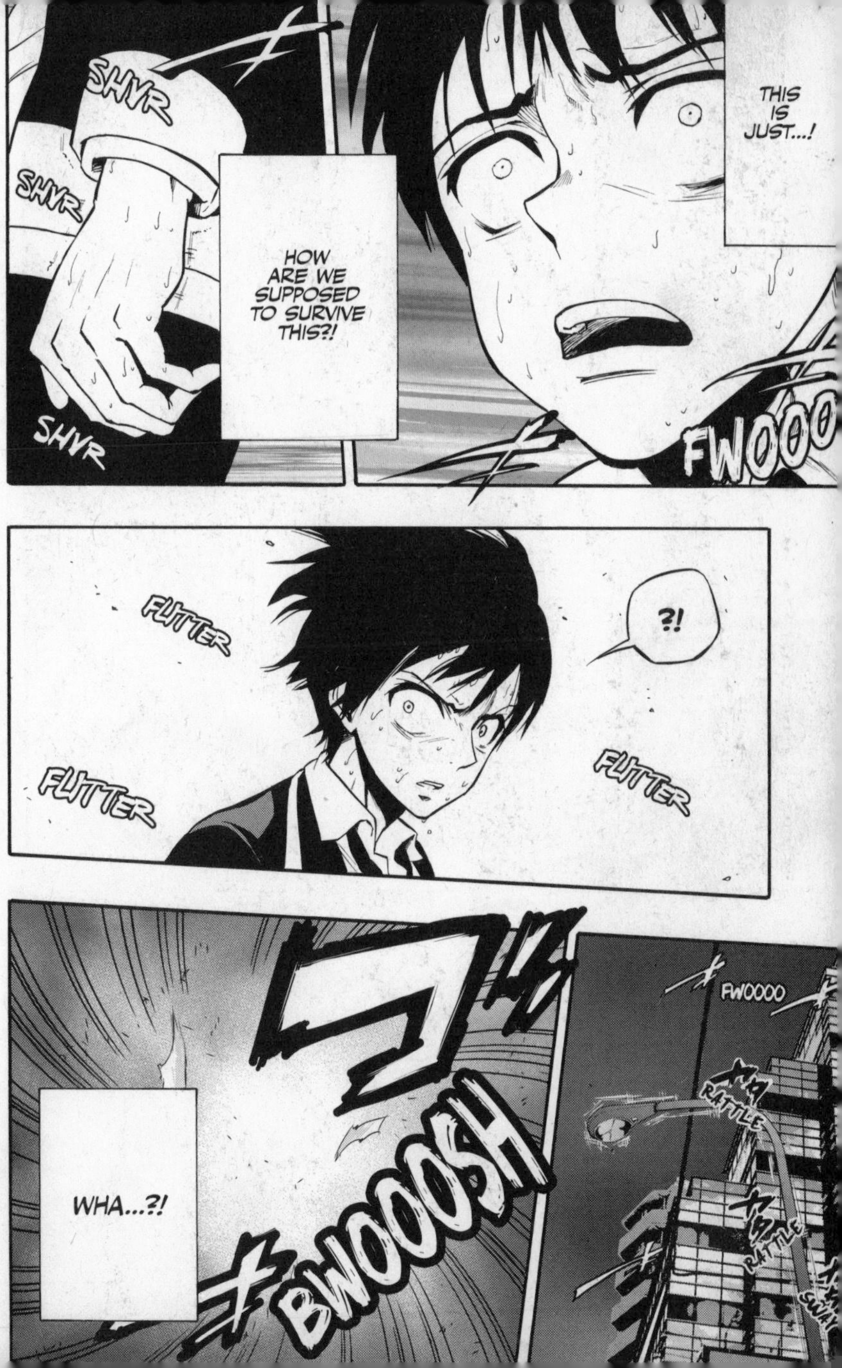
THIS IS JUST...!
FWOOO
SHVR
SHVR
HOW ARE WE SUPPOSED TO SURVIVE THIS?!
SHVR
?!
FLUTTER
FLUTTER
FLUTTER
FWOOOO
RATTLE
RATTLE
SWAY
BWOOOSH
WHA...?!

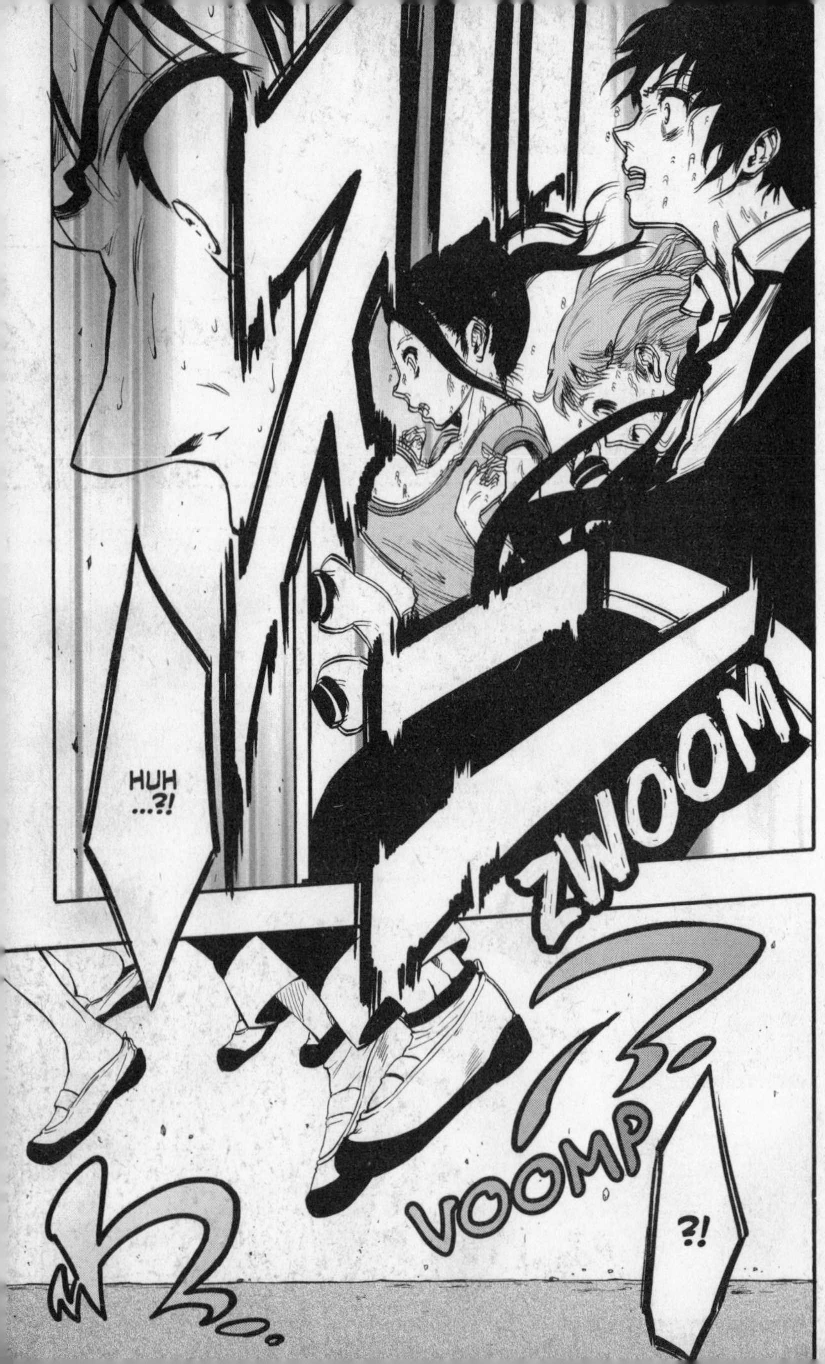
ZWOOM
HUH ...?!
?!
VOOMP

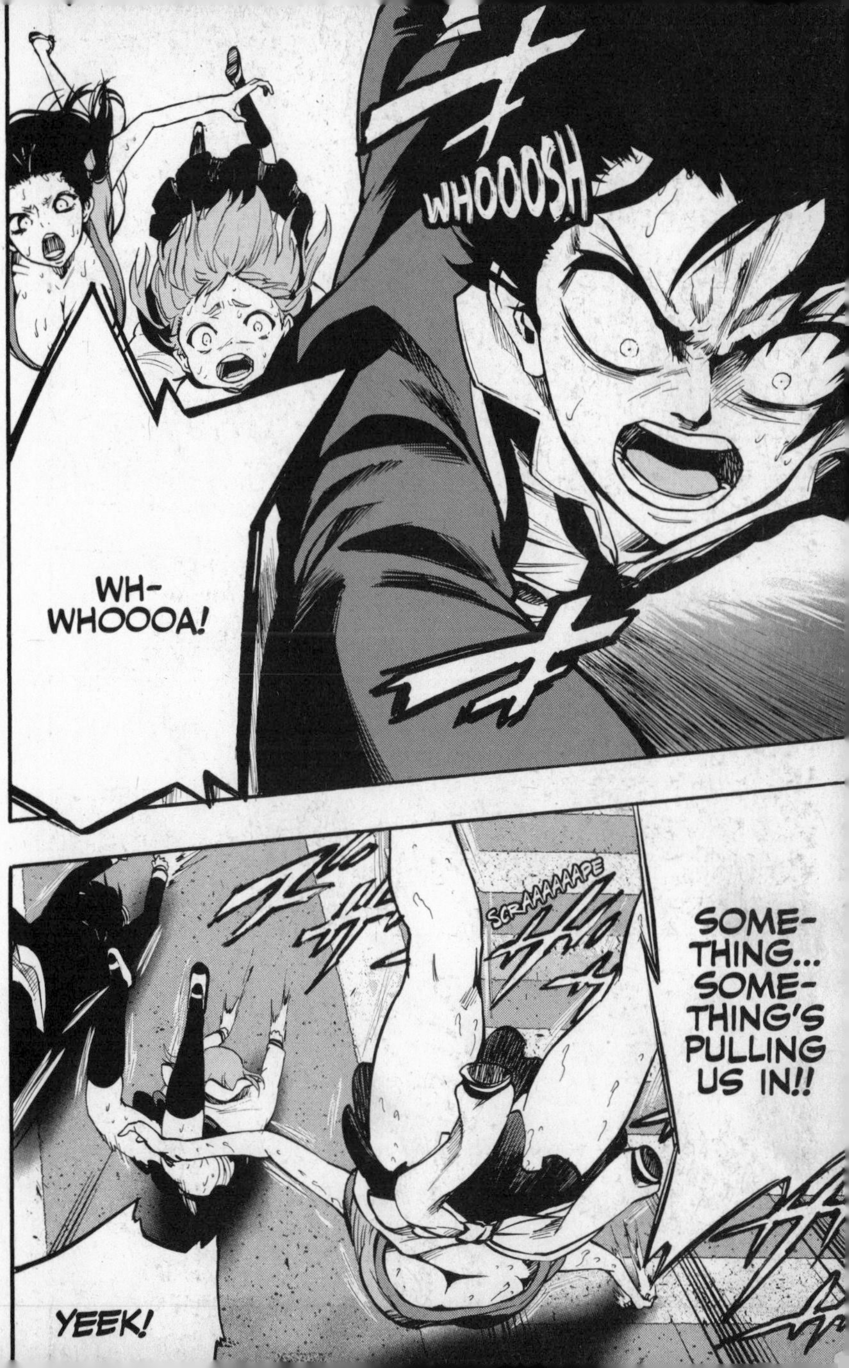
WHOOOSH
WH-WHOOOA!
SCRAAAAAAPE
SOME-THING... SOME-THING'S PULLING US IN!!
YEEK!

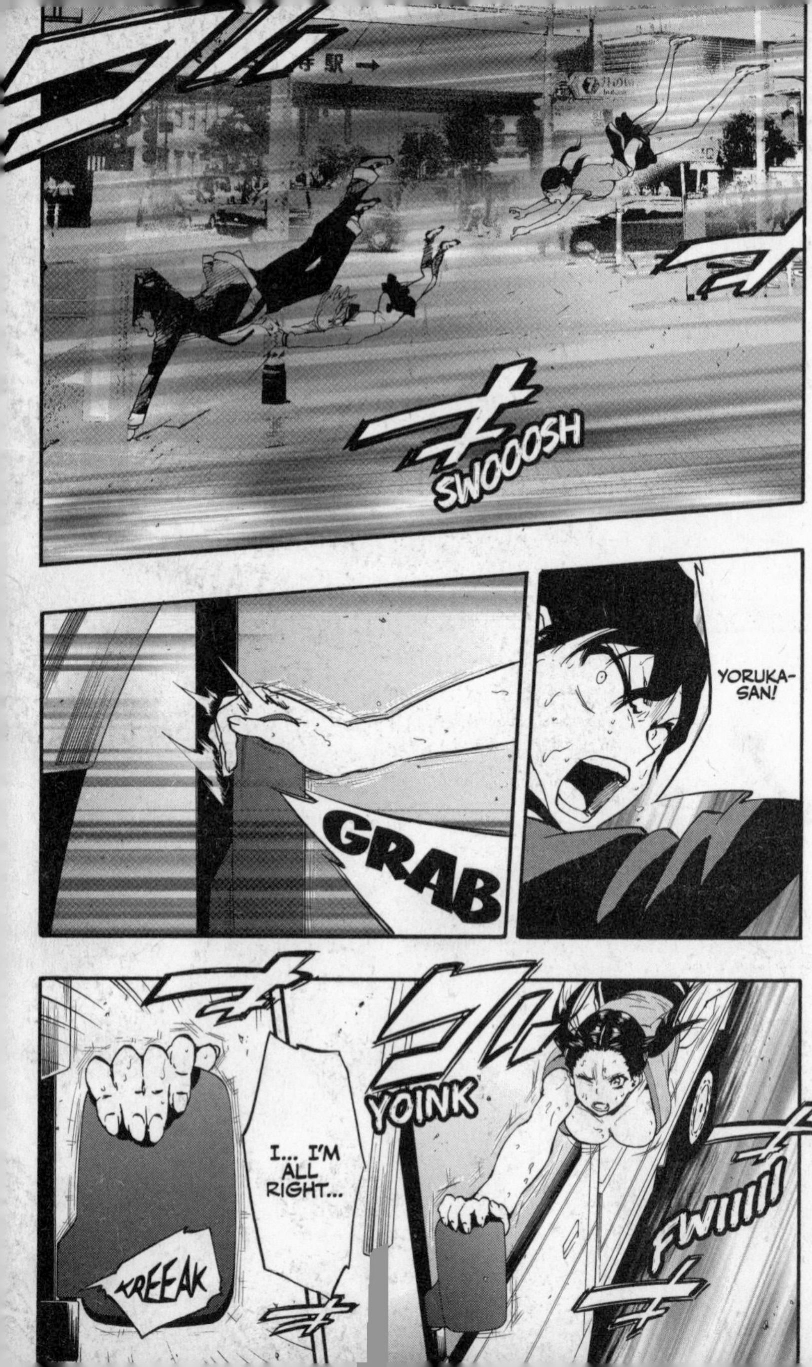
SWOOOSH
YORUKA-SAN!
GRAB
FWIIIII
YOINK
I... I'M ALL RIGHT...
KREEAK

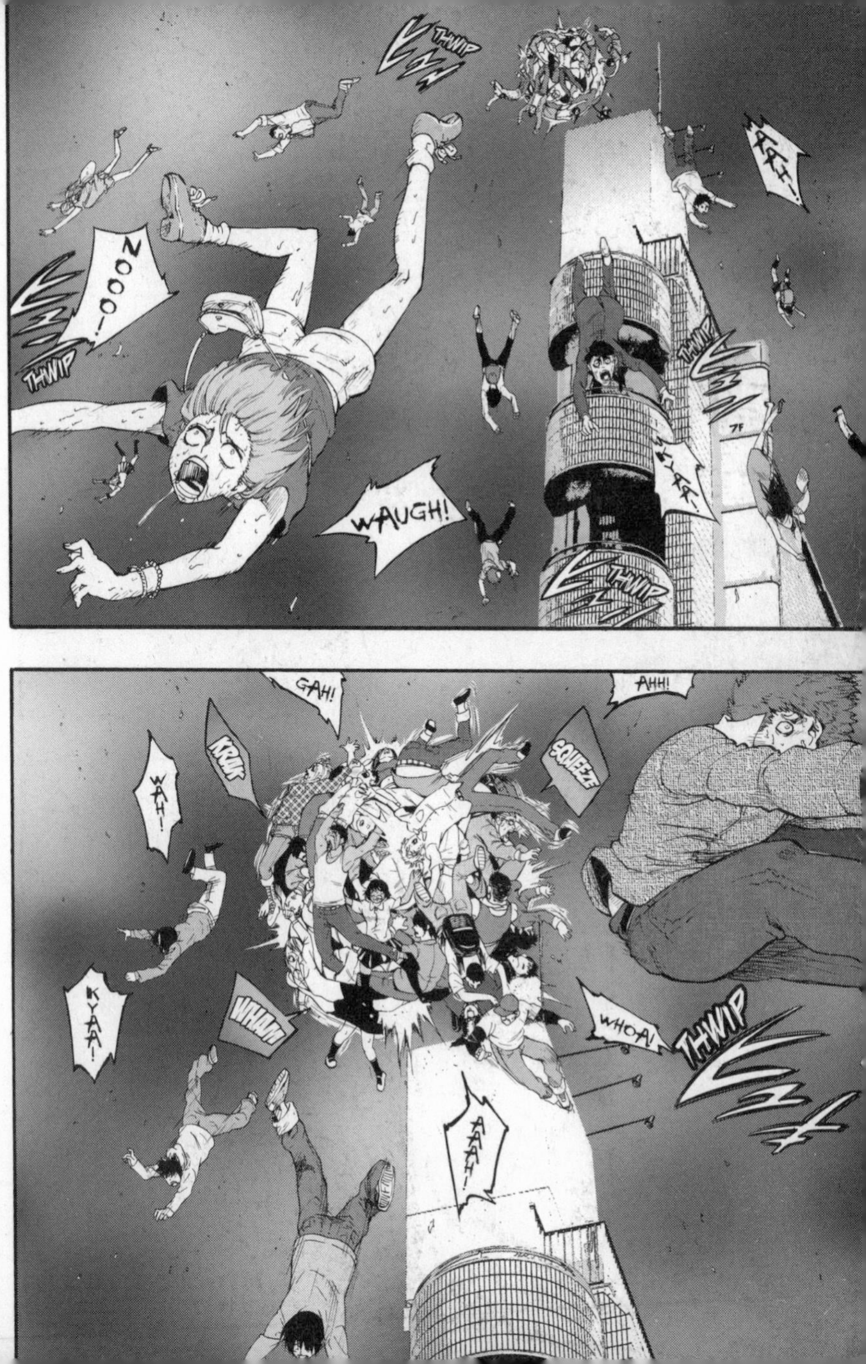
AAH!
THWIP
THWIP
KYAAA-
NOOOO!
THWIP
WAUGH!
THWIP
AHH!
GAH!
SQUEEZE
KRAK
WAH!
THWIP
WHOA!
WHAM
AAAAH!
KYAAA!

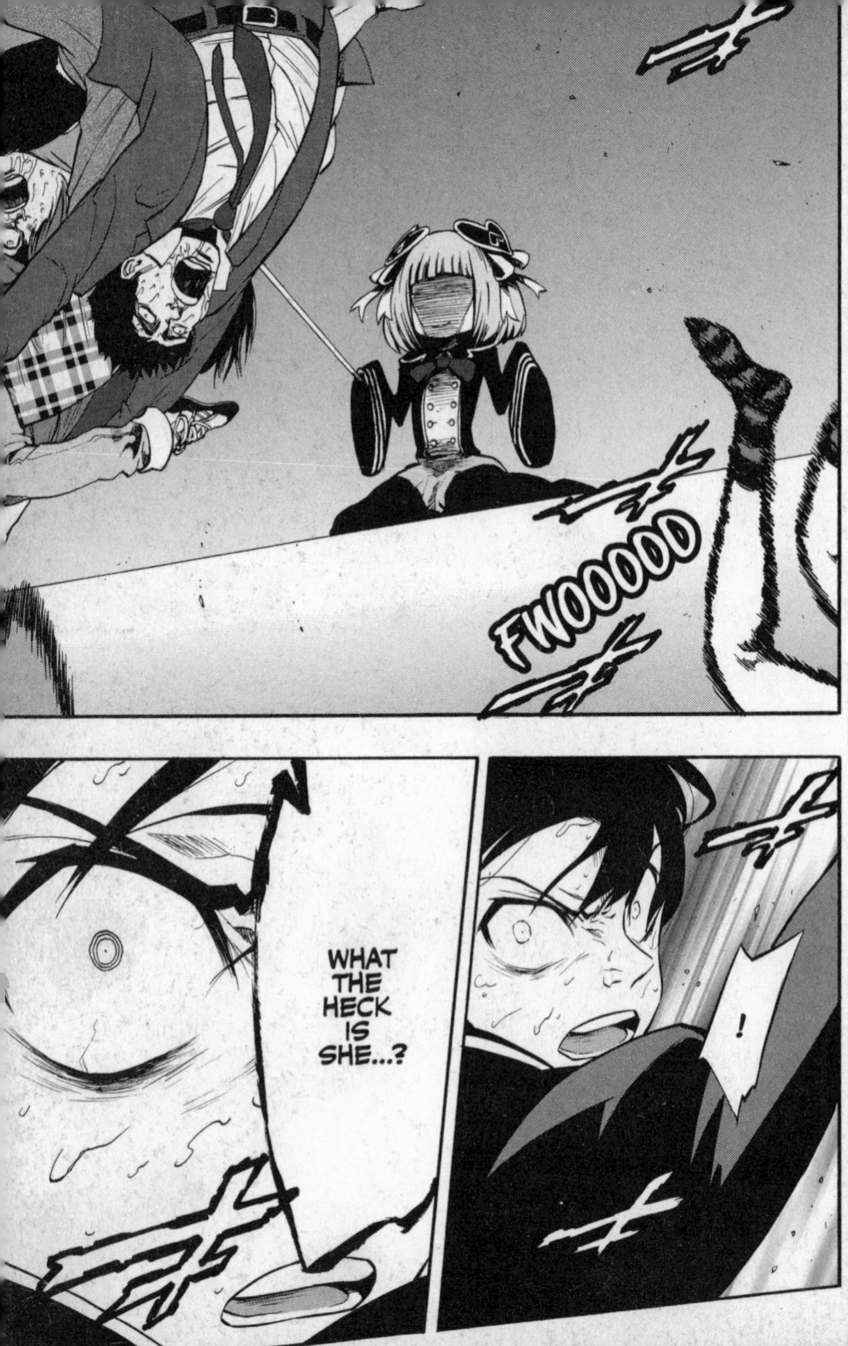
FWOOOOO
!
WHAT THE HECK IS SHE...?

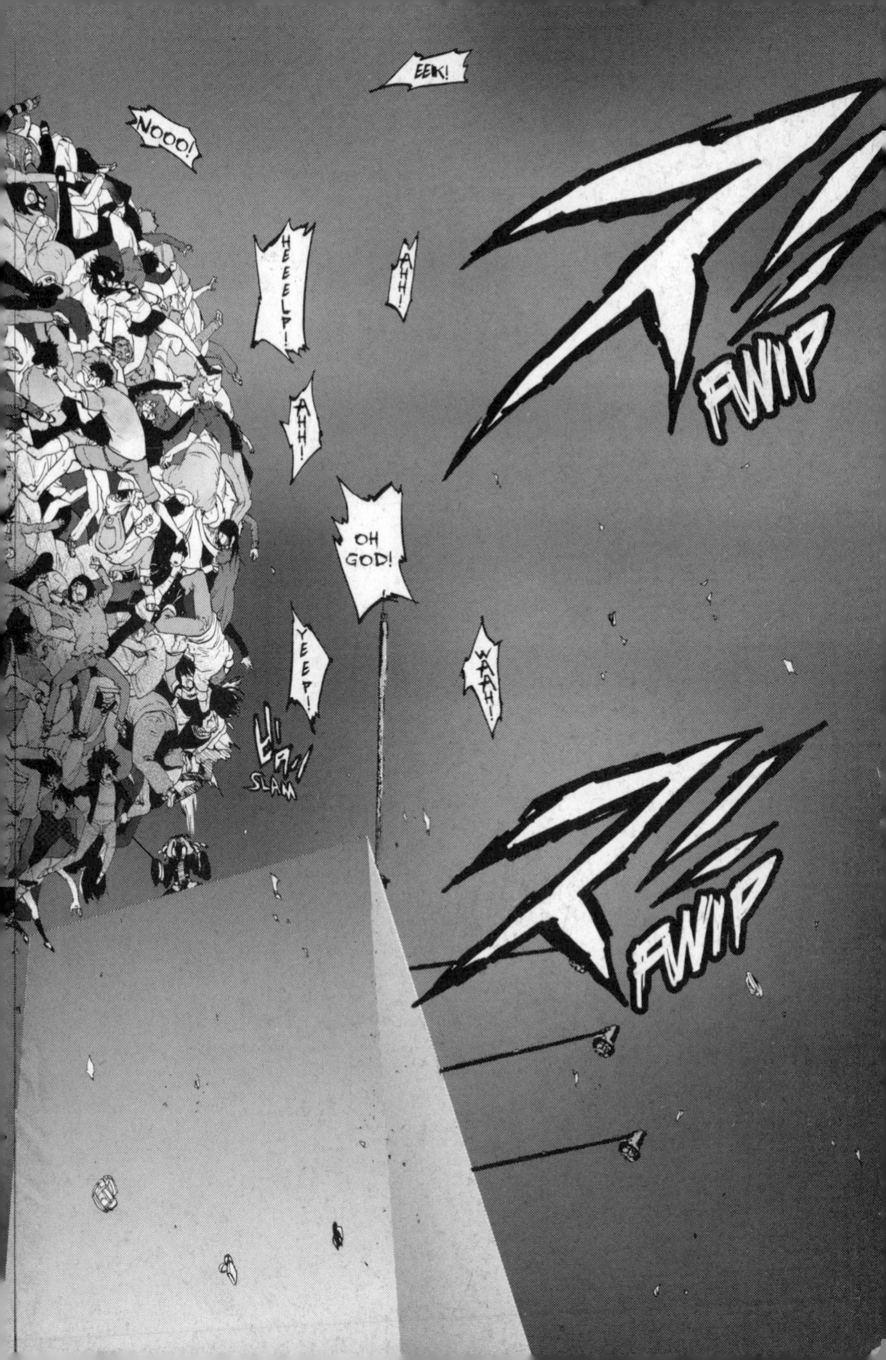
EEK!
FWIP
NOOO!
AHH!
HEEEELP!
AHH!
OH GOD!
WAAAH!
YEEEP!
SLAM
FWIP

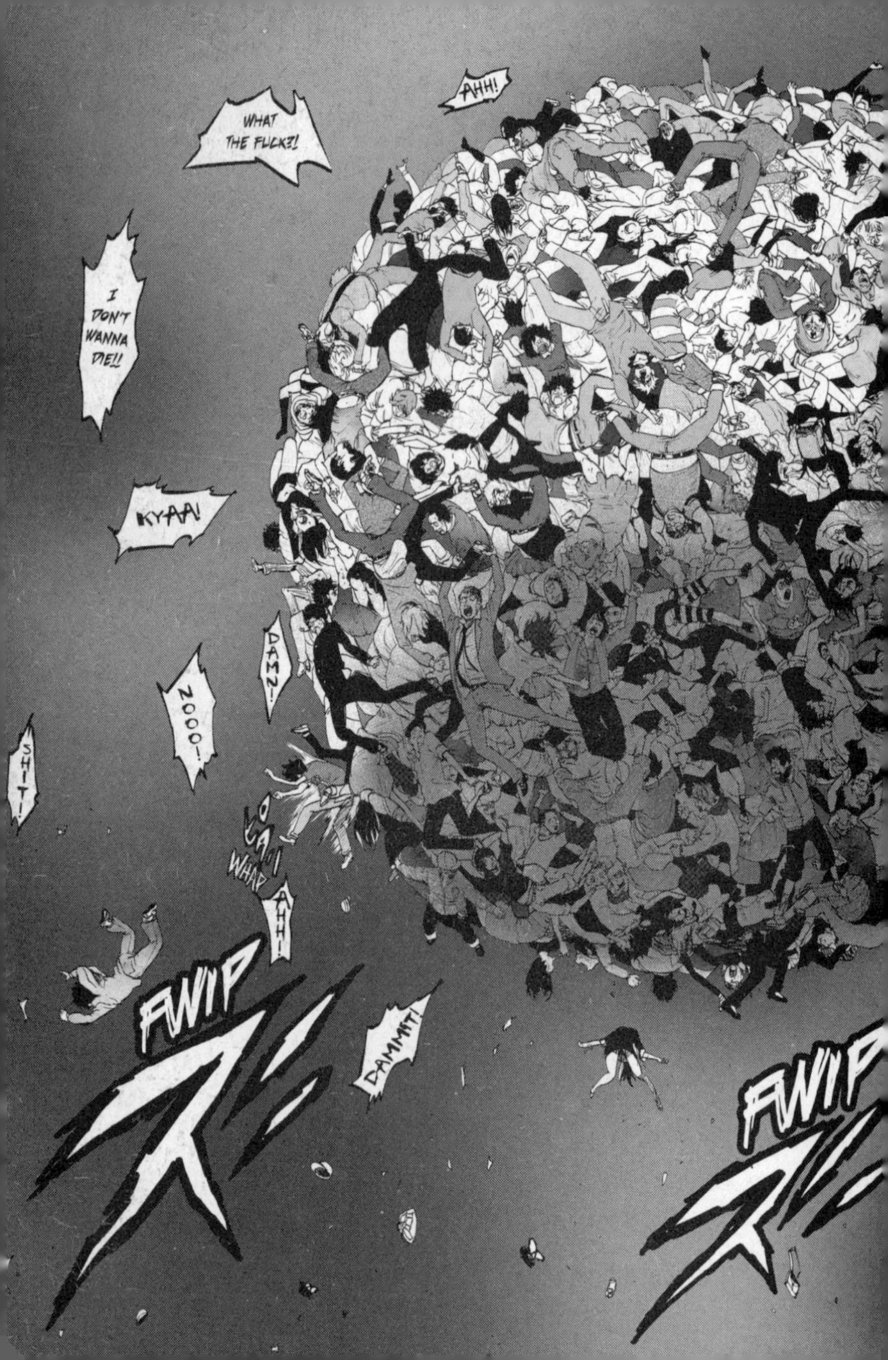
AHH!
WHAT THE FUCK?!
I DON'T WANNA DIE!!
KYAA!
DAMN!
NOOO!
SHIT!
WHAP
AHH!
FWIP
DAMMIT!
FWIP
FWIP

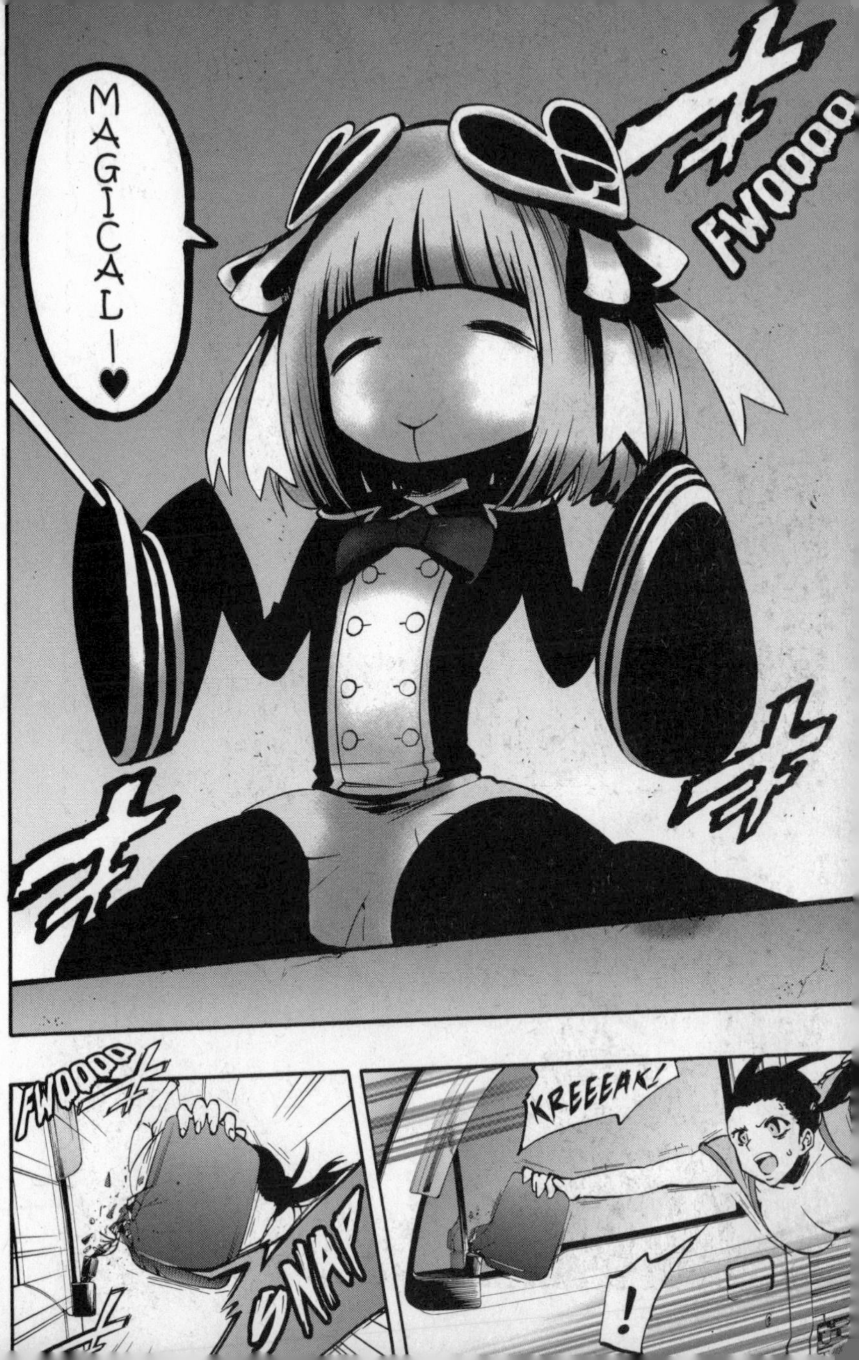
FWOOOO
MAGICAL!♥
KREEEAK!
!
FWOOOO
SNAP

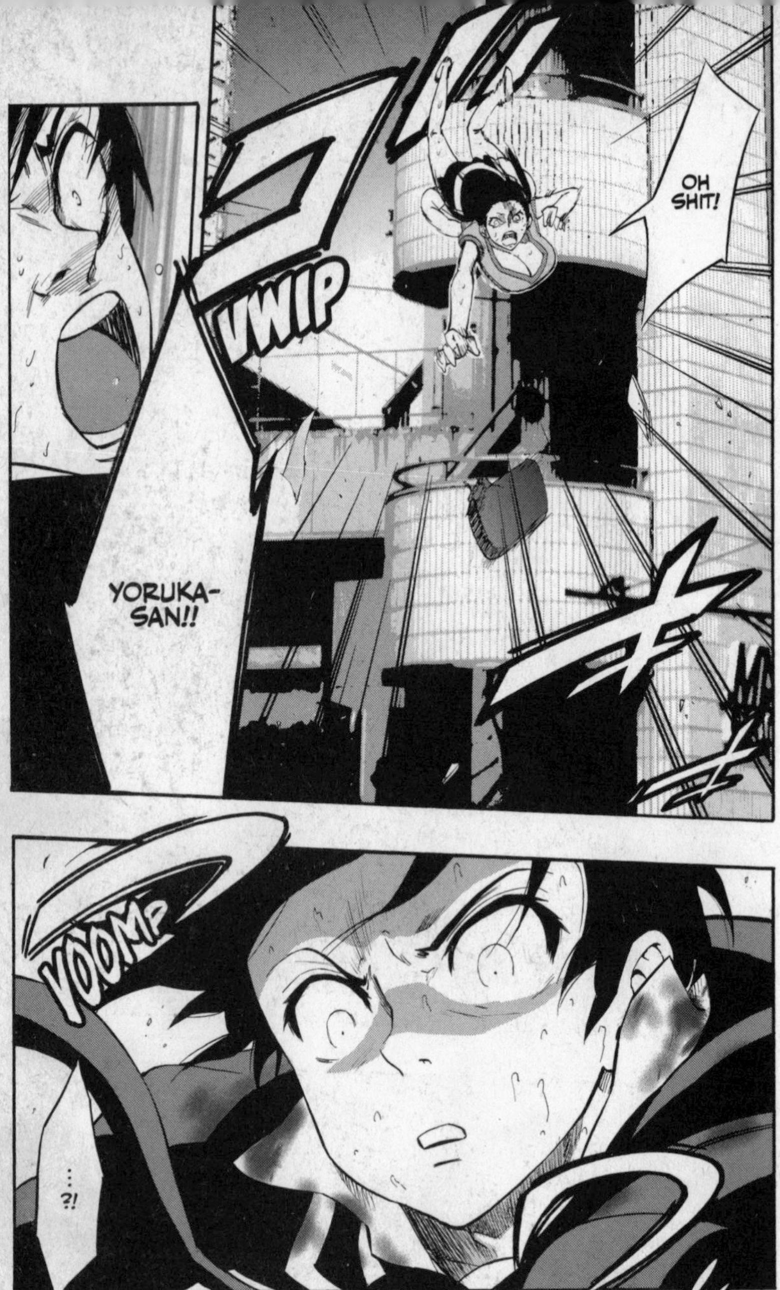
OH SHIT!
VWIP
YORUKA-SAN!!
VOOMP
...?!

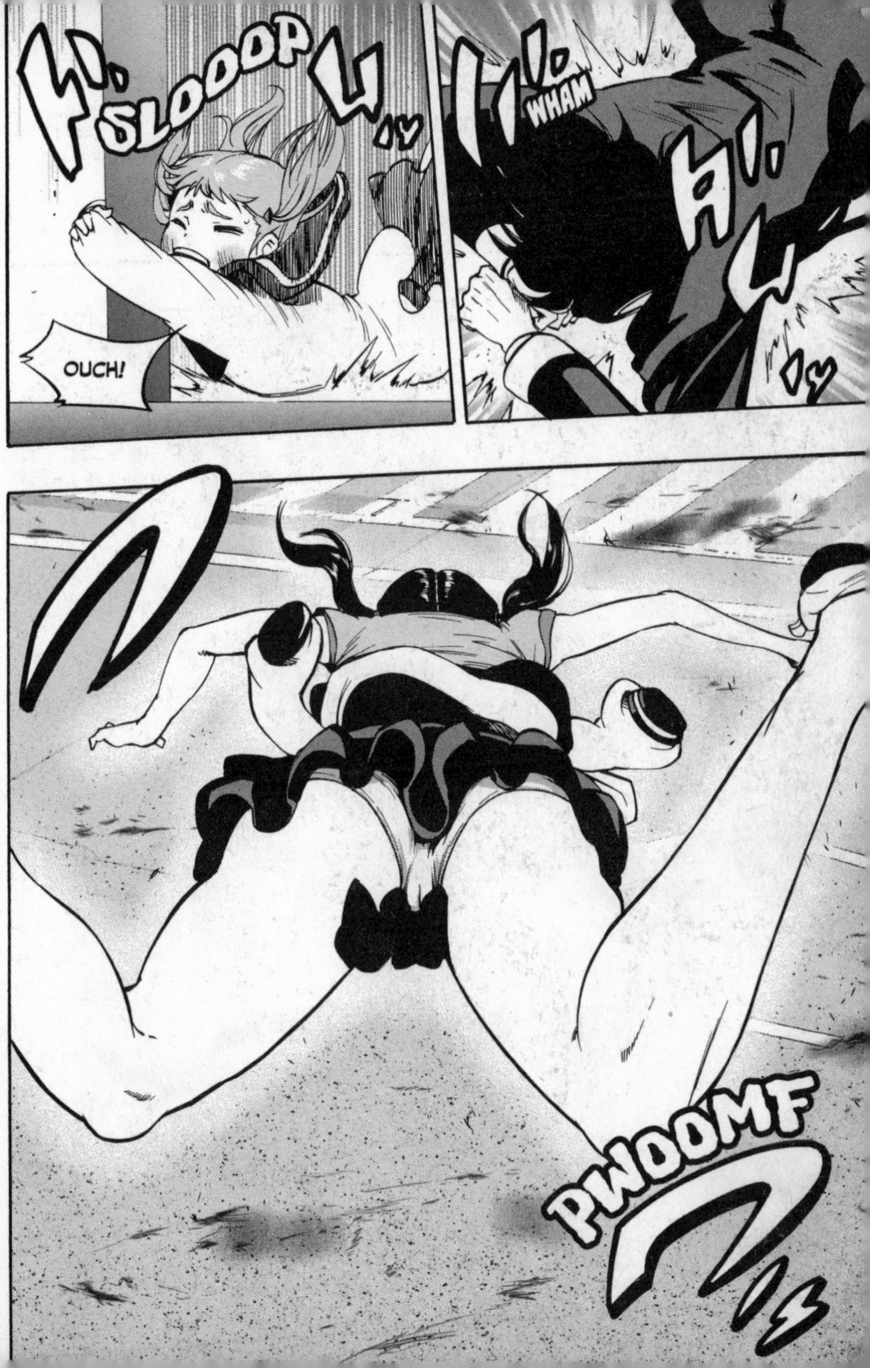
WHAM
SLOOOP
OUCH!
PWOOMF

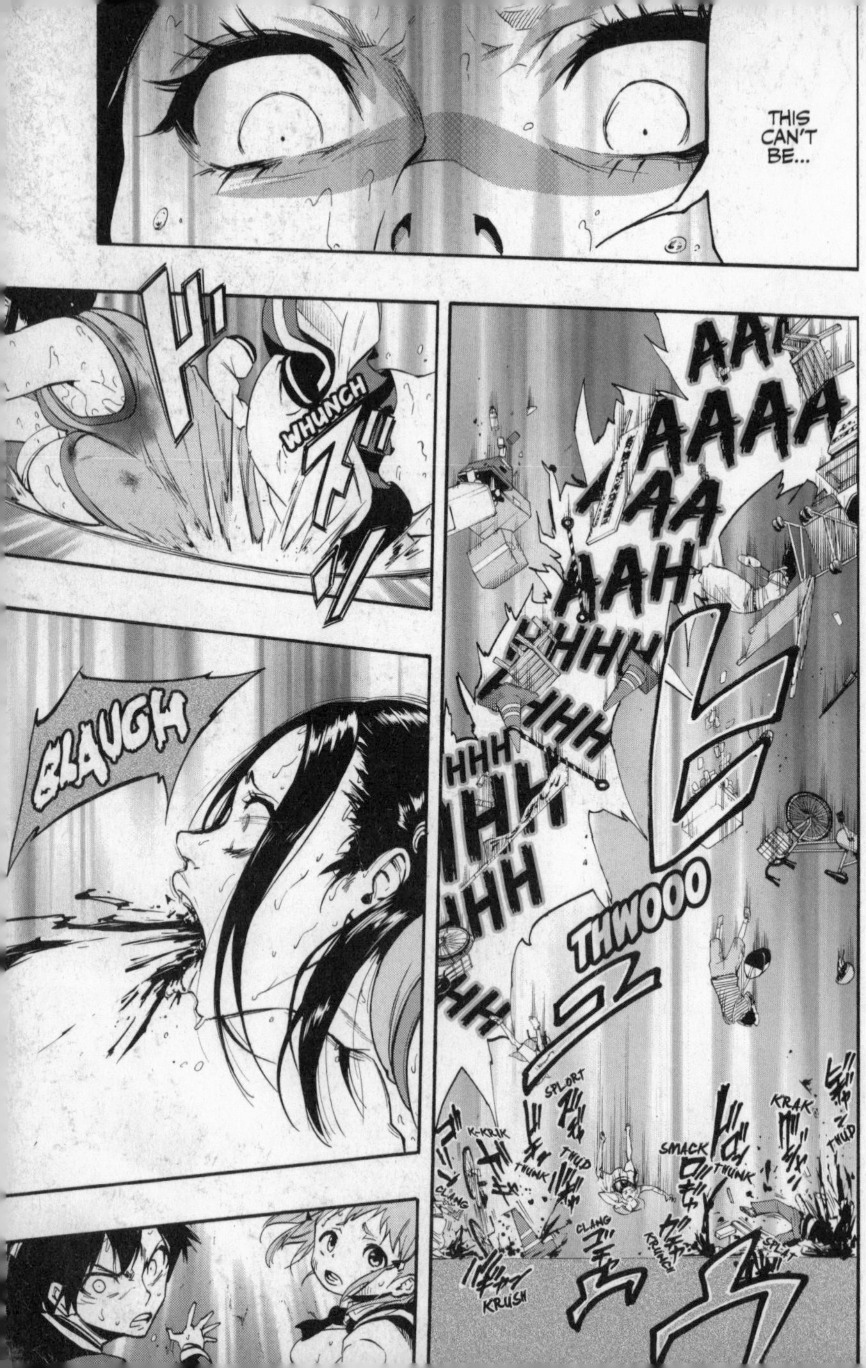
THIS CAN'T BE...
AAAAAAAAAAAHHHHHHHHHHHHHH
THWOOO
KRAK
THUD
SPLORT
SMACK
THUNK
THUD
K-KRIK
THUNK
CLANG
SPLAT
KRUNCH
CLANG
KRUSH
WHUNCH
BLAUGH

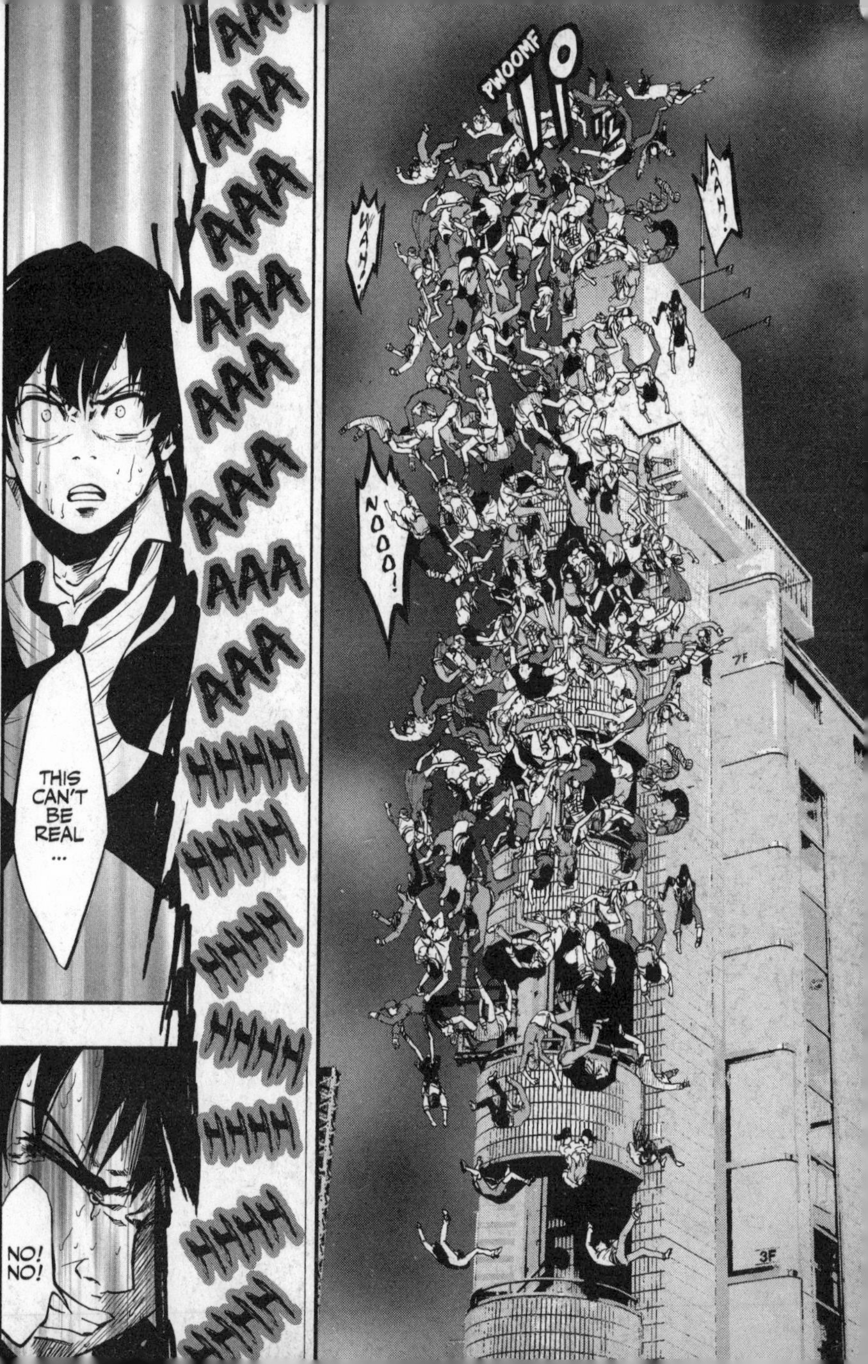
PWOOMF
AAH!
WAH!
NOOOO!
AAAAAAAAAAAAAAAAAAAAAAAAAAAAAHHHHHHHHHHHHHHHHHHHHHHHHHHHHHHHHHHHHHHHH
THIS CAN'T BE REAL...
NO! NO!

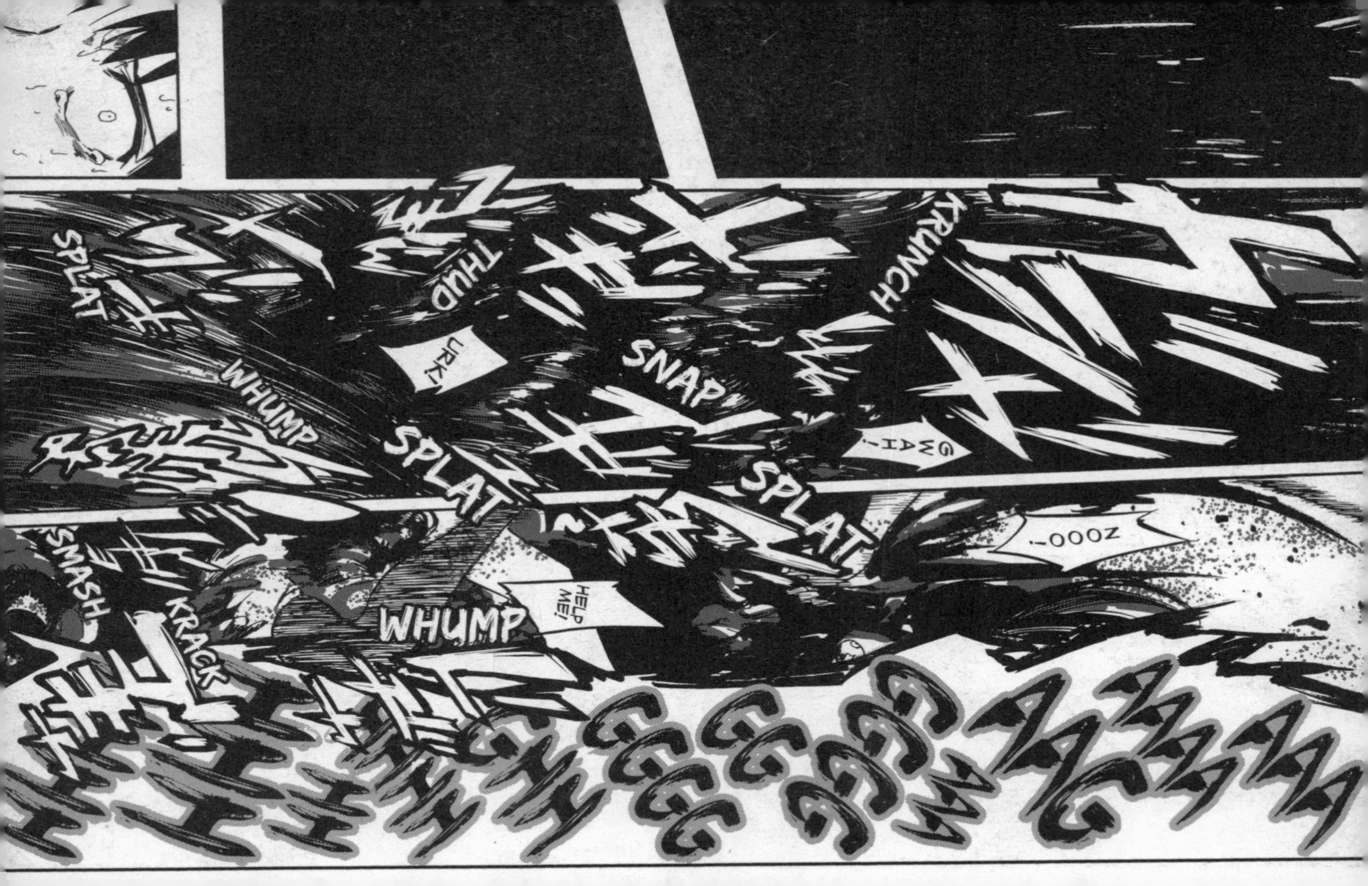

KRUNCH
GWAH!
SNAP
SPLAT
SPLAT
URK!
THUD
WHUMP
SPLAT
NOOO!
HELP ME!
WHUMP
KRACK
SMASH
AAAAAAAAAAGGGGGGGGGGGGHHHHHHH

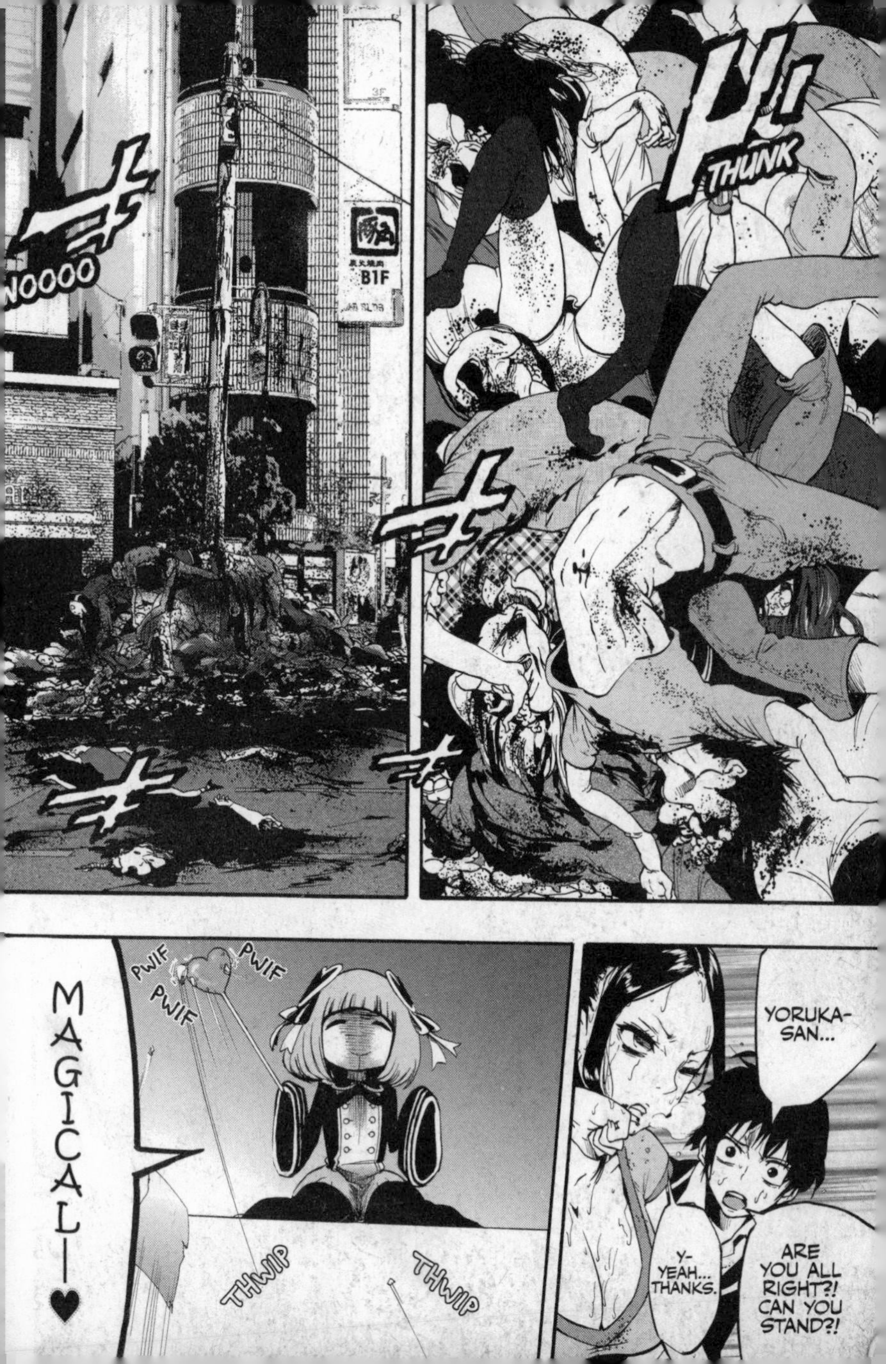
NO
THUNK
B1F
NOOOO
YORUKA-SAN...
ARE YOU ALL RIGHT?! CAN YOU STAND?!
Y-YEAH... THANKS.
PWIF
PWIF
PWIF
MAGICAL♥
THWIP
THWIP

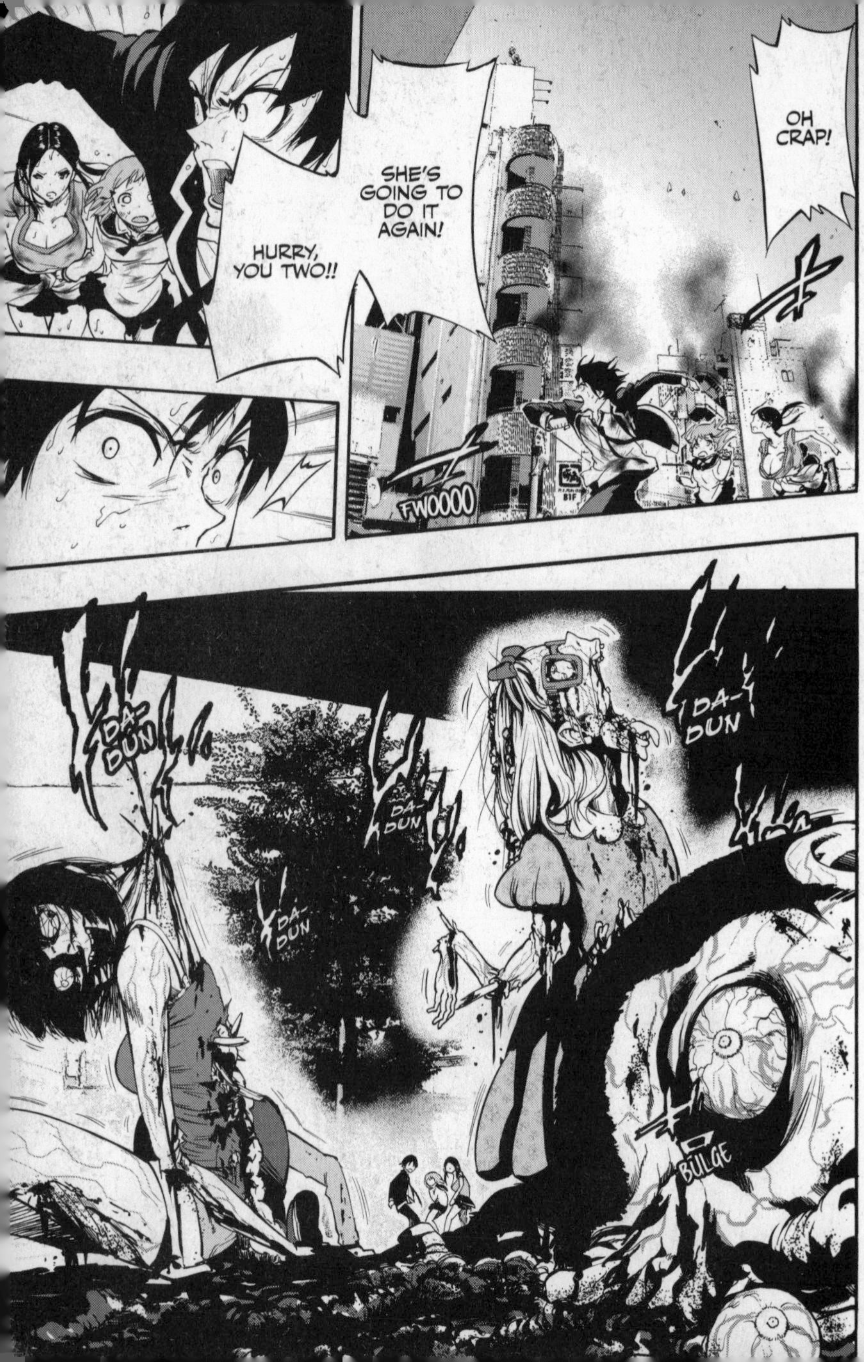
OH CRAP!
SHE'S GOING TO DO IT AGAIN!
FWOOOO
HURRY, YOU TWO!!
DA-DUN
DA-DUN
DA-DUN
DA-DUN
BULGE

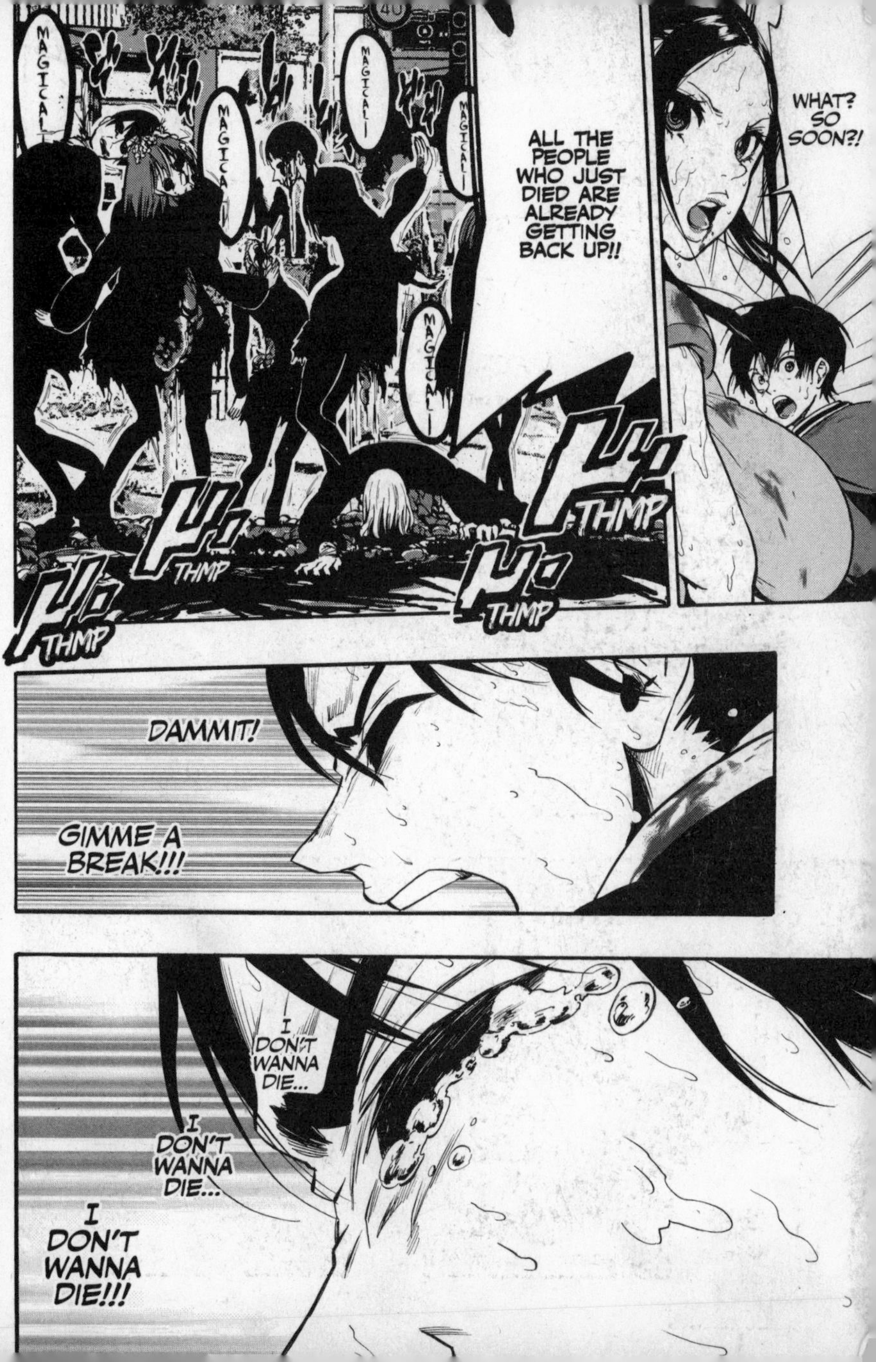
WHAT? SO SOON?!
ALL THE PEOPLE WHO JUST DIED ARE ALREADY GETTING BACK UP!!
MAGICAL!
MAGICAL!
MAGICAL!
MAGICAL!
MAGICAL!
MAGICAL!
THMP
THMP
THMP
THMP
DAMMIT!
GIMME A BREAK!!!
I DON'T WANNA DIE...
I DON'T WANNA DIE...
I DON'T WANNA DIE!!!

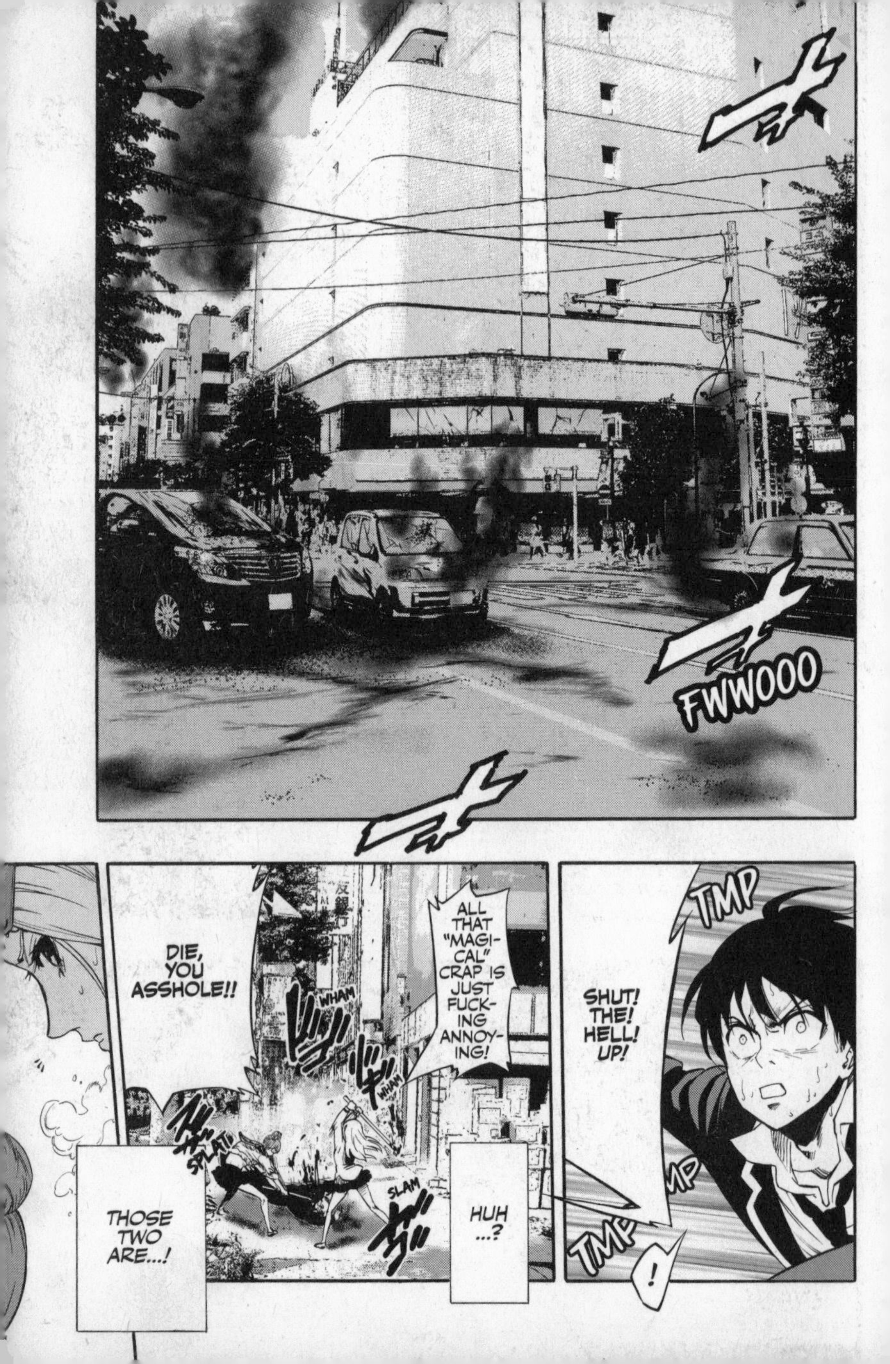
FWWOOO
TMP
SHUT! THE! HELL! UP!
!
ALL THAT "MAGICAL" CRAP IS JUST FUCKING ANNOYING!
DIE, YOU ASSHOLE!!
WHAM
WHAM
SPLAT
SLAM
HUH ...?
THOSE TWO ARE...!

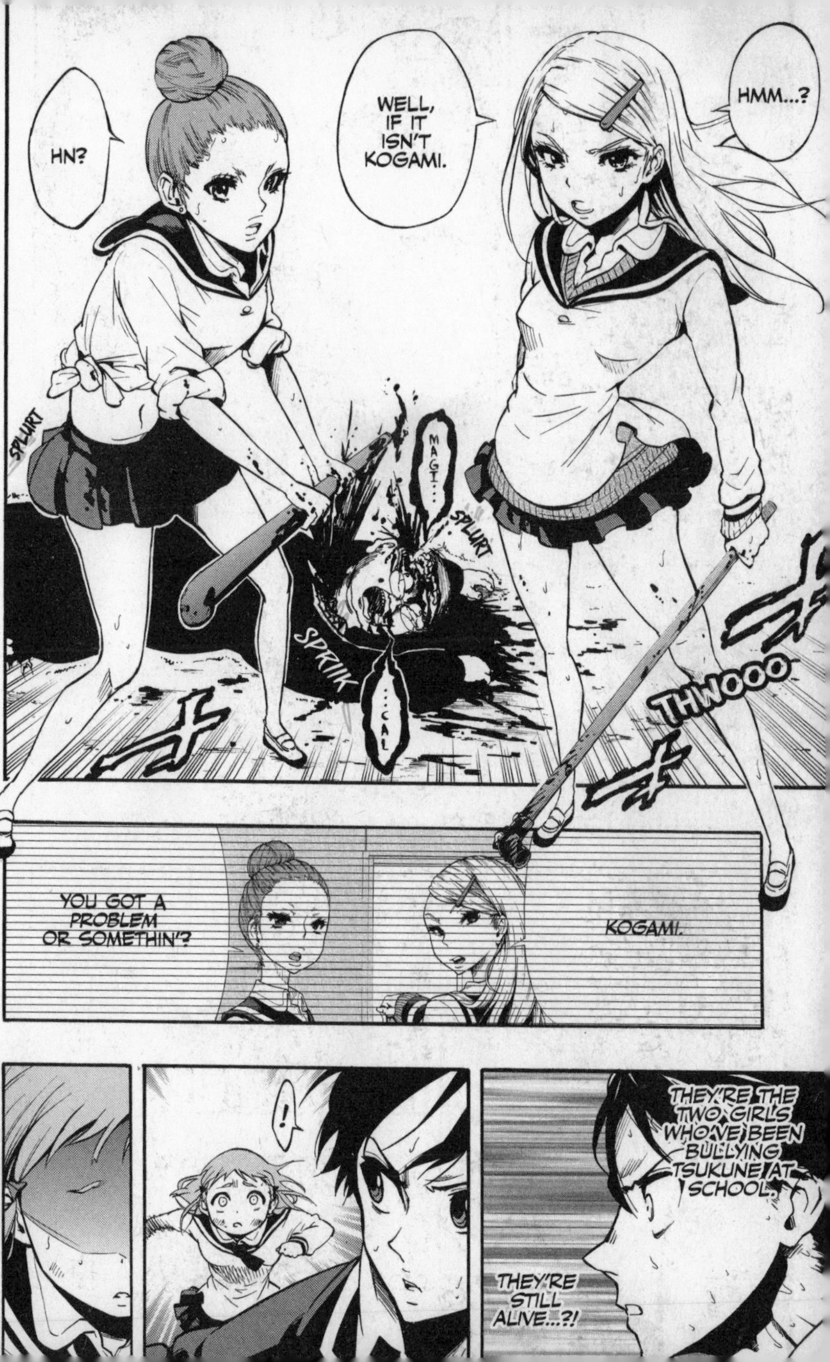
HMM...?
WELL, IF IT ISN'T KOGAMI.
HN?
THWOOO
SPLURT
MAGI...
...CAL
SPRIIK
SPLURT
KOGAMI.
YOU GOT A PROBLEM OR SOMETHIN'?
THEY'RE THE TWO GIRLS WHO'VE BEEN BULLYING TSUKUNE AT SCHOOL.
THEY'RE STILL ALIVE...?!
!

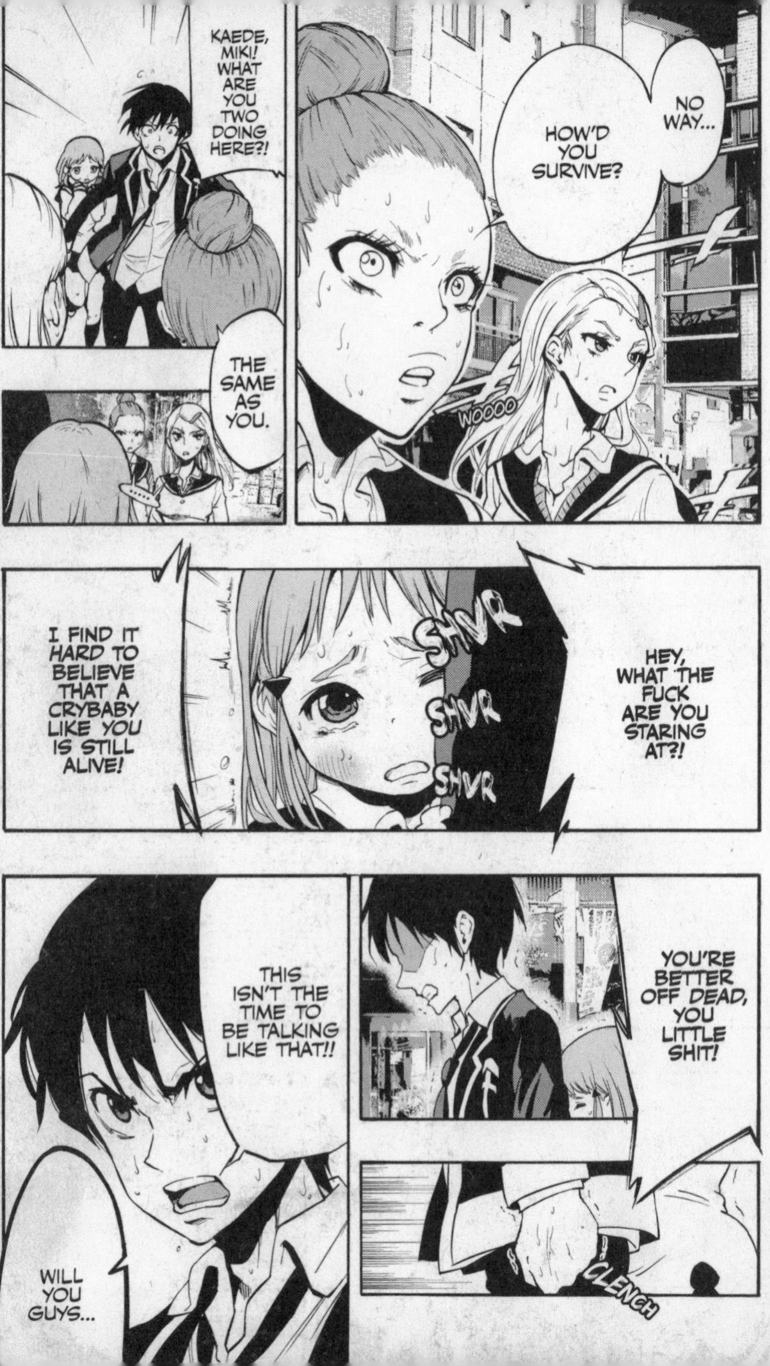
NO WAY...
HOW'D YOU SURVIVE?
WOOOO
KAEDE, MIKI! WHAT ARE YOU TWO DOING HERE?!
THE SAME AS YOU.
.....
HEY, WHAT THE FUCK ARE YOU STARING AT?!
SHVR
SHVR
SHVR
I FIND IT HARD TO BELIEVE THAT A CRYBABY LIKE YOU IS STILL ALIVE!
YOU'RE BETTER OFF DEAD, YOU LITTLE SHIT!
THIS ISN'T THE TIME TO BE TALKING LIKE THAT!!
CLENCH
WILL YOU GUYS...

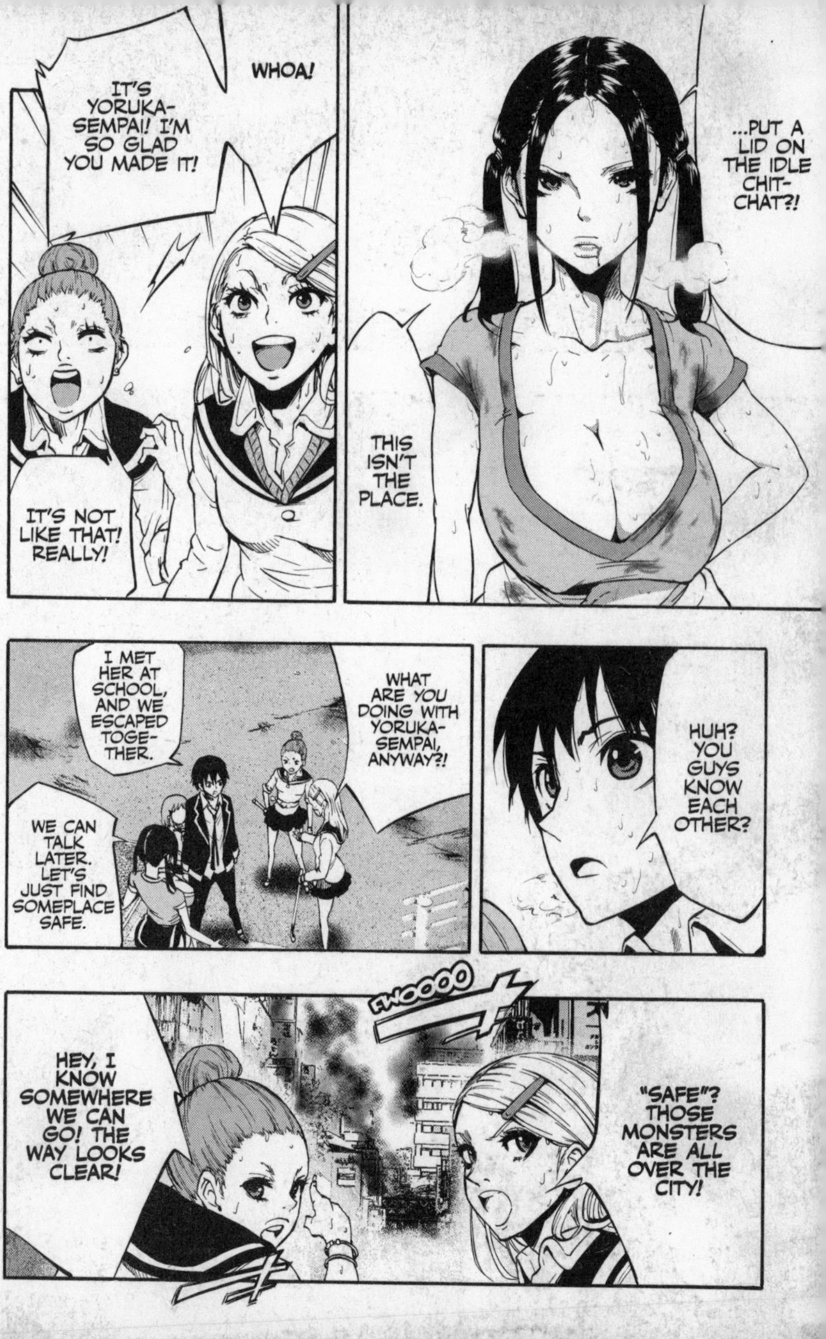
...PUT A LID ON THE IDLE CHIT-CHAT?!
THIS ISN'T THE PLACE.
WHOA!
IT'S YORUKA-SEMPAI! I'M SO GLAD YOU MADE IT!
IT'S NOT LIKE THAT! REALLY!
HUH? YOU GUYS KNOW EACH OTHER?
WHAT ARE YOU DOING WITH YORUKA-SEMPAI, ANYWAY?!
I MET HER AT SCHOOL, AND WE ESCAPED TOGE-THER.
WE CAN TALK LATER. LET'S JUST FIND SOMEPLACE SAFE.
FWOOOO
"SAFE"? THOSE MONSTERS ARE ALL OVER THE CITY!
HEY, I KNOW SOMEWHERE WE CAN GO! THE WAY LOOKS CLEAR!

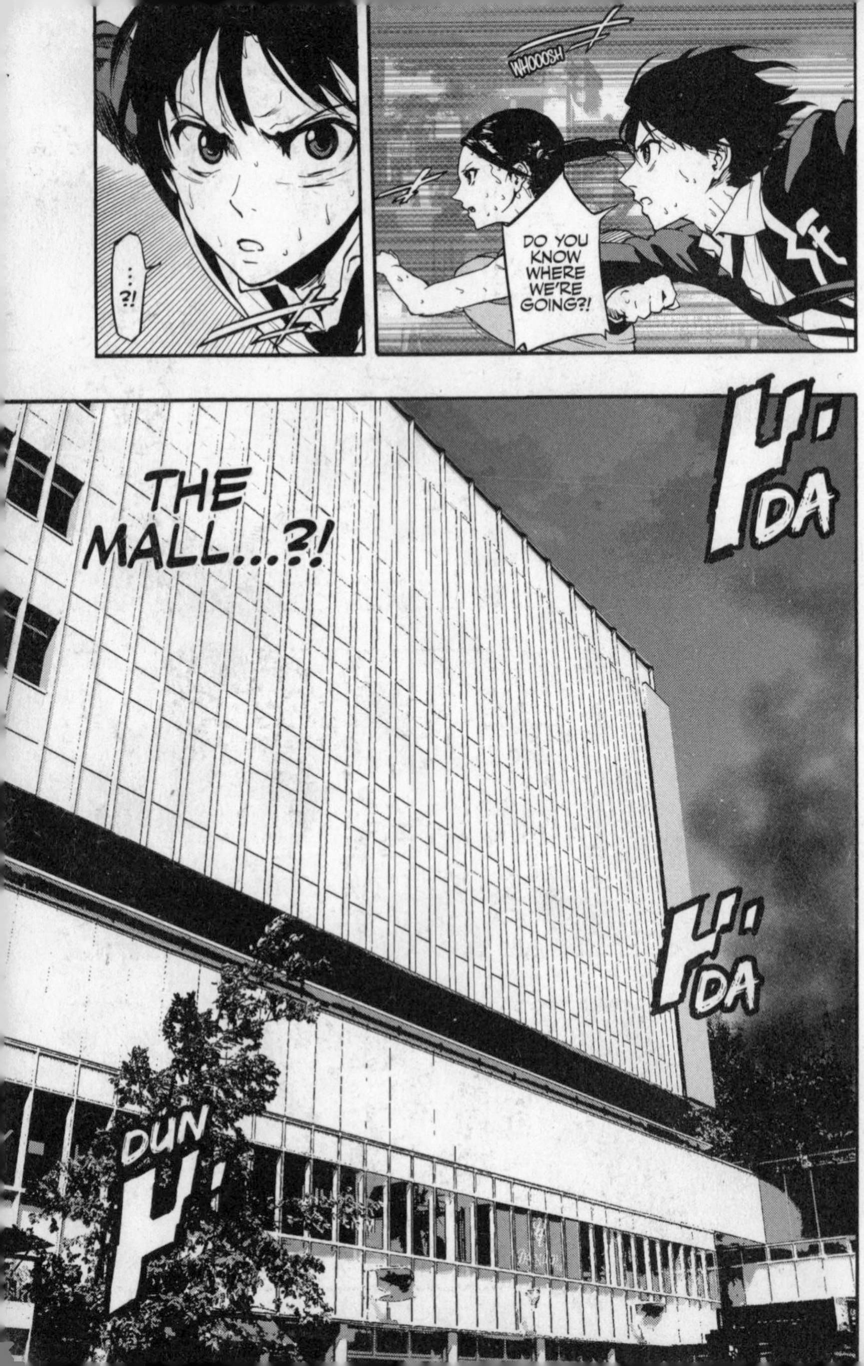
WHOOOSH
DO YOU KNOW WHERE WE'RE GOING?!
...?!
DA
DA
THE MALL...?!
DUN

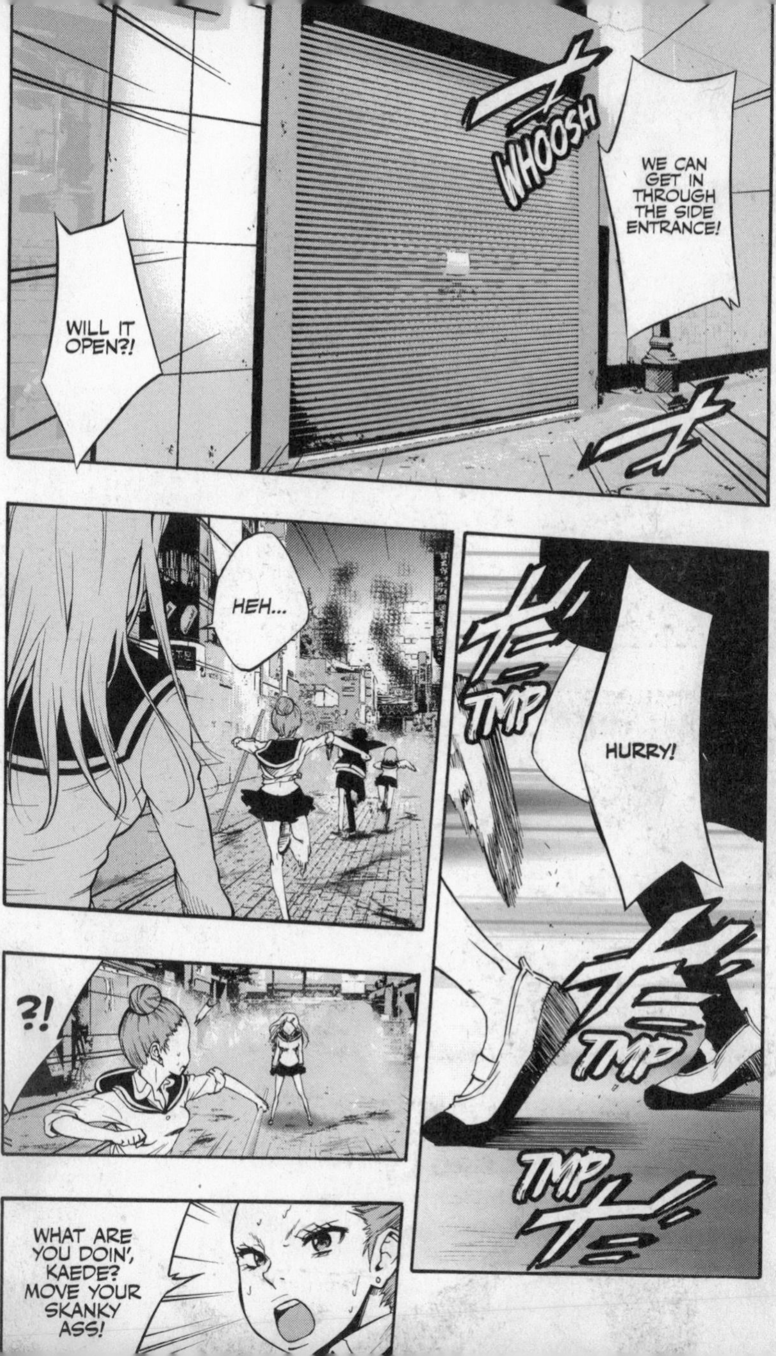

WE CAN GET IN THROUGH THE SIDE ENTRANCE!
WHOOSH
WILL IT OPEN?!
TMP
HURRY!
TMP
TMP
HEH...
?!
WHAT ARE YOU DOIN', KAEDE? MOVE YOUR SKANKY ASS!

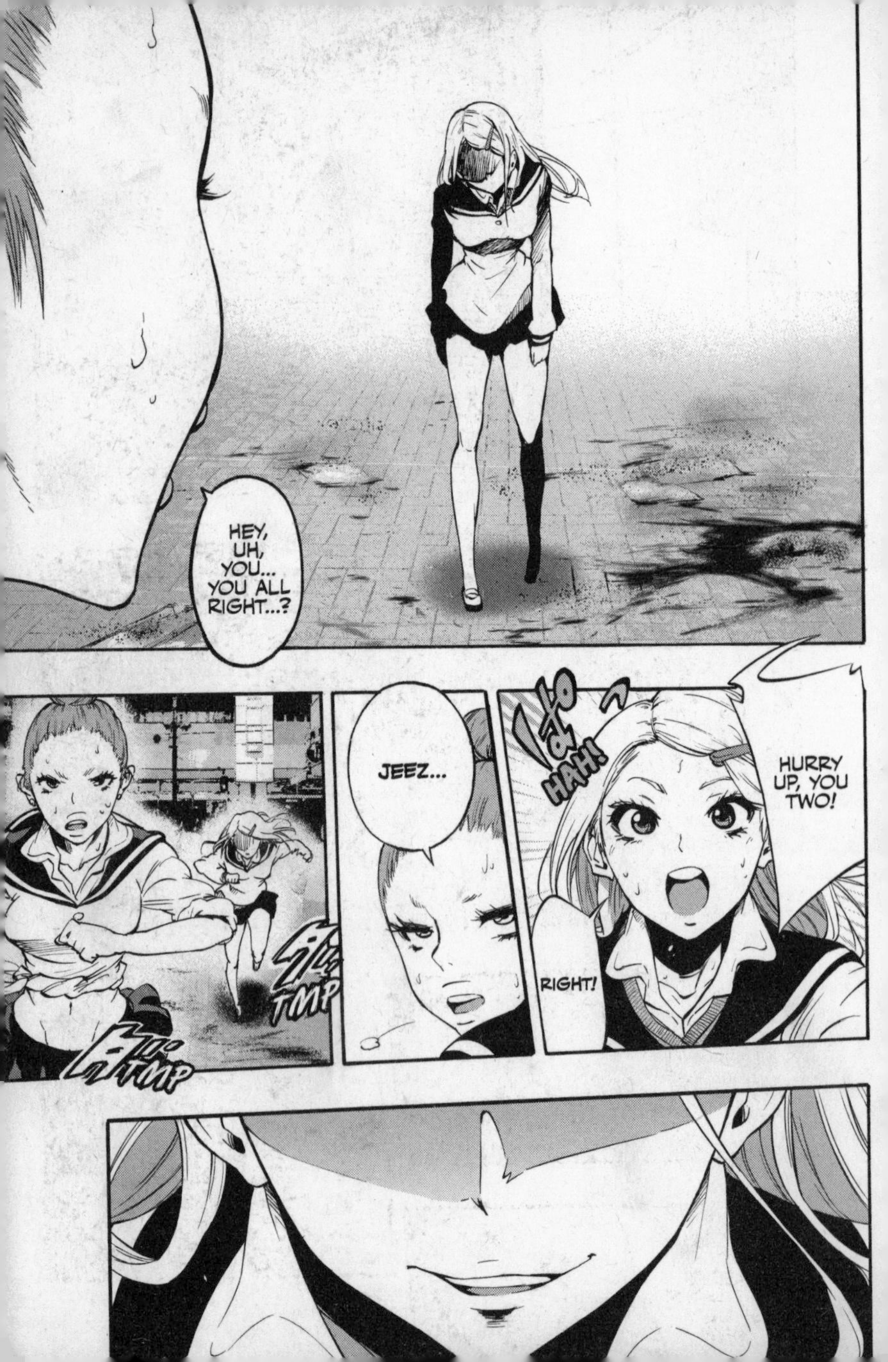
HEY, UH, YOU... YOU ALL RIGHT...?
HURRY UP, YOU TWO!
HAH!
RIGHT!
JEEZ...
TMP
TMP

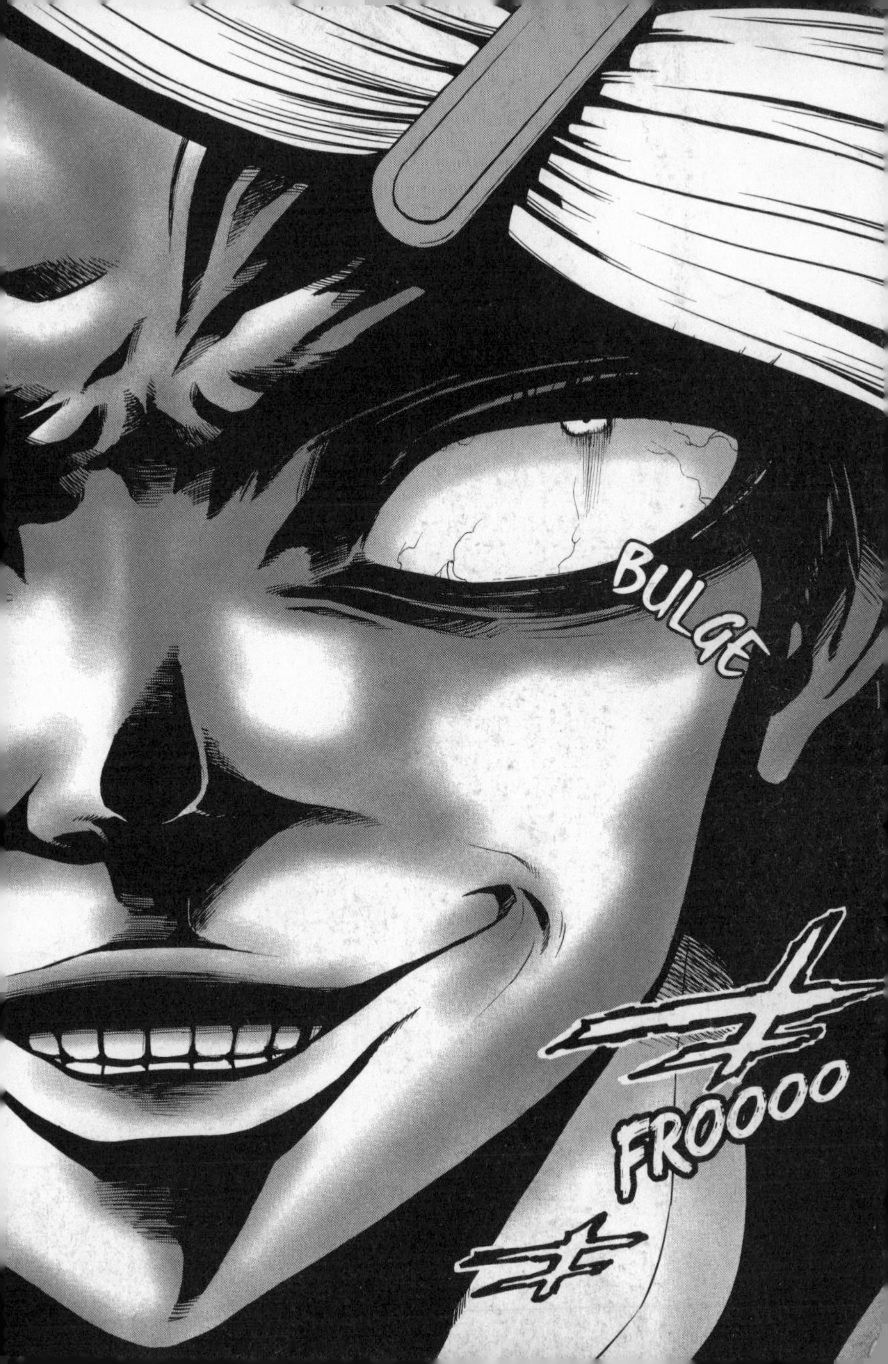
BULGE
FROOOO

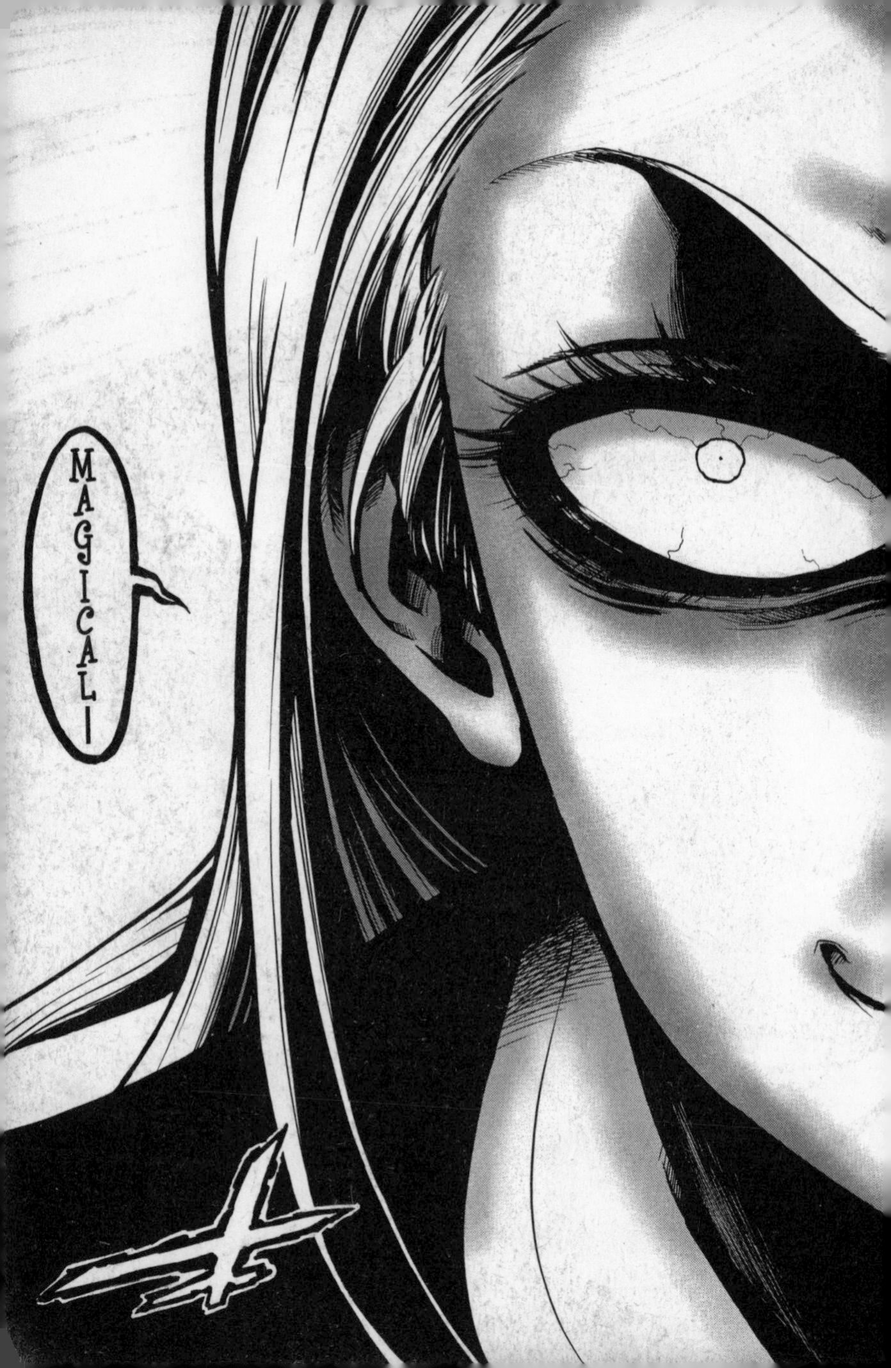
MAGICAL!

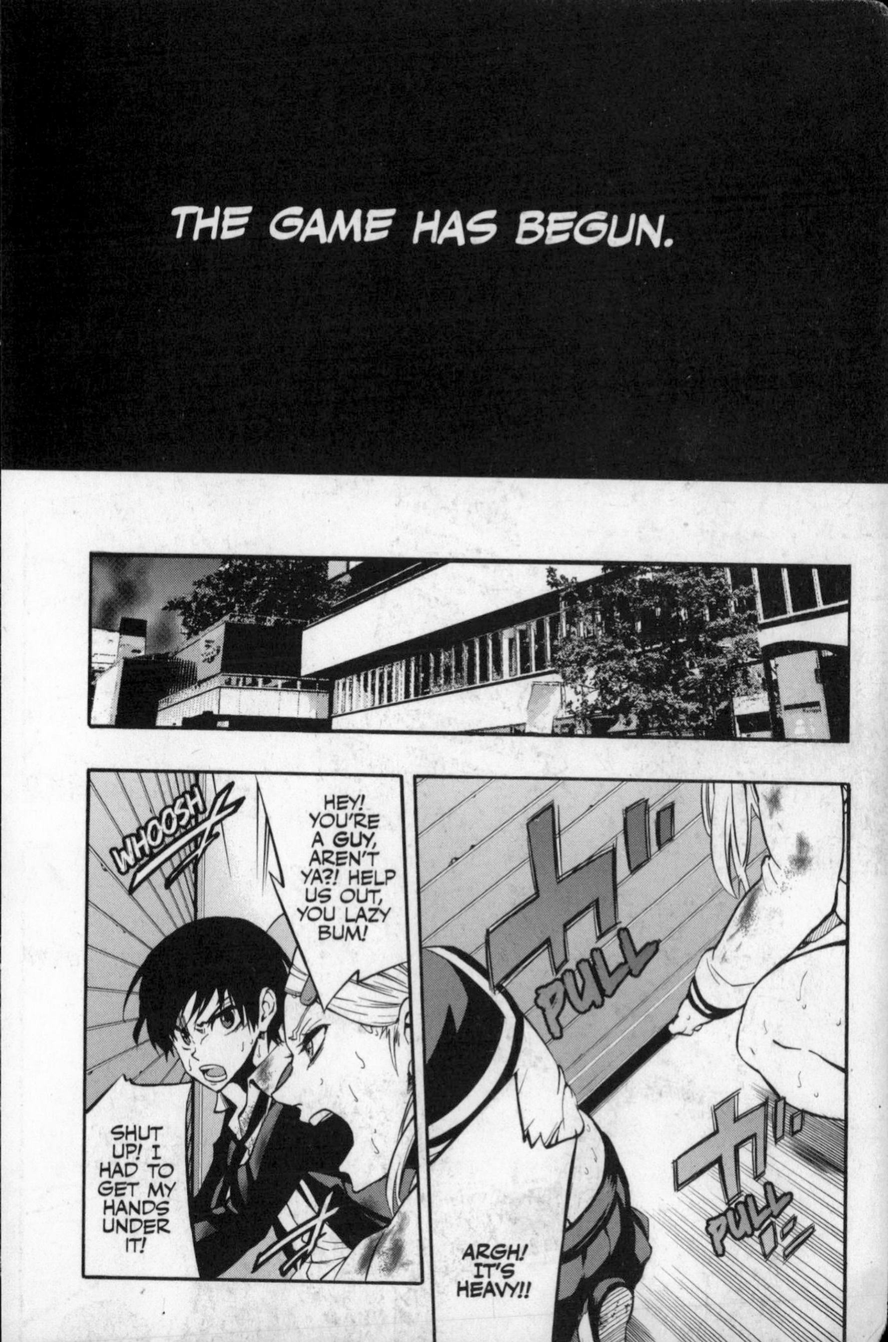
THE GAME HAS BEGUN.
PULL
PULL
ARGH! IT'S HEAVY!!
HEY! YOU'RE A GUY, AREN'T YA?! HELP US OUT, YOU LAZY BUM!
WHOOSH
SHUT UP! I HAD TO GET MY HANDS UNDER IT!

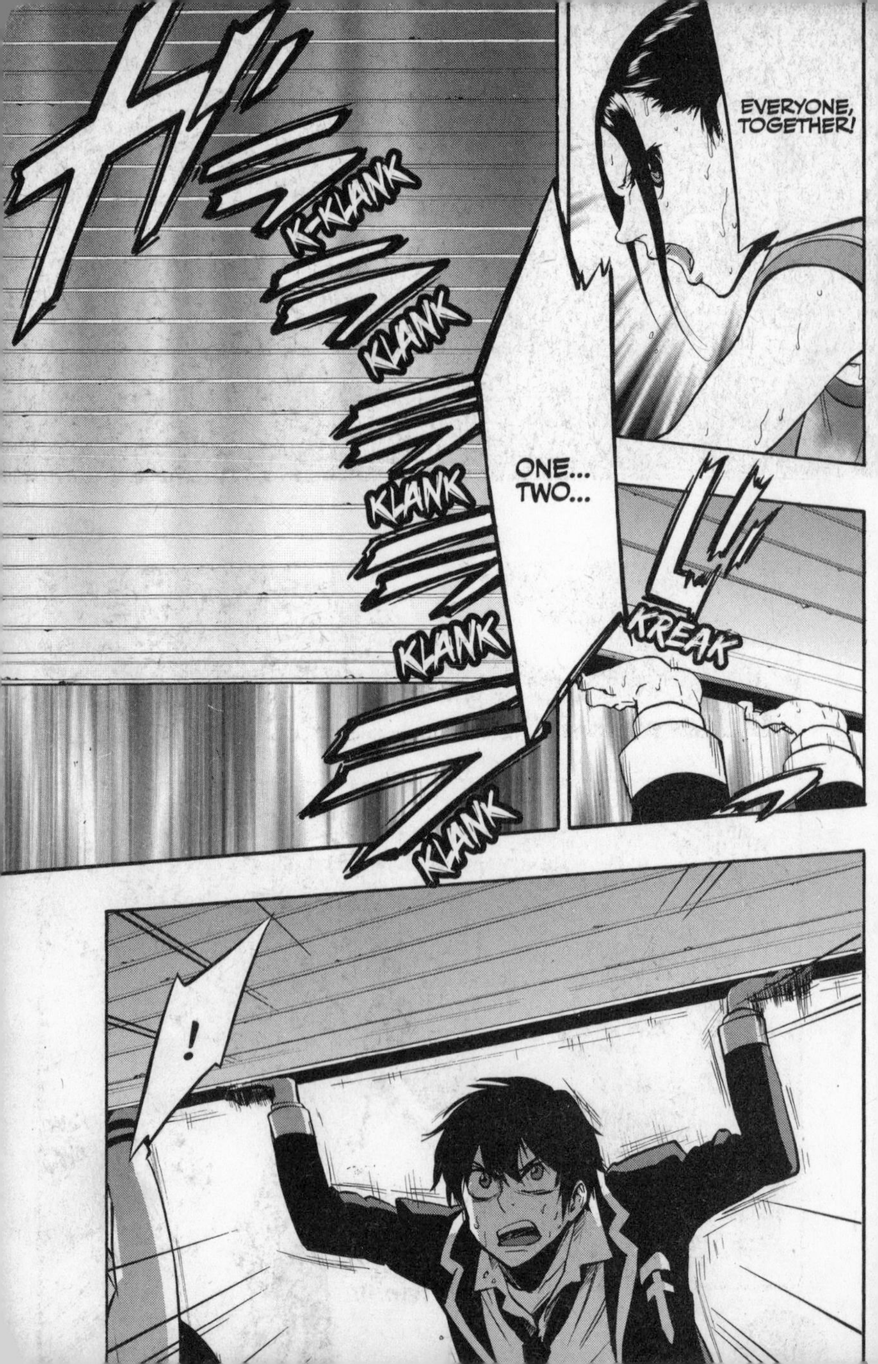
EVERYONE, TOGETHER!
ONE... TWO...
KREAK
K-KLANK
KLANK
KLANK
KLANK
KLANK
!

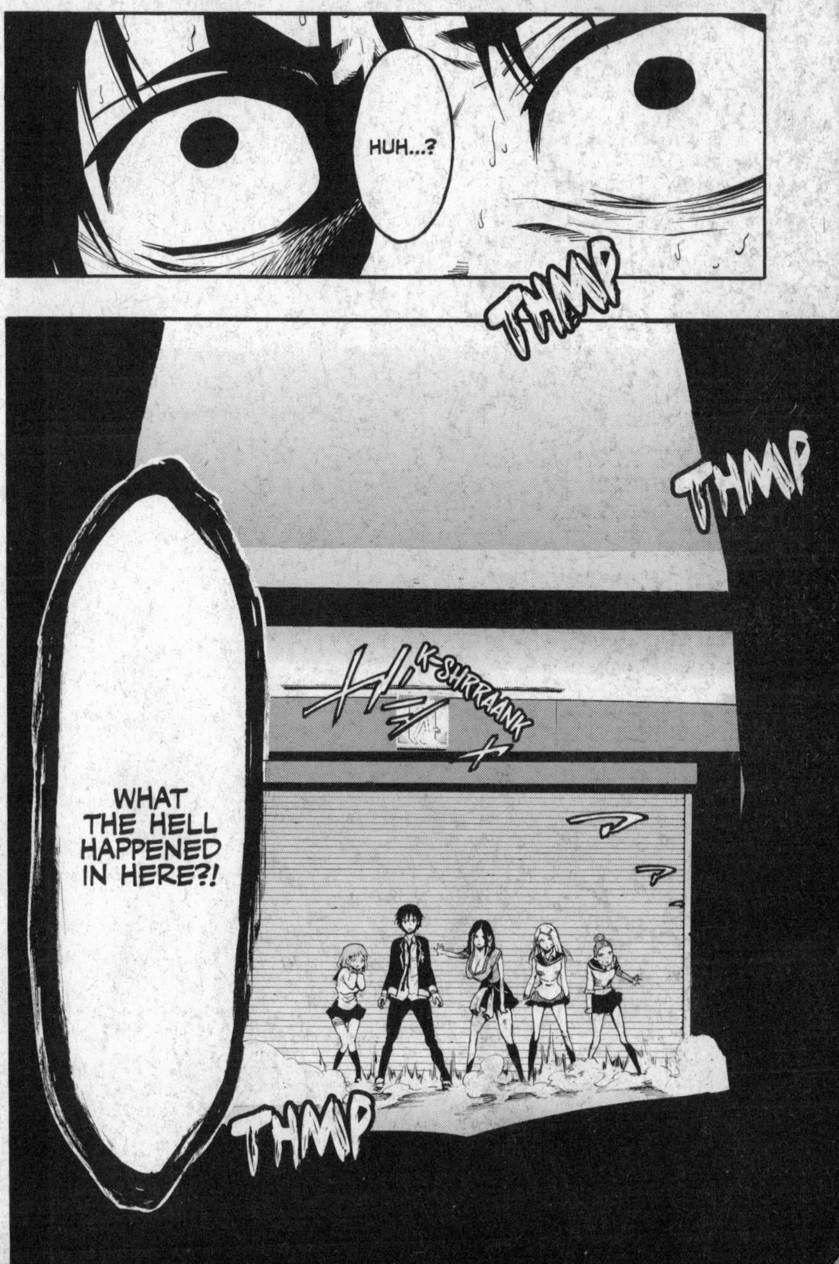
HUH...?
THMP
THMP
K-SHRRAANK
WHAT THE HELL HAPPENED IN HERE?!
THMP

TO BE CONTINUED...

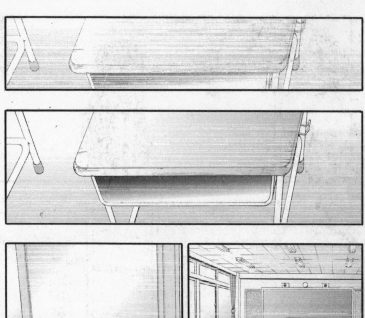

TODAY...

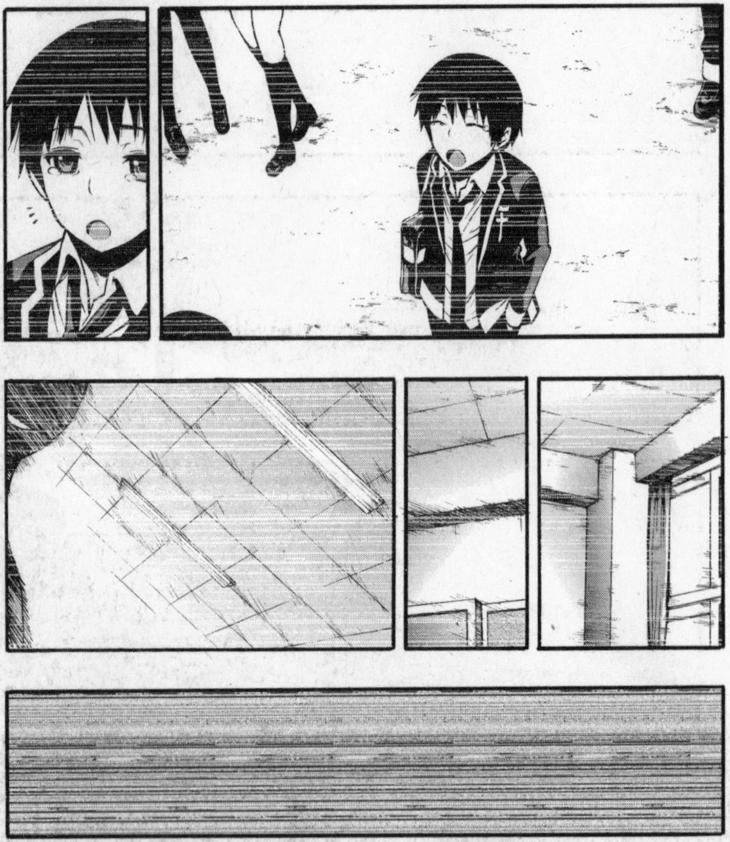

THE BEST DAY EVER
IS ABOUT TO BEGIN.

MAGICAL GIRL APOCALYPSE ~P.O.V~ 01

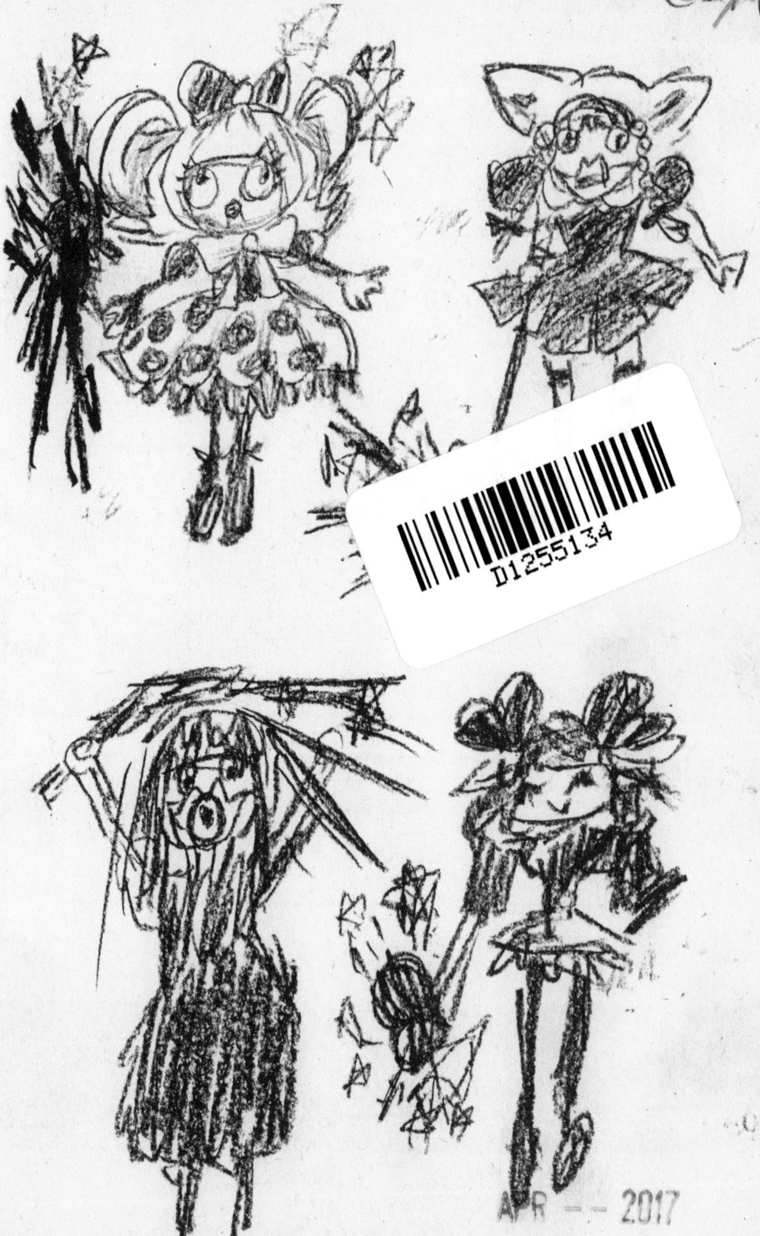